6th Edition

The Stage
and
the School

Harry H. Schanker

Katharine Anne Ommanney

GLENCOE

Macmillan/McGraw-Hill

Lake Forest, Illinois   Columbus, Ohio   Mission Hills, California   Peoria, Illinois

To Katharine

Title Page: *The Sprite Ariel, from William Shakespeare's* The Tempest, *and Boris Carnofsky as Prospero, The Keeper of the Magic Island, by the American Shakespeare prouction.*

Acknowledgments on pages v–viii are an extension of this copyright page.

Consultant
Lauren Kurki
Clark University
Worcester, Massachusetts

Reviewers

Douglas N. Bishop
Olympus High School
Salt Lake City, Utah

Nancy J. Poynter
Lake Highlands High School
Dallas, Texas

Dr. Leroy Hay
Manchester High School
Manchester, Connecticut

Father Frank Toste, C.S.C.
Peabody Public High School
Peabody, Massachusetts

Robbie Judd
Clear Creek High School
League City, Texas

Lawrence E. Zeiger
Point Loma High School
San Diego, California

Carol Poynter
Tate High School
Gonzalez, Florida

Ruth L. Tonner
Plymouth-Canton School District
Plymouth, Michigan

This book was set in 10½ pt. Cheltenham Light by Compset, Inc.
The color separation was done by TSI Graphics

ISBN 0-07-055145-6

Send all inquiries to:
GLENCOE DIVISION
Macmillan/McGraw-Hill
15319 Chatsworth Street
P.O. Box 9609
Mission Hills, CA 91346-9609

7 8 9 10 11 12 13   95 94 93 92

Acknowledgments

*W*e wish to thank the following authors, publishers, and agents for granting us permission to include copyrighted materials.

ANDERSON HOUSE PUBLISHERS for the following: Excerpt from *Elizabeth the Queen* by Maxwell Anderson; copyright © 1930 by Longmans, Green & Co. Copyright renewed 1957 by Maxwell Anderson. Excerpt from *Joan of Lorraine* by Maxwell Anderson; copyright © 1946 by Maxwell Anderson. For all excerpts: All rights reserved. Reprinted by permission of Anderson House.

Excerpt from *The Amen Corner* by James Baldwin. Reprinted by permission of Edward J. Acton, Inc.

DODD, MEAD & COMPANY, INC. for the following: Excerpts from *Whose Life Is It Anyway?* by Brian Clark. Reprinted by permission of Dodd, Mead & Company, Inc., from *Whose Life Is It Anyway?* by Brian Clark. Copyright © 1978 by Brian Clark. Excerpt from *Trifles* by Susan Glaspell. Reprinted by permission of Dodd, Mead & Company, Inc. from *Plays* by Susan Glaspell. Copyright © 1920 by Dodd, Mead & Company, Inc. Copyright renewed 1948 by Susan Glaspell. Excerpt from "Work" published in *The Hour Has Struck* by Angela Morgan.

DRAMATISTS PLAY SERVICE, INC. for excerpts from *Wine in the Wilderness*[1] by Alice Childress. © Copyright, 1969, by Alice Childress. For an excerpt from *Harvey*[1] by Mary Chase. Copyright, 1943, by Mary Chase (under the title *The White Rabbit*). Copyright renewed, 1970, by Mary C. Chase. Copyright, 1944, by Mary Chase (under the title *Harvey*). Copyright renewed, 1971, by Mary Chase.

MARI EVANS for "The Rebel" from *I Am a Black Woman*. Copyright © 1970 Mari Evans. Published by Wm. Morrow & Company, 1970. Reprinted by permission of the author.

FARRAR, STRAUS & GIROUX, INC. for an excerpt from *Talley's Folly* by Lanford Wilson. Copyright © 1979 by Lanford Wilson. Reprinted by permission of Hill and Wang, a division of Farrar, Straus and Giroux, Inc.

SAMUEL FRENCH, INC. for the following: Excerpt from *Prologue to Glory* by E.P. Conkle. Copyright © 1936, 1938 by E.P. Conkle. Copyright © 1963, 1966 (In Renewal) by E.P. Conkle. Excerpt from *The Belle of Amherst* by William Luce. Reprinted by permission of Samuel French, Inc.

HARCOURT BRACE JOVANOVICH, INC. for the excerpt from *I Remember Mama,* copyright © 1944, 1945 by John Van Druten; renewed, 1973, by the Carter Lodge, Executor of the estate of John Van Druten. Reprinted by permission of Harcourt Brace Jovanovich, Inc.

JAY S. HARRIS for an excerpt from *Butterflies Are Free* by Leonard Gershe. Copyright 1969, Samuel French, Inc. Reprinted by permission of Leonard Gershe.

HENRY HOLT AND COMPANY for excerpts from *Cyrano de Bergerac* by Edmond Rostand, translated by Brian Hooker. Copyright © 1923, 1937 by Henry Holt and Company, Inc., and renewed 1951 by Doris C. Hooker. Reprinted by permission of the publisher.

HOUGHTON MIFFLIN COMPANY for an excerpt from *J.B.: A Play in Verse* by Archibald MacLeish. Copyright © 1956, 1957, 1958 by Archibald MacLeish. Copyright © renewed 1986 by William H. MacLeish and Mary Grimm. Reprinted by permission of Houghton Mifflin Company.

METHUEN, LONDON for the excerpt from *Blithe Spirit* by Noel Coward. Reprinted by permission of Methuen, London.

MICHAEL IMISON PLAYWRIGHTS LTD. for the excerpt from *Blithe Spirit* by Noel Coward. Copyright © 1941 by Noel Coward.

INTERNATIONAL CREATIVE MANAGEMENT for an excerpt from *Dial "M" for Murder* by Frederick Knott. Copyright © 1954 by Frederick Knott (acting edition); copyright © 1953 by Frederick Knott; copyright as an unpublished work, 1952 by Frederick Knott. Copyrights renewed 1980, 1981, 1982. For an excerpt from *Everybody Loves Opal* by John Patrick. Copyright © 1961 and 1962 by John Patrick. Reprinted by permission of International Creative Management.

MORTON J. LEAVY of Leavy Rosensweig & Hyman, for an excerpt from *Spoon River Anthology,* the stage version by Charles Aidman.

LITTLE, BROWN AND COMPANY for the following: "The Rhinoceros" from *Verses from 1929 On* by Ogden Nash. Copyright © 1933 by Ogden Nash. First appeared in *The New Yorker.* For an excerpt from *The Chalk Garden* from *Four Plays* by Enid Bagnold. Copyright © 1953, 1956 by Enid Bagnold. All excerpts: Reprinted by permission of Little, Brown and Company.

LIVERIGHT PUBLISHING CORPORATION for an excerpt from *Liliom* by Franz Molnar. English text by Benjamin F. Glazer. Copyright © 1924 by Liveright Publishing Corporation. Copyright renewed 1952 by Liveright Publishing Corporation. Used with the permission of Liveright Publishing Corporation.

MACMILLAN PUBLISHING COMPANY for excerpts from *The Miracle Worker*[2] by William Gibson, excerpted from *The Miracle Worker,* Act II. Copyright © 1956, 1957 by William

Table of Contents

Part Three
Appreciating the Drama

Part One

Interpreting the Drama

························

Chapter 1

You and the Theater

You Will Learn

What theater language and conventions are.

What drama means.

What the ingredients of theater are.

Why criticism and evaluation are necessary for the theater.

What stage fright is and how to overcome it.

What theater discipline is.

Vocabulary

convention	dance pre-done	empathy	theater
humanities	situation	script	critique
drama	conflict	legitimate theater	stage fright

"*F*ive minutes to curtain!" That's right — you are about to go on stage. For some of you who use this book it will be your first venture "on the boards." For some it will be your first formal study of a subject you have been wanting to know more about. For others it will be an opportunity to learn about all the aspects of the theater you have grown to love as an actor, as a member of a backstage crew or committee, or as a member of an audience. And for some of you who have seen an incredible performance by an actor, an exciting play or musical, or a television program that left you saying to yourself "if only I could do that!" it may be the chance to fulfill a dream. No matter what your reason for taking this course, you probably have questions and apprehensions. The purpose of this chapter is to answer some of those questions and to allay some of those fears. Prepare yourself, because the curtain is going up.

Stage Language and Conventions

As does any specialized area, theater has a language all its own. For example, theater people still say "curtain going up," when most theaters have curtains that open from side to side. Theater also has many **conventions** — special

The ornate proscenium arch frames the stage and establishes the "wall" between the actor and the audience.
• • • • • • • • • • • •

or traditional ways of doing things. Because of this, each chapter of this book will introduce you to key ideas and to specialized theater vocabulary. There will even be some chapters that have lists of specialized vocabulary within them. A glossary at the end of the text will list and define all these terms. With these aids and with experience, you will soon be speaking, thinking, and even dreaming in the "language of the theater."

What Am I Doing Here?

The dramatic tradition is an ancient one. Drama is second only to dance as the oldest of the humanities. The **humanities,** which include music, art, literature, and philosophy, as well as drama, are those areas of human interest that attempt to answer the eternal questions: "Who am I? Why am I here? Where am I going?"

The word **drama** comes from a Greek word meaning "to do or to act," and that is why you are here — *to do.* Acting, building, directing, producing — *doing* is what theater is all about.

Where are you going? In your drama class, you will be both actor and audience. From pantomimic imitation, you will advance to creative action called improvisation. From these you will proceed to written scenes and plays.

How Did Drama Come into Being?

Drama had its origins in the human impulse to imitate. Judging from the records left behind, early humans imitated the significant events in their lives *after* those events took place. Successful hunts, victorious battles, earth-quenching rains were typical of the events acted out, often around a fire or within a circle of viewers. But, as we well know, not all hunts are successful, not all battles are won, and not all years are free of drought. Therefore, the first actors began to pantomime, dance, and chant how they would like things to turn out. This acting out of wished-for events was the forerunner of ritualistic drama or **dance pre-done.** The traditional tribal dances we see performed today by Native Americans are examples of the dance pre-done.

The Ingredients of Drama

There are only four essentials necessary for a dramatic experience:

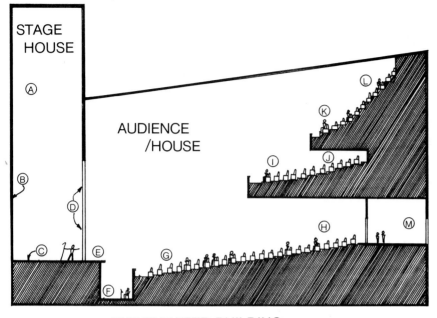

THE THEATER BUILDING
THIS DIAGRAM IS CALLED A SECTION DRAWING:
IMAGINE THE THEATRE SPLIT DOWN THE CENTER AND OPENED FOR VIEWING

Ⓐ FLY SPACE   Ⓖ ORCHESTRA SECTION
Ⓑ "BACK WALL"   Ⓗ PARQUET CIRCLE*
Ⓒ STAGE FLOOR   Ⓘ LOGE*
Ⓓ PROSCENIUM ARCH   Ⓙ MEZZANINE
Ⓔ THRUST OR APRON   Ⓚ FIRST BALCONY
Ⓕ ORCHESTRA PIT   Ⓛ UPPER OR SECOND BALCONY
                            Ⓜ LOBBY

* LIMITED USE.

DESCRIPTIONS OF SEATING AREAS CHANGE ACCORDING TO STYLE OF THEATRE ARCHITECTURE

1. Actors — someone to perform

2. Audience — someone to observe a performance

3. Place — a location to perform

4. Light — enough to see the performers

We really do not need a theater building with permanent seating, or a stage, or special lighting equipment. What we do need are an actor, an audience with a little imagination, and a **situation** — a problem or challenge the character or characters must face. The situation is not really interesting without two ingredients. **Conflict** is drama's most important ingredient. Conflict is a struggle between two opposing forces. A character struggles with himself or herself, with another character, or with a force. The second is a relationship that builds between actor and audience called empathy. **Empathy** is the emotional identification with someone or something outside one-self. It is "feeling in" with the character, not just "feeling for" the character, which is sympathy. If the audience enters into the world of the play, accepts it as real, and becomes involved in the actor's struggles and responds; and if the actor, in turn, is moved by the audience's response, the electricity of theater is generated.

When drama is written down it becomes a **script.** If it has a beginning, a middle, and an end we call it a play. However, drama is not to be confused with other literary forms such as a novel or poetry. Like a novel, a play almost always tells a story. Like poetry, a play may be written in poetic form, and like poetry, a play shares feelings. But drama is meant to be acted out, not simply to be read. In addition, we read most literature to interpret what we can from the printed page. Acted-out drama is interpreted for us by actors whose interpretation is an extension of the interpretation of a director. We may or may not like or agree with that interpretation, but that is how we become evaluators of theater.

In this book we will focus primarily on what is normally referred to as **legitimate theater.** Although the term was originally applied to the live professional stage, it is now used to distinguish live acting on the stage from other media forms such as motion pictures and television. There is something unique and captivating about "real" people performing on stage that has not been matched by the two-dimensional limitations of the screen.

Most theatrical performances are seen in buildings constructed primarily for dramatic presentations. Such buildings are called **theaters,** although most schools refer to such facilities as auditoriums. You should become familiar with the areas of a professional theater. Knowing them will be important to you not only for ordering tickets to a professional production, but also in wanting to learn about as many aspects of theater production as possible.

Criticism and Evaluation

As a student of theater you will become a better judge of the quality of the plays, movies, and television shows that you see. At the same time, you will be evaluated as you perform. An actor or technician who wishes to improve seeks positive criticism that will strengthen the theatrical product. One must learn what audiences like, accept, and reject because the audience is there to be pleased, and the director, actors, and crews are there to please the audience. Theater is presented *to* and *for* an audience. Simply doing what you want to do in performance, design, or writing is not good theater if it confuses, bores, embarrasses, offends, or fails to communicate with the audience.

The performance evolves through the director's critique—the ultimate goal being a unified performance shaped by the director's vision.

Accept criticism as a help to your growth as a performer. Sound criticism should not be aimed at you as a person, and you should try not to take it personally. When you are given the opportunity to evaluate a fellow actor or a performance, first try to find something that deserves praise — the voice, animation, interpretation; then comment on things that can improve if called to the performer's attention. A **critique** can be more positive than negative. Sometimes it is almost totally complimentary. A director may give many critical notes or comments, but the intent is to improve the performances, never to put the actors or crew down.

Stage Fright

One of the problems you might have to face is called **stage fright** or the nervous anticipation of going on stage to perform.

First, rest assured: most performers experience nervousness, sometimes near sickness, before going on stage, particularly for the first performance.

The performance of **Pajama Game** *by a summer youth organization.*
• • • • • • • • • • • • • • • •

Second, bear in mind that a certain amount of stage fright is good for your performance. It means you are concerned about doing a good job.

Stage fright is caused by the release of adrenalin by the body. Adrenalin dilates, or enlarges, the blood vessels, allowing a greater supply of blood to flow. During periods of stage fright, the extra blood flow causes "butterflies" and/or increased physical activity. The trick in conquering stage fright is to concentrate on the performance you are about to give and use that extra blood supply to give you that special "lift" that can enable you to perform at higher than rehearsal level.

In order to control and use the body's natural catalyst, you should do three things:

1. Be totally prepared. Make your nervousness a result of concern for a strong performance rather than a result of fear for lack of preparation.

2. Relax. Use some of the relaxation exercises found in this book.

3. Avoid situations in which you burn off the positive effects of adrenalin. Do not pace, run about, talk loudly, or anything else that will use up

your energy. Concentrate on your performance and character and control the release of the extra-ability adrenalin can give you.

Theater Discipline

Discipline is the heart of theater. Please do not let that word intimidate you. Theater discipline means be where you are supposed to be on time, learn lines on schedule, make quick, efficient scene changes, perform your best even when you do not feel well, pick up cues, make your performance appear as fresh and sharp as if it were the first time that line was ever spoken. In other words, most of theater discipline is self-discipline. It is your commitment to the theater that will prompt you to do your physical, vocal, and relaxation exercises on a regular basis. It will be your love for the theater that will encourage you to research your part, work long hours to complete your project or task, and demand excellence of yourself and those around you.

You and the Theater

As a result of your studies in drama, you will come to know more about yourself, your talents, your strengths, your weaknesses, and your effect on others. As a result, you will become more understanding of others. The actor becomes a student of human nature in order to present a truthful and realistic performance. Therefore, you will learn to observe real people, their motivating forces, their basic drives and needs, their hopes and dreams.

Your study of the theater should allow you to become a more expressive, communicative person on stage and off. You can become one of those special people who has an intense desire to share talents, insights, and excitement with others, to lift spirits, to cause a laugh or smile, to stir compassion and perhaps to draw forth a tear. You can become a "doer" in the world of theater and a giver of the warmth, thrill, joy, and power of the stage. When you find the magic that belongs to theater, you will know why thousands have felt it worth all the hours of rehearsal, the sacrifices that are often required, the butterflies of opening night, and the discipline and commitment demanded by a production schedule.

Are you ready? CURTAIN'S GOING UP!

Recalling Ideas

1. What does the word *drama* mean?

2. What are the origins of drama?

3. Explain the four essential ingredients of dramatic experience.

4. Define *conflict* and *empathy*.

5. Explain the term *legitimate theater*.

6. Why is criticism important?

7. How can you control stage fright?

Discussing Ideas

1. Discuss some of the reasons people take drama classes and participate in drama.

2. Discuss some of the questions and concerns people have about taking drama classes and participating in drama.

3. Explain why both actors and audience often find the legitimate theater more "captivating" than movies or television.

4. What is theater discipline? Why is it important to a good production?

Careers in the Theater

At the end of each chapter will be a brief section on careers in the theater. The number and variety of careers in theater are almost limitless. Those that come to mind immediately — acting and directing — are by no means the only important ones. Any production you see has crews of people working behind the scenes on lighting, props, stage settings, makeup, and costumes. In addition, every production requires people working on the business aspects: publicity, ticket sales, house management. All of these jobs require different talents and interests. Many people who love the theater and have devoted their lives to it have no desire to be on stage. Perhaps you will find yourself drawn to one of these behind-the-scenes careers.

Chapter 2

Improvisation

You Will Learn

What improvisation is.

How improvisation is one of the foundations for interpretation.

How improvisation and plays are based on character-centered and situation-centered action.

Why the development of specific character personalities will improve your improvisational experiences.

Vocabulary

improvisation	scene-stealing	situation-centered
spontaneity	character-centered	action
"illusion of the first	action	motivated sequence
time"		

*A*re you ready to act? The approach that should help you gain confidence "on the boards" is called **improvisation**. Improvisation is the impromptu portrayal of a character or a scene without rehearsal or preparation. You will make up character, lines, and action as you go along, without a formal script. You will have fun as you are learning some of the fundamentals of acting and getting better acquainted with your classmates. Imagination is the key to improvisation. You must learn to "say the most with the least"; that is, you must convey personality and physical traits, conflicts and desires, age and dress with a minimum of aids. Sometimes you may be allowed to use a few props, but character must be conveyed by voice, posture, and movement.

Drama is the link between thought and expression. It depends upon words and action rather than upon words alone. Drama began as descriptive action expressed by facial expression and bodily movement. It then became stylized dance. Finally, it developed into formal dramas. Words could not convey the full excitement of the great hunt or battle, and so bodily movements were added by the actor-storyteller. The playwright must turn action into words, and the actor must turn those words into action. When improvising, however, you must create both words and action. As a result of your improvising, you should have a better understanding of what goes into a play and should develop a keener appreciation of clever lines, good action, effective blocking, well-developed characters, and strong plots.

Spontaneity and freshness at each performance are the goals of the director of a play, the challenge to the cast, and the pleasure of the audience. However, after weeks of rehearsals or after many performances, the "**illusion of the first time**" is sometimes difficult to capture, and a play becomes stale. Improvisations are enjoyable in their you-never-know-what's-coming-next freshness. They should help you to appreciate the sparkle that comes with a first-time performance. You will learn to appreciate the most important factor in the execution of lines or action — timing. Play casts may rehearse for weeks to achieve the kind of fresh, natural timing that may come as you improvise.

Foundation of Interpretation

Improvisation is one of the foundations of interpretation. Even though improvisation is quite spontaneous it demands physical and mental control, adaptability, acceptance of and positive response to criticism, "directability," and cooperation with others.

Although improvising emphasizes the creative — the doing rather than the telling — the beginning performer often wants to experience the actual emotion rather than to portray it. The student must always bear in mind that a person may go only so far and still be acting. Beyond that point, the actor *is* rather than *is pretending to be.* This is where the discipline enters in. The character, like makeup and costume, must be removed by the actor after the scene is over. As an actor, you should grow as a result of the performance, but you must never let a characterization engulf your own identity. When that happens, you are no longer an actor.

"What is happening now" is the keynote of improvisation. Improvisation

Drama began as pantomimed descriptive action, became stylized dance, and then was ritualized into formal dramas. An improvised stage such as this one was common in England during the 1600s.

focuses your attention on natural actions and reactions and should force you to concentrate on immediate responses. All action should be motivated only by what you already know about the characters and situation and by what is brought forth as you improvise. You do not have the advantage — or disadvantage — of knowing what lines come next in a script. You must play it as it develops. You will learn how a scene may change direction as the result of a single line or action. You may even find it necessary to meet one of the toughest challenges that faces an actor: to "do nothing effectively" — that is, to be on the stage, visible, but not playing an active part in the scene. In such cases, you must get the audience to accept your presence without being distracted. To call attention to your presence would be **scene-stealing**. You will learn to appreciate the interrelationships of the characters and how essential it is that an actor be a member of a team.

You will appreciate even more a well-written script, which is the finished product of many improvisations that passed through the author's mind while designing the action. In fact, the trial run of most plays is a form of improvisation where the playwright sees "how it plays" and makes necessary changes in the script before the opening. You will also realize why it is said that a well-written play has no wasted words. Sincere characterization will develop during improvisation and become deeper and more convincing as you proceed toward formal acting. You will begin to feel the role and sense when you are only impersonating the character and when you or a fellow actor is "putting on the cloak but not the soul" of the part. There is a tremendous difference between character and caricature, and it is important for the beginning actor to learn that difference.

Character and Situation-Centered Action

There are two basic approaches to telling a story: **character-centered** and **situation-centered**. The character-centered approach places a character or group of characters in different situations. This approach emphasizes the character's response to those situations as they occur. *Man of La Mancha* and *Pippin* are examples of this. The character-centered approach is used in most daily and weekly television programs in which the same characters are seen

Originally written in the 15th century, Cervantes' character of Don Quixote survives on the modern stage as Man of La Mancha.

in episode after episode. If you develop a character or two for use in your improvisations, you will soon find your character responding naturally to each situation as it takes place in an improvisational exercise.

The situation-centered approach takes a single situation or series of situations and places a number of characters into the situation to demonstrate how different personalities will respond to the same event. Many improvisations are set up as situation-centered. Many television programs are situation-centered. This is why they are referred to as "sit-coms," or situation comedies. Plays like *Arsenic and Old Lace* and *Little Shop of Horrors* are situation-centered.

It is very demanding for young actors to build a character, work out a situation, carry on action, and create effective dialogue all at the same time and on the spur of the moment. Therefore, if you establish a character beforehand that you can use, the words and the action will come much easier.

When your character is described, no matter how simply, you should immediately ask, "Who am I? What kind of person am I? When does this action take place? How should the audience react to me? How am I different from the other characters?" "What are the fewest things I can do to convey the

Elizabeth Swados's Runaways *was developed at Joseph Papp's Public Theatre partially from the improvisations of the young actors involved in the production.*

most?" and, finally, "What does my character want?" You will soon learn that a raised eyebrow, a silent stare, a one-word response, or a groan may convey more than a dozen sentences. Try also to determine the mood of the scene. Ask yourself how your character can contribute to the complication and resolution of the idea to be presented.

In your characterization, do not yield to the common impulse to "play the character down." Shallow characterizations are weak characterizations. The Italian playwright Luigi Pirandello said that a person plays a "game of masks" in life, putting on a different mask for each person or occasion faced. Seldom does a person want anyone to see what is really behind the mask. The convincing actor lets the audience see the various masks of a character, but also allows them to see what is behind, even if only for brief moments. When this is carefully worked out, the audience sees a well-rounded, thoroughly developed personality.

The improvised·approach to acting is being adopted by many directors, and most directors encourage improvising while the actor is working toward the development of a character. Some directors are using an improvised approach completely. This creative experience has certain benefits for the developing actor, but the production usually suffers from lack of direction, unity, and coherence. A combination of inner-developed improvisations and outer-lead directions usually brings out the best in theater.

**Improvisation
Warm-up
Activities**
● ● ● ● ● ● ● ● ● ● ● ● ●

1. *The Mirror.* This is a fundamental exercise in acting training. Two persons face each other. One is the activator; the other, the responder. The activator moves the hands, the head, and eventually, any part of the body while pretending to look in a mirror. The responder matches the actions of the activator without making physical contact. The goals are to learn to work smoothly with a partner and to feel the single impulse of an action. Keep your movements steady and fluid. You are not to trick your partner. Again, the goal is working together.

2. *The Machine.* This is group improvisation that puts your imagination to the test. One person starts the machine by performing a physical action, such as pumping the arm or lifting a knee. Another person joins the first piece of the machine by linking a different physical action to the first. This continues until as many members of the group as possible become part of the machine.
   Variation 1. Make the machine a manufacturing process, so that raw materials are turned into a finished product.
   Variation 2. Add sound to the action. Each new action must be accompanied by its own new sound.

3. *The Exchange.* The class divides into groups of two persons, each facing the other. One partner begins moving toward the other partner, performing a simple task, such as pushing a wheelbarrow, bouncing a ball, or throwing newspapers.

As quickly as possible, the responder must pick up the action and imitate it, moving toward the activator. When both partners meet, they mirror the action of the other.

Concentration Activities
● ● ● ● ● ● ● ● ● ● ● ● ●

1. Each student is given a simple measurement task to perform. While the class watches, the student engages in the completion of the assigned task. This activity focuses attention of a specific action in view of an audience. Some sample actions are below.

Measure a room.	Measure a window.
Measure a chair.	Measure the floor.
Measure a door.	Measure a desk.

2. Each student chooses a personally familiar action to perform. Simple props are necessary. In acting out this action, there must be a sense of urgency within the student motivating her or him to perform the action and complete the task *now*. After completing the action, each student explains the reason behind the urgent need to rush. Some sample actions are below.

Hem a skirt.	Apply makeup.
Photograph a subject.	Write a letter.
Change a bicycle tire.	Hide a valuable.

3. Building on Activity 2, as the student performs the action, a second student comes into the scene. This second student also has an action to perform. Neither student, however, must be distracted by the other's behavior.

4. Building on Activity 3, conversation is added to the scene. Both students continue to perform their actions. However, they now talk to each other or mutter to themselves. Concentration on the actions must be maintained in spite of the complication of talking.

5. Pairs of students are assigned a simple location and a relationship. The relationship could be between brother and sister. The location could be in the family's garage. One student is already in the garage engaged in an activity, such as painting a chair. That student is in a certain mood. The second student arrives from a specific location and is in a specific mood. The scene builds around the two moods, the relationship, and the location of the present action.

Improvising Scenes

Before you begin working with a partner on an improvised scene, there are a few *do's* and *don'ts* to keep in mind. Following these simple rules will free your imagination and keep your improvisation moving.

Do's

1. Take your cues from your scene partner.

2. Play your scene from moment to moment.

3. Allow your intuition to be your guide.

4. Be spontaneous in your actions.

5. Say or do things that demand a definite response.

Don'ts

1. Never deny anything your scene partner says about you or the situation. If your partner says you have lovely yellow eyes, accept the statement as true and allow your imagination to help you respond.

2. Avoid asking questions. Questions turn an improvisation into a question-and-answer routine. Especially avoid "terminal questions" — those that can be answered with a "yes" or "no" or with a response that shuts down the flow of dialogue.

3. Avoid simple statements of information. Make statements about your feelings and observations.

4. Avoid explanations about situations and feelings. If you are happy, show it. If you are afraid of the dark, show that. *Telling* is storytelling, not acting. Acting is *doing*.

With the class divided into groups of two persons each, select one incident around which to build your scene, and decide whether it will be the opening event, the climax, or the conclusion of an imagined play. You can get your material from any source you wish. Some suggestions are the pictures in this book, newspaper clippings, cartoon captions, and anecdotes from magazines; events in your own or your parents' and friends' lives; or historical and literary sources.

Decide on the main idea you want to put over and on the general mood. You may do any kind of scene you want — comic or sad, fanciful or realistic — but each character must be a distinct type, totally different from the others. You should avoid such generalized scenes as those involving students in a dormitory or members of a basketball team. The greater the difference in age, personality, and type among the characters, the more contrast your scenes will contain.

Work out your stage setting carefully, knowing just where the entrances will be. You probably will have nothing more than a table and a few chairs to work around. You will not use any doors, windows, or heavy props. Suggest

Street theater works from an improvisational base. One never knows what will happen next.

entrances and major props by what you do. You may carry small articles you need. In turning the classroom into a street, a ballroom, a theater dressing room, an office, or whatever you choose, you are developing not only your own imagination but also that of the rest of the class. They will see whatever you make clear, first by your explanation and then by your performance.

Visualize your character in detail and try to feel emotions. Before you enter, take on the physical attitude of your character in accordance with the character's age, size, and mood. Walk in character as you enter, and remember that your audience is out front.

Onstage, talk loudly enough to be heard and do not hide behind other people or pieces of furniture. Try not to stand beside your scene partner all the time. Move about freely. Take plenty of time to speak and move, so that you can create a definite impression. Most important, keep in character all the time. Listen and speak as the character would in the situation, and lose yourself in appropriate actions and reactions.

As you get more practice in improvising scenes, you can begin to learn some of the subtleties of acting. You will find that you can stand still without fidgeting and that you can make definite gestures when you feel the need, avoiding the little, aimless ones. When you must move to a chair or toward another person, learn to go straight there without rambling. If you are to pick up an article, actually see it before you touch it. By observation you will learn that the head usually reacts first (sometimes simply the eyes), then the torso, and then the rest of the body.

The Motivated Sequence

The actor mirrors a natural **motivated sequence** that we follow in response to an internal or external stimulus — a thought, an action, a sound, what we hear, see, taste, feel, or smell:

1. We experience the stimulus.

2. The "idea connects." The brain registers the stimulus. This usually takes only a fraction of a second.

3. The body responds — The chest moves in the direction of the stimulus, the eyes look in that direction. If the stimulus is the kind that causes a reflex action, we may jerk back the head, or make a sound.

4. We react vocally and/or physically with our main response.

This whole sequence may be completed in less than a second, but all steps must be present if the reaction is to be believable. For example: It is early morning on a school day. You are asleep in bed. The alarm goes off (initial stimulus). You awaken (primary response), your brain tells you "the alarm is going off" (idea connection 1). You think, "It's Tuesday — school today!" (idea connection 2), and you glare at the clock (secondary response). "Yes, it really is 6 a.m." (idea connection 3). You reach out and shut off the alarm (main response).

If you follow a motivated sequence on stage, your actions will have a greater image of "truth" that the audience will accept. However, when you eventually have a script in your hand, you will discover how easy it is to jump to a response without following the sequence. Consequently, your director or your audience may say: "I don't believe what you are doing."

Individual Improvisations

After working with a partner, you may also want to try to develop individual characters in definite situations, reacting to imaginary persons or crowds, or showing particular moods. It is harder to work by yourself than with another person, but you can, by yourself, take more time to create a personality and to feel more deeply.

In these improvisations, keep relaxed and have fun. Do not allow yourself to feel embarrassed by the reactions of others. Do not let classmates who seem to fall right into a character without apparent effort discourage you from trying to do the same.

Individual Activities Using a Mirror

• • • • • • • • • • • • •

Your teacher will provide a full-length mirror to help you prepare for the following improvisational exercises.

1. You or your teacher will furnish props, such as canes, umbrellas, fans, glasses, and books. You will use one of these props. After 30 seconds of preparation time before the mirror, you will present a 30-second characterization built around the prop you used. It is recommended that the mirror be located away from the class's view so that you can concentrate alone. While one person performs, another can be preparing.
    Variation. Use the prop you have chosen for something other than its normal function. Improvise a character using the prop's new function. For example, you could change a cane into a laser beam.

2. You or your teacher will furnish a costume item, such as a hat, gloves, a coat, a scarf, a shawl, or a vest. Again, use the mirror to see how the costume can help convey a character. Then, using the costume item as a key to revealing your character, present a 1-minute characterization.

3. Bring a mask to class. It can be a Halloween mask or other commercial mask or a mask you have made for yourself. Use the mirror for preparation. Present the character the mask suggests for 30 seconds. You may then add sounds or speech.
    Variation 1. Add nonverbal sounds to the improvisation — a grunt, a hum, clearing the throat, a chuckle.
    Variation 2. Add words to the action.

If you keep practicing all sorts of characterizations on the spur of the moment at home, you will find doing improvisations in class much easier. Try being all sorts of people — Joan of Arc at her trial, a star during a television interview, an Olympic champion after a big event, and so on. Get yourself into all sorts of emotional states, laughing out loud and even crying if you can. With no one around, you will not feel silly. And the practice will show in your classwork because you will be more responsive and sensitive to changing moods and situations. You will find your voice and body becoming more flexible and expressive.

Remember: Improvise! Fill the "gaps" made by your own or another performer's actions or lines, and make "gaps" for others to fill. Feel free to experiment, using motivation as your impelling force. Imagination will be the key to characterization, so make every look, every line, and every action count. At times, you will realize that you have caught another personality, if just for a moment, and will know what it is to feel like an actor.

The following suggestions for improvisations provide a step-by-step progression from simple emotional responses to the improvised writing of a play.

Applications
• • • • • • • • • • • • •

Emotional Responses

1. Express the following feelings through, first, a facial response and, second, a facial response combined with a bodily reaction. Try to recall a personal experience that caused you to experience these feelings. From one to five participants at a time may do this exercise. Compare the responses. What similarities and differences are there?

love	jealousy	grief	shock
hope	ecstasy	embarrassment	sympathy
fear	kindness	understanding	patience
bitterness	scorn	irritability	fickleness
skepticism	rebuke	disbelief	mockery
longing	sarcasm	pleading	courage
greed	happiness	mourning	surprise

2. Place items like the following in individual paper sacks. Each member of the class must reach into a sack, feel the object that is in it, say "one thousand one" silently, and then convey the sensation received by a facial expression and a one-sentence reaction. After experiencing the sensations of sight, sound, touch, smell, and taste associated with the objects in the following list, practice recalling your sensory impressions without handling the real object. Such sensory recall is an essential tool for the actor. There will be times when you must drink hot coffee onstage without the luxury of real hot coffee. The heat, the taste, and the smell of the coffee must come from your imagination.

sandpaper	cold cream	raisins
cooked spaghetti	feathers	knitting yarn
a cotton ball	a flower petal	cracker crumbs
rough tree bark	a piece of lettuce	a marble
a pickle	crumpled cellophane	an ice cube

3. React to the following sentences with one gesture or bodily stance.

Your face is red!	Do you always look like that?
I hate you!	I think you're frightened.
You have pretty eyes.	You're standing on my toe.
I love you.	How much do you really weigh?

Vocal Responses

Make up a list of statements similar to the examples below. Exchange your list with that of a classmate, and react to one statement as five different people.

EXAMPLES OF STATEMENT: You have just said, "I don't like asparagus!"
RESPOND AS: Your mother, your doctor, your waiter, your hostess, your little daughter
STATEMENT: You have just said, "I've been asked to the prom!"
RESPOND AS: Your best friend, a jealous rival, your ex-boyfriend, the teacher whose class you have interrupted, your father, your mother, your sister, your brother

Change of Command

Two to five persons will begin improvising a scene based on a simple situation. One person, either your teacher or a member of the class, will act as director. As the scene develops, the director will call out various emotions to specific members of the performing group. As each individual is called, that person must immediately assume the emotion mentioned. The improvisation is to continue without pausing as the emotions are called out.

Variation. Other elements, such as age, situation, weather, time (day, year, historical period), or mood, may be changed.

I Want

This is a good two-person activity to develop a sense of conflict within a scene. Each student wants to fulfill a specific objective. One student may want the other's shoe, while the other student wants to leave the room. The object of the improvisation is to get what you want without asking for it.

Variation. Improvise the above activity as a well-known stock character, comic-strip character, or television character. Stock characters might be such types as hypochondriacs, wealthy snobs, athletic stars, misers, domineering individuals, intellectuals, and so on.

Famous People

1.   Make up a list of quotations, real or imaginary. Improvise the situation leading up to the quotation and end with the quotation.

   EXAMPLES:
   "Give me liberty, or give me death!"
   "Damn the torpedoes, full speed ahead!"
   "Ask not what your country can do for you, but what you can do for your country."
   "Which way did they go, George?"
   "I have always depended upon the kindness of strangers."

2. With a single stance, a single gesture, or a combination of the two, portray the following:

> Leonardo da Vinci painting the "Mona Lisa"
> Ben Franklin flying his kite
> Your favorite star accepting his or her first Oscar
> Annie Sullivan teaching Helen Keller sign language
> Nero playing his lyre while Rome burned
> Betsy Ross sewing the American flag
> Now create your own list from contemporary situations and people.

3. Improvise the dialogue and actions of famous people in the historical situations for which they are remembered.

4. Repeat your improvisation of Exercise 3, but change the ending.

5. Have several famous personalities respond in character to the same imaginary situation.

Scripts

1. From a description of the following situations, characters, or both, develop some scripts.

   a. Two salesclerks are discussing a department manager they dislike. The manager appears and accuses one of them of having stolen a necklace that has disappeared. Work out your own solution.

   b. A father meets his 15-year-old daughter in the hall at midnight on her return from a party that ended at ten-thirty. Show what happens when they meet.

2. The microcosm is "the world on the head of a pin" — people from varied walks of life thrown together by chance to face the same situation.

   a. An elevator is caught between floors. Work out your own characters, their reactions, and the conclusion.

   b. Do the same thing with people in a lifeboat together, in a taxi stuck in a traffic jam, and on a subway during a power failure.

Literary Sketches

1. Improvise a scene from *Crimes of the Heart* by Beth Henley.

2. Improvise a scene from one of Guy de Maupassant's short stories, such as "The Necklace" or "A Piece of String."

3. Improvise a scene from "The Lady or the Tiger" by Frank R. Stockton.

4. Improvise a scene where the Fox and the Cat tell Pinocchio of the wonders of Candyland.

5. Improvise the Mad Hatter's tea party or the trial scene from *Alice's Adventures in Wonderland.*

6. Improvise Dorothy's first meetings with the Scarecrow, the Tin Woodsman, and the Cowardly Lion in *The Wizard of Oz.*

7. Improvise a scene from a Greek myth, such as "Jason and the Golden Fleece."

8. Improvise one of Aesop's fables.

If You Were. . .
After deciding what roles each person will play in the scene, reenact some event, real or imaginary, such as the following:

1. You are members of the Roman Senate when Julius Caesar has just been stabbed to death. Each of you must recall something Caesar did to you that makes you support or reject the conspirators.

2. At lunch, someone rushes in with the news that a spaceship has just landed in City Park. Speculate on ship, occupants, origin, and so forth.

3. Just given an engagement ring, tell the world about it, including your former admirers and your fiancé's former admirers.

4. The Lady Godiva has just learned that she must ride nude through the town before the Duke of Godiva will reduce the townspeople's taxes.

5. You are the only five survivors at the Alamo.

Rumors Are Flying
Begin with a simple rumor and expand it, each person adding a new detail, character, twist, and so on. Tell the next person about it by improvised action until you have created a working script.

Potpourri
Now, after everyone has been in at least two improvisations, dream up new situations, rewrite scripts you have previously used, or make new scripts from news articles or works of literature. Use some of the characters the class has created, and let them play out the new situations.

The Basic Improvisational Exercise

In most drama improvisations, the performers are given a brief scenario giving characters and situation. Select three females and two males for the following exercise. The facilitator, in this case most likely the teacher, will give these instructions: "It is 4:30 p.m. There are five persons on an elevator — one is a famous movie actress on her way to a 4:40 audition; one is a courier delivering an urgent legal brief; one is a professional football player who is to be interviewed on the 5 p.m. sportscast; one is a window washer headed for the twelfth floor to do the windows at the end of the hall as the last task of the day before leaving work to catch the 5:12 uptown bus; the last is a five-year-old going to see a parent on the sixth floor. Just as the elevator leaves the third floor where the window washer got on, there is a power failure, stranding the passengers between floors. IMPROVISE!

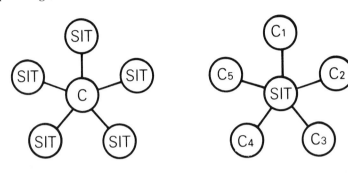

Every stage happening is based on one of two conditions: (1) a single character facing multiple situations, or (2) multiple characters facing a single situation.

After this improvisation has been performed, each member of the class should write two character/situation scenarios for members of the class to perform. The author may serve as the facilitator for his/her improvisation.

Creating the Improvised Play

Divide the class into groups of five to eight persons. In a discussion, each group is to work out a script that could be made into a simple, improvised play. Decide on the theme of your play, the characters, the basic conflicts, and the style. After improvising the script several times to establish some blocking, lines, and workable scenes, fill in your outline until you have a skeletal script. Improvise two or three more times, and you will be able to set down a written script created by the improvised approach to acting.

Recalling Ideas

1. What is improvisation?

2. Define *spontaneity*. Explain why it is a pleasure to an audience.

3. What is situation? What role does it play in improvisation?

4. What is "the illusion of the first time"? Why is it sometimes difficult to capture?

5. Why is "to do nothing effectively" one of the toughest challenges an actor faces? What is the connection between this challenge and "scene stealing"?

6. Identify the two basic approaches to telling a story. Explain each.

7. List the steps in the motivated sequence.

Discussing Ideas

1. Discuss how character is conveyed through voice, posture, and bodily movement. Is one of these methods more important than the others?

2. Discuss the role that imagination plays in improvisation. How can imagination aid in producing spontaneity?

3. Discuss the difference between experiencing an emotion and portraying an emotion. When does an actor cease to be an actor?

4. Many directors have accepted the improvised approach to acting. Discuss the benefits and drawbacks of this approach. Discuss how a combination of this approach with outer-lead direction might result in better theater.

Careers

Almost everyone who works in the theater should have a background in the theater arts. However they may also need intensive training in business, journalism, or another field. In this career section, educational and training options for theater artists are given. Additional requirements are discussed in connection with specific jobs at the end of each chapter.

Some experts believe that, since drama deals with all aspects of human experience, theater artists first need a liberal arts education. They recommend that work in the theater arts follow that education. Others, who believe that a liberal arts education is not needed, recommend only professional training. Still others favor a combination of liberal arts and theater training.

Many colleges and universities provide some theater arts courses, such as theater history, but do not train undergraduates as performers. Others combine such courses as playwrighting; directing; dancing; and scene, costume, and lighting design with liberal arts courses.

Professional training programs are offered by colleges and universities, conservatories, and studios. Students in those programs spend most of their time in theater courses. Some of the best known are connected with the American Conservatory Theater, the California Institute of the Arts, the Juilliard School, and Yale University.

Many performers first seek work in resident or alternative theater companies, while other hopefuls go to New York or Hollywood. Because competition is keen, and it can be difficult to make a full-time living in the theater, many opt to teach drama at the high school or college level and participate in community and regional theater. Others have discovered a variety of ways to pursue careers that connect them to the theater. Some of those occupations will be explored in this book.

Chapter 3

Pantomime and Mime

You Will Learn

What pantomime is.

How to do relaxation exercises.

How to walk on stage.

How to make stage crosses and turns.

How to take a stage fall.

How to gesture effectively on stage.

What the basic principles of pantomime are.

How to prepare a group pantomime.

What the differences are between pantomime and mime.

How to do mime exercises and actions.

Vocabulary

pantomime	gesture	rotations
nonverbal communication	mime	isolations
cross	inclination	

*P*antomime is the art of acting without words. It is often called the "art of silence." Because all actors are seen before being heard or understood, the art of acting without using speech is part of the first phase of your acting training. Indeed, pantomime was the first form of acting. Throughout the ages, pantomime has gone hand in hand with dance and was the forerunner of classical ballet.

Traditional pantomimes have delighted European and Asian audiences for centuries. However, it was Marcel Marceau, the French actor, who made Americans aware of the power of mime. His cross-country tours of full-evening programs on stage and his appearances as guest star on television introduced many people to this ancient art form. If you ever see him on film, watch carefully every expression and movement, for they are perfect examples of the original art.

Value of Pantomime

When young actors first go on stage, they tend to rely mainly on their voices in order to communicate with an audience. They forget that in everyday living they spend a great deal of time with **nonverbal communication** — they frequently communicate without words. They use facial expressions, gestures, and body language constantly. The art of "silent acting" is even more expressive and common on stage.

The Kabuki theater of Japan is a stylized form of pantomime. Kabuki actors are rigorously trained to use bodily coordination, gesture, and facial expression to tell classical Japanese tales.

You should remember that technique in pantomime is never an end in itself. It is only a valuable means of making your stage movements and facial expressions more meaningful and your voice and speech more effective. Because the trend in modern media is for action to take the place of words, directors are always looking for actors who can communicate physically.

Purpose of Pantomime

Your work with pantomime logically follows your experience with improvisation. A responsive, expressive body is one of the actor's chief tools. For most people, physical coordination and poise are more a matter of training than heredity. The value of pantomime is to encourage meaningful movement, significant gesture, and animated facial expression. These can be developed through a program of exercises that are designed to keep your muscles nimble, to develop coordination, and to promote body control.

Pantomime demands a flexible and expressive body. Because of the close relationship between physical and emotional attitudes, it is important that you learn to use your body correctly and effectively through a program of regular exercise until the right habits are established and become automatic. Actors understand that the body is the outward expression of the inner personality. At the same time, the inner personality is also partly the result of physical attitudes.

The character of Cyrano de Bergerac demands a large stage presence and flamboyant manner which present themselves through gesture.
• • • • • • • • • • • • • • •

Since an actor's personal appearance is important in character portrayal, the first work in pantomime deals with normal posture, movement, and gesture. Smoothness in physical action is the happy medium between overrelaxation or flabbiness and overtension or rigidity. Coordination of all parts of the body is a basic requirement of expressive movement and bodily action.

Physical Training for Pantomime

Any exercise that develops physical coordination is valuable for you as you prepare to perform. Fencing and dancing are required courses in most drama schools. Tennis, golf, swimming, and skiing are good hobbies. Jogging, aerobic exercises, isometric exercises, which can be practiced at any time, and deep breathing of yoga are among the many forms of physical exercise recommended. Whenever possible, do not take a car, an elevator, or a bus — walk. Walking is still one of the best forms of exercise.

At all times, your body should move or sit as a whole. From the top of your head to the tips of your fingers and toes, your body should be expressive. As a matter of fact, it is always expressive, but not always in the way you might desire. For example, a slovenly walk, a rigid or slouching posture, irritatingly aimless gestures, or a wooden face reveal your personality just as clearly as do purposeful, vigorous movements and a radiant, mobile face. Nine times out of ten, the world will take you at your "face value." You are judged first by your appearance and manner, only much later by what you say and how you say it.

Relaxation

Behind bodily poise and skill in action is relaxation. This is a matter of inner composure and mental awareness as well as physical flexibility. Successful actors, like athletes, must not be tense, emotionally or physically. You should learn right away to let go consciously all over, from the top of your head to the soles of your feet, whenever you feel a sense of strain on the stage or in real life. A few deep breaths and loosening muscles all over also help.

Before starting a daily practice of physical exercises, you must get your body relaxed. The following exercises will help you. Repeat each exercise four times — first to the right and then to the left, or forward and then backward.

1. Raise, lower, and rotate your head without moving your shoulders. Let it roll freely, without the slightest tension.

2. Rotate shoulders forward then backward.

3. Move your arms in wide circles, first close to the body and then at shoulder height.

4. Rotate your lower arms from the elbow, clockwise and then counter-clockwise. Hold your arms straight down and slightly away from your body.

5. Rotate your hands from the wrist.

6. Lift your arms with wrists leading, first to the side, then to the front.

7. Shake your hands vigorously, keeping them completely relaxed.

8. Open and close your fists, stretching the fingers apart and then drawing them together.

9. Do the "five-finger exercises." Hold your hands out in front of you. Place the heels of your hands side by side with the open palms facing you. Make each hand into a fist. Roll back each finger one at a time — little, ring, middle, index, and thumb. Alternate one finger of the right hand with one finger of the left hand. Return hands to fists, closing one finger at a time. Try to make a smooth, wave-like action, beginning with the left thumb and then releasing one finger at a time all the way to the right thumb. Reverse the action.

10. Bend your body forward, back, and to each side.

11. Clasping your hands together, push your arms vigorously above your head. Then rotate your body to the left and to the right, keeping your head within your arms.

12. Rotate each leg in circles, kick as high as possible, and swing each leg forward and back.

13. Rise on your toes, bend your knees, and sit on your heels.

14. Rotate each foot at the ankle.

15. Pick up marbles with your toes.

A complete plan for relaxation in conjunction with your voice work is given on pages 64 to 65. It is advisable to practice these exercises after the exercises above.

Posture

Your posture is fundamental, not only to your health but also to your personal appearance. Often good posture offsets a plain face, and certainly in the

Posture and bearing contribute to the total picture of the character on stage. The manipulation and control of this dramatic element communicates inherent character as well as emotional reaction in a scene.
. . . .

theater it is of far greater importance. Therefore, the next step in training the body deals with normal posture, movement, and gesture.

To stand properly, hold your body erect with chest high, chin up, back flat, and arms and legs straight but not tense. Keep one foot slightly in front of the other, the weight centering on the ball of the forward foot. The following exercise will help you develop good posture. It should be repeated many times.

1. Stand erect with your weight on the balls of your feet.

2. Bend forward, perfectly relaxed, with your loosely hanging arms almost touching the floor.

3. Place your right hand on your chest and your left hand at the small of your back.

4. Raise your body to an upright position, expanding the diaphragm so that you feel your hands being pushed apart.

5. Finally, bring your head to an upright position. Hold the chin perpendicular to the throat.

6. Drop your arms to the sides. Shift your weight to the ball of one foot and move forward. Keep your chest high, head erect, and the small of your back flat.

Walking

In walking, maintain good posture. Face the world squarely with shoulders back, chest high, and the axis of your body directly over the feet. "Thinking yourself tall" may help you to add strength to your character. Although the heel strikes the ground a fraction of a second before the toes, your movement should spring from the balls of your feet, and it should be easy, poised, and rhythmical.

The length of your step will be set by many elements, such as your height, build, and physical energy. However, avoid striding, tiny steps, or plodding. Moving straight ahead with your weight on the balls of your feet is the natural way to walk, and walking in a straight line keeps the moving silhouette narrow. Except when playing parts that call for it, never place your feet more than two inches apart. Your body should swing easily from the hips, and your arms should swing in easy opposition to your legs. Beware of habitually looking at the ground.

When you turn, rotate on the balls of your feet, shifting your weight from one foot to the other. Never turn on your heels or cross one foot over the other, tripping yourself. Turn your entire body, including your head.

Remember to hold yourself erect when standing or walking. Avoid the common habits of leaning forward, holding one shoulder higher than the other, looking down as you walk, dragging your feet, walking on your heels, keeping your feet apart as you walk, or tensing any part of your body.

These exercises from daily life are designed to help you stand and walk correctly.

Imagine you are standing:

1. At the microphone in your auditorium, ready to give a speech.
2. In the doorway of a potential employer, waiting for an interview.
3. In the garden, watching a songbird in a tree.

Imagine you are walking:

1. On a sandy beach with a fresh wind blowing over the waves.
2. On Fifth Avenue in New York City, with the skyscrapers and church spires rising above you.
3. In a forest of tall trees on a brisk day.
4. Across a platform to receive an award.
5. On stage, trying out for a part.

Walking up and down stairs is excellent exercise. Think yourself tall, keeping your head and chest high. Rest your hand lightly on the banister. Try not to look at the stairs, especially if you are wearing heels or a long, full skirt.

Sitting

Getting to, into, and out of a chair is often a problem. First, decide where and why you are about to sit. Next, without making it obvious that you are doing so, locate the chair out of the corner of your eye. Decide the best route to the chair, stool, or bench that you will occupy. Normally you will walk there directly, but sometimes you will have to get around people and obstacles. When you arrive, turn so that the calf of your leg touches the chair. Then sit.

When sitting, maintain an erect position. Keep the back of your spine at a 90° angle to the seat. On stage, you will usually sit forward in a chair, particularly if it is padded or if you are playing an older person. However, if the chair is firm and your character would do so, you may lean easily against the back of the chair. Your hands will ordinarily rest in your lap or on the arms of the chair. Crossing your arms on your chest or folding them restricts your breathing and looks tense. Avoid playing with buttons, jewelry, or your hair. Just sit erect. Your feet may be crossed at the ankles, or one foot may be placed slightly in front of the other. Avoid crossing your legs, spreading your feet apart, and resting your hands or elbows on your knees.

In rising, let your chest lead, not your head. Keep your weight balanced on the balls of your feet, placing one foot slightly forward and using the rear one as a lever in pushing yourself up, once again keeping the axis straight. Never hang on to the arms of the chair or push yourself up from them. Take a deep breath while rising. This relaxes the throat, gives a sense of control, keeps the chest high, and leads into a good standing position.

Crossing and Turning

The middle area of the stage is called center, the front is downstage, and the back is upstage. The actor's right is stage right and his or her left, stage left as the actor faces the audience. To **cross** means to move from one position to another. On entering the stage, the actor leads with the upstage foot to keep the body open toward the audience. If you enter from stage right, start on your left foot. If you enter from stage left, start on your right foot. This takes some practice because we learn in early childhood to always start on the left foot. When you stop, stop with the upstage foot forward; and when you move again, start with that forward foot. Normally all turns are made to the front. When making turns, rotate on the balls of your feet.

Try these exercises in crossing and turning, walking, sitting, and rising.

Marcel Marceau is recognized as the foremost exponent of the art of mime. His one-man shows are divided by their form and content. In the part of his show called "Style Exercises," Marceau shows the individual struggling with natural elements, as in "Walking Against the Wind," or else making symbolic statements as in "Youth," "Maturity," "Old Age," and "Death."

In Thornton Wilder's The Happy Journey to Trenton and Camden, *the family's automobile trip is mimed on a bare stage. The actors work together to portray the bouncing of the car, backing up to read a missed road sign, rolling down a window, and swerving to avoid a dog. Stopping for gas includes the attendant's mime of the old style side-lifting car hood, and giving the car a quick buff while father keeps an eye on the imagined rear-view mirror.*

Marceau's body of work includes the character Bip. Bip is typically involved in one of life's struggles. In "The Mask Maker," Marceau is a man with a split personality. Through the use of his many faces, Marceau confronts the problem of illusion versus reality.

Freedom of movement and relaxation are important to conveying a sense of well-being and ease on the stage.

1. Enter stage right to speak at a microphone downstage center. Cross to center and turn downstage. Stand with one foot slightly advanced with your weight forward. To leave, turn right, shift your weight to the right foot, and go off stage right.

2. Enter stage right and cross to center. Remember that you have forgotten something and turn front, rotating on the balls of your feet. Start on the right foot and exit.

3. Enter left and walk diagonally upstage to up center where there is an imaginary bookcase. Get a book and go off right, starting on the right foot.

4. Enter stage right as if to meet a friend. Cross to chair at left center. Without looking at chair, turn front, touching chair with calf of upstage leg. Shift weight to upstage foot and lower body into the chair, keeping head and chest high. See your friend approaching stage left. Rise, pushing with the leg closest to the chair. Move to front center. Meet your friend and exit left.

Falling

Some roles will require you to fall onstage. The keys to safe and effective stage falls are: (1) breaking the body into segments — head, torso, hips, thighs, and legs — and lowering each segment to the floor; (2) controlling the body so that you are very close to the floor before you actually "fall"; and (3) absorbing the fall with the soft parts of the body — the forearms, thighs, legs — rather than the bony projections — elbows, hipbones, knees. Practicing the following exercise will enable you to fall safely and convincingly.

1. Relax, and sway or stagger backward.

2. Sway forward, dropping the hands and arms.

3. Relax from the ankles and bend the knees.

4. Pivot slowly and, as you do so, go closer and closer to the floor. Lower the shoulder that is closest to the floor and sink down.

5. Land on the side of the leg. Roll on the hip. Catch your weight on your forearm.

6. Lower the head to the ground.

Gesture

The movement of any part of the body to help express an idea is called a **gesture.** It may be a lift of the eyebrow, a toss of the head, or a sweeping movement of the arm and hand. A change of attitude is usually expressed first by the eyes, then by the response of the mouth and facial muscles, then by the reaction of the torso, and lastly by the motion of the arm, hand, and fingertips. These movements are so rapid that they seem simultaneous, but in training exercises, you must try to follow their natural sequence.

A few practical suggestions regarding the use of the arm and hand may help you develop controlled gestures. However, you should remember that all technical practice must eventually become second nature if your gestures are not to appear artificial and affected.

Use relaxation exercises to free your tight muscles and establish habits of graceful coordination. Almost every body movement begins with the chest.

Even the most natural of gesture and stance may be choreographed to create a certain effect. As in A Chorus Line, *the manner in which the actors stand while lined up for an audition tells us a little about their characters.*

An arm movement passes from the chest through the shoulder, the elbow, and wrist, and "slips off" the ends of the fingers. It is most important that every arm gesture finish at the fingertips. Nothing is more ineffective than an arm movement in which the fingers are curled flabbily at the ends or are stiff like paddles. The movement should be from the body, and the wrist should lead hand gestures. The key to smooth gestures is getting the elbows away from the body slightly before making the gesture. Every gesture must have a definite purpose. If there is no purpose, there should be no gesture. Since the sole purpose of a gesture is to emphasize or clarify a thought or feeling, it is better to do nothing at all than to make meaningless movements. Try to cultivate definite, clear-cut gestures.

When doing the following exercises, use your entire body, but focus your attention on the objects mentioned. See the object, touch it, react to it mentally, and finally take action. Let your eyes and mouth show your reactions. Show the shape, weight, and size of any object you pick up. After you have shown that you have picked it up, be sure to hold it or put it down definitely.

1. You are walking in a garden. Pick flowers from plants, bushes, and vines, and pull weeds. Select fruit from a tree, taste it, and throw it away. Select another piece and eat it.

2. You arrive at an airport shortly before take-off time. You are carrying a suitcase, an umbrella, a box of candy, and magazines. You drop your suitcase, and everything spills out. Put down everything else you are carrying in the process of recovering the contents of your suitcase. Retrieve everything and lift the suitcase last of all.

Acting Without Words

Pantomime is the basis of characterization, which in turn is the basis of acting. People express themselves in their bodily actions before they speak, so it is natural that the first step in acting is to create personalities without the use of words.

The close relationship between the physical and the emotional begins at birth and continues through life. Note that some listless people do slump, draw down their face, look at the ground, and drag their feet. If, therefore, you want to impersonate such a character, you can do those things and give a pretty good imitation. However, it would be better dramatically to imagine you are so utterly lazy, bored, and weary with life that your chest will naturally slump, your face droop, and your feet drag.

In other words, try to feel the emotion first and allow it to gain control of

Inner energy and concentration can create a sincere physical response. Cornelia Otis Skinner in her one woman show, The Wives of Henry VIII, *used body language to help portray and emphasize the differences between various characters.*

your body, but then consciously respond from your head to your feet. You will probably respond awkwardly at first. Then apply the technical principles and train yourself to respond not only sincerely but expressively as well.

General Principles

General principles of the techniques of pantomime are based on what human beings do physically in response to emotional stimuli. Your richest source of authentic material for pantomimes is careful observation of people in daily life, individually or in crowds. Watch facial expressions, mannerisms, gestures, and ways of walking. You may find it profitable to analyze the movements of television, movie, and stage actors. Also note how your own bodily responses reflect your feelings.

There are two phases of your work with pantomime. You have studied the first — exercises to relax your muscles and free your body for quick expression of feeling. The second phase is the creation of characterizations in which feeling prompts a bodily response. Both activities demand concentration of thought and interest in detail. You will find it takes a great deal of time and practice to create the exact effect you desire.

Physical Principles

There are a few established principles that affect acting. They are based on what people often do in real life as well as on the best way to communicate a feeling or idea. The following are some of these principles. Try to apply them as you work out your pantomimes.

1. The chest is the key to all bodily action.

2. The wrist leads most hand gestures.

3. Keep the arms away from the body when gesturing. Except on specific occasions when it is necessary for communication purposes, do not gesture above the head or below the waistline.

4. Opposite action emphasizes physical movement. Pulling the arm back before delivering the blow makes the punch more emphatic.

5. Arms and hands should always be moved in curves, never in straight lines, unless you are deliberately trying to give the impression of awkwardness or being ill-at-ease.

6. Positive emotions, such as love, honor, courage, and sympathy, are evidenced by a high chest and head, free movement, broad gestures, and animated facial expression.

7. Negative emotions, such as hate, greed, fear, and suffering, contract and twist the body and are evidenced by a shrunken chest, tense movement, restricted gestures, and drawn features.

8. Facial expression — the use of the eyes, eyebrows, and mouth — usually precedes action.

9. Whenever possible, make all gestures with the upstage arm, the one away from the audience, and avoid all tendency to cover the face.

10. Some exaggeration of bodily response is essential to being clearly understood.

11. Always keep the audience in mind and direct reactions to it.

12. All action must be definite in concept and execution, and all movement must be clearly motivated.

Standard Pantomimic Expressions

The suggestions below are standard pantomimic expressions. After you have familiarized yourself with them, choose one that stimulates your imagination and create a character and situation to fit it.

Body as a Whole

1. Feet together, weight on both feet, with head and body lifted slightly represent aloofness, indifference, or trained self-control.

2. Weight carried to the front foot with the head and body leaning slightly forward represents interest, persuasion, sympathy, enthusiasm, and positive emotions.

3. Weight carried to the rear foot with the head and chest pulled back and turned away represents fear, hesitation, deep thought, amazement, and negative emotions.

4. Shrunken chest and bowed head with shoulders forward and down represent old age, envy, greed, pain, sorrow, and other negative emotions.

The Four Basic Hand Gestures

1. *Palms up* are appropriate for pleading, presenting ideas, and offering sympathy. Let movement reach fingertips.

2. *Palms down* are appropriate for negation, refusal, condemnation, fear, horror, and negative ideas.

3. *Clenched fists* represent anger and effort at control.

4. *Pointed finger* and extended arm are useful for pointing out, commanding, and directing.

Feet and Legs

1. Feet apart with legs straight denotes arrogance, strong confidence, or defiance.

2. Feet apart with legs bent denotes lack of bodily control, old age, great fatigue.

3. Tapping the foot depicts irritation, impatience, nervousness.

4. Twisting one foot denotes embarrassment.

5. Feet apart, head high, and hands or fists on hips represent conceit, scorn, contempt, self-assertiveness, or challenge.

Head and Face

1. Head raised, eyebrows lifted, eyes wide, and mouth open represent fear, horror, joy, and surprise.

2. Head raised, eyebrows lifted, and mouth drawn down depict comic bewilderment or a quizzical state.

3. Head down, eyebrows down, and mouth set or twisted by biting lips show worry, meditation, and suffering.

4. Raised eyebrows, wide eyes, smiling or open lips may depict innocence, stupidity, or flirtatiousness.

Carol Channing recording Ludwig Bemelman's Madeline *for Caedmon Records. Notice that, though she has no audience, Ms. Channing reacts to the reading with her whole body.*

Characterization

Characterization in pantomime involves placing a character in a situation and showing that character's feelings through nonverbal expression. This entails two mental processes — imitation and imagination. You must develop a memory bank of emotions by carefully observing other people. When you see a person involved in a highly emotional situation, observe facial expressions, gestures, and body language. Draw upon your observations when creating parts to be sure your characterization is true to life. However, this is only the beginning, for you must use your imagination to place and maintain yourself in the part you are playing.

After you have put on some comfortable clothes that leave your body free for action, run through the relaxing and other practice exercises. Then imagine yourself in situations such as the following.

Activities to Show Emotional Response
• • • • • • • • • • • • •

Emotion affects our bodies in various ways. In practicing these exercises, be sure that you feel the emotion first. Then let your face and body respond.

1. You are alone in your home. Go to the television set and adjust it. You find that you are watching the climax of a horror picture. Suddenly you hear a sound at the window. As you listen, the sound continues. The window slowly opens and a hand appears. You seize a book and hurl it at the hand, which promptly disappears. You tiptoe to the window, shut it, lock it, close the drapes, and fall into a chair, relieved but frightened.

2. Practice falling several times (see page 38). Then imagine yourself in the following situations.

    a. You receive a wound in the shoulder. Fall from loss of blood.

    b. You step on roller skates left on the floor. Fall, get up, and put away the skates, limping from a sprained ankle.

    c. You suddenly feel faint and fall. Then you recover, get up, and stagger to a chair, sitting down weakly.

    d. You are walking downstairs. You slip and fall down several steps.

3. You have quarreled with your girlfriend or boyfriend. You are standing by a window, looking out, frowning, and biting your lip. Your chest is sunken; your body is slumped. The phone rings. Your face lights up, with eyes wide and lips smiling. Then you run to the phone and lift the receiver, holding it in your upstage hand. Let your face reflect the conversation. When you hang up, you show by your movements whether the quarrel is over or not.

4. You are a feeble man or woman coming out to sit in the sun. You walk with short, uncertain steps. Your head is down, and your face, drawn. You sit down slowly with great effort and gradually relax as the sun warms you. Someone calls you, and you express your irritation by frowning and shaking your head. Then you rise, pushing yourself up from the chair. Hurry away as fast as your stiff limbs will allow, expressing worry and agitation.

Individual Pantomimes

Now you can begin working out real pantomimes involving careful planning, rehearsing, and presentation in class. The individual pantomimes may be divided into imitations of people you know and imaginary characterizations.

Preparation

In your pantomime of a real person, you should first determine that individual's chief characteristics. Is that person friendly? Timid? Boisterous? Suspicious? Glamorous? Physically vigorous? Discontented? Next, note mentally the details of the person's habitual facial expression, especially the eyes and mouth. Observe how that person holds the head, moves the hands, and walks. Decide what makes that person different from any other human being. Then place your character in a situation. (You need not have actually seen your character in such a situation, but you must be able to imagine how that person would react to it.) Take plenty of time to think through the exact reactions to your imaginary situation. Visualize them as if you were watching your character on a television screen. Finally, imitate what you have imagined your character would do.

In your imaginary characterizations, you should follow much the same procedure. You will, however, have to begin by inventing the details that will characterize the person you plan to play. What is your character's age? What are the physical traits? How does your character dress? What makes your character a distinctive individual? Only when you can see your character as clearly as someone you actually know will you be able to make your character live.

Whether your character is real or imaginary, you must work out in detail the situation in which you plan to place your character. Have your character enter a definite environment in a clear-cut state of mind and body. Invent something that will change the mood. The conclusion should leave no uncertainty in the mind of your audience about the mental state of the character when leaving the stage.

You will also need to visualize in detail the setting of your pantomime. Be sure you know the exact position of the doors, windows, furniture, and props you will use. Make the location of things clear to your audience. Put objects back where you got them. Use your body as the reference point for what you use. For example, relate to the things in your setting as being eye-, chest-, waist-, or knee-high.

Size, shape, weight, resistance, texture, and *condition* are important elements in pantomime. Show your audience the exact *size* of an object wherever possible. In conveying its size to your audience, consider the height, length, and width of the object. Small objects, such as cups, books, and food, can be outlined with the hands. Large objects, such as furniture or shrubbery, require the involvement of your whole body. Extremely large objects, such as trees or houses, need to be outlined through eye and head movements. Some objects may change in size during your pantomime, such as an ice cube that melts or a balloon that loses air.

Objects have different shapes. Some are round; some are square. Other common shapes are ovals, rectangles, and triangles. Convey *shape* as you do size, through the use of eyes, hands, and whole body.

Every item you handle has *weight.* A sack of popcorn does not weigh the same as a sack of sugar. A cement brick weighs more than a sack of sugar but far less than a gold brick. Your pantomimed muscular tension conveys an object's weight. Never let the audience have a vague notion of weight. For example, the idea that "something is being carried" is not specific enough. You must show that "a small, lightweight square box" is being carried, picked up, or put down.

Objects also have a quality called resistance. *Resistance* is the firmness or solidity of an object. A wall is solid and does not give way when you push on it. A balloon blown up changes in solidity when it bursts in your hands. A down-filled pillow gives far more when it is grasped in your hands than does a basketball. Pushing a baby carriage demonstrates less resistance than pushing a stalled automobile. Resistance also involves the object's response to your actions. If you pull a rope, does something go up or come toward you? If you pull an artificial rose petal, does it come off easily or must you yank it?

The surfaces of objects have a definite texture. Determine the *texture* of your object. Is it rough or smooth? Jagged or rounded? Is the surface sandy? Pebbly? Prickly? Concentrate on that texture as you touch your object. Allow your senses to respond to what you are touching. The more sensorily involved with your object, the more expressive your reactions will be. And you will convey through your facial expressions and body language your sensory reactions to your object. Touching a velvet cushion is very different from touching a cactus.

Many ideas or things that you use in your pantomimes will be in a particular state or have a particular condition that must be expressed through your actions. For example, changing states or conditions are hot to cold, solid to liquid, youth to age, happiness to sadness, life to death. Specific degrees of a state or condition are sweetness, sourness, spiciness, brightness, or loudness. Motion is a condition you must also remember. Youth and the aged move differently. An antelope moves with grace as compared to a gorilla, which lumbers awkwardly. Planes are propelled into the air at takeoff, while ships glide away from a pier at launching time.

Last of all, assume the physical appearance of your character as nearly as you can. Feel yourself to be your character's age and size. Let your character's state of mind take possession of you until your face, hands, and feet are reacting as your character's would in the imagined situation.

While working out your individual pantomime, keep the following directions constantly in mind.

1. Decide whether you will begin your pantomime on stage in a neutral position — head down or looking straight ahead, arms down, hands folded in front or facing upstage in a similar position — or whether you will enter from the wings.

2. Set your mental image in detail, knowing exactly how much space you are to use, the location of the furniture, and the shape, weight, and position of every imaginary prop you will be using. If you move an object, make very clear its shape, weight, and new position. After you have made your audience see your setting and props, you must remember not to break the illusion by shifting an article without clear motivation and action.

3. Visualize the appearance and emotional state of your character in minute detail.

4. Imagine yourself to be dressed in the clothes of your character. Make your audience see the weight, shape, and material of each garment and its effect upon you in your particular mood and situation.

5. Remember that in all dramatic work, the thought comes first — think, see, and feel before you move. Let your eyes respond first, then your face and head, and finally, the rest of your body. This is a *motivated sequence.*

6. Keep your action simple and clear-cut.

7. Always have a key action early in the pantomime that establishes who you are and what you are doing. Pantomime should not be a guessing game.

8. Keep every movement and expression visible at all times to your entire audience.

9. Never make a movement or gesture without a reason. Ask yourself: "Does it make clear who I am, how I feel, or why I feel as I do?" Take time to make every movement clear and definite.

10. Try out and analyze every movement and gesture until you are satisfied that it is the most truthful, effective, and direct means of expressing your idea or feeling.

11. Make only one gesture or movement at a time but coordinate your entire body with it and focus the attention of the audience upon it. The "setting" of each action is the heart of nonverbal physical action.

12. Rehearse until you know that you have created a clear-cut characterization and that the action began definitely, remained clear throughout, and came to a conclusion.

13. Plan your introduction very carefully. It may be humorous or serious, but it must arouse interest in your character and the situation in which your character is placed. It also must make clear all the details of the setting and preliminary situation.

14. Plan the ending very carefully. You should leave the stage in character.

Suggestions for Individual Pantomimes

If you find it difficult to get started, the following suggestions may help you. At first, it is not a bad idea to run through them all in rather rapid succession to get yourself limbered up physically and imaginatively. Then select one and work it out in detail, elaborating on mannerisms and concentrating on details. After creating a single study that satisfies you with its clarity, build up a sequence of events that brings about a change of mood and situation. Finally, build up to a definite emotional climax and conclusion. Such a pantomime will require hours of preparation before it will be ready for class presentation.

1. Standing erect, with your feet close together, suggest the following:
    a. A butler or maid
    b. A model displaying the latest fashions

2. With legs wide apart and a comfortable posture, represent the following:
    a. A warm-hearted host standing in front of the fireplace beaming at the guests.
    b. A political candidate addressing a friendly meeting

3. With alert posture, one foot somewhat ahead of the other and your weight definitely placed on the ball of the forward foot, represent the following:
    a. A high school student watching a football game
    b. An energetic cheerleader at a pep rally
    c. A politician pleading for votes

4. With a similar posture, except that the weight is definitely shifted to the rear foot, impersonate the following:
    a. An old person afraid to cross the street
    b. A mother disgusted with the caterpillar her child is showing her

5. Walk across the room, kneel, and kiss a lady's hand in the following manner:
    a. A knight of the Middle Ages in armor
    b. A cavalier of the court of Charles II, with a long curled wig, a stiff, outstanding coat with ruffled sleeves, and a plumed hat

6. Walk across the room and curtsy in the manner of the following characters:
    a. A colonial lady at a formal party wearing a full-skirted gown and towering headdress
    b. A beauty of the old South during the Civil War

7. Cross the room, sit in a chair, and rise as the following characters:
    a. A criminal in the witness box at the trial
    b. A miser counting money and listening for eavesdroppers
    c. A gossip retelling the latest scandal
    d. A parent at the bedside of a sick child
    e. A king or queen dismissing his or her court

8. Suggest, by smiling, the following characters:
    a. A seasick traveler trying to appear sociable
    b. A teacher greeting some new students

9. Suggest, by facial expression, the following situations:

   a. A chef opening a rotten egg

   b. A small child taking a nasty-tasting medicine

10. Present the following characters as completely as you can. Sit or walk, as you choose, and include enough action to show each one in a real situation:

    a. An egotistical, self-confident businessperson

    b. A conceited rock star

    c. A swaggering campus leader

    d. A distinguished society leader

Group Pantomimes

Group pantomimes should follow your individual ones and eventually lead you into the acting of a short play. They will, therefore, demand even more careful planning and rehearsal time than you have devoted to your individual pantomimes. They may be based on plays, novels, stories, or such secondary sources as photographic magazines, newscasts, and films. Feel free, also, to draw upon the daily life about you.

On stage actors, while concentrating on their own movement, should also be constantly aware of the movement of other actors on stage and their relationship to them.
• • • • • • • • • • • • • • • • •

Plan your story as you would a one-act play. Center it on one interesting situation that has a carefully worked out exposition, rising action, climax, and a logical and clear-cut conclusion. Create an interesting setting and five or six strongly contrasted characters. Be sure that each character is a real personality. Motivate all entrances, exits, and side action, and be sure that all characters are seen at all times. Avoid bunching, huddling behind furniture, or standing in stiff lines. Your stage picture should be well balanced and attractive, and attention should always be focused on the center of interest. Rehearse together until you have a unified whole in which each character is a living, breathing person. Do not rush your action, for the audience must be able to follow the development of all the roles. Take plenty of time to tell your story effectively and pictorially. Remember that you are limited to visual means of presenting your ideas. Try to build your plot around an emotional situation with considerable human interest. Avoid trite material. Be original, imaginative, and hardworking.

Suggestions for Group Pantomimes
• • • • • • • • • • • • •

The following suggestions may be useful to you. Be sure you plan the entrances and exits carefully and keep the action clear and unhurried. See that each character is a distinct personality and that the stage picture is well balanced at all times.

1. A boy and a girl quarrel and make up.

2. A group of six children play hide-and-go-seek. One must be chosen to be "it." The others hide.

3. Several persons apply to a personnel director for a position.

4. A baby-sitter takes charge after the parents have departed.

5. A photographer takes a family picture of four generations.

6. A shy young man pays his first call on a girl, who does not know how to put him at ease.

Applications
• • • • • • • • • • • • •

1. Write on separate pieces of paper ten suggestions for pantomimes that can be presented by a single person. Two should show just one mood. Two should reveal a transition from one mood to another. Two should require a definite entrance and exit. Two should necessitate sitting and rising. Two should require falling down and getting up again. Bring these suggestions to class and mix them up. Let each class member draw one and present it in class. You may go around the class as many times as you wish.

2. Give as many individual and group pantomimes as possible before the class. Analyze each performance to see whether it has convincing characterization, clarity, reality, and effectiveness. These questions, among others, should be discussed:

   a. Has the pantomime been carefully prepared?

b. Are the characters interesting, lifelike, and vivid? Do you become emotionally involved with them?

c. Do the gestures and movements seem sincere, convincing, clear, and properly motivated?

d. Does all the action help flesh out and clearly represent the characters and their situation for you?

e. Is the action clear-cut, realistic, prolonged sufficiently, and exaggerated enough to be seen by the whole audience?

f. Can you visualize the setting, the props for the characters, and the clothing of the characters?

g. Does the pantomime have a definite beginning and ending?

Mime

Although many performers make no distinction between mime and pantomime, **mime** is a special art form, an offspring of pantomime. Mime is abstract and highly stylized. Because it is abstract, mime does not imitate physical action as it occurs in real life. Rather, it gives an illusion of that action. In fact, it is through that lack of exactness that its greater meaning is conveyed. Mime replaces exactness with *conventions* — abstractions that communicate symbolic or literal meanings. For example, the mime does not walk as we ordinarily do. None of the mime walks — and there are several — look like normal walking. The mime walk is an *illusory walk,* giving only the idea of walking.

Pantomime deals with reality, while mime goes beyond reality. Thus, mime is not limited by the real world. A mime may look at the world from the point of view of a cat. This does not necessarily mean that the mime is acting out being a cat. Through catlike actions and behavior, the mime may help us see, think, and feel from the cat's point of view.

A mime is more concerned with the expression of an idea than with the exact pantomime of a specific action. Some mime themes might be expressed in a few simple words: "Loneliness," "Young Dreams," or "A Born Loser." Or the theme may be expressed in a phrase or a statement: "Old Friends Are Gone, Only the Birds Remain," "I'm Young, and I Can Do Anything," or "Down Inside, I Know That No Matter How Well Things Seem To Be Going, I'll Fail in the End."

In mime, the action conveys the theme. In pantomime, the action conveys only action. For example, simply flying a kite can be a fine pantomime. But snagging it on a tree after struggling to get it soaring high in the sky may be a mime's way of saying: "Our aspirations often become entangled with the things of this world."

The mime is not concerned with the element of time. *Mime is frozen in time* — the present. The mime concentrates on a sequence of actions in time, each action performed in its proper sequence and completed before moving on to the next. The mime must know the physical and dramatic origins of each mimic action. What muscle groups and body parts are necessary to perform the action? When in the sequence of dramatic events is this action needed?

Each primary mime action is preceded by a preparatory action. This preparatory action is usually a movement opposite to the action the mime wishes the audience to follow. It is much like the windup of a baseball pitcher prior to the delivery of the ball. For instance, the mime, before reaching out for an object, would first draw the arm back somewhat. This exaggerates the action and focuses the audience's attention on the action. This principle can be applied to most physical action.

Both the pantomimist and the mime work with imaginary objects — a flower, a glass, or a ball. But the mime may also use parts of the body or the whole body to become an object or express an idea. The opening of the hands forms a butterfly or a book; the clasping of the arms and hands around the body becomes the hugging of a friend or lover; the writhing of the entire body becomes the motion of a snake. Pantomime is always silent, but mime may use nonverbal sounds, such as escaping air, a telephone busy signal, or the screech of tires.

Everything in mime must be exaggerated. This exaggeration lifts mime above simple repetition of an action. Most hand actions are executed with a *setting* of the action. Mimes refer to this setting as *the click*. For example, if you were to take an imaginary drinking glass, at the moment at which the glass is grasped, your fingers should "snap" around the glass. This snap establishes the glass's shape, size, and resistance in one action. The setting of the action is seen quite readily when a mime suggests the presence of a wall. Each hand snaps into place from the wrist as contact with the wall is made. The snap shows the wall, its flatness, and its resistance.

The mime works from five basic facial expressions: *happy, sad, surprised, angry, afraid.* That is why traditional mimes emphasize the eyes and the mouth in their makeup.

Conventional Mime Actions

Mime is made up of many traditional conventions. One of the most basic mime conventions is that of the *illusory walk.* There are several mime walks that are commonly used. The simplest is done in the following manner. Stand with your feet pointed out at a 45° angle. Place your weight on your right foot. Lift your left heel so that you are on the ball of the left foot. Then, shift your weight to your left foot by dropping the left heel and at the same time raising the right heel. Once you have the feet shifting rhythmically, add an arm swing. The arms swing in an exaggerated, but not overdone, manner, crossing in front of the body. The illusion of walking appears when you move opposite arms and feet. Swing the right arm when you lift the left foot and the left arm when you lift the right foot.

A second illusory walk begins with the same starting position. The left foot is lifted and stretched out away from you at a 45° angle and then brought back toward you in a sliding motion. The third illusory walk is much like the second except that when the left foot is brought back to the starting position, the knee is turned inward and the foot is lifted behind and away from you with a snap. At the same time that the left knee is turned inward, the right knee is turned out to prepare for its step. Although the third illusory walk is difficult to master, the illusion is quite effective. It is also the walk used by many of the famous mimes.

In all the mime walks, there should be a lifting of the body just as the weight is shifted from one foot to the other. This is very important to the illusion. The exaggerated arm movement is also important. Speeding up the walk, leaning the body forward, and swinging the arms across in front of the body (much like in ice skating) will create the illusion of running.

Another mime convention is the *rope pull.* Stand with your body facing "two o'clock" with your left foot forward, knee bent, and your weight on it. Reach out as far as you can with your left hand, and grasp a 1-inch rope. Take the rope with your right hand just in front of the left hip. Now *pull.* Your weight shifts to your right foot, and the left hand is in front of your right hip. The rope should be straight through the two hands, which are parallel to the floor. The rope should maintain its diameter throughout the pull. Now comes the tricky part! Let go with the right hand, reach over the left, and grasp the rope about a foot in front of the left hip. Then, with a quick movement, shift your weight back onto your left foot as you reach out as far as you can with your left hand to take the rope for another pull. It is the quick "one-two" of the right hand-left hand switch that creates the illusion of pulling a large rope.

Another mime convention is the *ladder climb.* Remember that the rungs of a ladder form a sort of picture frame that can help you create the illusion as the audience "sees" your face move from frame to frame. When you climb a ladder, your arms and legs work together on the same side. Bend the elbows slightly, raise your arms above your head, and grasp the rung of the ladder with both hands. Now lift your right foot. Then lower it. As you lower your left foot, bring your left arm straight down. The left hand is still grasping the rung of the ladder. Look up, see the next rung, take it with your right hand, lift the right foot, and bring hand and foot down together, watching the rung as it passes before your eyes. Coming down is a little more challenging because there is more illusion to create. Place your hands on the ladder rungs as before. Lift the left foot and suspend it on the rung. Look down (about shoulder level) at the rung you are going to grasp. Let go with the left hand and take the rung below as you step down. As the left hand comes down, the right hand must go up to the "rung above" position, and the right foot must be lifted ready to step down. Obviously, the hands are passing each other, but the illusion is that of descending.

Still another mime convention is *climbing up and down stairs.* First, go up the stairs. Use the first mime walk for this illusion. Grasp the handrail about eye level with your right hand. If you are not sure about the size of the rail, take hold of your left wrist, get the feel of that size, and use that for the rail. Now, as you walk — usually taking three steps — bring the hand down past your body at the angle of the rail until your hand is just past your hip. Then reach up and take the rail again. Remember the click before each new action starts. Continue up the stairs. Coming down the stairs is easy, too. Just reach down in front of you at a comfortable distance (about midthigh), grasp the rail lightly with the right hand, and move the hand up beside you to about the midchest level. As you bring the arm up, extend the elbow out. This will enable you to keep the rail straight.

Conventional Mime Makeup

Another convention associated with mime is the makeup. The classic mime tries to neutralize the face by painting it a white mask, stopping at the jawline, hairline, and in front of the ears. The detailed makeup is individualized by each mime, but all mimes make up the eyes and mouth, the two most expressive parts of the face. Some draw in brows, some add a tear, a flower, a star, or other character feature somewhere on the face. Most classic mimes

The classic mime neutralizes the face by making it a white mask. The white makeup stops at the jawline, hairline, and in front of the ears.

still use the conventional makeup, but there are many who perform without the white mask. The choice is yours.

Conventional Mime Costume

Costume for mime is also a convention. However, there are many kinds of mime dress. The most important item of clothing is a flexible shoe, such as a ballet shoe. Some mimes perform in leotard and tights or dance pants. Others wear jump suits. Some wear bib overalls and striped knit shirts. Professional mimes often use specially made costumes consisting of fairly tight stretch pants and a matching short-waisted jacket worn over a knit shirt. Marcel Marceau's Bip is one of the few to use a character costume.

In recent years, a Swiss-trained mime troupe called Mummenschanz opened the doors of mime to the use of special props and nontraditional subjects. Many of their props were really costumes, such as stretch sacks. However, their imaginative style and creative mimes challenged other mimes to expand the form of mime beyond the "costumeless, propless" tradition of classic mime.

Mime Exercises

Mime exercises are of three types: inclinations, rotations, and isolations (separations). An **inclination** is a bending of the body to the front, the side, or the rear. **Rotations** are a turning or pivoting of a part of the body, such as the head or chest. **Isolations** separate parts of the body for individual development and expression.

Mime exercises begin with the heels close together and the toes pointing out at a 45° angle. The mime divides the body into six major parts: head, neck, shoulders, chest, waist, and hips. These may be further subdivided for more refined exercises. Complete each movement before moving to the next. Do not rush.

Inclinations (Move Each Body Part One at a Time)

1. Incline the head, the neck, the shoulders, the chest, the waist, and then the hips to the right. As the hip inclines right, slide the left foot along the floor away from the body. Straighten up one step at a time. Then repeat the action to the left. Remember to slide the right foot out for the hip inclination.

2. Do a vertical inclination, keeping the body relaxed. Drop the head forward. Next, the neck. The chin should be resting lightly on the chest. Now the shoulders. You will look very round-shouldered. Now drop the

chest forward. Feel as if the chest has caved in just above the stomach. Now drop at the waist. This should put the back in a position parallel to the floor. Finally, drop from the hips. Depending upon your physical flexibility at this time, you should be touching your toes, the floor, or perhaps you can even place your hands flat on the floor. Now go back to your standing position, doing your inclinations slowly in reverse order.

Rotations (Move Each Body Part in Smooth Circles)

1. To rotate the head and neck, start by dropping the chin on the chest. Rotate the head and neck to the right, back, left, and front. Raise the head.

2. To rotate a shoulder, lift the shoulder and move it in a circle forward, down, and back to the original position.

3. To rotate the chest laterally, lift the chest and move it in a clockwise fashion. You may also rotate the chest forward and back.

4. To rotate the waist, move it in a circle clockwise.

5. Following the same procedure, rotate the hips clockwise.

6. Now repeat these five rotations but reverse directions. Follow each step as described above.

Isolations

1. Isolate the head by moving it straight forward, then straight back, to the left, and to the right. Keep the head level; do not incline it. Now rotate the head to the right, then to the left.

2. Isolate the right shoulder. Raise it up; lower it; move it forward; move it back. Rotate the shoulder forward. Rotate it to the rear.

3. Try isolating the leg from the hip. Then isolate the lower leg and after that isolate the foot itself.

Applications
• • • • • • • • • • • • •

1. Line up as two teams facing each other for a rope pull. Your teacher will call out which team pulls. Remember, when one team pulls, the other team must "give" by leaning forward.

2. You are in a box. Show the size and shape of the box.

3. Get a kite into the air. Tug on the string to get it higher and higher. The string breaks, and the kite drifts away. Watch it and then walk off stage sadly.

4. Design a mime. Give it a title. Write your title on a large piece of paper or cardboard, and set it up before the class. Turn in your mime statement and the outline of your mime to your teacher before you begin. Then present your mime to the class. You may enter from the wings, or you may begin from a neutral standing position.

5. A *combination* is the putting together of inclinations, rotations, and isolations. Try this combination. Isolate the right arm by lifting it from the body slightly. Raise it from the elbow until the arm is at shoulder level. The forearm should hang down toward the floor with the hand relaxed. Imagine that a string is attached to your wrist and raise the isolated forearm perpendicular with the body until it is parallel to the shoulder. The hand should still be hanging limply. Next, lift the left foot and place it toe-down across the right foot, shifting the weight to the right foot as you do so. Now, incline the head to the right and let your weight sag on the right arm. You should have a "mime lean" and appear as if you are leaning on a wall, a mantel, or shelf.

Recalling Ideas

1. Why is pantomime the first stage in training actors?

2. Name three forms of nonverbal communication that people use daily.

3. What skills does pantomime demand?

4. What is the purpose of gesture?

5. List the four basic hand gestures.

6. What does characterization in pantomime involve?

7. Explain how mime differs from pantomime.

8. Name and explain the three types of mime exercises.

Discussing Ideas

1. Discuss the importance of a responsive, expressive body to an actor. Why is expressiveness so essential?

2. Discuss the importance of gesture on stage. Explain why it is sometimes better to make no gesture at all.

3. Characterization in pantomime demands both imitation and imagination. Discuss the importance of each in character portrayal.

4. Mime does not imitate physical action as it occurs in real life but instead gives an illusion of that action. Discuss why this key feature of mime appeals to audiences.

Careers

For some careers, business skills may be as important as theater arts skills. For example, the **producer, director,** and **business manager** need to understand and use good business practices.

Producers acquire plays from **playwrights,** hire directors, rent theaters, and raise money to finance shows. They use **lawyers** to draw up contracts specifying the playwright's royalty and the amount of control the producer has over the play. They raise money (from $250,000 to over $1 million for Broadway productions) from investors. They negotiate contracts with everyone connected with the show, often dealing with unions representing those personnel.

Directors (1) analyze plays and determine interpretation, (2) oversee the efforts of playwrights, technicians, and designers, (3) cast performers, (4) supervise rehearsals, and (5) coordinate each element of the production. During rehearsals they may be assisted by a **rehearsal secretary, assistant director,** and **stage manager.** Directors are the final authority on performance, design, and cost.

Business Managers may assist producers. They may oversee the budget of each designer or manager and approve expenditures for rentals, materials, and other needs.

The producer needs a strong business background and some theater arts background, the director a good mix of both, and the business manager more business than theater skills. Business administration at the college level would be helpful for all.

Producers may enter their profession through financial investing, directors from the performing arts, and business managers from business or financial institutions.

Chapter 4

Voice and Diction

You Will Learn

Why relaxation, proper breathing, and good posture are the keys to a good speaking voice.

Why a daily vocal exercise program is important to the development and maintenance of a strong, flexible stage voice.

How to develop a rich, strong, and interesting voice.

Vocabulary

resonance	pitch	optimum pitch	voiceless
nasality	inflection	volume	voiced
quality	monotone	rate	pronunciation
		diction	schwa

*A*n expressive voice and clear, correct speech are not only indispensable tools for the actor, they are also assets in every walk of life. Personnel directors list them among the assets needed for positions that involve meeting the public and sharing ideas. As the British playwright George Bernard Shaw so amusingly points out in *Pygmalion,* social standing and educational background are judged by the way a person talks.

Unfortunately, American actors have long been criticized for the quality of their speech on stage. Both the general public and the professional critics have often complained about the lack of vocal quality and the sloppiness of pronunciation in both the professional and the amateur theater. Critics have often noted that the problem is perhaps due to the tendency in recent years to emphasize audience involvement by playing up bodily action at the expense of clear verbal communication.

Recently, the American stage has faced the problem of poor language use directly. Directors of regional and repertory companies throughout the United States are now demanding that young actors speak clearly and correctly. These directors have made it known that poor pronunciation and careless mumbling will no longer be tolerated.

This chapter will make it possible for the serious student of drama to meet the speaking requirements that directors demand. It presents a simple and practical daily routine of exercises that are designed to improve and polish speaking ability. It presents fundamental principles that you must understand and apply. If you understand these principles and practice the exercises regularly, you can dramatically improve your speech habits.

Developing an Effective Voice

There is nothing mysterious or complicated about developing an effective voice. It depends primarily upon bodily relaxation, proper breathing, and good posture. Few people realize the close relationship between the voice,

Orson Welles' resonant voice communicated conviction and authority. Even in the medium of radio, his power and presence could be felt.

the emotions, and the body. The voice of a person who is ill, tired, worried, angry, nervous, hurried, or tense reflects those feelings. The voice becomes high-pitched, monotonous, or colorless. On the other hand, a person who is poised, self-confident, and healthy is more likely to have a pleasing voice. Consequently, your first efforts should be directed toward building a vigorous, well-controlled body and a confident attitude.

Voice is produced by the air from the lungs passing over the vocal folds, which are thin curtains of muscles with delicate edges. These folds set up vibrations, or waves. The vibrations become sounds and are amplified when they strike the resonating chambers of the throat, head, nose, and mouth. Exactly what sounds are produced depends upon the shape of these chambers, and this shape is determined by the position of the tongue, soft palate, lips, and lower jaw. For correct speech and voice production, it is necessary for you to have deep central breathing; an open, relaxed throat; flexible tongue and lips; and a relaxed lower jaw.

Human beings breathe and make sounds correctly from birth by using the vocal apparatus in a relaxed and natural way. However, the environment — home, community, region, or country — determines the manner in which we speak. Unfortunately, this can be slurred, garbled, nasal, or dialectical. Therefore, every student of the theater should begin a program of voice training as soon as possible. The poor vocal habits that teenagers often develop can be eliminated within an amazingly short period of time by regular exercise and deliberate concentration while speaking.

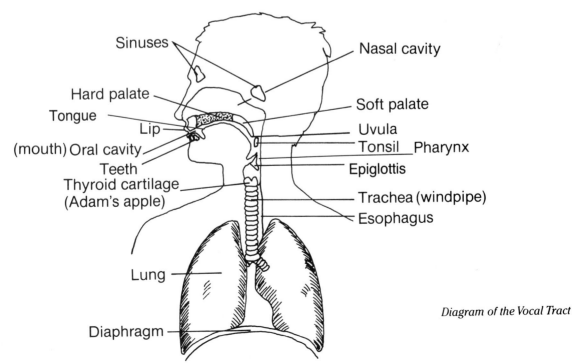

Diagram of the Vocal Tract

You will improve your ability to speak if you work at it every day. As part of your dramatics class homework, you should spend about 15 minutes a day, when you are feeling fresh and relaxed, in establishing good speech habits by regularly doing the exercises in this chapter.

Breath Control

Breath control determines the carrying power as well as the loudness of your voice. The first exercises should therefore deal with central breathing, consciously controlled.

No one can teach you how to breathe, for you have done so successfully since your birth, and you can breathe correctly when you are asleep or perfectly relaxed. There is some difference, however, between regular breathing and breathing for speech. In regular breathing, the inhalation (breathing in) and exhalation (breathing out) periods are of equal length. Breathing for speech requires a very brief inhalation period and a slow, controlled exhalation period. This is true because, for all practical purposes, speech is produced only when the breath is exhaled. In breathing for speech, therefore, you should inhale through the mouth, since this allows for more rapid intake of breath than does inhalation through the nose. You should work for a prolonged and controlled exhalation so that the outgoing breath will match your needs for sustained vocal tone. Controlled breathing is more important to the actor than deep breathing.

The first exercises for you to try in training your voice are those that will focus the breathing process in the center of your body and those that will strengthen and control the breath stream once it has been centered where it belongs. Practice these exercises every night and morning until central breathing gradually becomes automatic.

1. Place your hands on either side of the lower part of the rib cage. Now pant rapidly, laugh silently, and sniff in the air in tiny whiffs. Lie down and breathe deeply and regularly. Keep your hands in the same position.

2. Stand straight with an easy, well-balanced posture. Inhale slowly, making sure from the feeling under your hands that the whole rib cage is expanding. Hold your breath without straining for a count of six. Then exhale slowly and evenly while you mentally count, first to fifteen and then to twenty, twenty-five, and thirty. Be particularly careful to avoid muscular tension.

3. Repeat Exercise 2, gauging the evenness of your exhalation either by whistling or by making a soft sound as you breathe out, such as the

Actors in the French and English Restoration period needed to be masters of crisp articulation, vocal inflection, and breath control as their dialogue was often times dense and complex.

sound of *s* or *ah*. If the sound is jerky or irregular or fades at the end, repeat the exercise until you can keep the sound smooth and regular.

4. Use a favorite poem or prose passage for practice in breath control. Take a deep breath and see how far you can read in the selection before you have to take a second breath. Do not strain and be sure to relax after each effort. Your breath control will improve.

Relaxation

The degree of relaxation determines the beauty of the voice and the carrying power of the vowel sounds, which are made with an open, relaxed throat, a relaxed jaw, and flexible lips. Therefore, before any period of voice exercises, you must relax, consciously letting go both mentally and physically. Yawn! Stretch your whole body as an animal does after a nap. (Incidentally, watching a cat relax and move is an excellent exercise in itself for bettering your own reactions.) Feel the big muscles of your back, legs, and arms ease first. Imagine that a warm, relaxing shower is falling over your head. Imagine it passing over your forehead and wiping out the frown lines. Imagine it releasing the tension of the little muscles around your eyes, nose, mouth, and especially your cheeks, so that the lower jaw and lips are loose.

Next roll your head first to the left, then to the right, keeping the neck muscles relaxed. Then imagine the shower pouring over your whole body, relaxing your arms and fingertips, your chest, lungs, diaphragm, and even your toes. You should be yawning by this time, and that is one of the best voice exercises. With practice, you can learn to run through this process imaginatively when you are waiting to make a speech or standing in the wings before an entrance on the stage. You will also find it an excellent cure for stage fright. Also run through the posture exercises on page 34, and then do the breathing exercises on pages 62 and 63 before you begin vocal work. The importance of an erect, easily relaxed body should not be underestimated.

Practice of the following exercises demands careful use of your vocal apparatus.

For Relaxed Jaw

1. Let your head fall forward on your chest. Lift it up and back, letting the jaw remain loose. Drop it again and slowly roll the head over the right shoulder, back, over the left shoulder, and forward, describing a circle.

2. Drop your head forward again. Place your hands lightly on your cheeks and lift your head with your hands, keeping the jaw relaxed and being careful to avoid using the jaw muscles. When your head is lifted, the jaw should hang open. It helps sometimes to try to make your face as expressionless as possible. Looking blank will help relax the muscles.

3. Babble like a baby, saying *dä-dä-dä-dä lä-lä-lä-lä* brightly and feeling relaxed and happy, moving only the tip of the tongue. (In these and following exercises, refer to the list on pages 81 and 82 for pronunciation of vowel sounds.)

For Open Throat

1. Yawn freely, getting the feeling of an open, relaxed throat.

2. Take in a deep breath, relax your jaw, think of your throat as large, and exhale slowly.

3. Say: "I can talk as if I were going to yawn. Hear me talk as if I were going to yawn."

4. Say *lō-lā-lē-lä-lōo* gradually increasing the energy for each repetition. Give the vowels fullness and roundness, and relax your jaw. Sing the syllables on one note. Increase your volume by breathing deeply but do not tighten your throat. Use the tip of your tongue for the *l's.*

5. Repeat the following expressions, keeping the throat open: *lä-lä-lä-laughs, lä-lä-lä-lose, lä-lä-lä-loaves.*

Warm-up exercises that relax the throat and encourage flexibility of the mouth aid in creating a high quality performance.

For Flexible Lips

1. Say *ōō-ō-ô-ŏ-ä*, opening your lips from a small circle to a large one. Then reverse, saying *ä-ŏ-ô-ō-ōō*. These sounds may be sung with the piano, taking them all on one note. Keep the tongue flat in your mouth with the tip at the lower teeth. Keep your throat well open and your jaw relaxed.

2. Say *mē-mō-mē-mō-mē-mō-mē-mō*. Then sing these sounds with the piano.

For Flexible Tongue

1. Say rapidly: *fŭd-dŭd-dŭd-dŭd-däh-fŭd-dŭd-dŭd-dŭh-däh-fŭd-dŭd-dŭd-dŭd-däh-frill*. Trill the *r* in *frill*.

2. Keeping your jaw well relaxed, repeat the following sounds, watching with a hand mirror to see that your tongue is slowly arched as you go from one position to the next: *ä-ŭ-ēr-ä-ă-ĕ-ā-ĭ-ē*.

3. Say *ĭra-ĭra-ĭra-ĭra-ĭra-very*. Trill the *r* in *very*.

Resonance

The vibrant tone produced when sound waves strike the chambers of the throat, head, nose, and mouth is called **resonance.** The best practice for resonance is humming with an open, relaxed throat. The cavities of the head will vibrate automatically if you hum while throwing the voice forward through the facial mask. In English, only *m, n,* and *ng* should be sounded through the nose. All other sounds should be produced through the mouth. If the nasal passages are closed by a cold or raised soft palate, the sound becomes dull and blocked. This much-criticized **nasality** of many American voices is due to vowel sounds being forced through the nasal cavities, cutting down resonance, and leaving the voice flat. A disturbing twang results.

For Resonance

1. To locate your larynx and feel the vibration of the vocal cords, place your fingers *lightly* on your Adam's apple and say *b*. Then say *p* and *d*, then *t* and *v*, then *f* and *s*, and then *z*. Note the vibration on the *b, d, v,* and *z*. Also note the vibration on the vowel sounds *ā, ī, ē, ō,* and *ū*.

2. To feel the effect of obstructing the resonators, sing the word "hum" and then repeat it while you pinch your nose closed. Say "good morning," opening your mouth and your throat. Say it as if you were on the verge of tears and were swallowing them. Say it holding your nose closed. Say it with your teeth tightly set. Say it while drawing back your tongue in your mouth.

3. Say these words with full resonance: *ring, sing, ding-dong, bells, wind.*

For Speech and Breathing

1. Breathe in, relaxing your throat and lower jaw. Count "one" as you exhale. Repeat and count "one, two." Continue until you can count to twenty on one breath. Be careful not to tighten up. It may take you several weeks before you can reach twenty, but take time so that you can do it without straining. Any tension is bad.

2. Breathe in. Relax your throat and lower jaw. Say "Hong Kong" as you exhale, prolonging the vowel and *ng* sounds.

3. Breathe in. Relax your throat and lower jaw. Say "Hear the tolling of the bells — iron bells" as you exhale, prolonging the vowels and the *ng* and *n* sounds.

4. Breathe in. Relax your throat and lower jaw. Without straining, try to retain the position of your diaphragm as you exhale, saying slowly, "Roll on, thou deep and dark blue ocean, roll."

Voice Characteristics

There are four characteristics of the voice that must be used correctly if you are to become an effective and expressive speaker. These are *quality, pitch, volume,* and *rate.* Their development constitutes voice training.

In order to bring Shakespeare to the modern stage, actors, such as James Earl Jones in Timon of Athens, *must speak more precisely than in other forms of present day drama.*

Quality

The individual sound of your particular voice is called its **quality.** Its beauty and richness can be improved by keeping the resonating chambers of your throat and head open. Your daily speech habits are most important. Never speak with a tight throat, and always try to use a low, clear tone. Relax your throat frequently with a yawn, and breathe through your nose when you are not speaking. Never strain your voice.

The quality of your voice depends, for the most part, upon resonance and the correct formation of vowel sounds by the speech organs.

The vowel sounds, so important in the quality of your tone, are all made with the lower jaw relaxed. The position of the lips and tongue determines the sound. In pronouncing all vowels, you must keep the tip of the tongue at the base of the lower teeth. *Ah* is the most open sound, with the tongue flat and lips loose. By rounding the lips, you produce the sounds of ŏ *(ŏn),* ô *(lôrd),* ō *(ōh),* o͝o *(lo͝ok),* and o͞o *(lo͞ose).* Allow the middle of the tongue to arch up and forward until it almost touches the roof of the mouth to produce the sounds of ŭ *(ŭp),* ẽr *(makẽr),* ă *(ăt),* ĕ *(lĕt),* ā *(āte),* ĭ *(ĭt),* ē *(bē).*

It is important for the actor to remember that voice quality is definitely affected by emotion. For example, the voice may quiver with fear, sweeten with sympathy, and harden with anger. In addition, the age of your character will affect the quality of the voice. For instance, with old age, the vocal apparatus is usually less flexible, and the disposition has been obviously affected for better or worse by life's experiences. These things must be made apparent in your characterizations.

Applications
● ● ● ● ● ● ● ● ● ● ● ● ●

Practice reading aloud the following exercises, first feeling the appropriate emotion and then speaking.

1. Repeat a single word—*no, yes, dear, really*—conveying the following emotions: surprise, scorn, irritation, sarcasm, boredom, suspicion, eagerness, love, doubt, weariness, determination, horror, pain, despair, and joy.

2. Assume the character of a happy child, a cross older person, a dictatorial employer, a discouraged job-seeker, an eloquent minister, a distinguished actor, a plotting criminal, and a hysterical survivor of an earthquake. Speak the following sentences as each of these characters would.

   a. Now is the time to make your choice.

   b. Yes, I see the sunset!

   c. Whatever will be will be.

   d. Stop! Think it over before you do anything rash!

3. Say the following words, recalling personal experiences to give them "color," the special tone quality resulting from feeling and imagination: *home, icy, flag, ocean, roar, sunset, welcome, golden, jingle, melancholy, magnificent, dog, star*.

4. Read the following selections, concentrating mainly on the vowel sounds. Try to make each vowel in an accented syllable as full and rich as possible. Sound these vowels alone many times and then put them back in the words. (Note: In these and in all other excerpts and passages, the student is urged to read the complete work, if possible, in order to understand fully the mood and meaning of the selection.)

   a. FROM *Romeo and Juliet* by William Shakespeare

   JULIET The clock struck nine when I did send the Nurse;
       In half an hour she promised to return.
       Perchance she cannot meet him — that's not so.
       O, she is lame! Love's heralds should be thoughts,
       Which ten times faster glides than the sun's beams . . . .

   b. FROM *The Tempest* by William Shakespeare

   PROSPERO Our revels now are ended. These our actors,
       As I foretold you, were all spirits, and
       Are melted into air, into thin air:
       And, like the baseless fabric of this vision,
       The cloud-capp'd towers, the gorgeous palaces,
       The solemn temples, the great globe itself,
       Yea, all which it inherit, shall dissolve
       And, like this insubstantial pageant faded
       Leave not a rack behind.

Pitch

The relative highness or lowness of the voice at any given time is called **pitch.**
Each person's voice has a characteristic pitch level from which it moves up
and down. Women's voices are pitched on a higher level than those of men,
and children's voices are higher still. Pitch is determined by the rapidity with
which the vocal folds vibrate. This vibration, in turn, is influenced by the
length of the vocal folds, their elasticity, the degree of tension in them, their
thickness, and the amount of breath pressure applied.

Most persons use only four or five notes in ordinary speaking, but a good
speaker can use two octaves or more. Many girls and women pitch their
voices, consciously or unconsciously, at too high a level, not realizing that a
low voice is far more musical and easily heard. As a rule, therefore, girls
should do their vocal exercises on the lower pitch levels.

The pitch of the voice gives meaning to speech. When speakers are excited,
interested, and enthusiastic in conversation, they unconsciously lift the pitch
on important words to emphasize them and lower the pitch on unimportant
words to subordinate them. Pitch gives life to reading aloud and speaking. It
depends largely upon an interest in living and in what you are saying and
doing.

As you speak, you often alter your pitch. There are two primary ways of

*An awareness of one's
pitch leads to
manipulation of the
voice. (Charles Brown
in Douglas Turner
Ward's* Home.*)*

doing this. In the first, the *step,* you shift abruptly from one pitch level to another between words, parts of sentences, or sentences to express a distinct break in thought or feeling. In the second, the *inflection,* you gradually raise or lower the pitch level within a vowel, a word, or a sentence. A rising inflection shows incompleteness of thought or uncertainty and is often used in asking a question. A falling inflection indicates completeness and definiteness and is often used in answering a question. The rising-falling inflection is used to convey both subtle shades and sharp differences of meaning within words.

Variety in pitch, called modulation or **inflection**, makes the voice musical. Monotony in pitch, speaking in a **monotone**, resulting either from speaking continuously on one level or from giving every sentence exactly the same inflection, is a fatal flaw in speaking. Without variety in pitch, speakers are unable to hold the attention of their audiences. Ministers, teachers, and lawyers sometimes fall unconsciously into pitch patterns and monotonous inflections, which lessen their influence to a marked degree. Monotony in pitch may be due to two technical deficiencies: a person's inability to hear pitch changes, or a lack of vocal flexibility. The former is probably caused by a defect within the hearing mechanism and should be discussed with a speech therapist, who may administer a test for *tonal deafness.* Lack of flexibility, however, can be overcome by practice and conscious attention. It is due largely to lack of vitality and enthusiasm in thought and feeling or in vocal and bodily response.

As a student of dramatics, you must learn to control the number, length, and direction of pitch changes. Try to notice your own and other people's changes in pitch in normal conversation and how these changes affect the communication of thoughts and feelings. Notice what anger, exhaustion, irritation, worry, joy, and excitement do to the pitch of people's voices. You will find that the pitch is usually higher when a person is angry, that dominant people use falling inflections for the most part, and that timid ones use brief, rising inflections. Sneering and sarcasm are often shown by rising-falling inflections, which convey subtle meanings.

Applications
● ● ● ● ● ● ● ● ● ● ● ● ●

1. Find what your range and **optimum** (ideal) **pitch** is by matching tones with a piano. Begin by reading a selection in your normal voice. As a friend plays up the scale, match each note. Record the highest note you can reach without strain. Then go down the scale and record the lowest note you can reach comfortably. This is your range. In the middle of the range is your optimum pitch. This optimum pitch is often two or three notes lower than your normal speaking voice.

2. Count from one to ten, beginning as low as you can and going as high as you can without strain. Then reverse the count and come down. Be sure that it is pitch and not loudness that makes the difference in each count.

3. Count slowly from one to ten, giving the vowel in each number a long falling inflection. Repeat with a long rising inflection on each. Then alternate the two exercises.

4. Select a nursery rhyme and recite it as a comforting parent, an old-fashioned Shakespearean actor, a bored teenager, and a frightened child.

5. Read the following sentences with the widest possible range. Put emphasis on the important words and syllables by raising the pitch, using both the step and inflection shifts. Drop definitely on unimportant words.

   a. What a terrific idea!

   b. To speak effectively, you must raise your voice on the important words.

   c. In direct conversation, we change the pitch of the voice constantly.

   d. Did you hear what I said? Then go!

   e. No, I will not go!

6. Stand behind a screen or curtain and give the following lines, having someone check on your variations in pitch.

   a. No, never. Well, hardly ever.

   b. To be or not to be, that is the question.

   c. Do unto others as you would have them do unto you.

   d. Give me liberty or give me death!

7. Analyze the following selections and decide what inflections to use in order to bring out the predominant mood and inner meaning of each. If possible, use a tape recorder and read aloud the lines. Then study the pitch of your voice and try again, concentrating particularly on inflection and modulation.

   a. FROM *The Taming of the Shrew* by William Shakespeare

     PETRUCHIO   Good-morrow, Kate, for that's your name, I hear.
     KATHARINE   Well have you heard, but something hard of hearing:
       They call me Katharine that do talk of me.
     PETRUCHIO   You lie, in faith; for you are called plain Kate,
       And bonny Kate, and sometimes Kate the curst,
       But Kate, the prettiest Kate in Christendom.

   b. FROM *Twelfth Night* by William Shakespeare

     VIOLA   I left no ring with her. What means this lady?
       Fortune forbid my outside hath not charm'd her!
       She made good view of me; indeed, so much
       That sure methought her eyes had lost her tongue,
       For she did speak in starts distractedly.
       She loves me, sure; the cunning of her passion
       Invites me in this churlish messenger.
       None of my lord's ring! Why, he sent her none.
       I am the man; — if it be so — as 'tis —
       Poor lady, she were better love a dream. . . .

Volume

The relative strength, force, or intensity with which sound is made is called the **volume.** You must not confuse volume with mere loudness, for you can utter a stage whisper with great intensity, or you can call across a room with little intensity. Volume depends upon the pressure with which the air from the lungs strikes the vocal folds. While a certain amount of tension is required to retain the increased breath pressure, this tension should be minimal. If your throat is as relaxed as possible, you will not become hoarse when speaking with increased volume, or even when shouting, and your words will be resonant and forceful.

To speak loudly enough to be heard in the largest auditorium without forcing the words from your throat, you must breathe deeply and centrally. Think that you are talking to a person in the back row of the theater. Such concentration will cause you to open your mouth wider, speak more slowly, and enunciate more clearly. When you use a microphone, remember that no greater volume is necessary than might be used in ordinary conversation — no matter how large the auditorium may be.

Force is of two types. A sudden, sharp breath pressure creates *explosive* force, which is useful in commands, shouts, loud laughter, and screams.

The language in Eugene O'Neill's A Touch of the Poet, *shows the lilt and inflections of Irish dialect. The actors — Kathryn Walker, Jason Robards, and Geraldine Fitzgerald — spoke realistically in dialect without sacrificing intelligibility.*

When the breath pressure is held steady and the breath released gradually, the force is said to be *expulsive.* This type of force is necessary in reading long passages without loss of breath and in building to a dramatic climax.

Like the other voice characteristics, volume is closely related to the expression of ideas and emotions. Fear, excitement, anger, hate, defiance, and other strong emotions are usually accompanied by an explosive intensity. On the other hand, quiet, calm thoughts call for a minimal amount of force.

Volume is used in combination with other voice characteristics to suggest various feelings. For example, a quiet voice accompanied by a flat quality suggests dullness, indifference, and weariness. A quiet voice with a full tonal quality may express disappointment, shock, despair, bewilderment, and sometimes even great joy.

When you are on the stage, it is important to remember that you must use more energy to convey impressions of all kinds than is necessary off the stage. Thus, if you are merely chatting comfortably at home with a friend, your voice will have relatively little intensity. Put that identical scene on the stage, try to make it equally informal, and you will have to increase your vocal intensity considerably — otherwise the scene will fall flat. Keep the person farthest away from you in the audience constantly in mind and "bounce" your lines off the person on stage to whom your lines are spoken. You will find that if you "think" where your voice is to go and keep the throat relaxed, your projection will improve without vocal strain.

Using greater force to emphasize the important words in a sentence is the most common means of clarifying a thought. You can change the meaning of a sentence by shifting the force from one word to another, thus expressing innocence, surprise, anger, and other emotions. In acting, the entire thought of a line can be clarified or obscured by emphasizing a word or phrase. Key words brought out forcibly can make a character's personality understandable to the audience.

Applications
● ● ● ● ● ● ● ● ● ● ● ●

1. Pant like a dog. While you do so, feel the movement of your diaphragm with your hands. Then say "ha-ha" as you pant.

2. Take a full breath and call "one" as if you were throwing a ball against a wall at some distance. Exhale, relax, inhale, and call "one, two" in the same manner. Count up to ten in this way but be careful to relax between each effort. Get your power from a quick "kick" of the rib cage rather than from tightening the throat. In the same way, use the words *no, bell, on, never,* and *yes.*

3. Repeat the letters of the alphabet, increasing your energy whenever you come to a vowel. Then reverse the exercise, beginning with a strong, firm tone and gradually reducing the energy involved. Keep all the sounds on the same pitch.

4. Say the sentence "I am going home" as though you were saying it to the following people:

   a. A friend sitting next to you

   b. A person 10 feet away

   c. Someone across the room

   d. Someone in the back row of your auditorium

5. Change the meaning of the following sentences in as many ways as you can by using force to emphasize different words. Explain your exact meaning.

   a. I didn't say that to her.

   b. You don't think I stole the book, do you?

6. Read these passages aloud, making the mood and meaning clear by the amount of force you use and the words you emphasize. Use volume sufficient for a large auditorium by getting enough breath, keeping an open throat, and sounding the vowels clearly. Do this while standing, keeping your weight balanced, your head lifted slightly. Speak "through your eyes."

   a. FROM *The Merchant of Venice* by William Shakespeare

     PORTIA   The quality of mercy is not strained.
       It droppeth as the gentle rain from heaven
       Upon the place beneath. It is twice blest;
       It blesseth him that gives, and him that takes.
       'Tis mightiest in the mightiest; it becomes
       The throned monarch better than his crown.
       His sceptre shows the force of temporal power,
       The attribute to awe and majesty,
       Wherein doth sit the dread and fear of kings;
       But mercy is above this sceptred sway;
       It is enthroned in the hearts of kings,
       It is an attribute to God himself;
       And earthly power doth then show likest God's
       When mercy seasons justice.

   b. "The Rhinoceros" by Ogden Nash

       The rhino is a homely beast,
       For human eyes he's not a feast,
       But you and I will never know
       Why nature chose to make him so,
       Farewell, farewell, you old rhinoceros,
       I'll stare at something less prepoceros!

c. "The Rebel" by Mari Evans

When I	coming to see
die	if I
I'm sure	am really
I will have a	Dead
Big Funeral	or just
Curiosity	trying to make
seekers . . .	Trouble

Rate

The speed at which words are spoken, in speech, is called **rate.** Each person has a characteristic rate of speech, which is usually more rapid in informal conversation than in public speaking or in work in dramatics. Like quality, pitch, and volume, rate is also an important means of suggesting ideas and emotional states. A steadily increasing speed creates a feeling of tension and excitement, while the deliberate delivery of important passages impresses the hearer with their significance. Light, comic, happy, and lyric passages are usually spoken rapidly. Calm, serene, reverent, tragic, and awesome passages are delivered more slowly.

Pauses

Practically all our sentences in both speaking and reading are divided into groups separated by pauses of varying lengths. The breathing pause is a necessity because we must have breath in order to speak. One of the worst faults a beginner can have is gasping for breath, thus breaking the thought of a sentence. You must train yourself at once to get your breath between thought groups when reading or speaking in front of an audience. You undoubtedly manage it properly in normal conversation, unconsciously putting into groups words that belong together before you catch your breath. You will find it harder to do this on the stage. The number of words in a group necessarily varies with the thought. A single word may be important enough to stand alone, or there may be twelve or more in a group; ordinarily there are four or five. Too many breath groups tend to create choppy speech. Punctuation can be of great assistance, for it often clarifies meaning as well as grammatical relationship.

Logical grouping and pausing is a matter of making the thought clear and depends upon your knowing exactly what you are saying. The secret of interpretative power is the ability to realize an idea — to visualize, emotionalize, and vitalize it for yourself — and then give the audience an opportunity to do the same thing. Logical and dramatic pauses demand thought and feeling on your part, or you will not have your audience thinking and feeling with you. Therefore, work out your thought groups carefully. Remember: *pauses are often more effective than words.* After the pattern is set, approach each group as if for the first time every time you speak or read aloud. This is one of the secrets of giving a sense of spontaneity and freshness to every performance throughout a long run.

Go back over the passages you have been reading in the exercises in this chapter and decide where the thought groups divide. Then reread aloud the passages, watching your timing. Hold the important words longer than others and slip rapidly over the unimportant ones. Let the idea speed you up or slow you down and take time to feel the emotions and moods. A skillful use of phrasing and pausing is one of your most valuable tools in putting over ideas and arousing emotion, and the more you practice reading aloud, either from prepared selections or at sight, the more effective you will become.

Using the Voice in Interpretation

Emphasis and *subordination* are the light and shadow of interpretation in acting. The key words of every passage must be highlighted to be heard and understood by everyone in the audience. To stress such words, you must first feel their emotional context to give them color. They can be made to stand out in the following ways: (1) *by delivering them with greater force,* (2) *by holding them for a longer period,* (3) *by lifting or lowering them in pitch,* and (4) *by giving the vowels a rich resonant quality and the consonants a strong, crisp attack and finish.* They can also be set off by pauses before or after, or sometimes both before and after. To subordinate unimportant words or phrases, "throw them away" by saying them rapidly at a lower pitch with less volume.

Stress also involves tone placement and projection. There are two rather different but not conflicting ideas regarding the matter of placement of tone. One is that tone should be placed in the mask of the face — the area of the face where you feel vibrations when you hum. This is done by forming sounds of speech with the position of the lips, lower jaw, and tongue. The other is that the voice should be thrown as far as the size of the auditorium requires. This is accomplished by breathing deeply, opening the mouth, and forming the sounds accurately, while consciously putting attention on the person farthest away. In both cases, the throat is never tightened but kept open. The term *swallowing words* is used when the sound is prevented from reaching the resonating chambers of the head. This happens when the throat is closed by tension or by carelessness in controlling the breath and the vocal folds cannot vibrate to produce sound.

Climax is another principle of great value in interpretation. A climactic passage must, of course, be well written by the author before it can be effectively spoken by the speaker. In such a passage, the emotional intensity of the lines is increased to a high point of feeling at the end. Naturally, to reach a high point, it is necessary to start at a relatively low one. In a strong emotional passage, begin with a relatively slow rate, deliberate utterance, low pitch, and little or medium vocal energy. Gradually increase the energy and speed and change the pitch until you reach the highest point of interest or feeling.

A flexible, responsive voice is the most valuable asset an actor or a speaker can have. Speaking is like painting. In both arts, the main purpose is to express an idea. The painter may use dull grays or a great variety of colors, exquisitely blended and harmonized. So, too, the speaker or actor may use a lifeless voice — monotonous in tone, energy, and pitch — or may utilize all the resources of vocal technique.

In the Applications that follow, try to use all the suggestions made in this chapter, first thinking and feeling and then using the intonation, inflection, and emphasis necessary to express the ideas behind the sounds and words. Be sure to take the time you need and be careful not to tighten your throat.

Priscilla Lopez as Harpo Marx, David Garrison as Groucho Marx, and Frank Lazarus as Chico Marx believably recreate the vocal characteristics of the famous Marx brothers in the musical comedy A Day in Hollywood/ A Night in the Ukraine.
● ● ● ● ● ● ● ● ● ● ● ●

Applications
• • • • • • • • • • • • •

1. Read aloud a fairy tale, stressing the vocal characteristics of each character and getting all the contrast possible.

2. Using the letters of the alphabet instead of words, tell a funny story, a moral tale, a short tragedy, and a ghost story.

3. Say "oh" to suggest keen interest, sudden pain, deep sympathy, utter exhaustion, delight, fear, irritation, anger, sarcasm, hesitation, embarrassment, good-natured banter, polite indifference, horror, and surprise.

4. Address the following sentences first to someone 5 feet away and then to someone 25, 100, and 300 feet away. Keep an open throat and control the breath from the diaphragm. Make full use of the vowel sounds.

   a. Run for your life!

   b. Fire! Help!

   c. Are you all right?

   d. Come here at once!

5. Read aloud the following passages. First, carefully analyze their meanings. Then determine the mood, the situation, and the emotion portrayed. Finally decide what quality, energy, change of pitch, and rate will best suit your interpretation.

   a. FROM "Work" by Angela Morgan

   > Work!
   > Thank God for the might of it,
   > The ardor, the urge, the delight of it —
   > Work that springs from the heart's desire,
   > Setting the brain and the soul on fire.

   b. FROM "The Fall of the House of Usher" by Edgar Allan Poe

   > During the whole of a dull, dark, and soundless day in the autumn of the year, when clouds hung oppressively low in the heavens, I had been passing alone, on horseback, through a singularly dreary tract of country; and at length found myself, as the shades of evening drew on, within view of the melancholy House of Usher.

   c. FROM *The Merchant of Venice* by William Shakespeare

   > THE PRINCE OF MOROCCO   All that glisters is not gold;
   > Often have you heard that told;
   > Many a man his life has sold
   > But my outside to behold:
   > Gilded tombs do worms infold.
   > Had you been as wise as bold,
   > Young in limbs, in judgment old,
   > Your answer had not been inscroll'd:
   > Fare you well; your suit is cold.

6. Study the following passages. Decide what type of person is speaking, what exactly is being said, what mood that person is in, and why that person is saying these lines. Read them aloud, trying to convey the exact meaning and mood.

a. FROM *The Diary of Anne Frank* by Frances Goodrich and Albert Hackett

ANNE'S VOICE   I expect I should be describing what it feels like to go into hiding. But I really don't know yet myself. I only know it's funny never to be able to go outdoors . . . never to breathe fresh air . . . never to run and shout and jump. It's the silence in the nights that frightens me most. Every time I hear a creak in the house, or a step on the street outside, I'm sure they're coming for us.

b. FROM *Julius Caesar* by William Shakespeare

JULIIS CAESAR   Cowards die many times before their death.
The valiant never taste of death but once.

c. FROM *Sanskrit*

> Look to this day
> For it is life — the very life of life.
> In it lie all the verities and realities of existence:
> > The bliss of growth,
> > The glory of action,
> > The wealth of beauty.
> For yesterday is but a dream,
> And tomorrow is only a vision,
> > But today well lived
> Makes every yesterday a dream of happiness
> And every tomorrow a vision of hope,
> > Look therefore to today!

Improving Your Diction

There are various definitions of **diction**, but for all practical purposes, it means the selection and pronunciation of words and their combination in speech. Technically, diction involves the correct articulation of sounds, which results in the proper formation of words; careful enunciation of syllables, which results in clear and distinct speech; and the musical rhythm that characterizes effective speech.

If your speech is to be an asset rather than a liability, in addition to correct and distinct utterance of sounds, you must also improve your choice of words in your normal daily usage. Your aim should be clear, correct, pleasing speech that carries well. There are some very common habits of sloppy speech you should avoid. They include mumbling, muttering, dropping words at the ends of sentences and letters at the ends of words, and indistinctness due to the lazy use of vocal apparatus, especially the tongue. There are some less common habits that may creep up on you after a little speech training. One is speech that is *pedantic* — too accurate, meticulous, artificial, or unnaturally theatrical. Another is speech that is *imitative* — expressive of characteristics you admire in someone else's speech that do not suit your own personality. Practice reading aloud every day using your own best speech and then relax and speak naturally. You will find the habitual use of your vocal apparatus improving.

Television offers an opportunity for the study of diction that no other generation has had. In the field of colloquial speech, television is especially useful. In news reports from all sections of the country and in panels of people from all areas, you hear conversational speech from everywhere. On both sides of the Atlantic, there are numerous dialects in the English of daily life. This colloquial or provincial speech is fascinating to listen to but confusing in communicating thought and should be avoided on the stage except when a role demands it.

The use of tape recorders is another advantage of this generation. Get someone to set up a recorder when you are unaware of it in order to record

For Colored Girls Who Have Considered Suicide When the Rainbow Is Enuf *by Ntozake Shange is classified as a choreopoem. In this contemporary verse play, the emotional intensity of the poetry comes through because the performers are masterful vocal interpreters.*

your ordinary diction. You can then analyze it for its good and its weak points. Also, early in the term record your reading of some of the selections in this book. Then remake them at the end and note your improvement.

Records and tapes offer opportunities for studying the diction of professionals. Many excellent records of plays, readings of poetry and prose, examples of the dialects in various sections of the country, and even lessons in speech improvement are available for your entertainment and instruction.

Ear training is almost as important as speech training. Therefore, accustom yourself to the best speech used in your community. As far as possible, listen to people who speak well, for speech habits are quite contagious.

Vowel Sounds

English vowel sounds are unobstructed tones through the mouth. They are given characteristic tone by the positions of the lips, tongue, jaw, and soft palate, which necessarily differ for each vowel sound.

The vowel sounds may be classified as front vowels, middle vowels, and back vowels, according to the position of the tongue as each is formed. Remember that the tip of the tongue remains at the base of the lower teeth in all vowels. In the front vowels, the front of the tongue is gradually raised until it almost touches the inner gum ridge, as with *ē* in *mē*. In the middle vowels, the front of the tongue is midway to the roof of the mouth, as with *ŭ* in *ŭp*. In the back vowels, the back of the tongue is raised, the jaw relaxed, and the lips rounded, as with *ōo* in *fōod*. In all the back vowels, the lips are rounded until only a small opening is left. Diphthongs are combinations of two vowel sounds, as in *how (ä + ōo)* or *hay (ā + ĭ)*. Prolong the vowel sounds and see how the quality changes from one sound to another. Listen carefully and perhaps tape-record yourself as you practice.

FRONT	MIDDLE	BACK
ē as in *ēve*	*ŭ* as in *ŭp*	*ä* as in *äh*
ĭ as in *hĭm*	*à* as in *àlone*	*ŏ* as in *ŏccur*
ĕ as in *ĕnd*	*û* as in *ûrn*	*ô* as in *lôrd*
ă as in *căt*	*ẽ* as in *makẽr*	*ō* as in *ōld*
		ŏo as in *hŏod*
		ōo as in *fōod*

(Note: Modern dictionaries use various symbols, explained in a pronunciation key, to represent vowel sounds. The system used here is a simplified one.)

Practice to distinguish among the vowel sounds as you read the words in the following lists.

1. feel, fill, fell, fall, fail, file, foil, foul

2. tea, tin, ten, tan, ton, turn, tarn, torn, tune, town

3. eat, it, at, ought, ate

4. peak, pick, peck, pack, puck, perk, park, pock, pork, poke, pike

Consonant Sounds

The consonant sounds are made by deliberately blocking the air passage at some point with the tongue, soft palate, or lips. If there is no vibration of the vocal folds, the consonant is said to be **voiceless**. If there is a vibration of the vocal folds, the consonant sound is **voiced**. You can tell whether a consonant sound is voiced or voiceless by placing your finger lightly on your throat and feeling whether there is any vibration.

Plosive Consonants

In these sounds, the air is stopped and suddenly released.

VOICELESS	VOICED	AIR STOPPED BY
p as in *pop*	*b* as in *bob*	Lip against lip
t as in *tame*	*d* as in *dame*	Tip of tongue against upper gum ridge
c or *k* as in *came*	*g* as in *game*	Back of tongue against soft palate

Fricative Consonants

In these sounds, the air passage is narrowed at some point and a slight friction results.

VOICELESS	VOICED	AIR PASSAGE NARROWED BY
f as in *fan*	*v* as in *van*	Upper teeth on lower lip
s as in *bus*	*z* as in *buzz*	Front of tongue against upper and lower teeth, which are almost closed
sh as in *sure*	*zh* as in *azure*	Tip of tongue turned toward hard palate; teeth almost closed
th as in *breath*	*th* as in *breathe*	Tip of tongue against upper teeth
wh as in *which*	*w* as in *witch*	Rounded lips and raised tongue

Nasal Consonants

In these sounds, the mouth is completely closed at some point, and the soft palate is lowered. Thus, the air is forced to pass through the nose.

m as in *mommy*   Mouth closed by lip on lip
ng as in *sing*   Mouth closed by back of tongue on soft palate
n as in *ninny*   Mouth closed by tip of tongue on upper gums

Practice to distinguish among the consonant sounds as you read the words in these lists.

1. pen, Ben, ten, den, ken, fen, when, wen

2. have, cat, gap, quack, land, nag, tap, dash, rat, map, pat, bat, fat, vat, thank

3. than, sad, sham, chap, jam, plaid, black, flat, slack, clan, glad, snack, stand

4. smack, span, scan, trap, dram, prank, bran, frank, crab, grab, thrash, shrapnel

5. strap, sprat, scrap, splash, swam, twang, wag, yap

6. hood, could, good, look, nook, put, book, foot, soot, should, brook, crook, wood

A number of vowel and consonant sounds are not formed in the standard way in the colloquial speech of various parts of the United States. The important thing to remember is how they are produced in standard English.

Difficult Consonants

The consonants that give difficulty include the following.

1. The *r* is a consonant sound when it comes before a sounded vowel, whether the vowel is in the same word or is the first letter in the next word. The tip of the tongue should be on the upper gum ridge of the hard palate in such words as *red, grumble, three,* and *breeze,* or in such expressions as *butter and bread, as far as you go,* and *there are three boys.* The tip of the tongue should be held at the base of the lower teeth and is not permitted to turn back to form what is called the "rolled *r*." In stage diction, the *r* is sometimes trilled when it comes between two vowels or when it is doubled as in such words as *American, marry, courage, orange.* However, the trilled *r* is now considered to be somewhat artificial.

2. The *l* is formed by pressing the tip of the tongue against the upper gum, with the air passing over the sides of the body of the tongue. Do not turn the tip of the tongue back in the mouth (retroflex), do not follow it

Patti LuPone and Robert Gutman as Juan and Eva Péron in the rock opera Evita *must use precise enunciation to portray this Argentinian couple. The voice and diction demands are particularly great in* Evita *since all dialogue is sung rather than spoken.*

with a *ŭ* in words such as *elm* and *film,* and do not put an *ĕ* before it in words such as *fool.*

3. Such combinations as "Didn't you?" "Wouldn't you?" "Haven't you?" "Shouldn't you?" and "Why don't you?" are often run together slightly. Practice them carefully to avoid separating them too much and yet not say: "Didncha?" or "Didn'tchew?" Accomplish this by lowering the jaw and dropping the tongue after the *t.* Try this: "Will you, won't you, won't you join the dance?" Repeat quickly three times.

4. Note the distinction between the *w* and *wh* sounds in such words as *wear* and *where, weather* and *whether, wight* and *white.* The *wh* is pronounced like *hw;* if you blow on your finger, you get the correct sound.

Applications

Read the following clearly, pronouncing the consonant sounds carefully.

a. "Thumbprint" by Eve Merriam

On the pad of my thumb
are whorls, whirls, wheels
in a unique design:
mine alone.
What a treasure to own!
My own flesh, my own feelings.

No other, however grand or base,
can ever contain the same.
My signature,
thumbing the pages of my time.
My universe key,
my singularity.
Impress, implant,
I am myself,
of all my atom parts I am the sum.
And out of my blood and my brain
I make my own interior weather,
my own sun and rain.
Imprint my mark upon the world,
whatever I shall become.

b. FROM "The Highwayman" by Alfred Noyes

Over the cobbles he clatters and clangs in the dark inn-yard.
He taps with his whip on the shutters, but all is locked and barred.
He whistles a tune to the window, and who should be waiting there
But the landlord's black-eyed daughter,
    Bess, the landlord's daughter,
Plaiting a dark red love-knot into her long black hair.

Difficult Vowels

The vowels that give difficulty include the following.

1. *à* as in *last, ask, after, path, dance, pass* (This sound is often confused with the short *ă*. The *ă* is formed by dropping the jaw.)

2. *ô* as in *audience, daughter, because, water, automobile, thought* (This sound is often confused with the short *ŏ*.)

3. *ōō* as in *root, soon, bloom, roof, soup, rude* (This sound is often confused with the short *ŭ* or the diphthong *iu*.)

4. *ŏ* as in *God, John, stop, was, yacht* (This sound is often confused with *äw* or *äh*.)

5. *ē* as in *sleek, creek, sheep, peek* (Often confused with *ĭ*.)

6. *ă* as in *have, man, began, shall, and, than, glad* (This sound is often confused with *à* or *ä* when a student is being particularly careful or when a *ŭ* is sounded after it.

7. The vowel sound in *perfect, purple, world, girl, learn, nerve* (This sound is often confused with *ŭ* or the diphthong *oi*.)

8. The diphthong *iu* as in *assume, Tuesday, student, duty, stupid, avenue* (This sound is often confused with $\bar{oo}$.)

9. The indeterminate *e* in unstressed syllables is barely sounded.

10. The ĕ sound as in *men, experiment, engineer, sincerity* (This sound is often confused with ĭ.)

Applications

● ● ● ● ● ● ● ● ● ● ● ● ●

Read the following clearly, pronouncing the vowel sounds carefully.

a. FROM "The Rime of the Ancient Mariner" by Samuel Taylor Coleridge

Water, water, everywhere,
   And all the boards did shrink.
Water, water, everywhere,
   Nor any drop to drink.

b. "How to Eat a Poem" by Eve Merriam

Don't be polite.
Bite in.
Pick it up with your fingers and lick the juice that may run down your chin.
It is ready and ripe now, whenever you are.

You do not need a knife or fork or spoon
or plate or napkin or tablecloth.

For there is no core
or stem
or rind
or pit
or seed
or skin
to throw away.

Pronunciation

Good **pronunciation** means using the correct vowel and consonant sounds in words and the placing of the accent on the stressed syllables.

The following commonly used words are only a very few of those that are constantly mispronounced.

1. Place the accent on the first syllable in the following words.
   ab'so lute ly   req'ui site   ad'mi ra ble
   mis'chie vous   in'flu ence   the'a ter

2. Place the accent on the second syllable in the following words.
   ho tel'   a dult'   ad dress'
   in quir'y   ro mance'   en tire'

3. Drop the silent letters in the following words.

of**t**en*	cor**p**s	**h**eir
to**w**ard	sub**t**lety	indi**c**tment
de**b**t	fore**h**ead	bus**i**ness

   Note the consonant and vowel sounds, as well as the accent marks, in the following list of words. Say each word according to the pronunciation given in the parentheses. The **schwa** is pronounced "uh" and is indicated in the dictionary by italics. It is always unaccented. Every vowel has a schwa sound. The *a* has two. A vowel marked with a half-long (ŭ, ŏ) is pronounced rapidly. The first pronunciation is considered preferable, but the others are also good usage.

hearth (härth)	Feb′ru·ar′y (fĕb′rŏŏ·ĕr′ĭ; fĕb′ŭ·ĕr′ĭ;
na·ïve′ (nä·ēv′)	fĕb′ŏŏ·ĕr′ĭ; fĕb′ŏŏ·ĕr·ĭ)
gen′u·ine (jen′ŭ·ĭn)	vau′de·ville (vô′de·vĭl; vōd′vĭl)
I·tal′ian (ĭ·tăl′yạn)	ir·rev′o·ca·ble (ĭ·rĕv′ŏ·kạ·b'l)
bade (băd; bād)	har′ass (hăr′as; hạ·răs′)
her′o·ine (hĕr′ŏ·ĭn)	bou·quet′ (bŏŏ·kā′; bō·kā′)
col′umn (kŏl′um)	fin′an·cier′ (fĭn′ăn·sēr′; fĭ′năn·sēr′;
ab·surd′ (ăb·sûrd′)	fĭ·năn′sĭ·ēr)
a′li·as (ā′lĭ·ăs)	chauf·feur′ (shō·fûr′; shŏ′fĕr)

*Silent in America; pronounced in the United Kingdom.

Vocal training and over 50 years of experience support the performance of the legendary actress Eva LeGallienne in Joanna Glass' play To Grandmother's House We Go.
● ● ● ● ● ● ● ● ● ● ● ●

Read aloud these sentences very carefully.

1. The speech of the children over the radio was scarcely intelligible and entirely lacking in spirit and enthusiasm.

2. Some sparks from the largest of the rockets burned holes in her scarlet jacket.

3. The President of the United States of America delivered the dedicatory address.

4. His vocabulary is as meager as when he was in elementary school, and he is entirely lacking in intellectual curiosity; this is a sad commentary on his secondary education.

5. Her thought that remaining in the automobile would allow them to see over the audience placed them in an awkward position.

6. They quarreled as to whether or not to take the spotted dog on the yacht.

7. Aunt Blanche answered the demand by advancing with her passport.

8. We hope next year to hear that she has started her career as an engineer rather than as a cashier.

Read the following as rapidly as you can, keeping the sounds clear.

1. The perfectly purple bird unfurled its curled wings and whirled over the world.

2. Amidst the mists and coldest frosts
   With stoutest wrists and sternest boasts,
   He thrusts his fists against the posts
   And still insists he sees the ghosts.

3. The weary wanderer wondered wistfully whether winsome Winifred would weep.

4. When and where will you go and why?

5. To sit in solemn silence in a dull, dark dock
   In a pestilential prison with a life-long lock,
   Awaiting the sensation of a short, sharp shock
   From a cheap and chippy chopper on a big black block!

6. They know not whence, not whither, where, nor why.

7. Judge not that ye be not judged, for with what judgment ye judge ye shall be judged.

8. The clumsy kitchen clock click-clacked.

9. The very merry Mary crossed the ferry in a furry coat.

Careful diction also involves discrimination in the choice and use of words. A wide and constantly increasing vocabulary, free from an overuse of slang, is a cultural asset you cannot afford to neglect. Standard usage and grammatical structure are taken for granted.

Principles of Voice and Diction for the Actor

1. Vowels are the sounds the actor can work with in interpretation. Vowels can be lengthened, shortened, and inflected.

2. Verbs are the strongest words in the language. Verbs should be stressed, except for *being* verbs.

3. Look for the *color words* — those which are vividly descriptive. Look especially for those words whose sounds suggest their meaning (onomatopoeia), such as *crash, stab, grunt, splash.*

4. Rarely stress negatives, pronouns, and articles.

5. When a word or phrase is repeated, each repetition is stressed more than the preceding.

Voice and Diction in Acting

A play comes to life by means of the voices and words of the actors. It is their ability to arouse emotion through the playwright's lines that creates the illusion of reality for the audience. Actors must make the meaning of every passage clear to all listeners by the proper projection of the words. It is their responsibility to avoid spoiling lines by blurring pronunciation, muffling enunciation, or speaking with a nervous rhythm. The inner soul of the characters they are creating must be expressed through clear-cut patterns of voice quality, pitch, and tempo. However, these must all be varied in keeping with an immediate situation and mood without loss of the character's individuality.

1. Work with the following passages until you have created a totally individual characterization for the speaker.

    a. FROM *Poor Maddalena* by Louise Saunders

        Those foolish mortals who spend their time chasing bright bubbles sure to burst. Only art my children, accomplishment, can lead them to discover

Applications
● ● ● ● ● ● ● ● ● ● ● ● ●

riches that may be stored away one by one, until they grow to treasure indestructible. If they but knew!

b. FROM *The Piper* by Josephine Preston Peabody

Will you go with him?
He will gentler to you than a father!
He would be brothers five, and dearest friend,
And sweetheart, aye and Knight and serving man.

c. FROM *Prologue to Glory* by E. P. Conkle

ABE LINCOLN I went through something like this once before! Someone you love — standing helpless — waiting. I sat day by day reading Ma parts of the Bible she liked best. On the sixth day she called me to her bed — talked of many strange things — principalities and powers — and things present — and things to come — urged me and Sairy always to walk in paths of goodness and truth — and told us many things would come t'him that served God — an' th' best way t'serve Him was t'serve His people. *(Pause)* She was amongst the lowliest of mankind. She walked the earth with her poor feet in the dust — her head in the stars — *(Pause)* Pa took me down into the woods t' make her a coffin. Pa was sawin' and I was hammerin' the pegs in. The hammer dropped at my feet; it was like someone was drivin' 'em into my heart. It's — just goin' through all that again — now!

2. Turn to the chapter on pantomime and put words into the mouths of the characters in the suggested situations. Practice changing your voice completely for each character, coordinating your voice and body as you present each situation.

3. Using the following play excerpts, paint voice pictures of each character by experimenting with voice quality, pitch, volume, rate, pauses, and emphasis.

FROM *The Importance of Being Earnest* by Oscar Wilde

GWENDOLEN Ernest, we may never be married. From the expression on mamma's face, I fear we never shall. Few parents nowadays pay any regard to what their children say to them. The old-fashioned respect for the young is rapidly dying out. Whatever influence I ever had over mamma I lost at the age of three. But though she may prevent us from becoming man and wife, and I may marry someone else, and marry often, nothing that she can possibly do can alter my eternal devotion to you.

FROM *The Merchant of Venice* by William Shakespeare

ANTONIO Give me your hand, Bassanio; fare you well,
Grieve not that I am fallen to this for you.

Recalling Ideas

1. Upon what three things does the development of an effective voice depend?

2. What is resonance? Tell how it can best be practiced.

3. Explain how nasality occurs.

4. Name and define the four characteristics of the voice that must be used correctly if one is to become an effective and expressive speaker.

5. What is the most valuable asset that an actor or speaker can have? Why?

6. Define *diction*. Explain what it involves.

Discussing Ideas

1. Discuss the connection between playing up bodily action and poor speech quality.

2. Discuss the general importance of improving diction. What benefits can improved diction bring to you as a person as well as an actor?

3. Think about your own speaking quality. Discuss the individual improvement exercises that would be of most help to you personally.

Careers

Narrators tell a story in the theater, motion pictures, radio, or television. **Announcers** work in clubs, theaters, and radio and television stations, introducing programs and making other announcements. **Newscasters** work in radio and television, giving the news, weather, and sports. Many narrators, announcers, and newscasters have college level training or degrees in communication.

Many teaching positions relate to the theater. **Elementary teachers** may instruct young students in creative drama, voice, instrumental music, or art. **High school teachers** may teach English, drama, or music. They may be in charge of the drama club and help produce student productions.

College teachers may be instructors, assistant or associate professors, or full professors. They may teach communication classes or any number of liberal or theater arts courses.

Special teachers teach specialized theater arts courses in such areas as improvisation, movement, pantomime, the speaking voice, makeup, and costume construction.

All public school teachers must be state certified. They need at least a bachelor's degree from a 4-year college, university, or teacher training institution. For many teachers, a master's degree is essential and, especially for college teachers, a doctor's degree may also be necessary. Most of these teachers will have a solid background in both liberal and theater arts.

Chapter 5

Acting

You Will Learn

What acting is.

Acting terminology.

About emotional and technical acting.

Types of roles.

How to create a character.

Acting techniques.

How to control stage fright.

Vocabulary

emotional or subjective
    acting
technical or objective
    acting
leading roles
protagonist
antagonist
juvenile
ingenue
supporting roles

straight parts
cast by type
character parts
typecasting
characterization
pause
originality
versatility
primary source
secondary sources

body language
master leading gesture
leading center
cheat out
share a scene
giving the scene
turning the scene in
taking yourself out of a
    scene
rising inflection

falling inflection	inconsistent consistency	part-whole memorization
sustained inflection		
circumflex inflection	playing the conditions	playing the moment
internalizing	playing the objectives	working backwards
externalization	playing the obstacles	paraphrasing
concentration	energy	substitution
observation	focus	improvising
emotional memory	uniqueness	cut-off lines
projection	subtext	fade-off lines
motivation	memorizing	picking up of cues
intent	whole-part memorization	laugh curve
stretching a character		knap

$\mathcal{S}$o now you're ready to act! For most students of drama, this is the moment you have been waiting for. You probably share the dream of every actor to create a role so convincing that the audience totally accepts your character as real, forgetting that you are only an actor playing a part. It is an even greater compliment to you as an actor if the audience becomes so absorbed in your role and in the play that they forget you are acting. In fact, you might even consider it less of a compliment if the audience were to exclaim, "What tremendous acting!"

You must work hard to be an effective actor, but you must also always keep in mind that your acting should never be so real that the audience loses the theatrical illusion of reality. The loss of the theatrical illusion is currently a problem in motion pictures and television. Remember always that theater is *not* life and acting is *not* life. Both are illusions that are larger than life. If both theater and acting are too real, the illusion is destroyed and replaced by what is normal. On stage, this is boring.

Shakespeare's Advice to Actors

The finest lessons in dramatic art come from the world's greatest actor-director-dramatist, William Shakespeare. They were given as advice to actors in Act III, Scene 2 of *Hamlet.* They are represented here in modern language for you to apply.

> Speak the lines of the author as written, distinctly and fluently, with an understanding of their meaning.

Naturalness and subtlety are important elements in the interpretation of roles in a realistic play such as Night Mother.

· · · · · · · · · · · ·

Do not use elaborate and artificial gestures.

Keep energy in reserve in order to build to an emotional climax smoothly and effectively.

Do not resort to farfetched action or noise simply to please unintelligent and unappreciative onlookers.

Never speak lines that are made up on the spur of the moment, especially in humorous roles, even when these lines are clever enough to make some stupid people in the audience laugh. Such lines draw attention away from the center of interest and ensure the loss of important lines. Such action is inexcusable and shows a most pitiful ambition in the fools who use it.

Modern directors usually give the same sort of advice as Shakespeare gave. In the first few rehearsals, beginning actors hear statements like the following over and over again: Get your lines. Speak clearly. Keep your hands still. Do not overact. Be natural and easy. Do not play to those in the audience who understand the least. Be controlled. Be yourself at your best. Stick to the script. Use your head. Act like a human being. Do not steal the scene from the main business.

Acting Terminology

You must become familiar with a number of expressions if you are to work comfortably on stage. Those most often used in connection with acting are listed and defined here.

ad-lib: To extemporize stage business or conversation.
at rise: Who and what are on stage when the curtain opens.
back or *backstage*: The area behind the part of the stage that is not visible to the audience.
bit: An acting role with very few lines.
blocking yourself: Getting behind furniture or other actors so that you cannot be seen by the audience.
building a scene: Using dramatic devices such as increased tempo, volume, and emphasis to bring a scene to a climax.
business: Any specific action other than movement performed on the stage, such as picking up a book or turning on a TV.
C: The symbol used to identify the center of the stage.
countercross: A shifting of position by two or more actors to balance the stage picture.
cover: To obstruct the view of the audience.
cross: The movement by an actor from one location to another onstage.
cue: The last words, action, or technical effect that immediately precedes any line or business; a stage signal.
curtain: The curtain or drapery that shuts off the stage from the audience; when written in all capital letters in a script, it indicates that the curtain is to be closed.
cut: To stop action or to omit.
cut in: To break into the speech of another character.
down or *downstage*: The part of the stage toward the audience.
dressing the stage: Keeping the stage picture balanced during the action.
exit or *exeunt*: To leave the stage.
feeding: Giving lines and action in such a way that another actor can make a point or get a laugh.
foil: An acting role which is used for personality comparison, usually with the protagonist or main character.
hand props: Properties such as letters or luggage, carried on stage by an individual player.

hit: To emphasize a word or line with extra force.

holding for laughs: Waiting for the audience to quiet down after a funny line or scene.

left and right: Terms used to refer to the stage from the actor's point of view, not that of the audience.

milk: To draw the maximum response from the audience from comic lines or action.

off or *offstage*: Off the visible stage.

on or *onstage*: On the visible stage.

overlap: To speak when someone else is speaking.

pace: The movement or sweep of the play as it progresses.

personal props: Small props that are usually carried in an actor's costume, such as money, matches, a pipe, or a pen.

places: The positions of the actors at the opening of an act or scene.

plot: To plan stage business, as to "plot" the action; to plan a speech by working out the phrasing, emphasis, and inflections.

pointing lines: Emphasizing an idea.

principals: The main characters in a play.

properties or *props*: All the stage furnishings, including furniture.

ring up: To raise the curtain.

role scoring: The analysis of a character.

script scoring or *scripting*: The marking of a script for one character, indicating interpretation, pauses, phrasing, stress, and so on.

set: The scenery for an act or a scene.

set props: Properties placed on stage for the use of actors.

showmanship: A sense of theater and the ability to present oneself effectively to the audience; stage charisma.

sides: Half-sheet pages of a script which contain the lines, cues, and business for one character.

stealing a scene: Attracting attention from the person to whom the center of interest legitimately belongs.

subtext: Character interpretations which are not in a script but are supplied by the actor.

tag line: The last speech in an act or a play, usually humorous or clever.

taking the stage: Giving an actor the freedom to move over the entire stage area, usually during a lengthy speech.

tempo: The speed at which the action of a play moves along.

timing: The execution of a line or piece of business at a specific moment to achieve the most telling effect.

top: To build to a climax by speaking at a higher pitch, at a faster rate, or with more force and greater emphasis than in preceding speeches.

up or *upstage*: The area of the stage away from the audience, toward the rear of the stage.

upstaging: Improperly taking attention from an actor who should be the focus of interest.

walk-on: A small acting part which has no lines.

warn: To notify of an upcoming action or cue.

Emotion and/or Technique

There are two major approaches to acting. In **emotional** or **subjective acting**, the actors play their parts in such a way that they actually weep, suffer, or struggle emotionally in front of the audience. As nearly as they can, they become the parts they play and experience all that their characters experience. In **technical** or **objective acting**, performance is based upon the perfecting of acting technique. In this approach, the actor analyzes the play's structure and the personalities of the characters. The actor then uses the learned skills of acting, movement, speech, and interpretation to create the role. Emotional response is not allowed to interfere with the creation of the role. Instead, conscious control is responsible for the results. The actor does not actually live the part. The actor acts it so well that the illusion of living the part is created. In the emotional approach, personal inner reactions

Even the use of everyday properties, such as the tea service in Robert Anderson's Tea and Sympathy, *must be fully rehearsed so as not to interfere with the flow of the action.*

· · · · · · · · · · · ·

form the actor's emotional response. In the technical approach, the process of study, analysis, and creative imagination form the assumed personality.

There is much to be said for both approaches to acting. Today, however, most actors use a combination of the two approaches. It is therefore best to identify yourself with your part so that you can interpret it naturally, simply, and spontaneously. At the same time, you can use your technical training to achieve a clear-cut, convincing, and consistent characterization. What this means is that as an actor you must train yourself to become the character you play for the length of the performance. When you take off the costume and makeup, however, you are happy to return to your own personality that can grow from every performance. Balance is what you should aim for. An uneven and uncontrolled performance could result if you lose yourself in the character you portray. And too technical an approach to characterization may result in a performance that is artificial, shallow, and unconvincing.

"The Method" is the most discussed and influential acting theory today. It was formulated by Konstantin Stanislavski, the Russian actor and director. He explained his theories on the art of acting and offered practical exercises in the techniques of vocal and bodily expression in his books *My Life in Art, An Actor Prepares, Building a Character,* and *Creating a Role.* His ideas have greatly influenced the theater in the Twentieth Century.

Very sincere people have interpreted and misinterpreted Stanislavski's theories. Many of these people have put too much emphasis on the actor's use

Konstantin Stanislavski

Sir Tyrone Guthrie

of self-analysis and personal emotional experiences in creating a role. They have neglected to pay as much attention to Stanislavski's equal insistence on disciplined control of the techniques of vocal and bodily expressiveness. As a result, many so-called Method actors become so involved with their inner resources that they fail to communicate with the audience. Their speech is often slovenly and their actions overdone. They make the mistake of believing that the emotional identification with a character is more important than learning the lines as written or responding alertly to others on stage.

Stanislavski's so-called "magic *if*" provides advice that should be most helpful to you in creating a characterization. Stanislavski advised that an actor should use his or her full powers of concentration to ask what he or she would do *if* the events in the play were actually happening and he or she were intimately involved in these events. In answering these questions, the actor analyzes both the actor's inner nature and the character's inner nature. Only then can the actor use the technical resources of voice and body movement to interpret the likely reactions of the character accurately. This analysis also leads to an understanding of the play itself.

Types of Roles

A playwright brings out the play's theme through the **leading roles**. They include the **protagonist**, who must solve the problem that arises in the play or go down to defeat in the conflict. There is also the **antagonist**, who may be a pure villain or the gods or Fate or any other force that opposes the goals of the protagonist. Other leading roles are the **juvenile**, the term for a young romantic male lead between the ages of 16 and 30, and the **ingenue**, the young romantic female lead. While many young actors are often disappointed if they are not cast in leading roles, **supporting roles** are often more challenging and demanding. The challenge of these roles lies in the type of person to be portrayed, not in how long or short the part may be. One of the most important supporting roles is that of the foil, a character with whom another character, usually the protagonist, is compared. There may be more than one foil in a play. Together, the leads and supporting roles are referred to as the principals.

Both leading and supporting roles may be either straight or character parts. **Straight parts** are people of any age. The actors chosen for straight parts usually resemble in appearance and personality the persons that the playwright had in mind. The actors in straight parts are really playing themselves and are said to be **cast by type**. Most leading roles are straight parts.

The three high school cheerleaders in Vanities *by Jack Heifner are the principals in this scene as well as in the ensemble. These three actresses are the only actors in the play.*

Character parts almost always include some eccentric trait. It might be physical, psychological, or mental. These parts demand a high degree of ability to play them well. Such roles rarely resemble their actors in either appearance or personality. To play them well requires genuine acting ability.

When an actor is identified with a certain personality, such as the girl next door, the business tycoon, the always confused fool, or the faithful companion, and is cast over and over again in that same kind of role, that type of casting is called **typecasting**. There is a difference between typecasting and casting by type. For example, if a role calls for a man with a Santa Claus-like build, and the actor chosen happens to be a portly, white-bearded gentleman in his late sixties, the director has probably cast by type. However, if a similarly built man with dark hair and beard has been cast in his last twenty roles as a "heavy," this actor has very likely been typecast as a villain.

Minor roles demand as much careful attention to detail as supporting roles. The difference lies only in the number of lines and scenes involved. An actor who has only a few lines is said to have a bit part. An actor who appears briefly on stage with no lines at all has a walk-on part.

Creating a Character

Characterization is a creative process that demands that an actor grasp the fundamental personality of a part and then project it to the audience in such a way that the character becomes a living, convincing human being. Characterization is the be-all and end-all of acting.

The Background of Characterization

Your personal experiences and your existing dramatic talent determine your ability to play a particular role. As an actor, it is therefore your responsibility to increase your knowledge of the lives and emotions of real people in order to understand how they respond to the situations that people encounter in life. The constant study of human beings in all walks of life and in all types of literature is one of the actor's major responsibilities. It is an unending source of material and inspiration upon which to draw.

Successful projection of character depends upon the skillful use of techniques. But it also depends upon the actor's insights into a character's behavior and the actor's ability to express those insights in interpreting the character. The successful blending of technique and interpretation comes only with continued rehearsing and after experience with varied roles. Experience will teach you to use and to master some of the characteristics of acting. You will

Preparation for a role in a historical play involves not only study of the play and one's character, but also study of the time period. For a role such as the one Geraldine Fitzgerald plays in Eugene O'Neill's A Touch of the Poet, *it would be necessary to do research about innkeeping in 17th century Boston.*

learn the use of **pause** in order to sustain emotion while the voice and body are still. You will learn how to communicate **originality**, which colors and characterizes the work of every distinguished dramatic artist. You will learn to apply **versatility**, which always surprises and delights. These are some of the means that experienced actors use as they interpret the characters they portray. Look for them as you watch first-class actors work on the stage and in motion pictures and on television.

Studying the Play

To understand a role so that you can interpret it faithfully, you must study the play carefully. Usually the entire script is read through at the first rehearsal. The actors who have been assigned specific parts usually read those parts, although the director might also participate in the reading. This reading should bring out the author's purpose and theme. It should also identify the protagonist's main problems, the setting and type of each speech, and the structure of the plot, especially how it builds to a climax and holds interest to the end. Pay close attention not only to your own lines but also to those lines about your character that are spoken by others. Note the shifting of moods throughout the play and how your character is affected by them.

You will obviously want to know what kind of person you are in the play and why you behave as you do. You will also want to understand what your character wants and what stands in the way of what your character wants. Pay very careful attention to the lines your character speaks and to what your character does, for characters reveal themselves in what they say and do. Note any changes that take place in your character during the play.

Research

If the setting of a play is unfamiliar, study the place and the historical period. Learn all you can from books and pictures and, if possible, from people who have visited the place. Try to enter into the atmosphere of the location. If your character speaks a local dialect, try to talk to people from the locality or listen to recordings of speakers from the area. Notice their pronunciation and their inflections. You might also want to read other plays by the same author or by other playwrights of the same era. Look up historical references and check the meanings of unfamiliar words.

Character Sketch

You will find it helpful to write a character sketch or brief biography of your character to supply information not provided in the script. Go through the play

Research into the time period as well as the history of boxing was necessary for James Earl Jones in The Great White Hope. *How Jones's characters feels about the other characters is an important understructure to be explored. (Appearing with Jones are Jane Alexander and Jimmy Pecham.)*
● ● ● ● ● ● ● ● ● ● ● ● ● ●

thoroughly. Pay particular attention to what the author says about the character in the stage directions. Notice also what the character's lines reveal about him or her, what other characters say about the character, and how other characters respond to your character when they are on the stage with him or her. Pay attention as well to what other characters say about your character when he or she is not on stage with them. Look for any lines that might give you some clue to the role you have to play. For example, if you were playing the role of Julie in *Carousel,* you would know that Billie says, "Julie never changes" and that the statement is verified by The Heavenly Friend. Therefore, you would know that consistency is a strong personal trait of your character.

In developing your character sketch, use headings like the following: Physical Traits; Mental Traits; Spiritual Traits; Individual and Social Behavior; Emotional Motivations; Physical Motivations; Intellectual Motivations. Under each heading, list the traits, behaviors, and motivations that your character possesses. Then ask and answer some basic questions about your character, such as the following: What is my character's purpose? What is my character's function in the play? Am I playing a protagonist, an antagonist, or a foil? Is my character there for comic relief? What does my character want to do? What does my character want to be? What is my character's goal in the play as a whole and in each particular scene? State the answers to the last question in the form of a verb, such as *revenge, flatter, trap.*

As you complete your character sketch and become better acquainted with your part, ask yourself more questions: How well adjusted to others is my

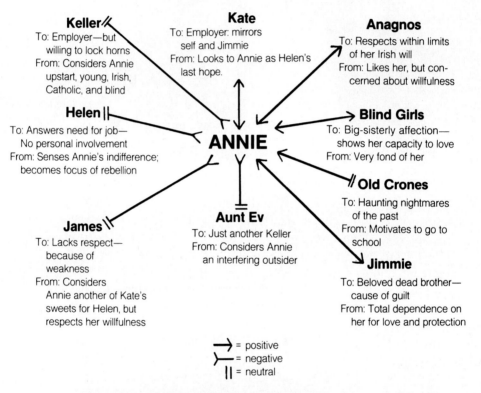

Keller
To: Employer—but willing to lock horns
From: Considers Annie upstart, young, Irish, Catholic, and blind

Helen
To: Answers need for job— No personal involvement
From: Senses Annie's indifference; becomes focus of rebellion

James
To: Lacks respect— because of weakness
From: Considers Annie another of Kate's sweets for Helen, but respects her willfulness

Kate
To: Employer: mirrors self and Jimmie
From: Looks to Annie as Helen's last hope.

Aunt Ev
To: Just another Keller
From: Considers Annie an interfering outsider

ANNIE

Anagnos
To: Respects within limits of her Irish will
From: Likes her, but concerned about willfulness

Blind Girls
To: Big-sisterly affection— shows her capacity to love
From: Very fond of her

Old Crones
To: Haunting nightmares of the past
From: Motivates to go to school

Jimmie
To: Beloved dead brother— cause of guilt
From: Total dependence on her for love and protection

→ = positive
⊢ = negative
|| = neutral

CHARACTER RELATIONSHIP DIAGRAM
The Miracle Worker
Annie Sullivan

character? Is my character shy or uninhibited? How intelligent is my character? In what ways has environment influenced my character? What are my character's particular problems? Is my character meeting or avoiding responsibilities? How and why? How does my character react to all of the other characters in the play? Does my character unknowingly avoid the main issues in situations? Is my character cynical, talkative, rowdy, tense, aggressive, charming, friendly, fearful, envious, courageous, or idealistic? Why? The answers to questions such as these will allow you to more deeply understand your character's personal and social background.

Role Scoring

Role scoring is a helpful process in character analysis. The process consists of twenty-five questions that you need to answer as you score your role. If you take the time to answer these questions, you will unlock important information about your character. (Some of these questions will be expanded upon later in the chapter.) The role scoring questions below were adapted by Paula Parker of Northwestern University in Illinois.

1. How does the title of the play relate to your character?

2. Is there a special texture that your character relates to? (For example, Grandma in Edward Albee's *The Sand Box* might relate to the texture of sand.)

3. What is your character's main sense of urgency? What strong impulse motivates your character to act? (For example, in *Romeo and Juliet*, Juliet's sense of urgency is shown when she becomes impatient with the Nurse for not telling her immediately about the plan for marrying Romeo.)

4. What is your character's secret? (Having a secret always adds a sense of mystery to a character.)

5. What rhythm do you associate with your character? (The steady swinging of a pendulum is an example of rhythm.)

6. What personal sound do you associate with your character? (Sighing, wheezing, and grunting are sounds that might be associated with a character.)

7. What is your character's leading gesture? (A leading gesture is an abstract movement that your character unconsciously uses throughout the play. An example of a leading gesture is the brushing of imaginary dust from clothing.)

Knowing your character's personality and exploring it in depth is a key ingredient to the success of intimate scenes which demand that actors listen and respond to each other as well as speak their lines.

8. What is your character's leading center? (The head? The heart? The stomach? You should gesture from your character's leading center.)

9. What color do you associate with your character? Why? (For example, you might associate a jealous character with green.)

10. What object do you associate with your character? Why? (For example, you might associate a pocket watch with a character who is a time-controlled person.)

11. What animal do you associate with your character? Why? (For example, you might associate a sly character with a fox.)

12. What are your character's two primary senses? What are yours? (They might be sight and hearing.)

13. If your character saw the play, what reaction might he or she have?

14. Does your character "mask" or cover up feelings and behaviors? If so, what does your character mask?

15. Does your character use any "as if" images? If so, what are they? (For example, a character may say, "I feel as if I were an unwanted kitten." "As if" images can be rather strange and unusual, but they should have a ring of reality about them.)

16. Does your character have a sense of humor? Is this sense of humor used in a positive or negative way?

17. In real life, would you or would you not be your character's friend? Why or why not?

18. What is your character's most positive trait?

19. What is your character's status in the world? Does your character have money and power?

20. What are your character's major wants and desires?

21. What is your character's major objective for each scene in which that character appears?

22. How does your character go about achieving those major objectives?

23. What is your character's life objective?

24. How does your character go about achieving his or her life objective?

25. Has your character changed by the end of the play? If so, in what ways?

Primary and Secondary Sources

It is always best not to see a motion picture or stage production of a play that you are preparing to appear in. If you do, you are likely to find yourself copying another actor's mannerisms rather than developing for yourself a sound understanding of the role and the play. A better way of building a characterization is to choose a person that you know who is similar to the character you are playing. This individual would become your **primary source.** You might want to adopt that person's posture, movements, habits, and voice inflections. In many situations, you might choose more than one primary source and combine characteristics from them. The books that you read to help shed light on your character are your **secondary sources.** They are helpful but good actors must always refer to life itself for appropriate models.

Script Scoring

Script scoring is the marking of a script to indicate pauses, pitch levels, emphasis, speed of delivery, phrasing, pronunciation, function within the context of the play, and character revelation. It is another useful tool in character analysis. The term comes from a musical score, which has similar markings to indicate tempo, rhythm, pauses, style and interpretation. In its simplest form, a scored script may be marked to show only pronunciation, pauses, emphasized words and phrases, movement, and stage business. There are no

Ah, no, young sir! /

You are too simple. Why, you might have said— /

Oh, a great many things! Mon dieu, why waste   *Mon dyü (My God)*

Your opportunity? For example, thus:— ///

AGGRESSIVE: I, sir, if that nose were mine, /   *C – Cyrano's subconscious wish*

I'd have it amputated on the spot! //

FRIENDLY: How do you drink with such a nose? /

You ought to have a cup made specially. //   *L – prepare for audience reaction*

DESCRIPTIVE: Tis a rock a crag a cape /

A cape? say rather a peninsula! //   *C – Cyrano's ego concept*

INQUISITIVE: What is that receptacle

A razor-case or a portfolio?

KINDLY: Ah, do you love the little birds

So much that when they come and sing to you,

You give them this to perch on?   *L – prepare for audience reaction*

Symbol Key

+	slight pause	ꜛ	pitch level rising
/	1-second pause	ꜜ	pitch level lowering
//	2-second pause	∿	speed up reading
///	3-second pause	∿	slow down reading
⌒	phrase	↗	rising inflection
—	simple stress	↘	falling inflection
=	greater stress	L	laugh line
≡	greatest stress	C	character line
		P	plot line
		T	theme line

hard-and-fast rules for script scoring, nor is there any agreement about what symbols or marks should be used to score a script. The actor is free to use a personal marking system that will be of help to him or her. Here is a detailed script scoring of the first few lines of the famous "nose" speech from Edmund Rostand's *Cyrano de Bergerac.*

Building Up Your Part

There are two stages in building up your part. The first stage begins when the director gives the cast his or her own view of the play, its characters and the relationships among them, its theme, and its style. Then, as you study the play and analyze the playwright's characters, you develop your own concept of the part. The second stage begins as you go to rehearsals with the entire cast under the director's guidance. It is, of course, in rehearsing that your character develops into a living person as you react to others and incorporate the principles of acting in preparation for a performance.

Once you have settled on the general interpretation of your part, you must then grow into it physically, intellectually, and emotionally. Keep in mind that your character's actions and speech are your means of making that character real to your audience. Your voice, your movements, and your imagination are the tools you will use to make your character come alive on the stage.

Physical Acting

According to the experts, at least seventy percent of our daily communication occurs through physical action. Nonverbal communication, communication without the use of words, is often called **body language.** Physical acting relies on body language. It allows actors to communicate far more than the words of a script alone can convey. Since beginning actors generally rely too heavily on the voice, physical acting is usually something that most new actors need to work on and improve.

The Bubble

To get some idea of how people use their physical bodies, it is helpful to imagine that each of us operates within a bubble. This bubble is an imaginary circle that people establish around themselves. Imagine that each character portrayed on the stage is surrounded by a personal bubble in which he or she "lives." The size of each bubble is determined by the personality of the character. Shy, withdrawn, and frail   personalities have small bubbles.

The stance as well as the voice help communicate an actor's characterization of a role. They should reflect the character's feelings and reactions towards the action of the play.
• •

Swaggering, bold, and daring personalities have large bubbles. Since customary gestures are made within the bubble, less forceful characters do not really need much room for their uncertain movements. More forceful characters, on the other hand, often need bubbles that are large enough to contain the arms fully extended.

The imaginary bubbles that surround each person are cultural as well as individual. In American society, a six-foot or greater distance between an individual and others is considered "formal." Three to five feet is said to be "friendly." Less than two feet is called "intimate." Without being aware of it, people are automatically territorial creatures. They guard their territories and do not expect others to come closer than three feet without being invited. That is why we stand so straight and rigidly on elevators, trains, and buses. We are fearful that a sudden lurch might accidentally cause us to bump into someone else, thereby violating that person's personal space. Audiences are very much aware of the bubble space. They realize at once that when two personal bubbles overlap, there is likely to be either a confrontation or an embrace.

Master Leading Gesture

As you work on your physical acting, you will want to develop a **master leading gesture,** a distinctive action that is repeated and will serve as a clue to a character's personality. The master leading gesture might be a peculiar walk or laugh or some other distinctive form of behavior. Even the position of your feet while you are standing, walking, or sitting can be a master gesture.

Body Lead

Almost every character on stage begins movement or "leads" with a part of the body that is appropriate for the character's personality. A lead looks as if a string attached to a part of the body is pulling that part away from the other parts. This **leading center** can be either a slight or an exaggerated movement, depending upon the character and the style of the play. The body part that a character leads with is determined by the character's major personality trait. For example, intelligent people lead with the forehead. Snobbish individuals lead with the nose. Daring personalities lead with the chin. Brave characters lead with the chest. Well-fed characters lead with the stomach. Characters in plays from certain historical periods and characters in children's theater often greatly exaggerate the body lead.

Entrances and Exits

Because entrances introduce your character into a scene, you must prepare for them long before you come on stage. Plan exactly how you wish to appear. Pay particular attention to your posture. Remember that posture will be determined by your character's age, mood, and attitude toward the other characters onstage. Be sure that every detail of your costume and makeup are exactly as they should be.

Be sure that hand props are where they are supposed to be so you will not be worrying about them onstage. As you wait for your entrance, do not stand in front of a backstage light or you will cast your shadow on stage. Also, be sure that you do not block the exit.

Pace and style of movement add to a characterization and also telegraph the actors' intent to the audience.

You must always plan your entrance so that you have enough time to come onstage and speak exactly on cue. If the set has steps that you must climb or walk down when making your appearance, be sure to walk up or down them carefully. Think about where your character was and what your character was doing before your entrance. Know exactly why you are coming on stage. If you must enter through a door, open it with your hand nearest the hinges and close it with the other hand as you step in. If the action of the play permits it, and if you have a line to say, pause in the doorway and deliver it. Such a pause can be very effective.

Keep the audience in mind at every entrance but don't appear to do so. Enter on your upstage foot, so that your body is turned downstage. If several characters enter together and one of them is speaking, the character who is speaking should come last so that he or she does not have to turn to talk to the others.

Exits are as important as entrances. Plan ahead for them. Always leave the stage in a definite state of mind and with a definite place to go. Keep in character until you are completely out of sight. If you go through a door, use the hand nearest the hinges to open it. If you have an exit line or a reason to turn back, turn on the balls of your feet, and deliver the line or glance pointedly, still holding the doorknob. Otherwise, go directly offstage, closing the door with the hand farthest from the hinges.

Cross

You will recall that a movement from one stage position to another is called a cross. In general, actors usually move in gently curving patterns that resemble an "S." Sometimes, if the movement is agitated or urgent, a straight line cross will be necessary. The curved pattern always allows actors to open up to the audience more easily. It also suggests that the stage space, which in reality is about one and a half times as large as the actual space that people normally have, is more similar to actual space. Audience members viewing the play from a balcony notice this more readily than the audience on the stage level.

It is always best to cross between lines or to break up the line and move during the breaks. Never move during important lines or when involved in stage business. Do not move on a laugh line or while the audience is laughing. Always cross below furniture and characters who are standing. Cross above characters who are seated. It is always more forceful to move toward the audience or other characters than it is to move away. Standing is more forceful than sitting. Seated characters must expend more energy to build a scene.

Gestures should usually be made with the upstage arm for maximum forcefulness. Turns should be made toward the front. Move forward on the upstage

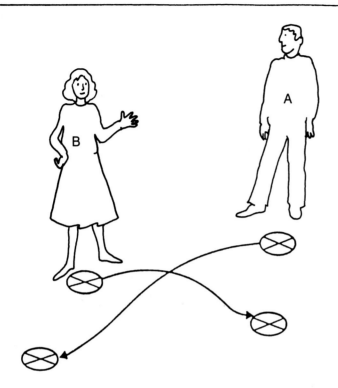

COUNTERCROSS
When character A crosses from his UL position to DR, character B will move from UC to LC to balance the stage, to offset the movement of A, and to avoid being blocked by A's new position.

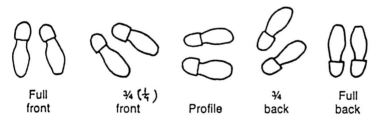

| Full
front | ¾ (½)
front | Profile | ¾
back | Full
back |

Decreasing Emphasis

THE ACTOR'S POSITIONS

foot and kneel on the downstage knee. When speaking, never cover your face with your hands or with a prop like a fan or telephone. A two-character scene must be carefully rehearsed to be sure that one actor does not cover the other and also to be sure that both do not hold the same position for too long or use similar gestures.

The Countercross

When one character moves, the stage picture loses its balance. Therefore, for each cross on stage, there is usually a movement in the opposite direction by another character. This is called a countercross. It does not have to cover a distance equal to the first movement. Crossing and countercrossing are an important part of rehearsing, and they must be carefully worked out so that they look natural on stage. It is always best not to move on important lines, either of your own or of another character because movement distracts the audience from the words spoken. Try to cross between speeches on a definite piece of business. Countercross easily and naturally when giving way to someone else.

Sitting and Rising

Sitting and rising must be done naturally and effectively. Continually practice crossing to a chair or sofa and sitting down in character until it feels comfortable and becomes natural. Avoid looking behind you for the chair or sofa before you sit. Locate the edge of the chair or sofa with the back of the calf of your leg. Then sit down, remaining in character as you do so. Sit with your feet and knees together unless you are playing a middle-aged or older part. Never cross your knees or feet and never spread your feet apart with the knees together unless your character would do so. When rising, put one foot slightly in front of the other and push yourself up with the back foot, letting the chest lead. Do not grasp the arms of a chair to push yourself up unless the character you are playing would get up in that way.

Stage Positions, Movement, and Grouping

Movement and grouping on stage are very important because the audience sees both before the actors utter a single word. How the actors move and how they are grouped on stage allow the audience to grasp the spirit of a situation before any lines are spoken.

Stage Positions and Movements

When you play a scene you should be aware of four basic staging techniques. Actors normally **cheat out** by pivoting the torso and turning the face towards

Body position for sharing a scene is slightly "cheated out" from the face to face position of normal conversation.

the audience. Two characters may cheat out when they **share a scene.** You share a scene with another actor when you stand or sit parallel to each other. A shared scene should be played three-quarter front or in profile. However, profile is rather weak because it does not allow the audience to see your face. Also, a profile scene is a confrontation-type scene. It can be played for only a short time before a strong emotional reaction, such as a fight or an embrace, must result.

A second basic staging technique is **giving the scene.** It occurs when the audience's attention is shifted from one actor to another. This is accomplished when one actor crosses downstage and then turns slightly upstage toward the other actor. This movement gives the scene to the upstage actor, who now holds the dominant stage position.

Turning the scene in is a third basic staging technique. This type of staging is important in scenes in which more than two characters appear. In these kinds of scenes, the audience's attention must focus on the actor who is the real center of dramatic action. This happens when the actors who are not the key characters in a particular scene shift the angle of their bodies more upstage and then look directly at the scene's key character.

A fourth basic staging technique is called **taking yourself out of a scene.** This occurs when the actor turns away from the audience into a three-quarter back or full back position. The actor may then gaze out a window, leaf through the pages of a book, or engage in some other stage business, such as reading a magazine.

Sharing

A and B are on even line.
Both ¾ front.

Taking

A moves into position
upstage of B.

Giving

A turns ¾ upstage to B.

Taking Out of Scene

A turns full back.

Dominant Stage Positions

Grouping

The proper grouping of characters depends upon maintaining the center of interest. A triangular positioning with the important character of the moment standing at the highest point of the triangle works out well. Frames, such as doorways and archways, also set an actor off. Everyone is conditioned to move their eyes from left to right. Down right is therefore a stronger position than down left. Actors must keep the stage picture constantly in mind. If they do, everyone in the audience will be able to see clearly because they will not cover other actors, huddle in tight groups, or stand in straight lines.

Stage Business

Stage business is an essential part of acting that involves the use of hand props, costume props, stage props, other actors, and even part of the set (doors, windows, lighting fixtures, and so forth). Handling a cup and saucer, a pair of glasses, or a handkerchief will, of course, vary from characterization to characterization. It takes training and a lot of practice to handle props well. This is especially true of such historical props as swords, fans, parasols,

Props have a way of introducing the unexpected on stage. One must be prepared for varied outcomes when working with children and animals. In this scene from Sugar Babies, *Carol Channing had to work with pigeons.*

canes, and swagger sticks. If such items are not handled properly, their use will appear awkward and distracting. The audience will then focus on the props instead of the actor using them. Stage business like writing a letter, drinking from a cup, and stirring a fire demands concentration and much practice before they look natural. Good stage business aids a characterization and enhances an entire production. Too much stage business, however, especially that which is out-of-character and nonmotivated, is meaningless and even harmful.

Eating and drinking on stage present special problems. Real food is rarely used on stage, so an actor needs imagination to convince an audience that the food or drink is real. When you drink on stage, think about what the real drink is like. If you are supposed to be drinking a cup of cocoa, think about how hot it is. If it is really hot, you will sip it carefully. If it is lukewarm, you might gulp it down before it gets colder. Does it have a marshmallow on top? Is it instant or made from scratch? How full is the cup? When you eat on stage and dark bread has been substituted for steak, imagine what kind of steak it is, how it has been cooked, whether it is tender and juicy, or tough and dry.

There are three basic rules to remember when eating on stage.

1. Do not eat or drink any more than is necessary.

2. Unless the script calls for it, do not try to deliver lines with food in your mouth.

3. Learn how to dispose of food that is in your mouth. For example, practice disposing of it unnoticeably into a napkin.

Vocal Acting

A full discussion of the voice is found in Chapter 4. However, a few basic principles that affect characterization should be noted here.

Rising and Falling Pitch

Most characters can be classified as either "pitch up" or "pitch down" personalities. This means that most of the time a character's vocal patterns are either falling or rising. Falling pitch is typical of the speech of characters who are self-assured, dominating, authoritative, and overbearing. Rising pitch is typical of the speech of characters who lack confidence, are followers rather than leaders, are fearful, intimidated, or confused.

Four Patterns of Inflection

Closely related to the general rising and falling pitch patterns are the four inflections — rising, falling, sustained, and circumflex. **Rising inflection** is used to indicate questioning, surprise, or shock. **Falling inflection** usually signals the end of a statement. It is also used to express depression, finality, or firmness. **Sustained inflection** — staying on the same note — suggests calmness, decisiveness, or steadiness of purpose. **Circumflex inflection** blends two or three sounds for a vowel that normally has a single sound. This inflection allows an actor to suggest a change of meaning of a word or to stress a particular meaning. This twisting of sound can alter the literal meaning of a word and even reverse the meaning entirely. One of the best known examples of the circumflex inflection is found in Marc Antony's funeral oration in *Julius Caesar.* Each time Antony says the word *honorable,* he inflects the vowel sounds more and more until the word suggests the meaning "dishonorable."

Try saying the following lines. Inflect the italicized vowels with a circumflex.

Applications
• • • • • • • • • • • • •

1. She is *so* grateful.

2. It h*u*rts a lot.

3. It's *so* str*a*nge.

4. L*oo*k at those fl*a*mes!

5. *See*, I t*o*ld you she was surpr*i*sed.

Your voice, your body, and your imagination are the tools that make your character come alive onstage. In Shakespeare's Coriolanus, *Gloria Foster is one with her character.*
• •

In a choreopoem such as For Colored Girls Who Have Considered Suicide When the Rainbow Is Enuf, *vocal expertise carries the performance.*
. . . .

Pitch Response

As far as volume, pitch, tempo, and stress are concerned, an individual always responds to others. When we rehearse alone, we may guess how we believe a line will be delivered by another actor. But when we go into rehearsal, we may find that the planned delivery does not match up with the lines as given by the other actors. For example, if someone shouts at you, you automatically shout back. As a scene builds, the volume levels usually get louder and louder. If the pace of a conversation quickens, people naturally begin to speak more rapidly. As an actor, you must respond to the emotion, pitch, and volume levels of the other actors on the stage. However, you must always do so within the personality and mind-set of the character you are playing. Some personalities will respond to a given situation in a manner that is almost directly opposite to the way in which most people respond. While most characters will raise the volumes of their voices in response to shouting, a particular character might whimper in response. You must not allow the flow of emotion from other characters to pull you out of your own characterization. You must guard against unconsciously or uncontrollably mirroring another actor. The appropriate responses of particular characters must be carefully worked on in rehearsals.

The Keys to Characterization

There are fifteen keys to characterization. Each should be of help to you as you learn to develop the characters you play.

Internalizing

The first key to characterization is called **internalizing.** When an actor internalizes a character, the actor gets within the character and learns what the character is really like down deep inside. The actor has already answered questions like these about the character: "Who am I? What am I? Why am I? What do I want?" The answers to these questions are collected by studying the play carefully, understanding the director's insights, writing a character biography, researching the part and the play, and scoring the role. Having done all of these things, the actor knows how the character thinks.

Internalizing bears fruit when an actor develops the ability to respond in character to any given situation. This ability prevents panicky mistakes on stage. Should an accident of some sort occur, an actor who is deeply in character will know how to respond in character. An actor who has not internalized the role completely, is likely to respond inappropriately as himself or herself.

Externalization

The second key to characterization is **externalization.** This is the process by which the true personality of a character is made visible to an audience. This is done through careful interpretation, nonverbal expression, voice quality, pitch, rate, and physical action. For example, in *The Caine Mutiny Court Martial,* Captain Queeg's conviction that he is being persecuted is externalized through the ball bearings that he carries in his pocket. Whenever the Captain becomes nervous and panicky, he removes the ball bearings from his pocket and begins fidgeting with them in his hand. As a result, the audience can see evidence of the inner man breaking down.

Concentration

The third key to characterization is **concentration.** This is the ability to direct all your thoughts, energies, and skills into what you are doing at any single moment. It often helps to remember that every line comes from the middle of some larger thought. Lines are not isolated and independent from other thoughts and actions. As an actor, you must learn how to concentrate simultaneously on character, lines, and action. You must sustain that concentration over each performance and over the length of the production's run.

Observation

The fourth key to characterization is **observation.** Observe people carefully, noting how they communicate fine shades of emotions. Notice in particular how they use their small facial muscles. Notice also their distinguishing physical characteristics and their unique voice and diction patterns. Do what most professional actors do: Begin an actor's notebook and record your observations. Also, include pictures of real people that you might want to use as makeup models in the future. Record in your notebook as well comments and suggestions made by directors and other actors. As you become more skilled in observation, you will begin to see the many little things that people do that reveal their inner thoughts and feelings.

Emotional Memory

The fifth key to characterization is the use of **emotional memory.** Emotional memory is the recalling of specific emotions that you have experienced or observed. You have had direct or indirect experience of fear, joy, jealousy, timidity, anger, love, and many more emotions. However, emotions might be adjusted to fit your character, situation, time, and environment. As an actor, you draw upon those emotional memories to give life to the characters that you play. Keep in mind, however, that people can experience more than one level of emotion at a time. People, for example, are sometimes happy and sad at the same time. It is challenging when a part calls for the expression of conflicting emotions. When that happens, you must reach into your emotional memory bank to determine how to play a role so that the audience can see the tug-of-war between the two feelings within your character.

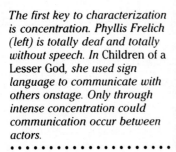

The first key to characterization is concentration. Phyllis Frelich (left) is totally deaf and totally without speech. In Children of a Lesser God, *she used sign language to communicate with others onstage. Only through intense concentration could communication occur between actors.*

EMOTIONAL MEMORY

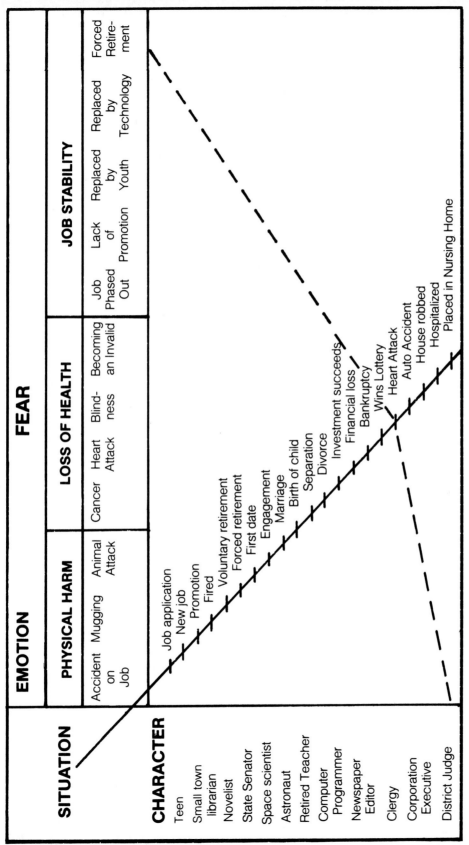

This is a sample of how the EMOTIONAL MEMORY can function. The left hand column lists character possibilities. The base emotion in this diagram is *fear*. Only three causes of fear have been selected, and these have been broken down to illustrate the many specific fears that might be experienced. The solid diagonal line represents some possible situations. The dotted line represents a specific character (District Judge), situation (suffers a heart attack), and fear (forced retirement).

Even a quiet moment must be projected from the inner energy an actor builds through the internalization of a role.

Projection

Once inner feelings are externalized, they must then be projected to the audience. **Projection** is the sixth key to characterization. Strong volume is a part of projecting, but projection is more than loudness. Projection is "reaching out" to the last person in the last row of a distant balcony. You project your character through dialogue and action made larger than life. It is this larger-than-life exaggeration that carries the skillfulness of a polished performance beyond the stage. Projection of character generates an electricity between actor and audience that carries the dynamics of theater.

Motivation

The seventh key to characterization is **motivation.** Motivation is the "why" of characterization. To be believable, your actor's behavior must be driven by an inner force. The inner force is intent. **Intent** is what the character wants to do. Motivation is why the character wants to do it. Motivations impelling a character to act are influenced by personal convictions, mind-set, self-interest, past experience, situation, environment, friends, and loved ones. Good acting always makes a character's motivation clear to an audience.

Stretching a Character

Ordinary personalities on stage are very limited and rather boring. **Stretching a character** is therefore the eighth key to characterization. Stretching a character is the process of making a role unique, individual, and interesting. The process should result in a character that is noticeably different from the other characters in a play. In stretching a character, the actor's aim is not to create an unbelievable exaggeration. Instead, the actor's goal is to identify the character's primary personality trait and then to emphasize it. If the actor is portraying a villain, for example, he or she develops and emphasizes the cruelty that is the character's primary personality trait. Even if a character is stretched only slightly, the result can be a characterization that the audience will long remember. There is an old saying in the theater: "A tenth of an inch makes a difference."

The Inconsistent Consistency

The ninth key to characterization is called the **inconsistent consistency.** This key has to do with the special personality trait of a character that the actor chooses to emphasize. That trait is the character's inconsistency, the thing that makes him or her different from the rest of humanity. It might be a dialect, a limp, an arrogance, or a cackling laugh. Once it is chosen, it must not be dropped, even for a line or two or a minute or two. If the dialect slips away, if the limp shifts to the other leg, if the arrogance is mellowed, or if the cackle loses its fiendish quality, the characterization is bound to suffer. The actor, and especially the beginning actor, must strive to be consistent with their characters' inconsistencies.

Playing the Conditions

The tenth key to characterization is **playing the conditions**. The conditions are the elements of time, place, weather, objects, and the state of the individual. These conditions affect the manner in which characters meet their objectives and deal with the obstacles. *Time* can be the hour of the day, the day

The locale, the setting, and the time of day, each affect the actor's interpretation of the moment.

itself, the month, year, or season. There can be plenty of it, or it can be very limited. *Place* can be indoors or outdoors, familiar or unfamiliar, threatening or comforting. The *weather* may be hot or cold, sunny or rainy, calm or blustery. *Objects* may be familiar or unfamiliar, in adequate supply or few, in working order or broken. The *state of the individual* may be extremely fatigued or well rested, wounded or healed, freezing or sweltering, healthy or ill. Actors must keep all of these conditions in mind as they interpret their characters, for each of these conditions influences or can influence the way a character responds.

Playing the Objectives

The eleventh key to characterization is **playing the objectives.** This includes all of the ways and means that a character uses to reach a goal that he or she has established. The method used to attain a goal might be a physical act, such as a slap, a kick, or a kiss. It might be a mental act, such as a decision, a deliberate strategy, or an assumption. The method used might also be an object, such as a gun, a key, or a secret code. It might also be an action, such as writing a letter, making a phone call, or planting an explosive device. An actor must be completely familiar with a character's objectives and must be totally aware of all the means that the character uses to reach them. Only in this way can the actor properly stress and present each of these means as it occurs in the play.

Playing the Obstacles

The twelfth key to characterization is **playing the obstacles** or, in other words, the ways in which a character faces each crisis or obstacle. An actor must note carefully how the personality of the character deals with these situations. For example, an actor must notice whether a character tackles an obstacle head on by considering it thoughtfully or whether the character ignores it, denies that it exists, transfers it to someone else, loses control, becomes rattled, or runs away from it. Each personality approaches a similar obstacle differently. An actor must know his or her character's response so that it can be forcefully communicated to an audience.

Energy

The thirteenth key to characterization is **energy.** Energy is the fuel that drives acting, both individual performance and group performance. Energy enlivens a performance, makes forceful character portrayal possible, and creates greater empathy between the actor and the audience. Physical energy pro-

Energy as the drive behind the performance is controlled, and the control is more exciting than "letting it all hang out." Anger and explosive scenes which are seemingly easy to play are the hardest to play effectively. Even when one's character is out of control, the actor should not be.

. . . .

duces the freshness, sparkle, and spontaneity that theater depends upon. The finest actors learn how to control energy and how to conserve it. Because most plays build steadily to a major climax, the key scenes of most characters occur well along in the play. Every performer must therefore control the use of energy and save some for important scenes.

Focus

The fourteenth key to characterization is **focus**. Focus directs the actor's attention, action, emotion, or line delivery to a definite target. There are many forms of focus. There is the internal focus on character that includes focus on thought. There is the focus on scene which concentrates on the central idea toward which a scene moves. There is the focus on stage position which turns a scene in and concentrates audience attention on the key player in a scene. There is the visual focus that an actor creates with the eyes, leading the audience to concentrate on whatever the actor is gazing at. There is vocal focus that projects the voice to the members of the audience furthest from the stage or that bounces a line off another player and then out to the audience. There is the focus of feeling that exists when an actor concentrates on a physical or emotional pain. This focus of feeling is called the "point of pain." If the character has a physical pain in the chest, the actor focuses on the specific spot where the pain exists — the chest. If the character is suffering from a broken heart, the hurt is focused on the heart.

The playwright's writing, the director's staging, and the actor's delivery of lines can all create focus. The author may focus a scene on certain characters (their internal and external conflicts, their emotional stresses, their relationships) or on the situation in which these characters are involved. The director may focus attention on a key actor by placing that actor in a doorway, in an elevated location, or upstage of all the other actors. However, the main responsibility for focusing attention is the actor's. By stressing particular lines, gestures, mannerisms, facial expressions, or behaviors, the actor focuses audience attention on the key ideas of theme, plot, or characterization.

Uniqueness

The fifteenth and final key to characterization is **uniqueness**. Every actor who plays a character should be unique in that role, not merely a close copy of someone else. Each actor and each director will have a different picture of the play and its characters. The director envisions each character as part of the total production. Within the director's image of a character, the actor must shape a personality special unto itself.

Acting Techniques

Subtext

The **subtext** is what your character thinks but does not say. The author provides the character's words in the script. You the actor provide the subtext. Actors should know what their characters are thinking when they are on stage and even what they are thinking offstage. Many actors write out a complete subtext. They think as their character would think while other actors are delivering their lines. If you think in response to what you hear, your face and body will respond naturally. This is why it is important to learn lines completely very early in the rehearsal process. Once the lines are learned, you can concentrate on the other character's lines and respond to them just as you would in a real-life situation.

Powerful scenes and relationships must appear to the audience as if they are happening for the first time.
· · · · · · · · · · · · · · · · ·

Memorizing

A chief responsibility that follows from getting a part is **memorizing** one's lines. Lines must be learned according to the director's schedule. Directors realize that an actor is severely limited as long as the script is still in hand. Therefore, the sooner the lines are memorized, the sooner the actor is free to concentrate on the action and to respond naturally to the other actors.

There are two approaches to memorizing. **Whole-part memorization** requires the actor to read the whole play through several times. The actor then reads a complete act several times, followed by several readings of those scenes in which the actor appears. (*Scene* here means an identifiable section of a play, usually from the entrance of a character to the exit of a character.) The actor focuses on individual lines only after whole units of the play are firmly in mind. This method develops an internal feel for the entire play and the other characters who are in it.

The second method is called **part-whole memorization**. This approach has the actor study cues and lines line-by-line until the script is memorized. This method has a number of disadvantages. First of all, since each line is learned by itself, the risk of forgetting exists with each line. Secondly, the play may seem very fragmented in the early rehearsals, for the differences between memorized lines and still-to-be-memorized lines are rather dramatic. Finally, the actors tend to focus more on cues than on the meaning of the other characters' lines.

Unless the director says otherwise, lines should always be memorized exactly as written. Sometimes beginning actors complain that they don't like a line or that a line doesn't sound right. With few exceptions, the problem is with the actor. The line or lines that the actor is complaining about will sound right once the actor gets more into character.

Forgetting What You Know

When you have studied a play thoroughly and rehearsed it over and over again, it becomes very familiar to you. You ought to know things that your character really wouldn't know. For example, you know how things are going to turn out, you know the content of conversations that your character did not participate in, and you know what takes place when your character is not on stage. To create the illusion of reality in a convincing manner, you must "remember to forget" all of these things.

Playing the Moment

Closely connected to "forgetting what you know" is **playing the moment.** Playing the moment means that you respond to each line, each action, and each character in the permanent present time that theater demands. The theater lives in the permanent "now," and you must not anticipate what is about to happen. An actor who plays the moment never turns to a phone before it actually rings and never opens a door before the knock. Beginning actors must remember not to shift emotions before the onstage action makes the emotional shift understandable. Maintain the "illusion of the first time" and the air of suspense that keeps the audience wondering what will happen next.

Working Backwards

Although actors must play the moment, **working backwards** is a helpful technique. This means that although an actor will not give away a character's future actions, he or she will find ways of making a character's future action believable. Audiences like surprises but will not accept dramatic character

In this scene from Julius Caesar, *what the actors are thinking but do not say, add to the depth of their performance.*

Though the actor who plays Willie Loman in Death of a Salesman *may never have had the same relationship with his family as Loman does, he must substitute similar experiences that will evoke the necessary emotional output.*

changes that are not at all prepared for. If a somewhat villainous character in a play will undergo a change of heart and show mercy instead of pure vengeance, disclose the possibility of this change early by emphasizing certain lines, by actions, or by tone of voice. Such a character, for example, might show an obvious compassionate side to an acquaintance or loved one early in the play. An actor must know where a character is headed and then work backwards to prepare an audience earlier on.

Paraphrasing

A useful technique to use when you are uncertain how a line should be delivered is **paraphrasing.** Paraphrasing is simply restating in your own words. You figure out the meaning of the line and state it in your words. Since the vocal patterns for similar thoughts are almost identical, the vocal pattern of your own phrasing and those of the line will be very much alike. This exercise gives you a very good idea of how the line should be delivered.

Substitution

When an actor uses a private experience as a replacement for an experience that a role calls for, it is called **substitution.** No actor could possibly have personally dealt with every emotional experience that a role includes. For example, an actor might be faced with the challenge of playing the role of a father who has to watch his own child die in his arms. The actor may never have been a father and may never have experienced the death of any loved one. However, the actor might have experienced the death of a beloved pet and knows something about the emotional content of that experience. In playing the scene, the actor recalls the death of the pet and therefore uses a similar experience to help capture and project the emotional response that the scene calls for.

Improvising

Whether alone or in a group at a rehearsal, **improvising** is a useful means of identifying with a situation or of experiencing the natural emotions of a role. It is particularly useful if you are working on a period play or if you are trying to develop a mature role that has lines and action that are very distant from your own personal experience. You can improvise once you know your character rather well, understand the general content of the lines and the reasons for the actions, and grasp the objectives and obstacles of a scene. If you are working alone, you can carry on a one-sided conversation that parallels the script. In a cast improvisation, you can play the whole scene. Under these circumstances, improvisation often allows you to understand more clearly how your character feels and what the other characters are feeling. It frequently enables you to see how the scene should be built when you return to the script.

Animal Types

A practice technique that can be used at home or in rehearsal is the playing of roles as animal personalities. Sometimes, a mannerism associated with a type of animal can be carried over to an actor's portrayal of a role. Various animals have physical actions and produce vocal sounds that can be worked into roles. Some of the animal types that can be used are the lion, bear, wolf, fox, rabbit, dog, cat, donkey, elephant, monkey, gorilla, turtle, alligator, snake, owl, vulture, chicken, duck, parrot, fly, and butterfly. This technique works especially well for children's theater. Ben Jonson's *Volpone* is an example of a play written with animal personalities in mind. This same technique may be extended to other nonhuman types, such as androids, the Tin Woodsman and Scarecrow of Oz, toys in a toyshop, and other inanimate objects.

Filling in the Blanks

Scripts often include incomplete lines or telephone conversations. These must be practiced carefully, for to handle them correctly demands precise

(ABOVE) *In Samuel Beckett's play* Cockaby, *Billie Whitelaw undergoes a transformation that demands discipline and control.* (LOWER LEFT) *Research into the life of the painter, George Seurat, adds dimension to the portrayal of this historical character in* Sunday in the Park with George. (LOWER RIGHT) *The* Dresser *is essentially a play within a play. The show centers on an actor's preparation for a performance and his longtime relationship with his dresser. The scenario allows the audience to examine the actor's role in the creation of an illusion.*

(ABOVE) *The father in Ionesco's* Jack or the Submission *presents the three-faced bride. Special techniques are involved in performing with the masks which are important in the stylization of this theater of the absurd production.* (BELOW) *In a fantasy role, an actor's performance demands imagination and awareness of characterization through the use of gesture. In* Cats, *each actor interprets the feline mannerisms of his or her character in an individual way.*

(UPPER LEFT) *The actors in* I'm Not Rappaport *create a sparkling performance by listening and responding to one another's characterizations.* (UPPER RIGHT) *The effective performance of a monologue involves total concentration and an in-depth understanding of the structure of the script.* (LOWER LEFT) *In order not to interfere with the action of a play, props should be used during rehearsal. The manner in which the gun is handled during its purchase in this scene from Buchner's* Woyzeck *allows the actor to subtly reveal his character's personality.* (LOWER RIGHT) *The grouping of the actors in this scene from Brecht's* Private Lives of the Master Race *focuses the audience's attention on the speaker. The body language of the actors communicates a quick insight into each of their characters.*

Henley's Crimes of the Heart *provides the actors with a challenging opportunity to portray roles of depth and humor. The actors playing the three sisters must portray their feelings toward each other with an understanding of their past life together.*

The family relationships in True West *erupt into violence and destruction. The breaking up of the set occurs in the heat of the action but does not appear orchestrated—though it is.*

The actors portraying trains in Starlight Express *were involved in many hours of rehearsal and experimentation before this unique performance was perfected.*

timing. There are two types of incomplete lines — **cut-off lines** and **fade-off lines**. Cut-off lines are lines that are interrupted by another speaker. In most scripts, cut-off lines are indicated by dashes (—). An actor who has a cut-off line should know what the rest of the line would be if it weren't cut off and should finish the line mentally. The actor who creates the cut-off line by interrupting, must decide upon a cue word ahead of the cut-off in order to interrupt at the right time.

<pre>
          cue word   cut-off
  MARY   I don't care if – – – (she does leave.)

  JANE   What do you mean you don't care!
</pre>

A fade-off line is one that the speaker trails off because he or she does not finish the line. This sometimes occurs because the speaker expects an interruption that does not come. It may also occur because the meaning is so obvious that it is pointless to express it. In most scripts, this kind of line is indicated by a series of dots (. . . .).

> MARY   I knew it was wrong all along, but . . . .
>
> JANE   *(after an awkward pause)* It's all right, Mary. It's all over now.

Phone conversations are common on stage. To make them believable they should include legitimate pauses during the other party's words. If your part includes a phone conversation, it is always best to write out the conversation that occurs on the other end of the line. You can then memorize it and repeat it silently in between your spoken lines.

> MIKE   Hello? (Hello Mike?) Yeah, this is Mike. Who's this? (Mike, this is Bill — you know, Mary's fiancé?) Oh, yeah — Bill. What can I do for you? (Well, I just wanted you to know that it's off. It's over between us — Mary and me — you understand?) What? Oh, yeah, sure. It's over. I understand.

Line Delivery

General

Speaking lines communicates the playwright's meaning and style. Speaking lines also reveals the characters and their emotions in each situation. Of course, lines are closely associated with action and must not be lost or blurred by movements. Significant lines, such as character lines, theme lines, comic set-ups, and punch lines, must be heard by each person in the audience no matter where that person is seated. You should mark the significant lines plainly on your script as soon as you have studied every situation carefully. Recheck them after the first rehearsals during which movements will be determined. Avoid fixing imperfect inflections until action is set, for when they become automatic, you can seldom change them.

A rapid **picking up of cues** must be established as early in rehearsals as possible. The cues should be memorized along with the lines. Many beginning actors wait for their cue before they show any facial or bodily reaction. Your face should respond during the other person's lines. You will then be ready to speak on cue. A good technique is to take a breath during the cue. Failure to pick up cues quickly causes many amateur performances to drag in spite of many painstaking rehearsals. The loss of only a fraction of a second before each speech slows the action dramatically.

The ad-lib is an emergency measure that should only be used to avoid a dead silence. If it is necessary to ad-lib, the lines must be spoken as though they were a part of the script without any decrease in volume or inflection. If one actor forgets lines or begins a speech ahead of the appropriate point in

In a comic scene, pace and delivery must be explored in much the same way that a conductor might explore differing tempos in a musical piece.
· · · · · · · · · · ·

the action and skips important information, the other actors have to ad-lib the missing information while carrying on the conversation naturally. Entire conversations are often improvised in crowd scenes and in scenes that portray social gatherings. These conversations must be spoken very quietly to avoid drowning out the lines of the speaker who is carrying the scene. Frequently, reciting the alphabet with appropriate inflections can be used in background groupings to suggest conversation.

Pointing lines means placing the emphasis on exactly the right word and timing the rate and pauses so that the audience gets the full emotional impact. Stage conversation must be kept fluent. It must mirror the give-and-take of normal conversation. The difference lies in sharing the conversation with the silent witnesses in the audience. The audience should become so involved that their reaction of laughter or tears is involuntary. Pointing lines is particularly essential in comedy, for getting laughs in the right places makes or breaks a scene. Actors must work together to build up to the laugh line, so feeding cues properly is essential. Unless the preceding line or word leads to the point of the joke, the joke will fall flat. You can watch people in comic sketches on television getting laughs by leading into them. Notice how they combine pausing in the right place with using their faces to help get laughs. This they do without stealing the scene from the actor who should have it. In a play on the stage, it is inexcusable for the actor feeding the line or the actor making the point to laugh, although this is often done on television.

How a person's name is spoken shows how one character feels about another at a given moment. A name can be uttered with love, hatred, envy, flirtatiousness, or in any of countless ways that express how the speaker feels about the person. One reason playwrights use names so frequently in dialogue is that their use clarifies a speaker's feelings. The position of a name in a line determines whether the pitch will rise or fall. That is why actors should not change the position of a name in a line. Notice the difference in pitch as you read these lines.

"Tom, I can't understand how you could have done such a thing."
"I can't understand how you could have done such a thing, Tom."
"I can't understand, Tom, how you could have done such a thing."

Playwrights often place *ohs* or *wells* or similar "sound words" at the beginnings of lines and sentences. These terms serve as vocal transitions which allow an actor to raise or lower the pitch level of the lines without interfering with the meaning of key words. Try these sentences. Change the pitch level by the way you inflect each sound word.

(In shock)   Oh, how awful for you!

(In disgust)   Well, I always said he'd turn out bad.

(In admiration)   My, that's a lovely shawl!

(In polite agreement)   Yes, I would like another cup of tea.

(In reserved dismay)   Oh, dear, did I do something wrong?

(In mild denial)   Well, no, I wouldn't say that.

Playing Comedy

Much of the success of comedy depends upon the comic mood that the cast establishes. The cast must always communicate enjoyment as they maintain the fast pace that comedy requires. Individual actors must keep in mind a few techniques for playing comedy successfully. Lift the end of a punch line and leave it hanging, or play it "flat," or deadpan, in order to say to the audience, "Laugh now." Clinch the punch line with a facial or bodily reaction. It is helpful to develop an air of innocence because comic characters are often naive and unknowledgeable. Learn to feed a line to a fellow performer, so that the other actor can catch it in midair and clinch the laugh on the following line. Remember that laugh lines are usually short and that their length is determined by sounds as much as by words. A line too long or too short will kill a laugh. This is one major reason that explains why actors are told over and over again to deliver comic lines exactly as they are written. Adding or omitting one word can lose the laugh that the line is designed to get.

Topping becomes a particularly important factor in comedy. The actors top each other through increased volume, higher pitch, faster tempo, or greater emphasis. However, when a comic actor breaks a topping sequence, he or she may get a laugh through a sudden change of pitch, by saying the line in an almost expressionless manner, or with a look or gesture that seems inconsistent with the character or the situation. Remember: Timing must be perfect or the laugh can easily be killed. Comedians even learn how to "milk" audiences for laughs by adding some exaggerated bits of business to their punch lines.

The comic actor must play to the audience and must use the audience as a comic barometer. The saying "no two audiences are alike" is almost always true of comedy audiences. Barely detectable chuckles might result from a line or action on one night. On the next night, a roar of laughter greets the same line. Some audiences will laugh at almost nothing, some will laugh in outbursts, and some never stop laughing from the opening curtain to the final curtain.

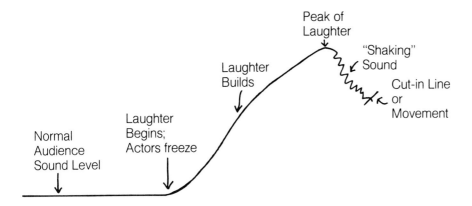

Laugh Curve.

Beginning actors often fail to hold for laughs. Even after weeks of rehearsal during which many hours are spent picking up cues, beginning performers often continue to rush from line to line without giving the audience an opportunity to react by laughing. An audience will naturally silence itself to hear lines. But an actor must anticipate where the audience is likely to laugh and then be prepared to freeze until the laughter dies naturally. The actor must listen for the **laugh curve**. This begins with the laughter of those members of the audience who catch on more quickly. The laughter then swells more rapidly as others join in, for laughter is contagious, until a peak is reached. Just after the peak, the laughter will start to fade and then will seem to linger. It is at this instant that the actor with the "cut in" line must kill the laughter. Usually the line is not all that important to the play. Its main purpose is to silence the audience. It is important that an audience not be allowed to "laugh itself out." If it did, its members would then sit back relaxed and satisfied and would be quite willing to wait awhile before being entertained again. The pace of the comedy would then be seriously slowed.

Laughing

Laughing on stage is extremely difficult. The best approach to learning how to do it effectively is to take a special interest in laughter. You must develop your ability to observe laughter closely, both in real life and on stage and television. Pay particular attention to unusual laughs. Try to notice the sounds and inflections that make up laughter. There are many kinds, including uproarious guffaws, artificial simperings, musical ripples, hysterical gurgles, and sinister snorts.

Laughter is as idiosyncratic of a character as other traits and qualities.
. . . .

Technically, a sudden contraction of the abdominal muscles produces a laugh. This forces the breath out in sharp gasps. These gasps are given sound as they pass through the larynx. The first step in learning to laugh is to pant like a dog. Tighten your abdominal muscles as you exhale and relax them as you breathe in. On your first try, you will probably only make faces, because you will probably try to say "ha" when you are drawing in the breath instead of when you are expelling it in sharp, quick spurts. As you practice, you will literally "laugh until your sides ache."

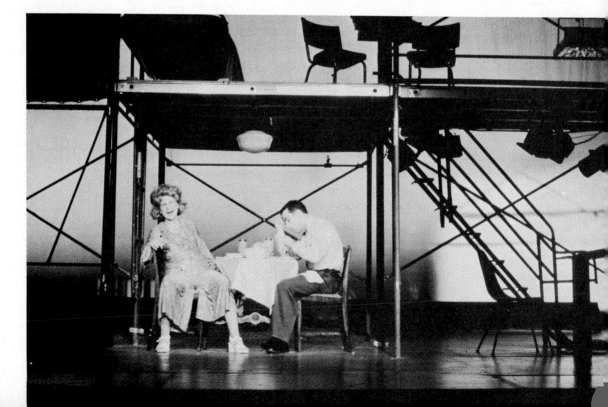

In order to master the laugh, you must relax first and then let yourself go. Take the vowel combinations heard in laughter — "ha-ha-ha, ho-ho-ho, he-he-he, hoo-hoo-hoo" — and say them in rapid succession with sharp contractions of the abdominal area. Do not stop or become self-conscious. Begin at a high pitch and run down the scale. Then begin at a low level and run up the scale. Finally, select any combination of vowel sounds and go both up and down, prolonging some vowel sounds and shortening others in various combinations.

Laughter may come before, during, or after lines. ("Ha-ha-ha, you don't say so! Ha-ha, ho-ho, that's the funniest thing, ha-ha-ha-ha, I ever heard, ho-ho-huh-huh.") If laughter comes within a line, be sure that meaning is not overwhelmed by the laughter.

Applications

1. Practice laughing like the following people: a giggling child on the telephone; a fat actor at a comic television show; a very polite lady reacting to a joke she has heard many times before; a villain who has at last captured the hero; a miser gloating over a box of money; an elementary school student seeing a friend trip over a brick; a farmer seeing a motorist whose expensive car has broken down; a charming girl very pleased with her date; a department store Santa Claus greeting a small child.

2. Say the lines below, accompanying each with laughter as (a) a five-year-old child; (b) a teenager; (c) a middle-aged conservative person; (d) an elderly, wealthy person.
   "That's the silliest thing I ever heard."
   "Look at that crazy monkey!"
   "But, that's so embarrassing!"

3. Deliver the following lines, laughing as you believe the character named would laugh.
   a. As the wicked witch in *Snow White*:
      "Taste this delicious apple, my dear."

   b. As the villain in a melodrama:
      "So, you can't pay the mortgage, eh?"

   c. As an egotistical movie star:
      "So, you really don't know who I am?"

   d. As a hulking football player:
      "You want to know if I can lift this sack?"

   e. As a practical joker at camp:
      "Who me? Why should I short-sheet your bed?"

4. Read the following passages from Shakespeare, accompanying the lines with appropriate laughing.

   a. FROM *The Merchant of Venice*

      PORTIA   God made him, therefore, let him pass for a man.

   b. FROM *As You Like It*

      JAQUES   A fool, a fool! — I met a fool i' the forest
      A motley fool; — a miserable world!

   c. FROM *As You Like It*

      CELIA   O wonderful, wonderful, and most wonderful, wonderful, and yet again wonderful!

   d. FROM *Twelfth Night*

      MARIA   Get ye all three into the box-tree: Malvolio is coming down this walk; he has been yonder i' the sun practicing behavior to his own shadow this half-hour; observe him for the love of mockery; for I know this letter will make a contemplative idiot of him. Close, in the name of jesting.

   e. FROM *The Merchant of Venice*

      GRATIANO   Let me play the fool;
      With mirth and laughter let old wrinkles come.

Crying

Crying on stage is much easier than laughing. The technique for crying is much the same as the technique for laughing. Gasp for breath, flexing the abdominal muscles in short, sharp movements. Words are often spoken on the gasping breath, so you must be careful to keep the meaning clear by not obscuring the key words. In sobbing without words, try using different vowel sounds through the gasps. Intensify and prolong the sounds to avoid monotony. Occasional indrawn and audible breaths for the "catch in the throat" are effective. "Swallowing tears" is simulated by tightening the throat muscles and really swallowing. In uncontrolled or hysterical crying, the vowel sounds will be stronger. If words are needed, they will be greatly intensified. Your entire body should react in crying. Your shoulders will shake and heave. Facial expression is most important. An appropriate expression can be created by puckering the eyebrows, biting the lips, and twisting the features to obtain the necessary effect.

Applications

1. Practice sobbing like each of the following: a young child who is put in the corner as punishment; a husband at the bed of his sick wife who is asleep; a spoiled child having a tantrum; a hysterical woman after a serious automobile accident; an old person alone on Christmas.

In this death scene from Amadeus, *the portrayal of grief is in keeping with the intensity of emotion warranted by the scene.*

2. Read the following passages. Cry through the words but be careful to keep the meaning clear.

   a. FROM *Pearls*, by Dan Totheroh
      A young girl has just learned that her brother is a thief.

      POLLY   I can't believe it. I can't — I can't — He's only a little boy — just a kid.

   b. FROM *The Time of the Cuckoo*, by Arthur Laurents
      An American tourist has just had an unfortunate flirtation with a charming Italian.

      LEONA   I'm Leona Samish. I *am* attractive. I'm bright and I'm warm and I'm nice! So *want me*! Want me! — Oh, why couldn't you love me, Renato? Why couldn't you just *say* you loved me?

Stage Combat

Stage combat is a very complex area of stage technique that requires considerable training and practice. Therefore, only a few general principles will be given here. Most importantly, most stage combat is *noncontact.* If executed properly, the audience responds as if actual physical contact had taken place. Combat should never be treated as a game, and participants should always take care of their partners.

There are three stages to most combat:

1. The Preparation — usually an action opposite to the direction of the blow, as the drawing back of the fist

2. The Blow — the execution of the blow, jab, or pull

3. The Reaction — a combination of sound, physical response, and freeze

Both actors should take in air before a blow is delivered so that both can respond vocally to the assault. Immediately following and timed to coincide with the landing of the blow is a second sound called a **knap**, a sliding, slapping sound or clap. The knap is usually made by the deliverer of the blow who may hit his or her own chest with the free hand. It is not the sound of a closed fist hitting the palm. The knap should not be seen by the audience, except in commedia dell'arte, when seeing the knap is part of the comedy. There must be a slight pause after each hit of combat for what occurs to register with the audience. The actor who receives the blow reacts facially and bodily immediately, freezes, and then lets out air with a pained sound.

Pulling the hair and choking are also used in stage combat. To pull the hair believably, an actor holds a closed fist against the back of a victim's head. The actor whose hair is being pulled distorts the face in anguish, twists the body in pain, and produces a sound of suffering. This is all that is necessary to convince the audience that the hair has been pulled. Choking, whether with two hands from the front or with the arm from the back, can be very dangerous if not done properly. It is best done by placing the hands or forearm on the collarbone instead of on the neck itself. The victim then reaches up and pulls the hands or forearm toward him or her, thereby controlling the pressure. At the same time, the actor doing the choking pulls the hands or forearm away from the victim as the victim grimaces in pain.

Romantic Scenes

Couples offstage normally require little help with romance, but onstage romantic scenes require careful rehearsal. They should even be rehearsed pri-

vately with the director before they are attempted in rehearsals with the entire cast.

There are four key parts to a successful stage kiss: (1) proper foot position; (2) correct body position; (3) exact time count; and (4) a smooth release. The script or the director will tell you what kind of kiss is needed in the scene — a motherly peck or a romantic embrace. The first part is getting into the embrace. The young woman usually faces the audience with her feet about six inches apart. The young man then steps toward the young woman on the foot closest to her, puts that foot between her feet and swings around so that they end up facing each other.

Body position is the second part of a stage kiss. For most romantic kisses little or no light should be seen between the couple. The young woman should be facing the audience, and the young man should be facing her, his back squarely toward the audience. The couple should decide ahead of time which way they will tilt their heads — to the right or to the left. Because the young man has his back to the audience and because in most instances he will be taller than his partner, the most expressive part of the kiss will be the young woman's hands, embracing the young man's back. They are what the audience will see. The couple does not have to make any actual physical contact at all; many professional actors do not. Correct foot and body position give the illusion of a real kiss.

The third and most important part of the kiss is the count. A sweet romantic kiss lasts one second; a reasonably romantic kiss lasts two seconds; and a very romantic kiss lasts from three to five seconds. Anything over five seconds will usually cause the wrong audience response.

Perhaps the most difficult part of the stage embrace is the parting or separation of the couple. First, it must be done with the same emotional value as the kiss established, usually a smooth slow release. Second, it is important for the couple to maintain physical contact with the hands until the "break" — the actual separation. To do this, the couple slowly pulls apart while sliding their hands down each other's arms. The break may occur at the forearms, or the couple may continue until they are holding hands. Then they may step away from each other, gently releasing the hands.

Dialect

Dialect presents interesting problems in many roles. National and regional speech differences show themselves in the pronunciation and selection of words and in the inflection of sentences. You should train your ears to catch the changes in quality, pitch, timing, stress, and rhythm and the occasional substitutions and omissions of sounds.

When you are beginning work with a role involving a dialectal shift in English, you might find records most valuable because you can play them again and again. Television is also becoming a growing source for the study of dialectical variances in speech. There are a few good books that will help you with dialects, idioms, and colloquial speech. Actors who master dialects are never without opportunities to act on stage, screen, and television. However, a dialect that is too precise can be very distracting to an audience. Dialects used on stage are rarely authentic, but are accepted stage versions of dialects.

A few suggestions may help you interpret the most commonly used dialects, but nothing can take the place of speaking with people who use the dialects until you catch the inflections, omissions, and patterns of sounds. Having a tape recorder with you on interviews will be of great value for later practice. Dialects can be imitated orally until they become more or less natural to the actor, but the audience must never be forgotten. Communication is the first consideration.

British

At its best, British speech is the basis for so-called stage diction. It can be heard in the BBC dramas on television or on records that were made by such players as Laurence Olivier, John Gielgud, or Edith Evans.

The British use a higher tonal pitch and a much wider range than Americans.

The *ä* is emphasized in such words as *bäsket, äunt, bänana, läugh*; in American speech these are usually *ă*. However the British do say *ă* in *chăp, făncy, ăn, mădam, hănd*. The *ä* appears in unexpected words like *räly* for *really*, in *Däbi* for *Derby*, in *Bäkli* as *Berkley*.

Most words, using $\overline{oo}$ add an unstressed *ĭ* so that *fōod* becomes *fĭood*; bl$\overline{oo}$ (blue) becomes *blĭoo*.

The short *ĭ* is used at the end of such words as *Tuesday* and *nobody* and the *ly* in *certainly* and other adverbs. Long *ee* is used in *been*; long *ā*, in *agāin*. Long *ī* is used in *eīther* and *neīther*. *Leisure* is *lĕsha*. The *ŏ* is made with the rounded lips and is never *aw* or *äh*.

The British generally stress the first syllable, therefore *secretary* is *sek'rŭhtrĭ, library* is *lī'brĭ; necessary* is *nĕ'sŭsrĭ*.

The *r* is dropped when it is preceded by a vowel and followed by a consonant or is the final sound: *father = fä'thuh; never = ne'vah; park = päk; remember = remem'buh; fire = fäh*.

The *r* between vowels or the doubled *r* is definitely trilled in such words as *very, American, orange, courage, marry*, and *spirit*. The authority that actors follow most carefully in British roles is Daniel Jones's *An English Pronouncing Dictionary*.

Cockney

This is British speech at its worst. Cockney is very difficult to master, yet it is one of the most common stage dialects. A record of *My Fair Lady* gives excellent examples in the speech of Eliza and her father. The outstanding vowel changes include the long *ī* for the long *ā*, as in *plīce* for *plāce*; the *oi* for long *ī*, as in *ice; ăow* for *ō* as in *năōw* for *know*; the short *ă* of *ask, laugh*, and *class* becomes *ä*. The sounded *h* at the beginning of words is dropped — *'abit, 'ome* — and added to the first word of a sentence if it begins with a vowel or to words beginning with a vowel sound — *hit for it*. The rhythms and phrasing are very difficult to acquire. Below is an example of Cockney speech, phonetically adapted.

From *Maid of France* by Harold Brighouse:

Thĕts äw$\overline{oo}$l roit. The bĕttuh the plice the bettuh the sū$\overline{ee}$t. Hit ĭnt ŭh fĕthŭh bed in the h$\overline{ooo}$l'ous at 'om, but hoiv sortŭh lawst the fĕthŭh bed ábĭt lītlĭ.

Irish

The Irish dialect is a lilting one, marked by much variety in pitch and inflection and a pace that is a little faster than American speech.

Vowel changes include notably *ĕh* for *ā*, *oi* for *ī*, *ĭ* for *ĕ*, *aw* or $\overline{oo}$ for *ŭ*, *ā* for *ē*. Thus, we have *foine* for *fine, whĭn* for *when, wăn* for *one, lōŏv* for *lŭv* (love), and *dāle* for *deal*. The pronouns *my* and *you* become *mō* and *yŭh*.

Consonant changes are more difficult to explain. The *r* is heavily rolled. The sound of *s* before another consonant is almost a *sh*; thus we have *shlape* for *sleep* and *shmile* for *smile*. The final *ing* is usually shorted to *in'*, and sometimes a *t* is substituted for *g*, resulting in *darlint* for *darling*.

Other European

Other European accents are too difficult to imitate without listening to people who use them habitually. A few suggestions may be helpful.

Italian is exceedingly musical and pleasant to hear, with many attractive inflections. The vowels are open and pure, but the short *ĭ* becomes *ē*, the *ä* is marked, and the short *ă* is seldom heard. The occasional *ŭh* sound added to consonant sounds is most pleasing, as in *soft-uh-ting* (soft thing) or *fruit-uh-stand*, and "I gottuh" as in T. A, Daly's delightful poem "I gotta love for Angela, I love Carlotta, too." All of Daly's poems offer excellent phrasing and pronunciations; he uses *dä* for *the*, *āy* for *ē*, and adds *uh*'s between words.

The German dialect is definitely gutteral; many of the sounds are made with the back of the tongue. *V* takes the place of *w*; and *d* is used for *t*, *p* for *b*, *äh-ēē* for *ī*, and *ō, ōō* for *ō*.

The Scottish dialect is somewhat gutteral and uses heavily rolled *r*'s. However, there is a lilting rhythm similar to that of the Irish dialect.

Swedish is inclined to be high in pitch, with recurring rising inflections and a flat tone, which is not nasal. The *oo* is *ū*, so *good* becomes *gude*; the voiced *th* is *d; w* is *v*; and *j* is *y*, as in *yūst* for *jŭst*. The *oo* and *o* sounds are formed by pursing the lips.

All the European dialects depend upon the original inflections and rhythms of their speech and the position of the parts of the sentence, which frequently differ very much from those of the English language. Authors can give some help in writing passages, but listening to people and recordings is essential to an actor using the dialects.

Yiddish

The popularity of *Fiddler on the Roof* and Neil Simon's comedies have increased the desire to learn this popular stage dialect. Yiddish is a mixture of Old High German and Hebrew and differs wherever it is used in the world. However, it is the American stage Yiddish that the actor should know.

The pitch is much higher than American speech, often rising into a falsetto and seldom dropping to low pitch levels. Most sentences end with a rising pitch, statements as well as questions. The quality is quite nasal, the pace fairly slow. The vowels *ā, à,* and *ă* become *ĕh*, *ē* becomes *ĭ, ĕ* is *ă, ī* is *ä, ĭ* is *ē.* Sometimes *b* becomes *p,* an internal *d* becomes *t,* and internal *g* is *k, i* is *ch,* the *ng* has a hard *g,* an internal *v* is *f,* and *w* is *v.*

American

Dialects vary in practically every state in the United States, but there are few distinguishing characteristics that apply to whole areas. As a general rule, the further a person is from an urban area, the slower the speech and the more nasal it becomes. The Western accent is very nasal and noticeably rolls the *r,* especially at the ends of words. The various Southern accents have vowels that are rich and round, but most are changed to diphthongs and triphthongs. The *ī* often becomes *äh,* as in *I, my,* and *like.* The final *er* is practically always *ah* because of the dropping of *r* at the ends of words. Thus, you might hear something like this: "Äh lähk that vēo͞o ovuh yonduh." The other most commonly used American stage dialects are those from Brooklyn, New Jersey, Boston, and Texas.

This scene from Big River, The Adventures of Huckleberry Finn, *is most effectively performed when attention is paid to the regional accent.*

Acting in the Round and Thrust

Learning to act in the round or on a thrust stage is now becoming a necessary part of dramatic training. The open stage, completely surrounded by seats, creates a close contact between the actors and the spectators. If you do not have a permanent stage, you can make an open stage in your classroom by placing chairs around a space and leaving one or two aisles for entrances.

Staging plays in the round demands careful planning and rehearsing. The director cannot depend upon a set for effects, and the audience is so close that every detail of costumes, furniture, and lighting must be right. The acting area must be lighted by spots that do not hit any member of the audience in the eyes. Acts can be ended by blacking out the lights or by incorporating exits into the play's action. Either will take the place of the usual stage curtain. The furniture must not block the action from any side, and scenes must be arranged so that they can be seen from all angles. The director must also plan to keep the actors moving and speaking as they cross and countercross rather than have them seated for long periods of time. Keeping the actors in motion allows their faces and voices to carry the meaning of the play to everyone. The actors often face each other off-set by at least two feet so that the audience can always see the face of one actor. If possible, the director must plan the action so that it can be seen from all sides at once.

The stage arena places more demands on the actors than the proscenium stage does. Each actor must be continually conscious of being surrounded by spectators who must see and hear everything. The actor must speak very clearly and project the voice so that everyone can hear even when the actor turns away from a part of the audience. Very accurate pointing of lines and accenting of key words must combine with a few clear-cut gestures that are effective from every angle. With the audience so close, any artificiality or ex-aggeration becomes so apparent that all sense of reality is lost. Also, fidgeting and aimless gestures are far more irritating at close range.

When acting in the round, the actors must move in curves and S patterns. This not only uses all the acting area efficiently, but it also gives the audience a continually changing and interesting view. Since there are no upstage/down-stage or right/left directions in arena staging, the acting areas must be identi-fied in a different way from UR (up right), DL (down left), or DCR (down right center). Some directors simply use clock directions for stage movements. Starting at the middle of the arena's one side, the twelve o'clock position is assigned. From there, all of the other directions can be worked out, according to the positions of the numbers on a clock's face. Another system that is fre-quently used is the dividing of the arena stage into quadrants. These quad-rants may be named according to compass locations, such as NE, SE, SW, NW; or by numbers, such as 1, 2, 3, 4; or by letters, such as A, B, C, D.

Plays for an arena production must be carefully selected. Entrances and exits are sometimes difficult in arena staging because the actor can be seen long before the acting area is reached and for some time after an exit from the stage. Entrances must permit effective approaches for actors before they speak, and exits must allow for convenient departures. Actions and lines must be suitable for the close attention of the audience. Sofas, benches, and low-backed chairs must be appropriate as a background for the actors since there is minimal scenery. A suitable play can move spectators deeply when it is well done in the round. If it is poorly selected, every fault is enlarged. A production that may be acceptable on the regular stage can be a failure in the round.

Rehearsing

Rehearsals are essential for full development of a play's unity, timing, and characterization. Rehearsals allow the director to shape the play. Rehearsals allow the actors to develop their characters in interaction with the other cast members.

Actors should come to rehearsals prepared to rehearse by using the methods that the director prefers. Directors are different. Some directors will block one movement at a time. Some directors will have the actors write down the

Acting in the round, as in this tent set up for summer theater, involves playing alternately to all sections of the audience and being aware of what is going on behind you.
• • • • • • • • • • •

It is important to dress as one will dress during the actual performance of the play as early in the rehearsal process as is possible.

• • • • • • • • • • • •

blocking for a page or scene and then have the actors walk through the scene. Some directors will have the actors move as they feel motivated to move and then correct awkward moves. Always bring a script to a rehearsal and write the blocking, the stage business, and the director's comments on the script *in pencil.*

In early rehearsals while the script is still being memorized, an actor may request a prompt when a line is forgotten simply by hesitating. Some actors will say "line" or "prompt." Some will snap the fingers. The director may establish the method for requesting prompts before the first rehearsal. The director may also instruct the prompter about how to give prompts. For example, the director might say, "Give the first word. Then give the first three. If that doesn't work, give the line."

An actor should clearly mark all of his or her lines in the script. If rented scripts are used, the markings should be made only with a soft lead pencil. If the scripts have been purchased, underlining the character's name or highlighting the lines are the preferred methods. Underlining all of the lines makes a script too difficult to read. Use a different color to mark movement or stage business or to note interpretation. Many directors prefer to number each speech of the page consecutively so that page and line numbers can easily be referred to in critiques and written notes.

Actors should always be prepared for frequent interruptions by the director during rehearsals. This is especially true of the early rehearsals. As rehearsals progress, lines should be so well memorized that a director can say, "Start with 'and furthermore.'" The actor is able to pick up the line at just that point and then go on.

It is during rehearsals that the tempo of a play is set. The rapid picking up of cues determines the play's tempo. If the tempo is slower than it should be, it is probably caused by the slight pauses between speeches. It is during rehearsals that actors must learn to come in on a final word without a pause.

It makes sense to wear clothing at rehearsals that is generally related to your character's personality. Avoid ultra-modern styles that are entirely out of keeping with your character. Wear clothes that are like those your character might choose. They will help to put you in the right mood for a scene. Shoes are very important, for your movements are greatly affected by footwear. Young men should wear a suit jacket if their characters would wear them. This will allow an actor to get the feel of wearing a coat. Too often a young actor who is given a jacket at dress rehearsal will jam the hands into the coat pockets or grab awkwardly at the lapels. Young women should wear appropriate rehearsal jewelry but remove any bracelets, necklaces, or wrist watches that are entirely out of character. A long necklace may be too tempting to fidget with. If possible, it would be helpful to wear a skirt of the same length as the costume will be.

If a cast works closely together at rehearsals, the members will experience the joy that real teamwork brings. As lines are tossed back and forth appropriately, the members will feel the different personalities reacting to each other and begin to understand that acting is a cooperative experience. Discovering how personality plays upon personality in a scene is what makes rehearsing so worthwhile.

Daily Practice

Stage techniques must become automatic and subconscious during rehearsals and performances. If you follow a daily practice schedule for as long as you are involved in dramatics, you will establish stage techniques and keep your body and voice at their best. Refer to Chapter 3 and 4 for exercises.

Daily Practice Schedule
Deep Breathing: at least twenty full breaths
Loosening-up Exercises: stretching, bending, twisting
Pantomime Exercises:

Shaking hands vigorously

Opening and closing fists

Moving fingers as in five-finger exercises

Turning hands from wrists in circles

Moving entire arms in circles

Moving arms from elbows in circles

Moving hands from wrists in circles, making formal gestures of giving, refusing, and pointing

Using body and arms, with gestures flowing from shoulder to fingertips, to show emotions, such as pleading, fear, and commanding

Vocal Exercises:

Relaxation of entire body; yawning to relax throat

Posture exercise

Jaw exercises

Lip exercises

Babbling

Humming

Breathing and counting

Tongue twisters

Chanting lines and stanzas of poetry

Reading poems

Reading stories aloud

Short Plays for High School Production and Study

Titles and authors of plays are followed by coded classifications with the following significations: Type of play: F = farce, C = comedy, D = drama, M = melodrama, T = tragedy; Number of parts for men and women; Play publisher: DPS = Dramatic Play Service, DPC = Dramatic Publishing Company, SF = Samuel French, Inc.; Scenery requirements: INT = interior, EXT = exterior. Coding also follows descriptions with ratings for A = acting difficult; B = book difficult; COS = period costumes or complex costumes required; DI = dialect. Other comments may also be included.

The American Dream by Edward Albee (C; 2M, 3W; DPS; INT; Theater of the absurd). A comment on American life and types, including Daddy, the dominated, suffering husband, and Mommy, the overbearing wife. (B)

Antic Spring by Robert Nail (C; 3M, 3W; SF; Bare stage). This is the humorous account of five teens and a little brother who go on a picnic, their trials and tribulations. (Simply staged.)

Aria da Capo by Edna St. Vincent Millay (Fantasy; 4M, 1W; SF; INT). A Harlequinade is interrupted by two shepherds who innocently kill each other and then the play goes on. (A; B)

Balcony Scene by Donald Elser (C&D; 4M, 4W; SF; INT). This play takes place in a balcony overlooking a funeral service. (Excellent for contest or classroom work.)

The Bald Soprano by Eugene Ionesco (C; 3M, 3W; SF; Bare stage; Theater of the absurd). This "anti-play" shows the deterioration of language resulting from the inability to communicate. (B)

Black Comedy by Peter Shaffer (F; 5M, 3W; SF; INT). One of the wackiest plays ever written: when the lights are on, they're off and vice versa. Difficult and challenging. (A; B; DI)

The Boor by Anton Chekhov (F; 2M, 1W; SF; INT). An unmannerly landowner comes to the house of a grieving widow to collect a debt. They squabble, bicker, and fall in love. (A; COS)

Box and Cox by J.M. Morton (F; 2M, 1W; SF; INT). Two men are rented the same room, one by day, the other by night. The situation makes for great farce. (Non-royalty)

The Case of the Crushed Petunias by Tennessee Williams (C; 2M, 2W; DPS; INT). A prim and proper spinster is offered "Life Unlimited" by a traveling salesman in this clever fantasy.

The Cave by Tim Kelly (D; 12 characters; DPS; S). An allegory that begins with an acting troupe warming up and develops into a vote to "proceed ahead or remain where they are."

The Chairs by Eugene Ionesco (C; 2M, 1W; SF; Bare stage; Theater of the absurd). A real challenge. (B)

The Devil and Daniel Webster by Stephen Vincent Benét (C; 6M + 12 jurists — no lines, 1W, extras; DPS; INT). The well-known story of the New England farmer who sells his soul to Mr. Scratch (the Devil). Daniel Webster pleads the case.

Early Frost by Douglas Parkhirst (D; 5W; SF; INT). The story of two sisters, one a little "strange," and the uncovering of a long-hidden secret. If played well, an excellent challenge for five women.

Endgame by Samuel Beckett (D; 3M, 1W; SF; INT; Theater of the absurd). The hopeless playing out of the "end game" of life takes place within the mind of the dying individual. (Very difficult. A, B)

Everyman (anonymous). (D; 17 characters; non-royalty). This is the most famous of Morality plays—the allegorical tale of Everyman who seeks a companion to go with him to meet Death.

Fumed Oak by Noel Coward (C; 1M, 3W; SF; INT). Nice guy, Henry Gow, turns over a new leaf — and leaves.

The Happy Journey to Camden and Trenton by Thornton Wilder (C; 3M, 4W; SF; Bare stage). A fine piece for student actors, the simply-staged comedy presents Americana in the manner of *Our Town.*

Hello, Out There by William Saroyan (D; 3M, 2W; SF; INT). An itinerant gambler is arrested and jailed, falsely charged with rape. Two very good parts.

Ile by Eugene O'Neill (D; 5M, 1W; DPS; Bare stage). A prideful whaling captain drives his crew to near mutiny and his wife mad in his attempt to get "ile." (A, DI)

Impromptu by Tad Mosel (C&D; 2M, 2W; DPS; Bare stage). One of the finest one acts for student performers. Existential in style, this play gives four characters the opportunity to improvise a play — life — but it is over before it really begins.

In the Zone by Eugene O'Neill (D; 9M; DPS; INT). A sailor who behaves suspiciously is lashed to his bunk while his shipmates read letters from a former sweetheart. (A)

Infancy by Thornton Wilder (C; 2M, 2W; SF; Bare stage). Two women push baby buggies in the park, their conversation showing their lack of understanding of human needs.

Lemonade by James Prideaux (C&D; 2W; DPS; Bare stage). Two middle-aged women try to escape their mundane lives by selling spiked lemonade.

The Lesson by Eugene Ionesco (C; 1M, 2W; SF; INT; Theater of the absurd). A young female student comes to a professor for a lesson, but the lesson ends in murder. (A, B)

The Lottery adapted by Brainerd Duffield from Shirley Jackson (D; 8M, 5W, extras; DPC; Bare stage). A powerful adaptation of the short story which demonstrates the horror of blind adherence to tradition and superstition. The inhabitants of a small village gather to determine who will be the human sacrifice for the summer crops.

The Marriage Proposal by Anton Chekhov (F; 2M, 1F; INT). The classic farce about the young man who comes to propose, but ends up fighting with the young woman over boundary lines. (Non-royalty)

Mr. Flannery's Ocean by Lewis John Carlino (C; 2M, 4W, 1 boy, 1 girl; Bare stage). A fine distinction of characters. Jim Flannery "owns" the ocean and finally gives "her" away. (A, DI)

The Monkey's Paw by W.W. Jacobs and Louis Parlar (M; 4M, 1W; SF; INT). Based on one of the great suspense tales — the paw grants three wishes, but the wisher is worse off than at the beginning.

Neighbors by Zona Gale (C; 2M, 6W; SF; INT). The tender story of small town life and a friendless child.

A Night at an Inn by Lord Dunsany (M; 8M; INT). An Eastern idol takes retribution on the thieves that stole its ruby eye.

Objective Case by Lewis John Carlino (C&D; 2M, 2W; DPS; Bare stage). This play conceals a story of need and love in its fascinating existence in the realm between realism and expressionism. Brilliantly written and challenging. (A, B)

The Old Lady Shows Her Medals by James M. Barrie (D; 2M, 4W; SF; INT). The sensitive account of Mrs. Dowey who claims to have a son in the army (World War I). A Private Dowey comes along to "be her son" and then leaves for the war, never to return. (A, COS, DI)

Pink and Patches by Margaret Bland (C; 1M, 3W; SF; EXT). A mountain girl yearns for clothing that is "new and pink," but ends up with patched hand-me-downs again.

The Private Ear by Peter Shaffer (C; 2M, 1W; SF; INT). A companion piece to *The Public Eye.* A young man invites a young woman to dinner, but when he romances her, he fails miserably. (Mature)

The Public Eye by Peter Shaffer (C; 2M, 1W; SF; INT). A private detective is hired to follow a man's wife. The husband and wife depart for a "second honeymoon" and the detective takes over his client's office. (Mature)

The "Recognition Scene" from Anastasia by Guy Bolton (D; 2W; SF; INT). The confrontation between the Dowager Empress and the girl claiming to be granddaughter of the Czar. (A, COS, DI)

Red Carnations by Glenn Hughes (C; 2M, 1W; EXT or Bare stage). A clever satire, easily produced. Three characters, a man, a girl, and a boy enter into a three-sided conversation.

Riders to the Sea by John Millington Synge (T; 1M, 2W, extras; SF; INT). One of the finest one act plays — certainly the best tragedy in one act. An old Irish woman waits for the sea to take the last of her sons. (A, B, DI)

The Rising of the Moon by Lady Gregory (C; 4M; SF; Bare stage). A drifter, running from the law, wins the sympathy of the officer tracking him down, and is allowed to escape. (Non-royalty)

The Sandbox by Edward Albee (C&D; 3M, 2W; DPS; Bare stage). A very brief play with a poignant comment on old age and dying. Borders on theater of the absurd.

Sorry, Wrong Number by Lucille Fletcher (D; 3M, 4W; DPS; INT). One of the best short thrillers, this is the story of a neurotic invalid who accidently overhears a murder plot. Too late, she realizes it is her own. (A)

The Spiral Staircase adapted by F. Andrew Leslie (M; 4M, 4W; DPS; INT). A long short play. Helen, who has lost her ability to speak becomes the intended victim of a killer who seeks to relieve the world of "physical misfits." Powerfully intense. (A)

The Still Alarm by George S. Kaufman (C; 5M; SF; INT). The humor of this low-key comedy lies in its "almost bored" approach to a hotel fire. Great sport. (A; DI)

Sunday Costs Five Pesos by Josephina Niggli (C; 1M, 4W; SF; EXT). A young girl breaks off her engagement and then tries to win her fiancé back.

Tell Me Another Story, Sing Me a Song by Jean Lenox Toddie (C&D; 2W; SF; Bare stage). A beautiful play for two females. This play takes a meaningful look at a mother and her daughter through childhood, adolescence, young adulthood, and old age. (A)

The Twelve Pound Look by James M. Barrie (C; 2M, 2W; SF; INT). Sir Harry Simms is about to be knighted and a typist is hired to respond to congratulatory letters. The typist turns out to be Sir Harry's first wife. (A)

Two Crooks and a Lady by Eugene Pillot (D; 3M, 3W; SF; INT). An old favorite, this play features clever characters in a simple-to-stage one act.

The Ugly Duckling by A.A. Milne (C; 4M, 3W; SF; Bare stage). An "adult" children's play that well demonstrates Milne's wit. Some fine characters. (A; COS)

The Valiant by Holworthy Hall and Robert Middlemass (D; 5M, 1W; SF; INT). Long a contest favorite. A man in prison awaits his execution. A girl visits him seeking her long-lost brother. She leaves, thinking her brother died a war hero. (A)

Where Have All the Lightning Bugs Gone? by Louis E. Catron (C&D; 1M, 1W; SF; EXT or bare stage). An excellent piece for student actors. A boy and a girl meet and fall in love, but more than that. Clever, meaningful lines. (A)

Where the Cross Is Made by Eugene O'Neill (D; 6M, 1W; DPS; INT). A tale of guilt and madness masterfully told. (A; DI)

Wine in the Wilderness by Alice Childress (C&D; 3M, 2W; DPS; INT). A poignant expression of the turmoil of the Black dilemma.

The Zoo Story by Edward Albee (D; 2M; DPS; Bare stage). The forceful encounter of a neat conventional man reading in the park with a young man whose personality is totally opposite. The younger man's attempts at communication are overwhelming and lead to a shocking ending. (A)

Remembering the Audience

The thrust staging of this production of Much Ado About Nothing *by the Delacorte Theatre in Central Park presents its own unique set of givens to the actors. During a curtain call, the cast can receive thanks as well as give thanks to the audience.*

As you study theater more deeply, audition for all kinds of parts, and spend a number of weeks at rehearsals, it is easy to focus on yourself exclusively and on what progress you are making. However, you must remember that actors perform for an audience and gain empathy from an audience. Actors must always keep the interests, needs, and enjoyment of the audience uppermost in their minds. The individuals who make up your audience are *auditory, visual,* and *kinesthetic* people.

But one of these qualities often predominates in a specific individual. Some will respond more to what they hear. Some will respond more to what they see. Others will respond more to the kinds of physical action that they identify with. Therefore, in order to appeal as strongly as you can to all of the members of your audience, your acting must be a blending of sound, sight, and action.

Recalling Ideas

1. What advice do directors often give to beginning actors?

2. Who was Konstantin Stanislavski? What is his "magic *if*"?

3. What is role scoring? What is script scoring? How does each help an actor on stage?

4. Define body language. Describe two ways that an actor can use body language on the stage.

5. What is a cross? Why is a cross usually followed by a countercross? What are four basic staging techniques?

6. What are effective ways of entering and exiting the stage?

7. List the three basic rules for eating on stage.

8. What do the terms *falling pitch* and *rising pitch* mean?

9. List the sorts of things you should record in your actor's notebook.

10. Describe the differences among playing the conditions, playing the objectives, playing the obstacles, and playing the moment.

11. What are some techniques for playing comedy?

Discussing Ideas

1. Compare the emotional, subjective approach to acting to the technical, objective approach. How would an actor use each approach to prepare for the part of a mother whose child is missing?

2. List the leading parts in three movies or plays. Identify the straight parts and the character parts.

3. Describe a role in a play, movie, or television drama that you consider a pitch-up part. Describe a role that you consider a pitch-down part. Which role do you think would be easier to play? Why?

4. What are the advantages of the whole-part method of learning lines?

5. What demands do special stages place on actors? Discuss in what ways an actor has to adjust for various stages.

Careers

The number of **stage managers** depends on the size of the show. A one-set production usually has one; larger productions, more.

Production stage managers are in charge of everything that happens backstage. They make sure that lights, sets, costumes, and sound equipment are completed and working in time for opening night. They coordinate rehearsal schedules, costume fittings, pre-opening press activities, and other company functions. After the show opens, they conduct understudy rehearsals, put new cast members into the show, and deal with actors' problems. They may direct the show in the absence of the **director.**

Production stage managers need a good background in sound, light, and set and costume design. Because they work with actors who are often tense, tired, and worried, they must be diplomats.

Stage managers run the show. They stand at an offstage desk in the wings and "call the show" from a promptbook, giving cues to the **technicians** who operate the light and sound equipment and the **stagehands** who move scenery and props. A closed-circuit camera and television monitor allows them to see the necessary parts of the theater and stage.

Assistant stage managers help call the show and handle many details involved in opening and running it. They take phone messages, compile cost contact sheets, sweep the floors during rehearsal, and check the stage equipment before each performance.

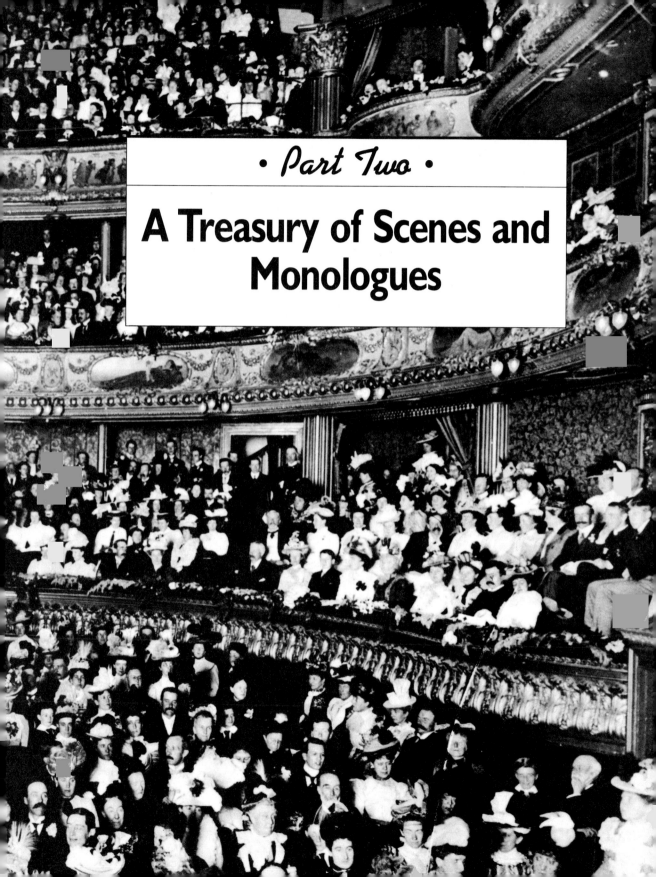

• Part Two •

A Treasury of Scenes and Monologues

Romeo and Juliet
by William Shakespeare

Romeo has met Juliet at a masked ball at her father's house and has fallen in love at first sight. After the ball, he goes to the Capulet garden. Juliet, standing on her balcony, confesses to the stars that she loves Romeo. Romeo overhears this private confession. The following is part of the balcony scene, the world's most famous love scene.

(Capulet's orchard. ROMEO *advances from the wall.)*

ROMEO He jests at scars that never felt a wound.
(Juliet appears above at her window.)
But soft! What light through yonder window
    breaks?
It is the east, and Juliet is the sun!
Arise, fair sun, and kill the envious moon,
Who is already sick and pale with grief
That thou, her maid, art far more fair than she.
Be not her maid, since she is envious;
Her vestal livery is but sick and green,
And none but fools do wear it; cast it off.
It is my lady, O, it is my love!
Oh, that she knew she were!
She speaks, yet she says nothing; what of that?
Her eye discourses. I will answer it. —
I am too bold, 'tis not to me she speaks.
Two of the fairest stars in all the heaven,
Having some business, do entreat her eyes
To twinkle in their spheres till they return.
What if her eyes were there, they in her head?
The brightness of her cheek would shame those
    stars,
As daylight doth a lamp; her eyes in heaven
Would through the airy region stream so bright
That birds would sing and think it were not night.
See, how she leans her cheek upon her hand!
O, that I were a glove upon that hand,
That I might touch that cheek!

JULIET Ay me!

ROMEO She speaks!
O, speak again, bright angel! For thou art
As glorious to this night, being o'er my head,
As is a winged messenger of heaven
Unto the white-upturned wond'ring eyes
Of mortals that fall back to gaze on him
When he bestrides the lazy-pacing clouds
And sails upon the bosom of the air.

JULIET O Romeo, Romeo, wherefore art thou
    Romeo?
Deny thy father and refuse thy name,
Or, if thou wilt not, be but sworn my love
And I'll no longer be a Capulet.

ROMEO *(Aside)* Shall I hear more, or shall I speak
    at this?

JULIET 'Tis but thy name that is my enemy.
Thou art thyself, though not a Montague.
What's a Montague? It is nor hand, nor foot,
Nor arm, nor face, nor any other part
Belonging to a man. Oh, be some other name!
What's in a name? That which we call a rose
By any other name would smell as sweet;
So Romeo would, were he not Romeo call'd,
Retain that dear perfection which he owes
Without that title. Romeo, doff thy name,
And for thy name, which is no part of thee,
Take all myself.

The Importance of Being Earnest
by Oscar Wilde

The Importance of Being Earnest is a satirical farce. Oscar Wilde is using his play to ridicule the social manners of nineteenth-century England. His characters tend to be stereotypes representing the types of individuals he perceived as being absurd in society as he knew it. In the following scene, Lady Bracknell confronts Jack Worthing. She holds certain character traits and family backgrounds as being essential in young men if they are to be acceptable potential husbands for her daughter, Gwendolen. Lady Bracknell quite vigorously rejects Jack as an appropriate suitor for Gwendolen.

LADY BRACKNELL *(Sitting down)* You can take a seat, Mr. Worthing. *(Looks in her pocket for a note-book and pencil)*

JACK   Thank you, Lady Bracknell, I prefer standing.

LADY BRACKNELL *(Pencil and note-book in hand)* I feel bound to tell you that you are not down on my list of eligible young men, although I have the same list as the dear Duchess of Bolton has. We work together, in fact. However, I am quite ready to enter your name, should your answers be what a really affectionate mother requires. Do you smoke?

JACK   Well, yes, I must admit I smoke.

LADY BRACKNELL   I am glad to hear it. A man should always have an occupation of some kind. There are far too many idle men in London as it is. How old are you?

JACK   Twenty-nine.

LADY BRACKNELL   A very good age to be married at. I have always been of opinion that a man who desires to get married should know either everything or nothing. Which do you know?

JACK   *(After some hesitation)* I know nothing, Lady Bracknell.

LADY BRACKNELL   I am pleased to hear it. I do not approve of anything that tampers with natural ignorance. Ignorance is like a delicate exotic fruit; touch it and the bloom is gone. The whole theory of modern education is radically unsound. Fortunately in England, at any rate, education produces no effect whatsoever. If it did, it would prove a serious danger to the upper classes, and probably lead to acts of violence in Grosvenor Square. What is your income?

JACK   Between seven and eight thousand a year.

LADY BRACKNELL   *(Makes a note in her book)* In land, or in investments?

JACK   In investments, chiefly.

LADY BRACKNELL   That is satisfactory. What between the duties expected of one during one's lifetime, and the duties exacted from one after one's death, land has ceased to be either a profit or a pleasure. It gives one position, and prevents one from keeping it up. That's all that can be said about land.

JACK   I have a country house with some land, of course, attached to it, about fifteen hundred acres, I believe; but I don't depend on that for my real income. In fact, as far as I can make out, the poachers are the only people who make anything out of it.

LADY BRACKNELL   A country house! How many bedrooms? Well, that point can be cleared up afterwards. You have a town house, I hope? A girl with a simple, unspoiled nature, like Gwendolen, could hardly be expected to reside in the country.

JACK   Well, I own a house in Belgrave Square, but it is let by the year to Lady Bloxham. Of course, I can get it back whenever I like, at six month's notice.

LADY BRACKNELL   Lady Bloxham? I don't know her.

JACK   Oh, she goes about very little. She is a lady considerably advanced in years.

LADY BRACKNELL   Ah, now-a-days that is no guarantee of respectability of character. What number in Belgrave Square?

JACK   149.

LADY BRACKNELL   *(Shaking her head)* The unfashionable side. I thought there was something. However, that could be easily altered.

JACK   Do you mean the fashion, or the side?

LADY BRACKNELL   *(Sternly)* Both, if necessary, I presume. What are your politics?

JACK   Well, I am afraid I really have none. I am a Liberal Unionist.

LADY BRACKNELL   Oh, they count as Tories. They dine with us. Or come in the evening, at any rate. Now to minor matters. Are your parents living?

JACK   I have lost both my parents.

LADY BRACKNELL   To lose one parent, Mr. Worthing, may be regarded as a misfortune; to lose both looks like carelessness. Who was your father? He was evidently a man of some wealth. Was he born in what the Radical papers call the purple of commerce, or did he rise from the ranks of the aristocracy?

JACK   I am afraid I really don't know. The fact is, Lady Bracknell, I said I had lost my parents. It would be nearer the truth to say that my parents seem to have lost me . . . I don't actually know who I am by birth. I was . . . well, I was found.

LADY BRACKNELL   Found!

JACK   The late Mr. Thomas Cardew, an old gentleman of a very charitable and kindly disposition, found me, and gave me the name of Worthing, because he happened to have a first-class ticket for Worthing in his pocket at the time. Worthing is a place in Sussex. It is a seaside resort.

LADY BRACKNELL   Where did the charitable gentleman who had a first-class ticket for this seaside resort find you?

JACK   *(Gravely)* In a hand-bag.

LADY BRACKNELL   A hand-bag?

JACK   *(Very seriously)* Yes, Lady Bracknell. I was in a hand-bag — a somewhat large, black leather hand-bag, with handles to it — an ordinary hand-bag in fact.

LADY BRACKNELL   In what locality did this Mr. James, or Thomas, Cardew come across this ordinary hand-bag?

JACK   In the cloak-room at Victoria Station. It was given to him in mistake for his own.

LADY BRACKNELL   The cloak-room at Victoria Station?

JACK   Yes. The Brighton line.

LADY BRACKNELL   The line is immaterial. Mr. Worthing, I confess I feel somewhat bewildered by what you have just told me. To be born, or at any rate bred, in a hand-bag, whether it had handles or not, seems to me to display a contempt for the ordinary decencies of family life that remind one of the worst excesses of the French Revolution. And I presume you know what that unfortunate movement led to? As for the particular locality in which the hand-bag was found, a cloak-room at a railway station might serve to conceal a social indiscretion — has probably, indeed, been used for that purpose before now — but it could hardly be regarded as an assured basis for a recognized position in good society.

JACK   May I ask you then what you would advise me to do? I need hardly say I would do anything in the world to ensure Gwendolen's happiness.

LADY BRACKNELL   I would strongly advise you, Mr. Worthing, to try and acquire some relations as soon as possible, and to make a definite effort to produce at any rate one parent, of either sex, before the season is quite over.

JACK   Well, I don't see how I could possibly manage to do that. I can produce the hand-bag at any moment. It is in my dressing-room at home. I really think that should satisfy you, Lady Bracknell.

LADY BRACKNELL   Me, sir! What has it to do with me? You can hardly imagine that I and Lord Bracknell would dream of allowing our daughter

— a girl brought up with the utmost care — to marry into a cloak-room, and form an alliance with a parcel? Good morning, Mr. Worthing!

(LADY BRACKNELL *sweeps out in majestic indignation.*)

JACK   Good morning!

Whose Life Is It Anyway?
by Brian Clark

Ken has been in an automobile accident that has left him completely paralyzed from the neck down. In the following scene, Ken shares his bitterness with Mrs. Boyle, a social worker trying to help him adjust to his severe handicap.

MRS. BOYLE   Why don't you want any more treatment?

KEN   I'd rather not go on living like this.

MRS. BOYLE   Why not?

KEN   Isn't it obvious?

MRS. BOYLE   Not to me. I've seen many patients like you.

KEN   And they all want to live?

MRS. BOYLE   Usually.

KEN   Why?

MRS. BOYLE   They find a new way of life.

KEN   How?

MRS. BOYLE   You'll be surprised how many things you will be able to do with training and a little patience.

KEN   Such as?

MRS. BOYLE   We can't be sure yet. But I should think that you will be able to operate reading machines and perhaps an adapted typewriter.

KEN   Reading and writing. What about arithmetic?

MRS. BOYLE   *(Smiling)* I dare say we could fit you up with a comptometer if you really wanted one.

KEN   Mrs. Boyle, even educationalists have realized that the three r's do not make a full life.

MRS. BOYLE   What did you do before the accident?

KEN   I taught in an art school. I was a sculptor.

MRS. BOYLE   I see.

KEN   Difficult, isn't it? How about an electrically operated hammer and chisel? No, well. Or a cybernetic lump of clay?

MRS. BOYLE   I wouldn't laugh if I were you. It's amazing what can be done. Our scientists are wonderful.

KEN   They are. But it's not good enough you see, Mrs. Boyle. I really have absolutely no desire at all to be the object of scientific virtuosity. I have thought things over very carefully. I do have plenty of time for thinking and I have decided that I do not want to go on living with so much effort for so little result.

MRS. BOYLE   Yes, well, we shall have to see about that.

KEN   What is there to see?

MRS. BOYLE   We can't just stop treatment, just like that.

KEN   Why not?

MRS. BOYLE   It's the job of the hospital to save life, not to lose it.

KEN   The hospital's done all it can, but it wasn't enough. It wasn't the hospital's fault; the original injury was too big.

MRS. BOYLE   We have to make the best of the situation.

KEN   No. "We" don't have to do anything. I have to do what is to be done and that is to cash in the chips.

MRS. BOYLE   It's not unusual, you know, for people injured as you have been, to suffer with this depression for a considerable time before they begin to see that a life is possible.

KEN   How long?

MRS. BOYLE   It varies.

KEN   Don't hedge.

MRS. BOYLE   It could be a year or so.

KEN   And it could last for the rest of my life.

MRS. BOYLE   That would be most unlikely.

KEN   I'm sorry, but I cannot settle for that.

MRS. BOYLE   Try not to dwell on it. I'll see what I can do to get you started on some occupational therapy. Perhaps we could make a start on the reading machines.

KEN   Do you have many books for those machines?

MRS. BOYLE   Quite a few.

KEN   Can I make a request for the first one?

MRS. BOYLE   If you like.

KEN   "How to be a sculptor with no hands."

MRS. BOYLE   I'll be back tomorrow with the machine.

KEN   It's marvelous, you know.

MRS. BOYLE   What is?

KEN   All you people have the same technique. When I say something really awkward you just pretend I haven't said anything at all. You're all the bloody same . . . Well there's another outburst. That should be your cue to comment on the light-shade or the color of the walls.

MRS. BOYLE   I'm sorry if I have upset you.

KEN   Of course you have upset me. You and the doctors with your appalling so-called professionalism, which is nothing more than a series of verbal tricks to prevent you relating to your patients as human beings.

MRS. BOYLE   You must understand; we have to remain relatively detached in order to help . . .

KEN   That's all right with me. Detach yourself. Tear yourself off on the dotted line that divides the woman from the social worker and post yourself off to another patient.

The Rainmaker
by N. Richard Nash

It is a summer evening at the Curry ranch. An extreme drought has hit the plains states when Starbuck arrives claiming to be able to bring rain, for a fee. He is presently boarding with the Curry family. In the following scene, Lizzie Curry has come out to the bunkhouse with bed linens.

STARBUCK   What are you scared of?

LIZZIE   You! I don't trust you!

STARBUCK   Why? What don't you trust about me?

LIZZIE   Everything! The way you talk, the way you brag — why, even your name.

STARBUCK   What's wrong with my name?

LIZZIE   It sounds fake! It sounds like you made it up!

STARBUCK   You're darn right! I did make it up.

LIZZIE   There! Of course!

STARBUCK   Why not? You know what name I was born with? Smith! Smith, for the love of Mike, *Smith!* Now what kind of handle is that for a fella like me? I needed a name that had the whole sky in it! And the power of a man! Star-buck! Now there's a name — and it's mine.

LIZZIE   No, it's not. You were born Smith — and that's your name.

STARBUCK   You're wrong, Lizzie. The name you choose for yourself is more your own than the name you were born with. And if I was you I'd choose another name than Lizzie.

LIZZIE   Thank you — I'm very pleased with it.

STARBUCK   Oh, no you ain't. You ain't pleased with anything about yourself. And I'm sure you ain't pleased with "Lizzie."

LIZZIE   I don't ask *you* to be pleased with it, Starbuck. I *am.*

STARBUCK   Lizzie? Why, it don't *stand* for anything.

LIZZIE   It stands for me! *Me!* I'm not the Queen of Sheba — I'm not Lady Godiva — I'm not Cinderella at the Ball.

STARBUCK   Would you like to be?

LIZZIE   Starbuck, you're ridiculous!

STARBUCK   What's ridiculous about it? Dream you're somebody — *be* somebody! But Lizzie? That's nobody! So many millions of wonderful women with wonderful names! *(In an orgy of delight)* Leonora, Desdemona, Carolina, Paulina! Annabella, Florinda, Natasha, Diane! *(Then, with a pathetic little lift of his shoulders)* Lizzie.

A Raisin in the Sun
by Lorraine Hansberry

Ruth and Walter live in a small apartment with their son, Travis, and Walter's mother and sister, Beneatha. In the following scene, Ruth and Walter try to understand what is happening to their marriage and their broken dreams.

WALTER   *(To* RUTH.*)* Who is Promeetheeius —? *(At sink with beer.)*

RUTH   I don't know, honey. Don't worry about it.

WALTER   *(Crosses above kitchen table. In a fury, pointing after* GEORGE.*)* See there — they get to a point where they can't insult you man to man — they got to talk about something ain't nobody never heard of! *(Crosses to sink.)*

RUTH   How you know it was an insult? *(To humor him.)* Maybe Promeetheeius is a nice fellow.

WALTER   *(Crosses below kitchen table.)* Promeetheeius! — I bet there ain't even no such thing! I bet that simpleminded clown —

RUTH   *(Rises, starts to* WALTER L.*)* Walter —

WALTER   *(Yelling.)* Don't start!

RUTH   Start what?

WALTER You're nagging! Where was I? Who was I with — How much money did I spend?

RUTH *(Plaintively.)* Walter Lee — why don't we just try to talk about it —

WALTER *(Not listening.)* I been out talking with people who understand me. People who care about the things I got on my mind.

RUTH *(Wearily.)* I guess that means people like Willy Harris. *(Crosses U.C., then above sofa.)*

WALTER Yes, people like Willy Harris.

RUTH *(Crosses R., back of sofa to laundry. With a sudden flash of impatience.)* Why don't y'all just hurry up and go into the banking business and stop talking about it!

WALTER *(Crosses U.L. above table.)* Why? — You want to know why? 'Cause we all tied up in a race of people that don't know how to do nothing but moan, pray and have babies! *(The line is too bitter even for him and he looks at her and sits down.)*

RUTH Oh, Walter — *(Softly.)* Honey, why can't you stop fighting me?

WALTER *(Crosses D.L. to sink. Without thinking.)* Who's fighting you? Who even cares about you — *(This line begins the retardation of this mood.)*

RUTH Well — *(She waits a long time and then with resignation starts to put away the laundry.)* I guess I might as well go on to bed — *(More or less to herself.)* I don't know where we lost it — but we have — *(Then to him as she crosses above sofa to C.)* I — I'm sorry about this new baby, Walter — I guess maybe I better go on and do what I started — I guess I just didn't realize how bad things was with us — *(Crosses R. front of sofa.)* I guess I just didn't realize — *(She picks up laundry basket and starts for R. bedroom, exits.)*

WALTER *(He lifts his head and watches her going away from him in a new mood which began to emerge when he asked her "Who cares about you?" Crosses R. above table to C.)* Baby, it's been rough, ain't it? *(She hears and stops but does not turn around and he goes on to her back.)* I guess between two people there ain't never as much understanding as folks generally think there is. I mean like between me and you — *(RUTH enters. She turns to face him.)* How we gets to the place where we scared to talk softness to each other. *(He waits, thinking hard himself.)* Why you think it got to be like that? *(He is thoughtful, almost as a child would be.)* Ruth, what is it gets into people ought to be close?

RUTH *(Above sofa.)* I don't know, honey. I think about it a lot.

WALTER On account of you and me, you mean. The way things are with us. The way something's come down between us.

RUTH There ain't so much between us, Walter — Not when you come to me and try to talk to me. Try to be with me — a little, even.

WALTER *(Standing front of chair L. of table. Total honesty.)* Sometimes — sometimes — I don't even know how to try.

RUTH *(Crossing slowly L. toward WALTER.)* Walter —

WALTER Yes —?

RUTH *(Coming to him, gently and with misgiving, but coming to him.)* Honey — Life don't have to be like this. I mean sometimes people can do things so that things are better — *(She crosses to him slowly and they embrace. She gropes for what she wants to tell him.)* You remember how we used to talk when Travis was born — about the way we were going to live — the kind of house — *(She is stroking his head.)* Well, it's all starting to slip away from us.

The Diary of Anne Frank
by Frances Goodrich and Albert Hackett

The Frank and the Van Daan families are hiding from the Nazis in an attic over a place of business. In this scene, Anne Frank and Peter Van Daan realize what young love is in war-torn Europe.

ANNE *(Looking up through skylight)* Look, Peter, the sky. What a lovely day. Aren't the clouds beautiful? You know what I do when it seems as if I couldn't stand being cooped up for one more minute? I *think* myself out. I think myself on a walk in the park where I used to go with Pim. Where the daffodils and the crocus and the violets grow down the slopes. You know the most wonderful thing about *thinking* yourself out? You can have it any way you like. You can have roses and violets and chrysanthemums all blooming at the same time. . . . It's funny. . . . I used to take it all for granted . . . and now I've gone crazy about everything to do with nature. Haven't you?

PETER *(Barely lifting his face)* I've just gone crazy. I think if something doesn't happen soon . . . if we don't get out of here . . . I can't stand much more of it!

ANNE *(Softly)* I wish you had a religion, Peter.

PETER *(Bitterly)* No, thanks. Not me.

ANNE Oh, I don't mean you have to be Orthodox . . . or believe in heaven and hell and purgatory and things . . . . I just mean some religion . . . it doesn't matter what. Just to believe in something! When I think of all that's out there . . . the trees . . . and flowers . . . and seagulls . . . when I think of the dearness of you, Peter . . . and the goodness of the people we know . . . Mr. Kraler, Miep, Dirk, the vegetable man, all risking their lives for us every day. . . . When I think of these good things, I'm not afraid any more. . . . I find myself, and God, and I . . .

PETER *(Impatiently, as he gets to his feet)* That's fine! But when I begin to think, I get mad! Look at us, hiding out for two years. Not able to move! Caught here like . . . waiting for them to come and get us . . . and all for what?

ANNE We're not the only people that've had to suffer. There've always been people that've had to . . . sometimes one race . . . sometimes another . . . and yet . . .

PETER *(Sitting on upstage end of bed)* That doesn't make me feel any better!

ANNE I know it's terrible, trying to have any faith . . . when people are doing such horrible . . . *(Gently lifting his face)* but you know what I sometimes think? I think the world may be going through a phase, the way I was with Mother. It'll pass, maybe not for hundreds of years, but some day. . . . I still believe, in spite of everything, that people are really good at heart.

Barefoot in the Park
by Neil Simon

Paul and Corie are newlyweds. Paul has just climbed five flights to the garret apartment Corie has rented.

CORIE The furniture will be here by five. They promised.

PAUL *(Dropping affidavits into case, looks at his watch)* Five? . . . It's five-thirty. *(Crosses to bedroom stairs)* What do we do, sleep in Bloomingdale's tonight?

CORIE They'll be here, Paul. They're probably stuck in traffic.

PAUL *(Crossing up to bedroom)* And what about tonight? I've got a case in court tomorrow. Maybe we should check into a hotel? *(Looks into bedroom)*

CORIE *(Rises and moves towards* PAUL*)* We just checked *out* of a hotel. I don't care if the furniture *doesn't* come. I'm sleeping in my apartment *tonight.*

PAUL Where? Where? *(Looks into bathroom, closes door, and starts to come back down the steps)* There's only room for one in the bathtub. *(He suddenly turns, goes back up steps and opens door to the bathroom.)* Where's the bathtub?

CORIE *(Hesitantly)* There is no bathtub.

PAUL No bathtub?

CORIE There's a shower . . .

PAUL How am I going to take a bath?

CORIE You won't take a bath. You'll take a shower.

PAUL I don't like showers. I like baths. Corie, how am I going to take a bath?

CORIE You'll lie down in the shower and hang your feet over the sink. . . . I'm sorry there's no bathtub, Paul.

PAUL *(Closes door, and crosses down into the room)* Hmmmm . . . Boy, of all the nights . . . *(He suddenly shivers.)* It's freezing in here. *(He rubs his hands.)* Isn't there any heat?

CORIE Of course there's heat. We have a radiator.

PAUL *(Gets up on steps and feels radiator)* The radiator's the coldest thing in the room.

CORIE It's probably the boiler. It's probably off in the whole building.

PAUL *(Putting on gloves)* No, it was warm coming up the stairs. *(Goes out door into hall)* See . . . It's nice and warm out here.

CORIE Maybe it's because the apartment is empty.

PAUL The *hall* is empty too but it's warm out here.

CORIE *(Moves to the stove)* It'll be all right once I get a fire going.

PAUL *(Goes to phone)* A fire? You'd have to keep the flame going night and day. . . . I'll call the landlord.

CORIE *(Putting log into stove)* He's not home.

PAUL Where is he?

CORIE In Florida! . . . There's a handy man that comes Mondays, Wednesdays, and Fridays.

PAUL You mean we freeze on Tuesdays, Thursdays, and Saturdays?

CORIE He'll be here in the morning.

PAUL *(Moving R.)* And what'll we do tonight? I've got a case in court in the morning.

CORIE *(Moves to* PAUL*)* Will you stop saying it like you always have a case in court in the morning. This is your first one.

PAUL Well, what'll we do?

CORIE The furniture will be here. In the meantime I can light the stove and you can sit over the fire with your law books and a shawl like Abraham Lincoln. *(Crosses to the Franklin Stove and gets matches from the top of the stove)*

PAUL Is that supposed to be funny? *(Begins to investigate small windows)*

CORIE No. It was supposed to be nasty. It just came out funny. *(She strikes match and attempts to light the log in stove.* PAUL *tries the windows.)* What are you doing? *(Gives up attempting to light log)*

PAUL I'm checking to see if the windows are closed.

CORIE   They're closed. I looked.

PAUL   Then why is it windy in here?

CORIE   *(Moves R. to PAUL)* I don't feel a draft.

PAUL   *(Moves away from windows)* I didn't say draft. I said wind . . . There's a brisk, northeasterly wind blowing in this room.

CORIE   You don't have to get sarcastic.

PAUL   *(Moving up into the kitchen area)* I'm not getting sarcastic, I'm getting chapped lips. *(Looking up, he glimpses the hole in the skylight.)*

CORIE   How could there be wind in a closed room?

PAUL   How's this for an answer? There's a hole in the skylight. *(He points up.)*

CORIE   *(She looks up, sees it and is obviously embarrassed by it.)* Gee, I didn't see that before. Did you?

PAUL   *(Moves to ladder)* I didn't see the *apartment* before.

CORIE   *(Defensively. Crosses to the railing and gets her coat)* All right, Paul, don't get upset. I'm sure it'll be fixed. We could plug it up with something for tonight.

PAUL   *(Gets up on ladder)* How? How? That's twenty feet high. You'd have to fly over in a plane and *drop* something in.

CORIE   *(Putting on coat)* It's only for one night. And it's not that cold.

PAUL   In February? Do you know what it's like at three o'clock in the morning? In February? Ice-cold freezing.

CORIE   It's not going to be freezing. I called the weather bureau. It's going to be cloudy with a light s — *(She catches herself and looks up.)*

PAUL   What? *(CORIE turns away.)* What? . . . A light what?

CORIE   Snow!

PAUL   *(Coming down ladder)* Snow?? . . . It's going to snow tonight? . . . In here?

CORIE   They're wrong as often as they're right.

PAUL   I'm going to be shoveling snow in my own living room.

CORIE   It's a little hole.

PAUL   With that wind it could blow six-foot drifts in the bathroom. Honestly, Corie, I don't see how you can be so calm about all this.

CORIE   Well, what is it you want me to do?

PAUL   Go to pieces, like me. It's only natural.

Elizabeth the Queen
by Maxwell Anderson

Elizabeth I of England is deeply in love with the Earl of Essex. The ambitious Essex has tried unsuccessfully to obtain the throne. Elizabeth asks Essex to be her consort, but Essex wants the crown. Neither Elizabeth nor Essex will bend, and she is forced to send him to his execution.

ESSEX   There's no way out. I've thought of it
　　Every way. Speak frankly. Could you forgive me
　　And keep your throne?

ELIZABETH   No.

ESSEX   Are you ready to give
　　Your crown up to me?

ELIZABETH   No. It's all I have. *(She rises.)*
> Why, who am I
> To stand here paltering with a rebel noble!
> I am Elizabeth, daughter of a king,
> The queen of England, and you are my subject!
> What does this mean, you standing here eye to
>   eye
> With me, you liege? You whom I made, and gave
> All that you have, you, an upstart, defying
> Me to grant pardon, lest you should sweep me
>   from power
> And take my place from me? I tell you if Christ
>   his blood
> Ran streaming from the heavens for a sign
> That I should hold my hand you'd die for this,
> You pretender to a throne upon which you have
> No claim, you pretender to a heart, who have
>   been
> Hollow and heartless and faithless to the end!

ESSEX   If we'd met some other how we might have
>   been happy . . .
> But there's an empire between us! I am to die . . .
> Let us say that . . . let us begin with that . . .
> For then I can tell you that if there'd been no
>   empire
> We could have been great lovers. If even now
> You were not queen and I were not pretender,
> That god who searches heaven and earth and
>   hell
> For two who are perfect lovers, could end his
>   search
> With you and me. Remember . . . I am to die . . .
> And so I can tell you truly, out of all the earth
> That I'm to leave, there's nothing I'm very loath
> To leave save you. Yet if I live I'll be
> Your death or you'll be mine.

ELIZABETH   Give me the ring.

ESSEX   No.

ELIZABETH   Give me the ring. I'd rather you killed
>   me
> Than I killed you.

ESSEX   It's better for me as it is
> Than that I should live and batten my fame and
>   fortune
> On the woman I love. I've thought of it all. It's
>   better
> To die young and unblemished than to live long
>   and rule,
> And rule not well.

ELIZABETH   Aye, I should know that.

ESSEX   Is it not?

ELIZABETH   Yes.

ESSEX   Good-bye, then.

Harvey
by Mary Chase

*Veta Simmons's brother, Elwood, has an invisible
six-foot tall rabbit named Harvey for a friend. Veta
is embarrassed and humiliated by her brother's behavior and goes to Dr. Sanderson to have Elwood
committed to a mental hospital.*

VETA   Doctor — everything I say to you is con-
fidential? Isn't it?

SANDERSON   That's understood.

VETA   Because it's a slap in the face to everything
we've stood for in this community the way
Elwood is acting now.

SANDERSON   I am not a gossip, Mrs. Simmons. I am
a psychiatrist.

VETA   Well — for one thing — he drinks.

SANDERSON   To excess?

VETA To excess? Well — don't you call it excess when a man never lets a day go by without stepping into one of those cheap taverns, sitting around with riffraff and people you never heard of? Inviting them to the house — playing cards with them — giving them food and money. And here I am trying to get Myrtle Mae started with a nice group of young people. If that isn't excess I'm sure I don't know what excess is.

SANDERSON I didn't doubt your statement, Mrs. Simmons. I merely asked if your brother drinks.

VETA Well, yes, I say definitely Elwood drinks and I want him committed out here permanently, because I cannot stand another day of that Harvey. Myrtle and I have to set a place at the table for Harvey. We have to move over on the sofa and make room for Harvey. We have to answer the telephone when Elwood calls and asks to speak to Harvey. Then at the party this afternoon with Mrs. Chauvenet there — We didn't even know anything about Harvey until we came back here. Doctor, don't you think it would have been a little bit kinder of Mother to have written and told me about Harvey? Be honest, now — don't you?

SANDERSON I really couldn't answer that question, because I —

VETA I can. Yes — it certainly would have.

SANDERSON This person you call Harvey — who is he?

VETA He's a rabbit.

SANDERSON Perhaps — but just who is he? Some companion — someone your brother has picked up in these bars, of whom you disapprove?

VETA *(Patiently.)* Doctor — I've been telling you. Harvey is a rabbit — a big white rabbit — six feet high — or is it six feet and a half? Heavens knows I ought to know. He's been around the house long enough.

SANDERSON *(Regarding her narrowly.)* Now, Mrs. Simmons, let me understand this —— you say ——

VETA *(Impatient.)* Doctor — do I have to keep repeating myself? My brother insists that his closest friend is this big white rabbit. This rabbit is named Harvey. Harvey lives at our house. Don't you understand? He and Elwood go every place together. Elwood buys railroad tickets, theater tickets, for both of them. As I told Myrtle Mae — if your uncle was so lonesome he had to bring something home — why couldn't he bring home something human? He has me, doesn't he? He has Myrtle Mae, doesn't he? *(She leans forward.)* Doctor — *(She rises to him. He inclines toward her.)* I'm going to tell you something I've never told anybody in the world before. *(Puts her hand on his shoulder.)* Every once in a while I see that big white rabbit myself. Now isn't that terrible? I've never even told that to Myrtle Mae.

SANDERSON *(Now convinced. Starts to rise.)* Mrs. Simmons —

VETA *(Straightening.)* And what's more — he's every bit as big as Elwood says he is. Now don't ever tell that to anybody, Doctor.   I'm ashamed of it. *(Crosses to C., to chair R. of desk.)*

SANDERSON *(Crosses to VETA.)* I can see that you have been under a great nervous strain recently.

VETA Well — I certainly have.

SANDERSON Grief over your mother's death depressed you considerably?

VETA *(Sits chair R. of desk.)* Nobody knows how much.

SANDERSON Been losing sleep?

VETA How could anybody sleep with that going on?

SANDERSON *(Crosses to back of desk.)* Short-tempered over trifles?

VETA You just try living with those two and see how your temper holds up.

SANDERSON *(Presses buzzer.)* Loss of appetite?

VETA No one could eat at a table with my brother and a big white rabbit. Well, I'm finished with it. I'll sell the house — be appointed conservator of Elwood's estate, and Myrtle Mae and I will be able to entertain our friends in peace. It's too much, Doctor. I just can't stand it.

Everybody Loves Opal
by John Patrick

A middle-aged, rather cantankerous Doctor stands examining Opal with a stethoscope. Opal stands with shoulders squared, eagerly co-operative.

DOCTOR Cough, please. *(OPAL coughs.)* Again. *(OPAL coughs violently, shaking her whole body.)* Have you ever had any respiratory trouble?

OPAL No.

DOCTOR *(Frowns, puzzled.)* Cough again, please. *(He listens. He shakes his head. Takes off stethoscope, crosses to coat rack for coat and hat.)* There is no point in continuing this examination. I couldn't possibly recommend the issuance of a policy on your life. *(Puts on coat and hat, picks up bag from couch. Crosses D. R. front of table.)*

OPAL Why not?

DOCTOR *(Turns to OPAL.)* You have the worst rattle in your lungs I've ever heard. I'd advise you to have an X-ray as soon as possible. I shouldn't wait. In a week or so — it might be too late.

OPAL *(Crosses to DOCTOR.)* I never been sick a day in my life!

DOCTOR Listening to the rattle in your lungs, I'm surprised you're alive today. *(Starts R. toward entrance.)*

OPAL *(Stops him.)* Judas! I know what's wrong. *(Reaches into her bosom and flushes out a small purse.)* That's my *coin* purse. You've been listening to my small change.

DOCTOR *(Takes purse from OPAL. Shakes it. Listens. Puts it on table.)* Um, hum. *(Glares at her. Puts on stethoscope again.)* Cough, please. *(Satisfied.)* Watch my finger. *(He moves his finger back and forth in front of her eyes.)*

OPAL *(Chuckles.)* I could see it better if you'd hold it still.

DOCTOR *(Puts stethoscope in bag. OPAL takes his coat and hat.)* Now, if you'll sit down, I'll fill out the application blank.

OPAL *(Crosses to coat rack. Puts coat and hat on rack.)* How about a nice cup of tea first?

DOCTOR I'm allergic to tea, thank you. *(He sits down, moving stiffly, as if his shoulders were musclebound.)* We'll proceed.

OPAL You got a stiff neck, doctor?

DOCTOR I have a cold that's settled in my shoulders. *(Spreads an application blank on the table and puts on his glasses.)*

OPAL If you'd lemme give your neck a little jerk, I could take that kink out of there for you. *(Crosses to table.)*

DOCTOR I have no desire to be maimed permanently. Sit down, please.

OPAL *(Sits C. of table.)* I just hate to see you suffer.

DOCTOR   *(Pen poised.)* Your name is —

OPAL   Opal Kronkie.

DOCTOR   How do you spell it?

OPAL   One quick little jerk and you wouldn't even feel it.

DOCTOR   Will you spell your name, please?

OPAL   K-r-o-n-k-i-e. I do it all the time for a butcher fren of mine. Nice fella. Real genuine. Had a boy that stuttered. They hanged him. *(Explains.)* He murdered somebody. I guess poor Gus gets kinks in his neck thinkin' about his boy. It don't seem right to hang a boy that stutters.

DOCTOR   *(Acidly.)* Miss Kronkie — do you *want* this insurance policy?

OPAL   *(Resignedly.)* Sure, I want it for my friends. *(One last effort.)* But *you* can't hardly turn your head either. You got a son?

DOCTOR   *(Grits his teeth.)* How old are you?

OPAL   Judas — I don't know.

DOCTOR   Forty-five? Fifty-five?

OPAL   Why doncha split the difference — say fifty?

DOCTOR   You don't know your exact age?

OPAL   Never did. You must be just miserable, doctor. Why don't you lemme give your head a twist.

DOCTOR   *(Persistently.)* Do you know when your *birthday* is?

OPAL   Halloween.

DOCTOR   That is *not* a date.

OPAL   What is it, then?

DOCTOR   You were born on Halloween?

OPAL   On the dot. Whenever I see the pumpkins out — I know I'm a year older.

DOCTOR   *(Sighs.)* I shall split the difference and say fifty. *(Seeing* OPAL *rise.)* Wait! I'm not finished!

OPAL   I know. I'm gonna move that stove up behind you. It'll warm your back. *(Humming to herself, She moves the kerosene stove closer behind the doctor's back. Surrendering to an overpowering urge, She reaches out to grasp the doctor's head. He turns stiffly in time to discourage her. Humming cheerfully again, She returns to her chair.)*

DOCTOR   What is your occupation?

OPAL   Collector.

DOCTOR   Art or garbage?

OPAL   Junk.

DOCTOR   Your parents' occupation.

OPAL   Junk.

DOCTOR   How far back?

OPAL   The Mayflower.

DOCTOR   Do you have any birthmark or deformity?

OPAL   Why?

DOCTOR   *(Grits his teeth.)* Identification.

OPAL   Do I have to say?

DOCTOR   Do you want this policy?

OPAL   *(Flushes.)* It's kinda embarrassin'. *(Ducks her head.)* Well, I was born with six toes on one foot.

The Miracle Worker
by William Gibson

Captain and Kate Keller have hired Annie Sullivan to teach their daughter Helen, who is blind and deaf. In this scene, Captain Keller is furious with Annie and wants his wife to fire her.

KELLER   Katie, I will not *have* it! Now you did not see when that girl after supper tonight went to look for Helen in her room —

KATE   No.

KELLER   The child practically climbed out of her window to escape from her! What kind of teacher *is* she? I thought I had seen her at her worst this morning, shouting at me, but I come home to find the entire house disorganized by her — Helen won't stay one second in the same room, won't come to the table with her, won't let herself be bathed or undressed or put to bed by her, or even by Viney now, and the end result is that *you* have to do more for the child than before we hired this girl's services! From the moment she stepped off the train she's been nothing but a burden, incompetent, impertinent, ineffectual, immodest —

KATE   She folded her napkin, Captain.

KELLER   What?

KATE   Not ineffectual. Helen did fold her napkin.

KELLER   What in heaven's name is so extraordinary about folding a napkin?

KATE   *(With some humor.)* Well. It's more than you did, Captain.

KELLER   Katie. I did not bring you all the way out here to the garden house to be frivolous. Now, how does Miss Sullivan propose to teach a deaf-blind pupil who won't let her even touch her?

KATE   *(A pause.)* I don't know.

KELLER   The fact is, today she scuttled any chance she ever had of getting along with the child. If you can see any point or purpose to her staying on here longer, it's more than —

KATE   What do you wish me to do?

KELLER   I want you to give her notice.

KATE   I can't.

KELLER   Then if you won't, I must.

Antigone
by Jean Anouilh

Anouilh's Antigone *is based on the Sophocles tragedy of the same name. Antigone's two brothers, Eteocles and Polynices, were engaged in a power struggle after the death of their father, Oedipus, the King of Thebes. This struggle resulted in the brothers killing each other. The present King of Thebes, Creon, has ruled that only Eteocles shall be given a noble burial, while Polynices shall be left as carrion for the birds. In the following scene, Antigone plans, despite the pleadings of her sister, Ismene, to bury Polynices. Antigone knows that such an act will result in her death.*

ISMENE   Antigone, I've thought about it a lot.

ANTIGONE   Have you?

ISMENE   I thought about it all night long. Antigone, you're mad.

ANTIGONE   Am I?

ISMENE   We cannot do it.

ANTIGONE   Why not?

ISMENE   Creon will have us put to death.

ANTIGONE   Of course he will. That's what he's here for. He will do what he has to do, and we will do what we have to do. He is bound to put us to death. We are bound to go out and bury our brother. That's the way it is. What do you think we can do to change it?

ISMENE   *(Releases* ANTIGONE's *hand; draws back a step)* I don't want to die.

ANTIGONE   I'd prefer not to die, myself.

ISMENE   Listen to me, Antigone. I thought about it all night. I'm older than you are. I always think things over and you don't. You are impulsive. You get a notion in your head and you jump up and do the thing straight off. And if it's silly, well, so much the worse for you. Whereas, I think things out.

ANTIGONE   Sometimes it is better not to think too much.

ISMENE   I don't agree with you! Oh, I know it's horrible. And I pity Polynices just as much as you do. But all the same, I sort of see what Uncle Creon means.

ANTIGONE   I don't want to "sort of see" anything.

ISMENE   Uncle Creon is the king. He has to set an example!

ANTIGONE   But I am not the king; and I don't have to set people examples. Little Antigone gets a notion in her head — the nasty brat, the wilful, wicked girl; and they put her in a corner all day, or they lock her up in the cellar. And she deserves it. She shouldn't have disobeyed!

ISMENE   There you go, frowning, glowering, wanting your own stubborn way in everything. Listen to me. I'm right oftener than you are.

ANTIGONE   I don't want to be right!

ISMENE   At least you can try to understand.

ANTIGONE   Understand! The first word I ever heard out of any of you was that word "understand." Why didn't I "understand" that I must not play with water — cold, black, beautiful flowing water — because I'd spill it on the palace tiles. Or with earth, because earth dirties a little girl's frock. Why didn't I "understand" that nice children don't eat out of every dish at once; or give everything in their pockets to beggars; or run in the wind so fast that they fall down; or ask for a drink when they're perspiring; or want to go swimming when it's either too early or too late, merely because they happen to feel like swimming. Understand! I don't want to understand. There'll be time enough to understand when I'm old. . . . If I ever *am* old. But not now.

Trifles
by Susan Glaspell

The farmer's wife has been arrested for murdering her husband. In the following scene, the sheriff and his deputies are searching the farmhouse for evidence while Mrs. Peters and Mrs. Hale neaten up the kitchen.

MRS. HALE   She liked the bird. She was going to bury it in that pretty box.

MRS. PETERS   *(In a whisper)* When I was a girl — my kitten — there was a boy took a hatchet, and before my eyes — and before I could get there — *(Covers her face for an instant)* If they hadn't held me back I would have — *(Catches herself, looks upstairs, falters weakly)* — hurt him.

MRS. HALE   *(With a slow look around her)* I wonder how it would seem never to have had any children around. *(Pauses)* No, Wright wouldn't like the bird — a thing that sang. She used to sing. He killed that, too.

MRS. PETERS   *(Moving uneasily)* We don't know who killed the bird.

MRS. HALE   I knew John Wright.

MRS. PETERS   It was an awful thing was done in this house that night. Mrs. Hale. Killing a man while he slept, slipping a rope around his neck that choked the life out of him.

MRS. HALE   His neck. Choked the life out of him. *(Her hand goes out and rests on the birdcage.)*

MRS. PETERS   *(With rising voice)* We don't know who killed him. We don't *know.*

MRS. HALE   *(Her own feeling not interrupted)* If there'd been years and years of nothing, then a bird to sing to you, it would be awful — still, after the bird was still.

MRS. PETERS   *(Something within her speaking)* I know what stillness is. When we homesteaded in Dakota, and my first baby died — after he was two years old, and me with no other then —

MRS. HALE   *(Moving)* How soon do you suppose they'll be through looking for the evidence?

MRS. PETERS   I know what stillness is. *(Pulling herself back)* The law has got to punish crime, Mrs. Hale.

MRS. HALE   *(Not as if answering that)* I wish you'd seen Minnie Foster when she wore a white dress with blue ribbons and stood up there in the choir and sang. *(A look around the room)* Oh, I *wish* I'd come over here once in a while! That was a crime. That was a crime! Who's going to punish that?

MRS. PETERS   *(Looking upstairs)* We mustn't — take on.

MRS. HALE   I might have known she needed help! I know how things can be — for women. I tell you, it's queer, Mrs. Peters. We live close together and we live far apart. We all go through the same things — it's all just a different kind of the same thing. *(Brushes her eyes, noticing the bottle of fruit, reaches out for it)* If I was you, I wouldn't tell her her fruit was gone. Tell her it *ain't.* Tell her it's all right. Take this in to prove it to her. She — she may never know whether it was broke or not.

MRS. PETERS   *(Takes the bottle, looks about for something to wrap it in; takes petticoat from pile of clothes; very nervously begins winding this around the bottle. In a false voice)* My, it's a good thing the men couldn't hear us. Wouldn't they just laugh! Getting all stirred up over a little thing like a — dead canary. As if that could have anything to do with — with — wouldn't they *laugh!*

The Chalk Garden
by Enid Bagnold

Miss Madrigal is Laurel's governess. Laurel is fascinated by crime. She believes there is something most mysterious about Miss Madrigal's past. In the following scene, Laurel tries to pry information from Miss Madrigal about who she is, what she has seen, and where she has come from.

LAUREL   So you've been to a trial?

MADRIGAL   I did not say I hadn't.

LAUREL   Why did you not say — when you know what store we both lay by it!

MADRIGAL   It may be I think you lay too much store by it.

LAUREL   *(Relaxing her tone and asking as though an ordinary light question)* How does one get in?

MADRIGAL   It's surprisingly easy.

LAUREL   Was it a trial for murder?

MADRIGAL   It would have to be to satisfy you.

LAUREL   *Was* it a trial for murder? *(Sits above her on sofa)*

MADRIGAL   *(Without turning around to look)* Have you finished that flower?

LAUREL   *(Yawning)* As much as I can. I get tired of

it. *(Wandering to the window)* In my house — at home — there were so many things to do.

MADRIGAL   What was it like?

LAUREL   My home?

MADRIGAL   Yes.

LAUREL   *(Doodling on a piece of paper and speaking as though caught unaware)* There was a stream. And a Chinese bridge. And yew trees cut like horses. And a bell on the weathervane, and a little wood called mine —

MADRIGAL   Who called it that?

LAUREL   *(Unwillingly moved)* She did — my mother. And when it was raining we made an army of her cream pots and battlefield of her dressing table — I used to thread her rings on safety pins —

MADRIGAL   Tomorrow I will light that candle in the green glass candlestick and you can try to paint that.

LAUREL   *(Looking up)* What — paint the flame!

MADRIGAL   Yes.

LAUREL   *(Doodling again)* I'm tired of fire, too, Boss.

MADRIGAL   *(As she notices* LAUREL *doodling)* Why do you sign your name a thousand times?

LAUREL   I am looking for which is me.

MADRIGAL   Shall we read?

LAUREL   Oh, I don't want to read.

MADRIGAL   Let's play a game.

LAUREL   All right. *(With meaning)* A *guessing* game.

MADRIGAL   Very well. Do you know one?

LAUREL   Maitland and I play one called "The Sky's the Limit."

MADRIGAL   How do you begin?

LAUREL   *(Sitting down opposite her)* We ask three questions each but if you pass one, I get a fourth.

MADRIGAL   What do we guess about?

LAUREL   Let's guess about each other? We are both mysterious.

MADRIGAL   *(Sententious)* The human heart *is* mysterious.

LAUREL   We don't know the first thing about each other, so there are so many things to ask.

MADRIGAL   But we mustn't go too fast. Or there will be nothing left to discover. Has it got to be the truth?

LAUREL   One can lie. But I get better and better at spotting lies. It's so dull playing with Maitland. He's so innocent. (MISS MADRIGAL *folds her hands and waits.)* Now! First question — Are you a — *maiden* lady?

MADRIGAL   *(After a moment's reflection)* I can't answer that.

LAUREL   Why?

MADRIGAL   Because you throw the emphasis so oddly.

LAUREL   Right. You don't answer. So now I get an extra question. Are you living under an assumed name?

MADRIGAL   No.

LAUREL   Careful! I'm getting my lie-detector working. Do you take things here at their face value?

MADRIGAL   No.

LAUREL   Splendid! You're getting the idea!

MADRIGAL   *(Warningly)* This is to be your fourth question.

LAUREL   Yes. Yes. I must think — I must be careful. *(Shooting her question hard at* MISS MADRIGAL*)* What is the full name of your married sister?

MADRIGAL   *(Staring a brief second at her)* Clarissa Dalrymple Westerham.

LAUREL   Is Dalrymple Westerham a double name?

MADRIGAL   *(With ironical satisfaction)* You've *had* your questions.

LAUREL   *(Gaily accepting defeat)* Yes, I have. Now yours. You've only three unless I pass one.

MADRIGAL   Was your famous affair in Hyde Park on the night of your mother's marriage?

LAUREL   *(Wary)* About that time.

MADRIGAL   What was the charge by the police?

LAUREL   *(Wary)* The police didn't come into it.

MADRIGAL   Did someone follow you? And try to kiss you?

LAUREL   *(Off her guard)* Kiss me! It was a case of Criminal Assault!

MADRIGAL   *(Following that up)* How do you know — if there wasn't a charge by the police?

LAUREL   *(Pausing a second. Triumphant)* That's one too many questions! *Now* for the deduction!

MADRIGAL   You didn't tell me there was to be a deduction.

LAUREL   I forgot. It's the whole point. Mine's ready.

MADRIGAL   And what do you deduce?

LAUREL   (*Taking breath — then fast as though she might be stopped*) That you've changed so much you must have been something quite different. When you first came here you were like a rusty hinge that wanted oiling. You spoke to yourself out loud without knowing it. You had been *alone*. You may have been a missionary in Central Africa. You may have escaped from a private asylum. But as a maiden lady you are an imposter. (*Changing her tone slightly — slower and more penetrating*) About your assumed name I am not so sure — *But you have no married sister.*

MADRIGAL   (*Lightly*) You take my breath away.

LAUREL   (*As lightly*) Good at it, aren't I?

MADRIGAL   Yes, for a mind under a cloud.

LAUREL   Now for your deduction!

MADRIGAL   Mine must keep.

LAUREL   But it's the game! Where are you going? (*Rises, steps down stage*)

MADRIGAL   (*Pleasantly*) To my room. To make sure I have left no clues unlocked.

LAUREL   To your past life?

MADRIGAL   Yes, you have given me so much warning. (*Exits*)

The Glass Menagerie
by Tennessee Williams

Amanda Wingfield raised her children, Tom and Laura, alone. Laura has grown up to be a very shy young woman largely as a result of her embarrassment over a deformed foot that makes her limp.

Laura's escape from her handicap is a glass menagerie, a collection of delicate glass animals, that she tends lovingly. Amanda, worried about Laura's future, has sent her to typing school. However, Laura hates the school and she has dropped out without telling her mother. In the following scene, Amanda has discovered Laura's deceit.

LAURA   Hello, Mother, I was —

(*She makes a nervous gesture toward the chart on the wall.* AMANDA *leans against the shut door and stares at* LAURA *with martyred look.*)

AMANDA   Deception? Deception?

(*She slowly removes her hat and gloves, continuing the sweet suffering stare. She lets the hat and gloves fall on the floor — a bit of acting.*)

LAURA   (*Shakily*) How was the D.A.R. meeting? (AMANDA *slowly opens her purse and removes a dainty white handkerchief which she shakes out delicately and delicately touches to her lips and nostrils.*) Didn't you go to the D.A.R. meeting, Mother?

AMANDA   (*Faintly, almost inaudibly*) — No — No. (*Then more forcibly*) I did not have the strength — to go to the D.A.R. In fact, I did not have the courage! I wanted to find a hole in the ground and hide myself in it forever!

(*She crosses slowly to the wall and removes the diagram of the typewriter keyboard. She holds it in front of her for a second, staring at it sweetly and sorrowfully — then bites her lips and tears it in two pieces.*)

LAURA   (*Faintly*) Why did you do that, Mother? (AMANDA *repeats the same procedure with the chart of the Gregg Alphabet.*) Why are you —

AMANDA   Why? Why? How old are you, Laura?

LAURA   Mother, you know my age.

AMANDA   I thought that you were an adult; it seems that I was mistaken.

(She crosses slowly to the sofa and sinks down and stares at LAURA.)

LAURA   Please don't stare at me, Mother.

(AMANDA closes her eyes and lowers her head. Count ten.)

AMANDA   What are we going to do, what is going to become of us, what is the future?

(Count ten.)

LAURA   Has something happened, Mother? *(AMANDA draws a long breath and takes out the handkerchief again. Dabbing process)* Mother, has — something happened?

AMANDA   I'll be all right in a minute, I'm just bewildered — *(Count five.)* — by life . . . .

LAURA   Mother, I wish that you would tell me what's happened.

AMANDA   As you know, I was supposed to be inducted into my office at the D.A.R. this afternoon. But I stopped off at Rubicam's Business College to speak to your teachers about your having a cold and ask them what progress they thought you were making down there.

LAURA   Oh . . .

AMANDA   I went to the typing instructor and introduced myself as your mother. She didn't know who you were. Wingfield, she said. We don't have any such student enrolled at the school!

I assured her she did, that you have been going to classes since early in January.

"I wonder," she said, "if you could be talking about the terribly shy little girl who dropped out of school after only a few days' attendance?" "No," I said, "Laura, my daughter, has been going to school every day for the past six weeks!"

"Excuse me," she said. She took the attendance book out and there was your name, unmistakably printed, and all the dates you were absent until they decided that you had dropped out of school.

I still said, "No, there must have been some mistake! There must have been some mix-up in the records?"

And she said, "No — I remember her perfectly now. Her hands shook so that she couldn't hit the right keys! The first time we had a speedtest, she broke down completely — was sick at the stomach and almost had to be carried into the wash-room! After that morning she never showed up any more. We phoned the house but never got any answer" — while I was working at Famous and Barr, I suppose, demonstrating those — Oh!

I felt so weak I could barely keep on my feet!

I had to sit down while they got me a glass of water!

Fifty dollars' tuition, all of our plans — my hopes and ambitions for you — just gone up the spout, just gone up the spout like that. *(LAURA draws a long breath and gets awkwardly to her feet. She crosses to the victrola and winds it up.)* What are you doing?

LAURA   Oh! *(She releases the handle and returns to her seat.)*

AMANDA   Laura, where have you been going when you've gone out pretending that you were going to business college?

LAURA   I've just been going out walking.

AMANDA   That's not true.

LAURA   It is. I just went walking.

AMANDA   Walking? Walking? In winter? Deliberately courting pneumonia in that light coat? Where did you walk to, Laura?

LAURA   All sorts of places — mostly in the park.

AMANDA   Even after you'd started catching that cold?

LAURA   It was the lesser of two evils, Mother. I couldn't go back up. I — threw up — on the floor!

AMANDA   From half past seven till after five every day you mean to tell me you walked around in the park, because you wanted me to think that you were still going to Rubicam's Business College?

LAURA   It wasn't as bad as it sounds. I went inside places to get warmed up.

AMANDA   Inside where?

LAURA   I went in the art museum and the bird-houses at the Zoo. I visited the penguins every day! Sometimes I did without lunch and went to the movies. Lately I've been spending most of my afternoons in the Jewel-box, that big glass house where they raise the tropical flowers.

AMANDA   You did all this to deceive me, just for deception? (LAURA *looks down.*) Why?

LAURA   Mother, when you're disappointed, you get that awful suffering look on your face, like the picture of Jesus' mother in the museum!

AMANDA   Hush!

LAURA   I couldn't face it!

(Pause. A whisper of strings)

AMANDA   *(Hopelessly fingering the huge pocket-book)* So what are we going to do the rest of our lives? Stay home and watch the parades go by? Amuse ourselves with the glass menagerie, darling? Eternally play those worn-out phonograph records your father left as a painful reminder of him.

We won't have a business career — we've given that up because it gave us nervous indigestion! *(Laughs wearily)* What is there left but dependency all our lives? I know so well what becomes of unmarried women who aren't prepared to occupy a position. I've seen such pitiful cases in the South — barely tolerated spinsters living upon the grudging patronage of sister's husband or brother's wife! — stuck away in some little mouse-trap of a room — encouraged by one in-law to visit another — little birdlike women without any nest — eating the crust of humility all their life!

Is that the future that we've mapped out for ourselves? I swear it's the only alternative I can think of! It isn't a very pleasant alternative, is it? Of course — some girls *do marry.* (LAURA *twists her hands nervously.)*

Haven't you ever liked some boy?

LAURA   Yes. I liked one once. *(Rises)* I came across his picture a while ago.

AMANDA   *(With some interest)* He gave you his picture?

LAURA   No, it's in the year-book.

AMANDA   *(Disappointed)* Oh — a high-school boy.

LAURA   Yes. His name was Jim. (LAURA *lifts the heavy annual from the claw-foot table.)* Here he is in *The Pirates of Penzance.*

AMANDA   *(Absently)* The what?

LAURA   The operetta the senior class put on. He had a wonderful voice and we sat across the aisle from each other Mondays, Wednesdays and Fridays in the Aud. Here he is with the silver cup for debating! See his grin?

AMANDA   *(Absently)* He must have had a jolly disposition.

LAURA   He used to call me — Blue Roses.

AMANDA   Why did he call you such a name as that?

LAURA   When I had that attack of pleurosis — he asked me what was the matter when I came back. I said pleurosis — he thought I said Blue Roses! So that's what he always called me after that. Whenever he saw me, he'd holler, "Hello, Blue Roses!" I didn't care for the girl that he went out with. Emily Meisenbach. Emily was the best-dressed girl at Soldan. She never struck me, though, as being sincere. . . . It says in the Personal Section — they're engaged. That's — six years ago! They must be married by now.

AMANDA   Girls that aren't cut out for business careers usually wind up married to some nice man. *(Gets up with a spark of revival)* Sister, that's what you'll do!

(LAURA utters a startled, doubtful laugh. She reaches quickly for a piece of glass.)

LAURA   But, Mother —

AMANDA   Yes? *(Crossing to photograph)*

LAURA   *(In a tone of frightened apology)* I'm — crippled!

AMANDA   Nonsense! Laura, I've told you never, never to use that word. Why, you're not crippled, you just have a little defect — hardly noticeable, even! When people have some slight disadvantage like that, they cultivate other things to make up for it — develop charm — and vivacity — and — *charm!* That's all you have to do! *(She turns again to the photograph.)* One thing your father had *plenty of* — was *charm!*

The Importance of Being Earnest
by Oscar Wilde

The Importance of Being Earnest *is a satirical farce ridiculing the social manners of nineteenth-century England. In the following scene, Cecily and Gwendolen meet for the first time. Both believe they are engaged to be married to Ernest Worthing. However, Cecily's Ernest is really Algernon Moncrieff, Gwendolen's cousin and Jack Worthing's friend. Gwendolen's Ernest is really Jack Worthing, who has been leading a double life. He is Jack in the country, and he is Cecily's guardian and Ernest in the city, where he met and fell in love with Gwendolen. For this scene to be effective, both young women should be played with a tongue-in-cheek attitude. Oscar Wilde created them to be farcical characters, fussily feminine, emotionally flighty, and pettily competitive.*

(Enter GWENDOLEN. *Exit* MERRIMAN.*)*

CECILY   *(Advancing to meet her)* Pray let me introduce myself to you. My name is Cecily Cardew.

GWENDOLEN   Cecily Cardew? *(Moving to her and shaking hands)* What a very sweet name! Something tells me that we are going to be great friends. I like you already more than I can say. My first impressions of people are never wrong.

CECILY   How nice of you to like me so much after we have known each other such a comparatively short time. Pray sit down.

GWENDOLEN   *(Still standing up)* I may call you Cecily, may I not?

CECILY   With pleasure!

GWENDOLEN   And you will always call me Gwendolen, won't you?

CECILY   If you wish.

GWENDOLEN   Then that is all quite settled, is it not?

CECILY   I hope so.

(A pause. They both sit down together.)

GWENDOLEN   Perhaps this might be a favorable opportunity for my mentioning who I am. My father

is Lord Bracknell. You have never heard of papa,
I suppose?

CECILY   I don't think so.

GWENDOLEN   Outside the family circle, papa, I am
glad to say, is entirely unknown. I think that is
quite as it should be. The home seems to me to
be the proper sphere for the man. And certainly
once a man begins to neglect his domestic duties he becomes painfully effeminate, does he
not? And I don't like that. It makes men so very
attractive. Cecily, mamma, whose views on education are remarkably strict, has brought me up
to be extremely shortsighted; it is part of her system; so do you mind my looking at you through
my glasses?

CECILY   Oh, not at all, Gwendolen. I am very fond
of being looked at.

GWENDOLEN   *(After examining* CECILY *carefully
through a lorgnette)* You are here on a short visit,
I suppose.

CECILY   Oh, no, I live here.

GWENDOLEN   *(Severely)* Really? Your mother, no
doubt, or some female relative of advanced
years, resides here also?

CECILY   Oh, no. I have no mother, nor, in fact, any
relations.

GWENDOLEN   Indeed?

CECILY   My dear guardian, with the assistance of
Miss Prism, has the arduous task of looking after
me.

GWENDOLEN   Your guardian?

CECILY   Yes, I am Mr. Worthing's ward.

GWENDOLEN   Oh! It is strange he never mentioned
to me that he had a ward. How secretive of him!

He grows more interesting hourly. I am not sure,
however, that the news inspires me with feelings
of unmixed delight. *(Rising and going to her)* I
am very fond of you Cecily; I have liked you ever
since I met you. But I am bound to state that now
that I know that you are Mr. Worthing's ward, I
cannot help expressing a wish you were — well,
just a little older than you seem to be — and not
quite so very alluring in appearance. In fact, if I
may speak candidly ——

CECILY   Pray do! I think that whenever one has anything unpleasant to say, one should always be
quite candid.

GWENDOLEN   Well, to speak with perfect candor,
Cecily. I wish that you were fully forty-two, and
more than usually plain for your age. Ernest has
a strong upright nature. He is the very soul of
truth and honor. Disloyalty would be as impossible to him as deception. But even men of the
noblest possible moral character are extremely
susceptible to the influence of the physical
charms of others. Modern, no less Ancient History, supplies us with many most painful examples of what I refer to. If it were not so, indeed,
History would be quite unreadable.

CECILY   I beg your pardon, Gwendolen, did you say
Ernest?

GWENDOLEN   Yes.

CECILY   Oh, but it is not Mr. Ernest Worthing who is
my guardian. It is his brother — his elder brother.

GWENDOLEN   *(Sitting down again)* Ernest never
mentioned to me that he had a brother.

CECILY   I am sorry to say they have not been on
good terms for a long time.

GWENDOLEN   Ah! that accounts for it. And now that
I think of it, I have never heard any man mention
his brother. The subject seems distasteful to
most men. Cecily, you have lifted a load from my

mind. I was growing almost anxious. It would have been terrible if any cloud had come across a friendship like ours, would it not? Of course you are quite, quite sure that it is not Mr. Ernest Worthing who is your guardian?

CECILY   Quite sure. *(A pause)* In fact, I am going to be his.

GWENDOLEN   *(Inquiringly)* I beg your pardon?

CECILY   *(Rather shy and confidingly)* Dearest Gwendolen, there is no reason why I should make a secret of it to you. Our little county newspaper is sure to chronicle the fact next week. Mr. Ernest Worthing and I are engaged to be married.

GWENDOLEN   *(Quite politely, rising)* My darling Cecily, I think there must be some slight error. Mr. Ernest Worthing is engaged to me. The announcement will appear in the *Morning Post* on Saturday at the latest.

CECILY   *(Very politely, rising)* I am afraid you must be under some misconception. Ernest proposed to me exactly ten minutes ago. *(Shows diary)*

GWENDOLEN   *(Examines diary through her lorgnette carefully)* It is certainly very curious, for he asked me to be his wife yesterday afternoon at 5:30. If you would care to verify the incident, pray do so. *(Produces diary of her own)* I never travel without my diary. One should always have something sensational to read on the train. I am so sorry, dear Cecily, if it is any disappointment to you, but I am afraid *I* have the prior claim.

Wine in the Wilderness
by Alice Childress

Tommy, a factory worker, meets Cynthia, a social worker, and Cynthia's husband, Sonny-Man, a writer. Cynthia and Sonny-Man know that a friend of theirs, Bill Jameson, an artist, is looking for a black woman to model for him. Tommy is exactly the kind of woman he has been looking for. In the following scene, Cynthia is trying to protect Tommy from getting emotionally involved with Bill, since he really is primarily interested in her as a model, not as a woman.

CYNTHIA   *(A bit uncomfortable)* Oh, Honey, . . . Tommy, you don't want a poor artist.

TOMMY   Tommy's not lookin' for a meal ticket. I been doin' for myself all my life. It takes two to make it in this high-price world. A black man see a hard way to go. The both of you gotta pull together. That way you accomplish.

CYNTHIA   I'm a social worker . . . and I see so many broken homes. Some of these men! Tommy, don't be in a rush about the marriage thing.

TOMMY   Keep it to yourself, . . . but I was thirty my last birthday and haven't even been married. I coulda been. Oh, yes, indeed, coulda been. But I don't want any and everybody. What I want with a no-good piece-a nothin'? I'll never forget what the Reverend Martin Luther King said . . . "I have a dream." I like him sayin' it 'cause truer words have never been spoke. *(Straightening the room)* I have a dream, too. Mine is to find a man who'll treat me just half-way decent . . . just to meet me half-way is all I ask, to smile, be kind to me. Somebody in my corner. Not to wake up by myself in the mornin' and face this world all alone.

CYNTHIA   About Bill, it's best not to ever count on anything, anything at all, Tommy.

TOMMY   *(This remark bothers her for a split second but she shakes it off.)* Of course, Cynthia, that's one of the foremost rules of life. Don't count on *nothin'!*

CYNTHIA   Right, don't be too quick to put your trust in these men.

TOMMY   You put your trust in one and got yourself a husband.

CYNTHIA   Well, yes, but what I mean is . . . Oh, you know. A man is a man and Bill is also an artist and his work comes before all else and there are other factors. . .

TOMMY   *(Sits facing* CYNTHIA*)* What's wrong with me?

CYNTHIA   I don't know what you mean.

TOMMY   Yes you do. You tryin' to tell me I'm aimin' too high by lookin' at Bill.

CYNTHIA   Oh, no my dear.

TOMMY   Out there in the street, in the bar, you and your husband were so sure that he'd *like* me and want to paint my picture.

CYNTHIA   But he does want to paint you, he's very eager to. . .

TOMMY   But why? Somethin' don't fit right.

CYNTHIA   *(Feeling sorry for Tommy)* If you don't want to do it, just leave and that'll be that.

TOMMY   Walk out while he's buyin' me what I ask for, spendin' his money on me? That'd be too dirty. *(Looks at books. Takes one from shelf)* Books, books, books everywhere. "Afro-American History." I like that. What's wrong with me, Cynthia? Tell me, I won't get mad with you, I swear. If there's somethin' wrong that I can change, I'm ready to do it. Eighth grade, that's all I had of school. You a social worker, I know that mean college. I come from poor people. *(Examining the book in her hand)* Talkin' 'bout poverty this and poverty that and studyin' it. When you in it you don't be studyin' 'bout it. Cynthia, I remember my mother tyin' up her stockin's with strips-a rag 'cause she didn't have no garters. When I

get home from school she'd say, . . . "Nothin' much here to eat." Nothin' much might be grits, or bread and coffee. I got sick-a all that, got me a job. Later for school.

CYNTHIA   The Matriarchal Society.

TOMMY   What's that?

CYNTHIA   A Matriarchal Society is one in which the women rule . . . the women have the power . . . the women head the house.

TOMMY   We didn't have nothin' to rule over, not a pot nor a window. And my papa picked hisself up and run off with some finger-poppin' woman and we never hear another word 'til ten, twelve years later when a undertaker call up and ask if Mama wants come claim his body. And don'cha know, mama went on over and claim it. A woman need a man to claim, even if it's a dead one. What's wrong with me? Be honest.

CYNTHIA   You're a fine person. . .

TOMMY   Go on, I can take it.

CYNTHIA   You're too brash. You're too used to looking out for yourself. It makes us lose our femininity . . . It makes us hard . . . it makes us seem very hard. We do for ourselves too much.

TOMMY   If I don't, who's gonna do for me?

CYNTHIA   You have to let the black man have his manhood again. You have to give it back, Tommy.

TOMMY   I didn't take it from him, how I'm gonna give it back?

Butterflies Are Free
by Leonard Gershe

Mrs. Baker has overprotected her blind son, Don, for most of his life. Only recently has he been able to convince his mother that he should have the opportunity to have an apartment of his own and care for himself completely. Jill is a neighbor in Don's apartment building. They met and discovered that they enjoyed each other's company. In the following scene, Mrs. Baker is once again trying to protect her son. She believes that Jill is the wrong woman for Don and will hurt him deeply. So Mrs. Baker is eager to convince Jill to get out of Don's life.

MRS. BAKER   *(Mumbling to herself.)* Mrs. Benson!!!

JILL   *(Opening her door.)* Yes?

MRS. BAKER   *(Is startled for a moment, but recovers, quickly. In friendly tones:)* Could you come in for a moment, Mrs. Benson?

JILL   *(Uneasily.)* Well, I have my audition. I should leave in about fifteen minutes. I don't know New York and I get lost all the time.

MRS. BAKER   *(Ingratiatingly. Steps toward* JILL *a bit.)* Don't you worry. I'll see that you get off in time. *(*JILL *enters, reluctantly, stands behind table.)* I thought you and I might have a little talk. You know — just girls together. Please sit down. *(*JILL *remains standing, avoiding too close contact with* MRS. BAKER.*)* Would you like a cup of coffee? Tea?

JILL   No, thank you . . . *(Crosses off platform to* L. *of sofa.)* but if that apple is still there.

MRS. BAKER   *(Crosses to refrigerator, gets apple and lettuce on plate, crosses to sink.)* I'm sure it is.

JILL   *(Crosses between sofa and coffee table to ladder, sits step.)* Where's Don?

MRS. BAKER   Shopping. *(Washes apple and polishes it with dish towel.)* You must be so careful to wash fruits and vegetables, you know. They spray all those insecticides on everything now. I'm not at all sure the bugs aren't less harmful. *(Crosses to* JILL *with apple.)* I like apples to be nice and shiny. *(Holds the apple out to* JILL, *who looks at it and then at* MRS. BAKER *oddly.)*

JILL   This reminds me of something. What is it?

MRS. BAKER   I have no idea.

JILL   You . . . handing me the apple . . . nice and shiny. . . . Oh, I know! Snow White. Remember when the witch brought her the poisoned apple? Oh, Mrs. Baker, I'm sorry. I didn't mean that the way it sounded. I know you're not a witch.

MRS. BAKER   Of course not. And I know you're not Snow White.

JILL   *(Takes the apple, rises, crosses below* MRS. BAKER, *through kitchen to* D. L. *post.)* I may have to wait hours before I read. I'll probably starve to death before their eyes.

MRS. BAKER   *(Crosses to kitchen, takes lettuce, picks off a few pieces, washes them, puts them on plate.)* You're going to get that part, you know.

JILL   What makes you so sure?

MRS. BAKER   Well, you're a very pretty girl and that's what they want in the theatre, isn't it?

JILL   *(Crosses below to* D. R. *post, away from* MRS. BAKER.*)* Today you have to have more than a pretty face. Anyway, I'm not really pretty. I think I'm interesting-looking and in certain lights I can look sort of . . . lovely . . . but I'm not pretty.

MRS. BAKER   *(Crosses with lettuce, sits* C. *sofa.)* Nonsense! You're extremely pretty.

JILL   *(Laugh.)* No, I'm not.

MRS. BAKER   Yes, you are.

JILL   *(Turns, leans post.)* No, I'm not. I've got beady little eyes like a bird and a figure like a pogo stick. *(Waits for a reaction from* MRS. BAKER. *There isn't one.)* Well? Aren't you going to deny you said that?

MRS. BAKER   *(Unperturbed.)* How can I, dear? Obviously, you heard it.

JILL   *(Crosses above director's chair.)* There are plenty of true things you can put me down with. You don't have to put me down with lies.

MRS. BAKER   You know what I like about you?

JILL   Uh-huh. Nothing.

MRS. BAKER   Oh yes. I like your honesty . . . your candor. You're really quite a worldly young woman, aren't you, Mrs. Benson?

JILL   I suppose I am. *(Crosses above "picnic," away from* MRS. BAKER.*)* I wish you wouldn't call me Mrs. Benson.

MRS. BAKER   Isn't that your name . . . Mrs. Benson?

JILL   But you don't say it as though you mean it.

MRS. BAKER   I'm sorry. Why don't I call you Jill? That's more friendly . . . and I'll try to say it as though I mean it. Now, Jill. *(*JILL — R. *turn, back to audience.)* . . .

MRS. BAKER   I was interested in seeing what you and Donny might have in common. He likes you very much.

JILL   *(Crosses U. end of coffee table.)* And I like him very much. He may very well be the most beautiful person I've ever met. Just imagine going through life never seeing anything . . . not a painting . . . or a flower . . . or even a Christmas card. I'd want to die, but Don wants to live. I

mean really live . . . *(Crosses onto platform to above table.)* and he can even kid about it. He's fantastic.

MRS. BAKER   Then you would want what's best for him, wouldn't you?

JILL   *(Crosses U.S. end of coffee table.)* Now, we're getting to it, aren't we? Like maybe I should tell him to go home with you. Is that it?

MRS. BAKER   Donny was happy at home until Linda Fletcher filled him with ideas about a place of his own.

JILL   *(Crosses through kitchen to above table.)* Maybe you just want to believe that he can only be happy with you, Mrs. Baker. Well, there are none so blind as those who will not see. *(Crosses D. L. post.)* There. I can quote Dylan Thomas AND Little Donny Dark.

MRS. BAKER   *(Rises, takes lettuce to counter.)* You constantly astonish me.

JILL   Well . . . we women of the world do that.

MRS. BAKER   *(Crosses to "picnic," picks up pillows and cloth, folds cloth.)* Funny how like Linda you are. Donny is certainly consistent with his girls.

JILL   Why do you call him Donny?

MRS. BAKER   It's his name. Don't I say it as though I mean it?

JILL   He hates being called Donny.

MRS. BAKER   *(Crosses to sofa, pillows at each end, crosses to counter, puts cloth on it.)* He's never mentioned it.

JILL   Of course, he has. *(Crosses off platform to D. end of sofa.)* You just didn't listen. There are none so deaf as those who will not hear. You could make up a lot of those, couldn't you? There are none so lame as those who will not walk. None so thin as those who will not eat . . .

MRS. BAKER *(Crosses off platform to* U.C.*)* Do you think it's a good idea for Donny to live down here alone?

JILL I think it's a good idea for *Don* to live wherever he wants to . . . and he's not alone. I'm here.

MRS. BAKER *(Crosses* U. *end of coffee table.)* For how long? Have you got a lease on that apartment?

JILL No.

MRS. BAKER So, you can leave tomorrow if you felt like it.

JILL That's right.

MRS. BAKER You couldn't sustain a marriage for more than six days, could you?

JILL *(Upset. Crosses* D. R.*)* My marriage doesn't concern you.

MRS. BAKER It didn't concern you much, either, did it?

JILL Yes, it did!

MRS. BAKER *(Crosses above director's chair.)* Have you thought about what marriage to a blind boy might be like? . . .

MRS. BAKER You've seen Donny at his best — in this room, which he's memorized . . . and he's memorized how many steps to the drugstore and to the delicatessen . . . but take him out of this room or off this street and he's lost . . . he panics. Donny needs someone who will stay with him — and not just for six days.

JILL You can stop worrying, Mrs. Baker. Nothing

serious will develop between Don and me. I'm not built that way.

MRS. BAKER But Donny *is* built that way.

JILL Oh, please — we're just having kicks.

MRS. BAKER Kicks! That's how it started with Linda — just kicks . . . but Donny fell in love with her . . . and he'll fall in love with you. Then what happens?

JILL *(Crosses below to* D. *end of sofa.)* I don't know!!

MRS. BAKER *(Crosses* U. *end of sofa.)* Then don't let it go that far. Stop now before you hurt him.

JILL What about you? Aren't you hurting him?

MRS. BAKER I can't. I can only irritate him. You can hurt him. The longer you stay the harder it will be for him when you leave. Let him come with me and you go have your kicks with someone who won't feel them after you've gone!!

JILL I'm not so sure you can't hurt him. Maybe more than anybody. *(Crosses above table.)* I think you deserve all the credit you can get for turning out a pretty marvelous guy — but bringing up a son — even a blind one — isn't a lifetime occupation. *(*MRS. BAKER *turns* U., *away from* JILL.*)* Now the more you help him, the more you hurt him. It was Linda Fletcher — not you — *(*MRS. BAKER *turns and looks at* JILL *slowly.)* who gave him the thing he needed most — confidence in himself. *(Crossing away* L.*)* You're always dwelling on the negative — always what he needs, never what he wants . . . always what he can't do, never what he can. *(Crosses* D. *end of sofa.)* What about his music? Have you ever heard the song he wrote? I'll bet you didn't even know he could write songs! *(Crosses above table.)* You're probably dead right about me. I'm not the ideal girl for Don, but I know one thing

— neither are you!! And if I'm going to tell anyone to go home, it'll be you, Mrs. Baker. YOU go
home!! *(Turns and exits into her apartment, closing door behind her.* MRS. BAKER *watches her go.)*

Romeo and Juliet
by William Shakespeare

---

*Romeo and Juliet have been married secretly by
Friar Lawrence. Nurse has been busy making arrangements for Romeo to be with his new bride.
Juliet is eagerly awaiting Nurse's report of when
Romeo will arrive. In the following scene, Nurse
must reveal a painful truth to Juliet — Romeo has
killed Tybalt and has been banished from Verona.*

JULIET   O, here comes my nurse,
  And she brings news; and every tongue that
    speaks
  But Romeo's name speaks heavenly eloquence.
  *(*NURSE *enters with cords.)*

JULIET   Now, nurse what news? What hast thou
    there? the cords
  That Romeo bid thee fetch?

NURSE   *(Throwing them down)* Ay, ay, the cords.

JULIET   Ay me! what news? why dost thou wring thy
    hands?

NURSE   Ay, well-a-day! he's dead, he's dead, he's
    dead.
  We are undone, lady, we are undone!
  Alack the day! he's gone, he's kill'd, he's dead!

JULIET   Can heaven be so envious?

NURSE   Romeo can,
  Though heaven cannot: O Romeo, Romeo!
  Who ever would have thought it? Romeo!

JULIET   What devil art thou, that dost torment me
    thus?
  This torture should be roar'd in dismal hell.
  Hath Romeo slain himself? say thou but 'I,'
  And that bare vowel 'I' shall poison more
  Than the death-darting eye of cockatrice:
  I am not I, if there be such am I;
  Or those eyes shut, that make thee answer 'I.'
  If he be slain, say 'I'; or if not, no:
  Brief sounds determine of my weal or woe.

NURSE   I saw the wound, I saw it with mine
    eyes, —
  God save the mark! — here on his manly breast:
  A piteous corse, a bloody piteous corse;
  Pale, pale as ashes, all bedaub'd in blood,
  All in gore-blood: I swounded at the sight.

JULIET   O, break, my heart! poor bankrupt, break at
    once!
  To prison, eyes, ne'er look on liberty!
  Vile earth, to earth resign; end motion here;
  And thou and Romeo press one heavy bier!

NURSE   O Tybalt! Tybalt, the best friend I had!
  O courteous Tybalt! honest gentleman!
  That ever I should live to see thee dead!

JULIET   What storm is this that blows so contrary?
  Is Romeo slaughter'd, and is Tybalt dead?
  My dear-loved cousin, and my dearer lord?
  Then, dreadful trumpet, sound the general
    doom!
  For who is living, if those two are gone?

NURSE   Tybalt is gone, and Romeo banished;
  Romeo that kill'd him, he is banished.

JULIET   O God! did Romeo's hand shed Tybalt's
    blood?

NURSE   It did, it did; alas the day, it did!

JULIET   O serpent heart, hid with a flowering face!
  Did ever dragon keep so fair a cave?

Beautiful tyrant! fiend angelical!
Dove-feather'd raven! wolvish-ravening lamb!
Despised substance of divinest show!
Just opposite to what thou justly seem'st,
A damned saint, an honourable villain!
O nature, what hadst thou to do in hell,
When thou didst bower the spirit of a fiend
In mortal paradise of such sweet flesh?
Was ever book containing such vile matter
So fairly bound? O, that deceit should dwell
In such a gorgeous palace!

NURSE   There's no trust,
No faith, no honesty in men; all perjured,
All forsworn, all naught, all dissemblers.
Ah, where's my man? give me some aqua vitae:
These griefs, these woes, these sorrows make me
old.
Shame come to Romeo!

JULIET   Blister'd be thy tongue
For such a wish! he was not born to shame:
Upon his brow shame is ashamed to sit;
For 'tis a throne where honour may be crown'd
Sole monarch of the universal earth.
O, what a beast was I to chide at him!

NURSE   Will you speak well of him that kill'd your
cousin?

JULIET   Shall I speak ill of him that is my husband?
Ah, poor my lord, what tongue shall smooth thy
name,
When I, thy three-hours wife, have mangled it?
But, wherefore, villain, didst thou kill my cousin?
That villain cousin would have kill'd my
husband:
Back, foolish tears, back to your native spring;
Your tributary drops belong to woe,
Which you, mistaking, offer up to joy.
My husband lives, that Tybalt would have slain;
And Tybalt's dead, that would have slain my
husband:
All this is comfort; wherefore weep I then?
Some word there was, worser than Tybalt's death,

That murder'd me: I would forget it fain;
But, O, it presses to my memory,
Like damned guilty deeds to sinners' minds:
'Tybalt is dead, and Romeo — banished;'
That 'banished,' that one word 'banished'
Hath slain ten thousand Tybalts. Tybalt's death
Was woe enough, if it had ended there:
Or, if sour woe delights in fellowship
And needly will be rank'd with other griefs,
Why follow'd not, when she said 'Tybalt's dead,'
Thy father, or thy mother, nay, or both,
Which modern lamentation might have moved?
But with a rearward following Tybalt's death,
'Romeo is banished,' to speak that word,
If father, mother, Tybalt, Romeo, Juliet,
All slain, all dead. 'Romeo is banished!'
There is no end, no limit, measure, bound,
In that word's death; not words can that woe
sound.
Where is my father, and my mother, nurse?

NURSE   Weeping and wailing over Tybalt's corse:
Will you go to them? I will bring you thither.

JULIET   Wash they his wounds with tears: mine
shall be spent
When theirs are dry, for Romeo's banishment.
Take up those cords: poor ropes, you are
beguiled,
Both you and I; for Romeo is exiled:
He made you for a highway to my bed;
But I, a maid, die maiden-widowed.
Come, cords, come, nurse: I'll to my wedding-
bed;
And death, not Romeo, take my maidenhead!

NURSE   Hie to your chamber: I'll find Romeo
To comfort you: I wot well where he is.
Hark ye, your Romeo will be here at night:
I'll to him; he is hid at Lawrence' cell.

JULIET   O, find him! give this ring to my true knight,
And bid him come to take his last farewell.

The Miracle Worker
by William Gibson

Annie Sullivan has been hired by the Keller family to teach their deaf and blind daughter, Helen. In this scene Kate Keller, Helen's mother, finds Annie signing with Helen.

KATE   *(Presently.)* What are you saying to her?

ANNIE   *(Glancing up, she is a bit embarrassed, and rises from the spelling, to find her company manners.)* Oh, I was just making conversation. Saying it was a sewing card.

KATE   But does that — *(She imitates with her fingers.)* — mean that to her?

ANNIE   No. No, she won't know what spelling is till she knows what a word is.

KATE   Yet you keep spelling to her. Why?

ANNIE   *(Cheerily.)* I like to hear myself talk!

KATE   The Captain says it's like spelling to the fence post.

ANNIE   *(A pause.)* Does he, now?

KATE   Is it?

ANNIE   No, it's how I watch you talk to Mildred.

KATE   Mildred.

ANNIE   Any baby. Gibberish, grown-up gibberish, baby-talk gibberish, do they understand one word of it to start? Somehow they begin to. If they hear it, I'm letting Helen hear it.

KATE   Other children are not — impaired.

ANNIE   Ho, there's nothing impaired in that head, it works like a mousetrap!

KATE   *(Smiles.)* But after a child hears how many words, Miss Annie, a million?

ANNIE   I guess no mother's ever minded enough to count.

Brighton Beach Memoirs
by Neil Simon

It is 1937. Kate (40ish) and Blanche (38) are sisters. Blanche is a widow. She and her two daughters live with Kate and her family. They have had an argument, and Blanche has decided to move.

KATE   Is she alright?

BLANCHE   Yes.

KATE   She's not angry anymore?

BLANCHE   No, Kate. No one's angry anymore. I just explained everything to Nora. The girls will help you with all the housework while I'm gone. Laurie's strong enough to do her share. I've kept her being a baby long enough.

KATE   They've never been any trouble to me, those girls. Never.

BLANCHE   I'll try to take them on the weekends if I can ... It's late. We could both use a good night's sleep. *(She starts out of the room.)*

KATE   Blanche! ... Don't go! (BLANCHE *stops.*) I feel badly enough for what I said. Don't make me feel any worse.

BLANCHE   Everything you said to me tonight was true, Kate. I wish to God you said it years ago.

KATE   What would I do without you? Who else do I have to talk to all day? What friends do I have in this neighborhood? Even the Murphys across the street are leaving.

BLANCHE   You and I never had any troubles before tonight, Kate. . . . It's the girls I'm thinking of now. We have to be together. The three of us. It's what they want as much as I do.

KATE   Alright. I'm not saying you shouldn't have it. But you're not going to find a job overnight. Apartments are expensive. While you're looking, why do you have to live with strangers in Manhatten Beach?

BLANCHE   Louise isn't a stranger. She's a good friend.

KATE   To me good friends are strangers. But sisters are sisters.

BLANCHE   I'm afraid of becoming comfortable here. I don't get out now, when will I ever do it?

KATE   The door is open. Go whenever you want. When you got the job, when you find the apartment, I'll help you move. I can look with you. I know how to bargain with these landlords.

BLANCHE   *(Smiles)* You wouldn't mind doing that?

KATE   They see a woman all alone, they take advantage of you . . . I'll find out what they're asking for the Murphy place. It couldn't be expensive, she never cleaned it.

BLANCHE   How independent can I become if I live right across the street from you?

KATE   Far enough away for you to close your own door, and close enough for me not to feel so lonely. (BLANCHE *looks at her with great warmth, crosses to* KATE *and embraces her. They hold on dearly.)*

BLANCHE   If I lived on the moon, you would still be close to me, Kate.

KATE   I'll tell Jack. He wouldn't go to sleep until I promised to come up with some good news.

BLANCHE   I suddenly feel so hungry.

KATE   Of course. You haven't had dinner. Come on. I'll fix you some scrambled eggs.

BLANCHE   I'll make them. I'm an independent woman now.

KATE   With your eyes, you'll never get the eggs in the pan.

You Can't Take It with You
by Moss Hart and George S. Kaufman

Mr. Henderson of the Internal Revenue Service calls on Grandpa Vanderhof, who has never filed an income tax return.

HENDERSON   *(Pulling a sheaf of papers from his pocket)* Now, Mr. Vanderhof, *(A quick look toward hall)* we've written you several letters about this, but have not had any reply.

GRANDPA   Oh, that's what those letters were.

ESSIE   *(Sitting on couch* R.*)* I told you they were from the government.

HENDERSON   According to our records, Mr. Vanderhof, you have never paid an income tax.

GRANDPA   That's right.

HENDERSON   Why not?

GRANDPA   I don't believe in it.

HENDERSON   Well — you own property, don't you?

GRANDPA   Yes, sir.

HENDERSON   And you receive a yearly income from it?

GRANDPA   I do.

HENDERSON   Of — *(He consults his records.)* — between three and four thousand dollars.

GRANDPA   About that.

HENDERSON   You've been receiving it for years.

GRANDPA   I have. 1901, if you want the exact date.

HENDERSON   Well, the Government is only concerned from 1914 on. That's when the income tax started. *(Pause)*

GRANDPA   Well?

HENDERSON   Well — it seems, Mr. Vanderhof, that you owe the Government twenty-four years' back income tax. Now, Mr. Vanderhof, you know there's quite a penalty for not filing an income tax return.

GRANDPA   Look, Mr. Henderson, let me ask you something.

HENDERSON   Well?

GRANDPA   Suppose I pay you this money — mind you, I don't say I'm going to pay it — but just for the sake of argument — what's the Government going to do with it?

HENDERSON   How do you mean?

GRANDPA   Well, what do I get for my money? If I go to Macy's and buy something, there it *is* — I see it. What's the Government give me?

HENDERSON   Why, the Government gives you everything. It protects you.

GRANDPA   What from?

HENDERSON   Well — invasion. Foreigners that might come over here and take everything you've got.

GRANDPA   Oh, I don't think they're going to do that.

HENDERSON   If you didn't pay an income tax, they would. How do you think the Government keeps up the Army and Navy? All those battleships . . .

GRANDPA   Last time we used battleships was in the Spanish-American War, and what did we get out of it? Cuba — and we gave that back. I wouldn't mind paying if it were something sensible.

HENDERSON   Sensible? Well, what about Congress, and the Supreme Court, and the President? We've got to pay *them*, don't we?

GRANDPA   Not with my money — no, sir.

HENDERSON   *(Furious. Rises, picks up papers)* Now wait a minute! I'm not here to argue with you. *(Crossing* L.*)* All I know is that you haven't paid an income tax and you've got to pay it!

GRANDPA   They've got to show me.

HENDERSON   *(Yelling)* We *don't* have to show you! I just told you! All those buildings down in Washington, and Interstate Commerce, and the Constitution!

GRANDPA   The Constitution was paid for a long time ago. And Interstate Commerce — what *is* Interstate Commerce, anyhow?

HENDERSON   *(Business of a look at* GRANDPA. *With murderous calm, crosses and places his hands on table)* There are forty-eight states — see? And if there weren't Interstate Commerce, nothing could go from one state to another. See?

GRANDMA   Why not? They got fences?

HENDERSON   *(To* GRANDPA*)* No, they haven't got fences. They've got *laws! (Crossing up to arch* L.*)* My . . . , I never came across anything like *this* before!

GRANDPA   Well, I might pay about seventy-five dollars, but that's all it's worth.

HENDERSON   You'll pay every cent of it, like everybody else! And let me tell you something else! You'll go to jail if you don't pay, do you hear that? That's the law, and if you think you're bigger than the law, you've got another thing coming. You're no better than anybody else, and the sooner you get that through your head, the better . . . you'll

hear from the United States Government, that's all I can say . . . *(The music has stopped. He is backing out of the room.)*

GRANDPA   *(Quietly)* Look out for those snakes.

*(*HENDERSON, *jumping, off* L.*)*

No Time for Sergeants
by Ira Levin and Mac Hyman

Will Stockdale is a private in the United States Army. His blundering and naive behavior have disrupted Army routine, so his sergeant has sent Will to the base psychiatrist hoping that the doctor will recommend that Will be transferred. In the following scene, Will responds to the doctor's questioning in an innocent, but sensible, manner.

*(*PSYCHIATRIST, *a major, signs and stamps a paper before him, then takes form from* WILL, *seated next to desk.* PSYCHIATRIST *looks at form, looks at* WILL. *A moment of silence)*

WILL   I never have no dreams at all.

PSYCHIATRIST   *(A pause. He looks carefully at* WILL, *looks at form.)* Where you from, Stockdale?

WILL   Georgia.

PSYCHIATRIST   That's . . . not much of a state, is it?

WILL   Well . . . I don't live all over the state. I just live in this one little place in it.

PSYCHIATRIST   That's where "Tobacco Road" is, Georgia.

WILL   Not around my section. *(Pause)* Maybe you're from a different part than me?

PSYCHIATRIST   I've never been there. What's more I don't think I would ever *want* to go there. What's your reaction to that?

WILL   Well, I don't know.

PSYCHIATRIST   I think I would sooner live in the rottenest pigsty in Alabama or Tennessee than in the fanciest mansion in all of Georgia. What about that?

WILL   Well, sir, I think where you want to live is your business.

PSYCHIATRIST   (*Pause, staring*) You don't mind if someone says something bad about Georgia?

WILL   I ain't heared nobody say nothin' bad about Georgia.

PSYCHIATRIST   What do you think I've been saying?

WILL   Well, to tell you the truth, I ain't been able to get too much sense out of it. Don't you know?

PSYCHIATRIST   Watch your step, young man. (*Pause*) We psychiatrists call this attitude of yours "resistance."

WILL   You do?

PSYCHIATRIST   You sense that this interview is a threat to your security. You feel yourself in danger.

WILL   Well, kind of I do. If'n I don't get classified Sergeant King won't give me the wrist watch. (PSYCHIATRIST *stares at* WILL *uncomprehendingly.*) He *won't!* He said I only gets it if I'm classified inside a week.

PSYCHIATRIST   (*Turns forlornly to papers on desk. A bit subdued*) You get along all right with your mother?

WILL   No, sir, I can't hardly say that I do —

PSYCHIATRIST   (*Cutting in*) She's very strict? Always hovering over you?

WILL   No, sir, just the opposite —

PSYCHIATRIST   She's never there.

WILL   That's right.

PSYCHIATRIST   You resent this neglect, don't you?

WILL   No, I don't resent nothin'.

PSYCHIATRIST   (*Leaning forward paternally*) There's nothing to be ashamed of, son. It's a common situation. Does she ever beat you?

WILL   No!

PSYCHIATRIST   (*Silkily*) So defensive. It's not easy to talk about your mother, is it.

WILL   No, sir. She died when I was borned.

PSYCHIATRIST   (*A long, sick pause*) You . . . could have told me that sooner . . .

WILL   (*Looks hang-dog.* PSYCHIATRIST *returns to papers.* WILL *glances up at him.*) Do you hate *your* Mama? (PSYCHIATRIST'S *head snaps up, glaring.*) I figgered as how you said it was so common . . .

PSYCHIATRIST   I do not hate my mother.

WILL   I should hope not! (*Pause*) What, does she beat you or somethin'?

PSYCHIATRIST   (*Glares again, drums his fingers briefly on table. Steeling himself, more to self than* WILL) This is a transference. You're taking all your stored up antagonisms and loosing them in my direction. Transference. It happens every day. . . .

WILL   (*Excited*) It does? To the Infantry?

PSYCHIATRIST *(Aghast)* The Infantry?

WILL You give Ben a transfer, I wish you'd give me one too. I'd sure love to go along with him.

PSYCHIATRIST Stop! *(The pause is a long one this time. Finally* PSYCHIATRIST *points at papers.)* There are a few more topics we have to cover. We will not talk about transfers, we will not talk about my mother. We will only talk about what *I* want to talk about, do you understand?

WILL Yes, sir.

PSYCHIATRIST Now then — your father. *(Quickly)* Living?

WILL Yes, sir.

PSYCHIATRIST Do you get along with him okay?

WILL Yes, sir.

PSYCHIATRIST Does he ever beat you?

WILL You bet!

PSYCHIATRIST Hard?

WILL And how! Boy, there ain't nobody can beat like my Pa can!

PSYCHIATRIST *(Beaming)* So *this* is where the antagonism comes from! *(Pause)* You hate your father, don't you?

WILL No . . . I got an uncle I hate! Every time he comes out to the house he's always wantin' to rassle with the mule, and the mule gets all wore out, and *he* gets all wore out . . . Well, I don't really *hate* him; I just ain't exactly partial to him.

PSYCHIATRIST *(Pause)* Did I ask you about your uncle?

WILL I thought you wanted to talk about hatin' people.

PSYCHIATRIST *(Glares, drums his fingers, retreats to form. Barely audible)* Now — girls. How do you like girls?

WILL What girls is that, sir?

PSYCHIATRIST Just girls. Just any girls.

WILL Well, I don't like just any girls. There's one old girl back home that ain't got hair no longer than a hounddog's and she's always —

PSYCHIATRIST No! Look, when I say girls I don't mean any one specific girl. I mean girls in general; women, sex! Didn't that father of yours ever sit down and have a talk with you?

WILL Sure he did.

PSYCHIATRIST Well?

WILL Well what?

PSYCHIATRIST What did he say?

WILL *(With a snicker)* Well, there was this one about these two travelin' salesmen that their car breaks down in the middle of this terrible storm —

PSYCHIATRIST Stop!

WILL — so they stop at this farmhouse where the farmer has fourteen daughters who was —

PSYCHIATRIST *Stop!*

WILL You heared it already?

PSYCHIATRIST *(Writing furiously on form)* No, I did not hear it already . . .

WILL Well, what did you stop me for? It's a real knee-slapper. You see, the fourteen daughters is all studyin' to be trombone players and —

PSYCHIATRIST *(Shoving form at* WILL*)* Here. Go. Good-by. You're through. You're normal. Good-by. Go. Go.

WILL *(Takes the form and stands, a bit confused by it all)* Sir, if girls is what you want to talk about, you ought to come down to the barracks some night. The younger fellows there is always tellin' spicy stories and all like that.

The Teahouse of the August Moon
by John Patrick

The setting of the play is Okinawa, where United States Armed Forces were based during World War II. Captain Fisby's main responsibilities are to teach the Tobiki villagers the principles of democracy and to help them learn to be more independent. In the following scene, Captain Fisby is packing for the trip to the village of Tobiki. He dislikes his new assignment and is irritable. Sakini, the local interpreter, is a shrewd rascal who knows how to take the best advantage of Captain Fisby and the United States Army.

(The jeep is piled with Fisby's belongings. Perched high on top of this pyramid sits a very old and very wrinkled NATIVE WOMAN. SAKINI *pays no attention to her as he goes around the jeep test-kicking the tires. And the* OLD WOMAN *sits disinterested and aloof from what goes on below her.)*

FISBY   Hey, wait a minute! What's she doing up there? *(He points to her. The* OLD WOMAN *sits with her hands folded serenely, looking straight ahead.)*

SAKINI   She nice old lady hear we go to Tobiki Village. She think she go along to visit grandson.

FISBY   Oh, she does. Well, you explain to her that I'm very sorry but she'll have to take a bus.

SAKINI   No buses to Tobiki. People very poor — can only travel on generosity.

FISBY   I'm sorry, but it's against regulations.

SAKINI   She not fall off, boss. She tied on.

FISBY   Well, untie her and get her down. She'll just have to find some other way to visit her grandson.

SAKINI   Her grandson mayor of Tobiki Village. You make him lose face if you kick old grandmother off jeep.

FISBY   She's the mayor's grandmother?

SAKINI   Oh yes, boss.

FISBY   Well, since she's already tied on, I guess we can take her. *(He looks at the bundles.)* Are all those mine?

SAKINI   Oh, no. Most of bundles belong to old lady. She thinks she visit three or four months so she bring own bed and cooking pots.

FISBY   Well, tell her to yell if she sees any low branches coming. *(He starts to get in.)* Let's get started.

SAKINI   Oh, can't go yet, boss.

FISBY   Why not?

SAKINI   Old lady's daughter not here.

FISBY   *(Glances at watch)* We can't wait for a lot of good-byes, Sakini!

SAKINI   *(Looking behind* FISBY*)* Oh, she come now — right on dot you bet.

(CAPTAIN FISBY *turns to witness a squat young* NA-TIVE WOMAN *who comes on pushing a wheelbar-row loaded with bundles. She stops long enough to bow low to* FISBY — *then begins to tie bundles onto the jeep.)*

FISBY Sakini, can't the old lady leave some of that stuff behind?

SAKINI Not her things, boss. Belong to daughter.

FISBY Wait a minute. Is the daughter planning on going with us, too?

SAKINI Old lady very old. Who take care of her on trip?

FISBY Well, I — *(The* DAUGHTER *takes the wheel-barrow and hurries off.)* Hey — you come back! Sakini — tell her to come back. We can't carry any more bundles.

SAKINI *(Calmly)* Oh, she not go to get bundles, boss. She go to get children.

FISBY Come here, Sakini. Now look — this sort of thing is always happening to me and I have to put a stop to it some place. This time I'm deter-mined to succeed. It's not that I don't *want* to take them. But you can see for yourself, there's *no room left for kids!*

SAKINI But daughter not go without children and old lady not go without daughter. And if old lady not go, mayor of Tobiki be mad at you. *(Turns to see the* DAUGHTER *hurry back with three children in tow. They all politely bow to* FISBY. *Their mother then piles them on the hood of the jeep.)*

FISBY For Pete's sake, Sakini, how does she expect me to see how to drive!

SAKINI Old lady got very good eyesight. She sit on top and tell us when to turn. *(At this point one of the* CHILDREN *climbs off the hood and points off-stage.)*

Whose Life Is It Anyway?
by Brian Clark

Ken Harrison has been totally paralyzed from the neck down as the result of an automobile accident. He is a sculptor and is devastated by the thought that he will never be able to work again. In the fol-lowing scene, Ken has asked a lawyer, Mr. Hill, to argue on his behalf for release from the hospital.

KEN Could you come away from the door? Look, do you work for yourself? I mean, you don't work for an insurance company or something, do you? . . .

HILL No. I'm in practice as a solicitor, but I . . .

KEN Then there's no reason why you couldn't rep-resent me generally . . . apart from this compen-sation thing . . .

HILL Certainly, if there's anything I can do . . .

KEN There is.

HILL Yes?

KEN . . . Get me out of here.

HILL . . . I don't understand, Mr. Harrison.

KEN It's quite simple. I can't exist outside the hos-pital, so they've got to keep me here if they want to keep me alive and they seem intent on doing that. I've decided that I don't want to stay in the hospital any longer.

HILL But surely they wouldn't keep you here longer than necessary?

KEN I'm almost completely paralyzed and I always will be. I shall never be discharged by the hos-pital. I have coolly and calmly thought it out and

I have decided that I would rather not go on. I therefore want to be discharged to die.

HILL   And you want me to represent you?

KEN   Yes. Tough.

HILL   . . . And what is the hospital's attitude?

KEN   They don't know about it yet. Even tougher.

HILL   This is an enormous step . . .

KEN   Mr. Hill, with all respect, I know that our hospitals are wonderful. I know that many people have succeeded in making good lives with appalling handicaps. I'm happy for them and respect and admire them. But each man must make his own decision. And mine is to die quietly and with as much dignity as I can muster and I need your help.

HILL   Do you realize what you're asking me to do?

KEN   I realize. I'm not asking that you make any decision about my life and death, merely that you represent me and my views to the hospital.

HILL   . . . Yes, well, the first thing is to see the Doctor. What is his name?

KEN   Dr. Emerson.

HILL   I'll try and see him now and come back to you.

KEN   Then you'll represent me? . . .

HILL   Mr. Harrison, I'll let you know my decision after I've seen Dr. Emerson.

KEN   All right, but you'll come back to tell me yourself, even if he convinces you he's right?

HILL   Yes, I'll come back.

Dial M for Murder
by Frederick Knott

Tony, an ex-tennis pro, married Margot for her money. He solicits the help of Swann, a past classmate from college, to murder Margot. However, things go wrong and Margot kills Swann with a pair of scissors in an attempt to defend herself. Margot is convicted of Swann's murder and sentenced to death. In the following scene, Max, a friend of Margot and a mystery writer, comes up with a plan to save Margot's life. What he must do is convince Tony to go along with the plan.

MAX   Tony, I take it you'd do anything — to save her life?

TONY   *(Surprised)* Of course.

MAX   Even if it meant going to prison for several years?

TONY   *(After a pause)* I'd do absolutely anything.

MAX   I think you can — I'm certain. *(Slowly)* If you tell the police *exactly* the right story.

TONY   The right story?

MAX   Listen, Tony. I've been working this out for weeks. Just in case it came to this. It may be her only chance.

TONY   Let's have it.

MAX   You'll have to tell the police that you hired Swann to murder her. *(Long pause.* TONY *can only stare at* MAX.*)*

TONY   *(Rises)* What are you talking about?

MAX   It's all right, Tony — I've been writing this stuff for years. I know what I'm doing. Margot was convicted because no one would believe her story. Prosecution made out that she was telling one lie after another — and the jury believed him. But what did his case amount to? Only three things. My letter — her stocking, and the idea that, because no key was found on Swann, she must have let him in herself. *(Pause)* Now Swann is dead. You can tell any story you like about him. You can say that you did know him. That you'd met him, and worked out the whole thing together. Now the blackmail. Swann was only suspected of blackmail for two reasons. Because my letter was found in his pocket and because you saw him the day Margot's bag was stolen.

TONY   Well?

MAX   You can now tell the police that you never saw him at Victoria. That the whole thing was an invention of yours to try and connect him with the letter.

TONY   But the letter was found in his pocket.

MAX   Because you put it there.

TONY   *(Pause)* You mean I should pretend that I stole her handbag?

MAX   Sure. You could have.

TONY   But why?

MAX   Because you wanted to find out who was writing to her. When you read my letter you were so mad you decided to teach her a lesson.

TONY   But I can't say that I wrote those blackmail notes.

MAX   Why not? No one can prove that you didn't. *(TONY thinks it over.)*

TONY   All right. I stole her bag and blackmailed her. What else?

MAX   You kept my letter and planted it on Swann after he'd been killed.

TONY   Wait a minute — when could I have done that?

MAX   After you got back from the party and before the police arrived. At the same time you took one of Margot's stockings from the mending basket and substituted it for whatever Swann had used. *(TONY thinks it over.)*

TONY   Max, I know you're trying to help but — can you imagine anyone believing this?

MAX   You've got to make them believe it.

TONY   But I wouldn't know what to say. You'd have to come with me.

MAX   No. I couldn't do that. They know the sort of stuff I write. If they suspected we'd talked this out they wouldn't even listen. They mustn't know I've been here.

TONY   Max! It's ridiculous. Why should I want anyone to murder Margot?

MAX   Oh, one of the stock motives. Had Margot made a will? *(Pause)*

TONY   I — yes, I believe she had.

MAX   Are you the main beneficiary?

TONY   I suppose so.

MAX   Well, there you are.

TONY   But thousands of husbands and wives leave money to each other, without murdering each other. The police wouldn't believe a word of it! They'd take it for exactly what it is. A husband desperately trying to save his wife.

MAX   Well, it's worth a try. They can't hang you for planning a murder that never came off. Face it. The most you'd get would be a few years in prison.

TONY   Thanks very much.

MAX   . . . And you'd have saved her life. That doesn't seem too big a price.

> **J. B.**
> by Archibald MacLeish

Two circus vendors, Zuss and Nickles, prepare to play the roles of God and Satan in the opening scene of this verse play based on the Book of Job. In the following scene, Nickles discovers the role he is about to play.

NICKLES   *(Hurt)*. If you would rather someone else . . .

MR. ZUSS   Did what?

NICKLES   Played Job.

MR. ZUSS   What's Job to do with it?

NICKLES   Job was honest. He saw God —
Saw him by that icy moonlight,
By that cold disclosing eye
That stares the color out and strews
Our lives . . . with light . . . for nothing.

MR. ZUSS   Job!
I never thought of you for Job.

NICKLES   You never thought of me for Job!
What did you think of?

MR. ZUSS   Oh, there's always
Someone playing Job.

NICKLES   There must be
Thousands! What's that got to do with it?
Thousands — not with camels either:
Millions and millions of mankind
Burned, crushed, broken, mutilated,
Slaughtered, and for what? For thinking!
For walking round the world in the wrong
Skin, the wrong-shaped noses, eyelids:
Sleeping the wrong night wrong city —
London, Dresden, Hiroshima.
There never could have been so many
Suffered more for less. But where do
I come in?
(MR. ZUSS shuffles uncomfortably.)
Play the dung heap?

MR. ZUSS   All we have to do is start.
Job will join us. Job will be there.

NICKLES   I know. I know. I know. I've seen him.
Job is everywhere we go,
His children dead, his work for nothing,
Counting his losses, scraping his boils,
Discussing himself with his friends and physicians,
Questioning everything — the times, the stars,
His own soul, God's providence.
What do *I* do?

MR. ZUSS   What do *you* do?

NICKLES   What do I do? You play God.

MR. ZUSS   I play God. I think I mentioned it.

NICKLES   You play God and I play . . .
(He lets himself down heavily on the rung of the ladder.)
Ah!

MR. ZUSS   *(Embarrassed)* I had assumed you knew.
(NICKLES looks up at him, looks away.)

MR. ZUSS   You see,
I think of you and me as . . . opposites.

NICKLES   Nice of you.

MR. ZUSS   I didn't mean to be nasty.

NICKLES   Your opposite! A demanding role!

MR. ZUSS   I know.

NICKLES   But worthy of me? Worthy of me!

Come Blow Your Horn
by Neil Simon

Alan has been living the life of the "man about town." His activities are interrupted by the arrival of his younger brother, Buddy. (Buddy Baker enters with a valise in hand. Buddy is the complete opposite of Alan. Reserved, unsure, shy.)

BUDDY   Hello, Alan — Are you busy? *(Enters apartment and looks around — crosses D. R. to L. of D. R. C. chair)*

ALAN   *(Offstage)* No, no. Come in, kid. *(He re-enters.)* What's up? *(Crossing to L. of* BUDDY, ALAN *sees suitcase.)* What's in there?

BUDDY   Pajamas, toothbrush, the works. *(Puts suitcase down next to chair)*

ALAN   You're kidding?

BUDDY   Nope.

ALAN   You mean you left? *(*BUDDY *nods.)* Permanently?

BUDDY   I took eight pairs of socks. For me that's permanently.

ALAN   I don't believe it. You can't tell me you actually ran away from home.

BUDDY   Well, I cheated a little. I took a taxi. *(Takes off coat and places it on suitcase)*

ALAN   You're serious. You mean my baby brother finally broke out of prison?

BUDDY   We planned it long enough, didn't we?

ALAN   Yes, but every time I brought it up you said you weren't ready. Why didn't you say something to me?

BUDDY   When? You weren't at work since Thursday.

ALAN   Hey, did Dad say anything? About my being gone?

BUDDY   Not at the office. But at home he's been slamming doors. The chandelier in the foyer fell down. Where were you?

ALAN   *(Crosses L. above coffee table)* Vermont.

BUDDY   Skiing?

ALAN   Only during the day. *(Sits on sofa and lights cigarette)*

BUDDY   *(Crosses L. to sofa; one knee on arm)* I don't know how you do it. If I'm at work one minute after nine, he docks my pay — and I get less to eat at home.

ALAN   Because he expects it from you. From me he says he expects nothing, so that's what I give him.

BUDDY   You're better off. At least you're not treated like a baby. You can talk with him.

ALAN   We don't talk. We have heart to heart threatening —

BUDDY   That's better than the subtle treatment I get. Last night I came home at three o'clock in the morning. He didn't approve. What do you think he did? *(ALAN shakes his head.)* As I passed his door, he crowed like a rooster. Cockle-doodle-doo.

ALAN   You're kidding? What'd you say?

BUDDY   Nothing. I wanted to cluck back like a chicken but I didn't have the nerve.

ALAN   Oh, he's beautiful.

BUDDY   And then yesterday was my birthday. *(Sits on sofa R. of* ALAN*)* Twenty-one years old.

ALAN   Oh, that's right. Gee, I'm sorry I wasn't there, Buddy. Happy birthday, kid. *(He shakes BUDDY'S hand warmly.)*

BUDDY   Thanks.

ALAN   I even forgot to get you a present.

BUDDY   I got one. A beaut. From Mom and Dad.

ALAN   What was it?

BUDDY   A surprise party. Mom, Dad and the Klingers.

ALAN   Who are the Klingers?

BUDDY   Oh, the Klingers are that lovely couple the folks met last summer at Lake Mahopac.

ALAN   Why? They're not your friends.

BUDDY   Think. Why would they have the Klingers there to meet me?

ALAN   They've got a daughter.

BUDDY   Oh, have they got a daughter.

ALAN   You mean they brought her with them?

BUDDY   In a crate.

ALAN   Let me guess. Naomi?

BUDDY   Close, Renee.

ALAN   Not much on looks but brilliant.

BUDDY   A genius. An I.Q. of 170. Same as her weight.

ALAN   And of course they had her dressed for the kill. They figured what she couldn't do, maybe Bergdorf could.

BUDDY   Nothing could help. So I spent the night of my twenty-first birthday watching a girl devour an entire bowl of cashew nuts.

ALAN   Oh, I'm sorry, kid.

BUDDY   *(Rises, crosses R. C. to chair.)* It's been getting worse and worse. He looks in my closets, my drawers. He listens to my phone calls. I don't know what it is I've done, Alan, but I swear he's going to turn me in. *(Sits L. arm of chair)*

ALAN   *(Puts out cigarette)* Well, it's simple enough. He's afraid you're going to follow in my footsteps.

BUDDY   I did. I thought it over all day and realized I had to leave. Well — here I am.

The Importance of Being Earnest
by Oscar Wilde

Jack Worthing has been living the dual life of the respected John Worthing in town and his ne'er-do-well brother Ernest in the country. In this scene, his friend Algernon confronts him with a cigarette case bearing a curious inscription.

ALGERNON   My dear fellow, Gwendolen is my first cousin; and before I allow you to marry her, you will have to clear up the whole question of Cecily.

JACK   Cecily! What on earth do you mean? What do you mean, Algy, by Cecily! I don't know anyone by the name of Cecily.

ALGERNON   *(To butler)* Bring me that cigarette case Mr. Worthing left in the smoking-room the last time he dined here.

JACK   Do you mean to say you have had my cigarette case all this time? I wish to goodness you had let me know. I have been writing frantic letters to Scotland Yard about it. I was very nearly offering a large reward.

ALGERNON   Well, I wish you would offer one. I happen to be more than usually hard up.

JACK   There is no good offering a large reward now that the thing is found.

ALGERNON   *(Taking case from butler)* I think it rather mean of you, Ernest, I must say. However, it makes no matter, for now that I look at the inscription inside, I find that the thing isn't yours after all.

JACK   Of course it is mine. You have seen me with it a hundred times, and you have no right whatsoever to read what is written inside. It is a very ungentlemanly thing to read a private cigarette case.

ALGERNON   Yes, but this is not your cigarette case. This cigarette case is a present from someone of the name of Cecily, and you said you didn't know anyone of that name.

JACK   Well, if you want to know, Cecily happens to be my aunt.

ALGERNON   Your aunt!

JACK   Yes. Charming old lady she is, too. Lives at Tunbridge Wells. Just give it back to me, Algy.

ALGERNON   But why does she call herself little Cecily if she is your aunt and lives at Tunbridge Wells? "From *little* Cecily with her fondest love."

JACK   My dear fellow, what on earth is there in *that*? Some aunts are tall, some aunts are not tall. That is a matter that surely an aunt may be allowed to decide for herself. *You* seem to think that every aunt should be exactly like your aunt! That is absurd! For Heaven's sake give me back my cigarette case.

ALGERNON   Yes. But why does your aunt call you her uncle? "From little Cecily, with her fondest love to her dear Uncle Jack." There is no objection, I admit, to an aunt being a small aunt, but why an aunt, no matter what her size may be, should call her own nephew her uncle, I can't quite make out. Besides, your name isn't Jack at all; it is Ernest.

JACK   It isn't Ernest; it's Jack.

ALGERNON   You have always told me it was Ernest. I have introduced you to everyone as Ernest. You answer to the name of Ernest. You look as if your name was Ernest. You are the most earnest-looking person I ever saw in my life. It is perfectly absurd your saying that your name isn't Ernest. It's on your cards. Here is one of them. "Mr. Ernest Worthing, B.4, The Albany." I'll keep this as a proof that your name is Ernest if ever you attempt to deny it to me, or to Gwendolen or to anyone else.

JACK   Well, my name is Ernest in town and Jack in the country, and the cigarette case was given me in the country.

ALGERNON   Yes, but that does not account for the fact that your small Aunt Cecily, who lives in Tunbridge Wells, calls you her dear uncle. Come, old boy, you had much better have the thing out at once.

JACK   My dear Algy, you talk exactly as if you were a dentist. It is very vulgar to talk like a dentist when one isn't a dentist. It produces a false impression.

ALGERNON   Well, that is exactly what dentists always do. Now, go on! Tell me the whole thing.

JACK   — Well, old Mr. Thomas Cardew, who adopted me when I was a little boy, made me, in his will, guardian to his granddaughter, Miss Cecily Cardew. Cecily, who addresses me as her uncle, from motives of respect that you could not possibly appreciate, lives at my place in the country, under the charge of her admirable governess, Miss Prism.

ALGERNON   Where is that place in the country, by the way?

JACK   That is nothing to you, dear boy. You are not going to be invited. I may tell you candidly that the place is not in Shropshire.

ALGERNON   I suspected that, my dear fellow. — Now go on. Why are you Ernest in town and Jack in the country?

JACK   My dear Algy, when one is placed in the position of guardian, one has to adopt a very high moral tone on all subjects. It's one's duty to do so. And as a high moral tone can hardly be said to conduce very much to either one's health or happiness, in order to get up to town I have always pretended to have a younger brother of the name of Ernest, who lives at the Albany, and gets into the most dreadful scrapes. There, my dear Algy, is the whole truth, pure and simple.

ALGERNON   The truth is rarely pure and never simple.

Brighton Beach Memoirs
by Neil Simon

The time is 1937. Stan (18) and Eugene (almost 15) are brothers. Stan has decided to leave home because he has lost his week's pay — $17.00 — in a poker game.

EUGENE   Aunt Blanche is leaving.

STAN   *(sits up)* For where?

EUGENE   *(sits on his own bed)* To stay with some woman in Manhattan Beach. She and Mom just had a big fight. She's going to send for Laurie and Nora when she gets a job.

STAN   What did they fight about?

EUGENE   I couldn't hear it all. I think Mom sorta blames Aunt Blanche for Pop having to work so hard.

STAN   *(hits pillow with his fist)* Oh, God! . . . Did Mom say anything about me? About how I lost my salary?

EUGENE   You told her? Why did you tell her? I came up with twelve terrific lies for you. *(STANLEY opens his drawer, puts on a sweater).*

STAN   How much money do you have?

EUGENE   Me? I don't have any money.

STAN   *(puts another sweater over the first one)* The hell you don't. You've got money in your cigar box. How much do you have?

EUGENE   I got a dollar twelve. It's my life's savings.

STAN   Let me have it. I'll pay it back, don't worry. *(He puts a jacket over sweaters, then gets a fedora from closet and puts it on.* EUGENE *takes cigar box from under his bed, opens it.)*

EUGENE   What are you putting on all those things for?

STAN   In case I have to sleep out tonight. I'm leaving, Gene. I don't know where I'm going yet, but I'll write to you when I get there.

EUGENE   You're leaving home?

STAN   When I'm gone, you tell Aunt Blanche what happened to my salary. Then she'll know why Mom was so angry. Tell her please not to leave because it was all my fault, not Mom's. Will you do that? *(He takes coins out of cigar box.)*

EUGENE   I have eight cents worth of stamps, if you want that too.

STAN   Thanks. *(picks up a small medal)* What's this?

EUGENE   The medal you won for the hundred yard dash two years ago.

STAN   From the Police Athletic League. I didn't know you still had this.

EUGENE   You gave it to me. You can have it back if you want it.

STAN   It's not worth anything.

EUGENE   It is to me.

STAN   Sure. You can keep it.

EUGENE   Thanks . . . Where will you go?

STAN   I don't know. I've been thinking about join... the army. Pop says we'll be at war in a couple of years anyway. I could be a sergeant or something by the time it starts.

EUGENE   If it lasts long enough, I could join too. Maybe we can get in the same outfit.

STAN   You don't go in the army unless they come and get you. You go to college. You hear me? Promise me you'll go to college.

EUGENE   I'll probably have to stay home and work, if you leave. We'll need the money.

STAN   I'll send home my paycheck every month. A sergeant in the army makes real good dough . . . Well, I better get going.

EUGENE   *(on the verge of tears)* What do you have to leave for?

STAN   Don't start crying. They'll hear you.

EUGENE   They'll get over it. They won't stay mad at you forever. I was mad at you and *I* got over it.

STAN   Because of me, the whole family is breaking up. Do you want Nora to end up like one of those cheap boardwalk girls?

EUGENE   I don't care. I'm not in love with Nora anymore.

STAN   Well, you *should* care. She's your cousin. Don't turn out to be like me.

EUGENE   I don't see what's so bad about you.

STAN   *(looks at him)* . . . Take care of yourself, Eug. *(They embrace. He opens the door, looks around, then back to* EUGENE*).* If you ever write a story about me, call me Hank. I always liked the name Hank. *(He goes, closing the door behind him.)*

Blithe Spirit
by Noel Coward

Charles Condomine is a writer. As part of his research on a book, he invited Madame Arcati, a spiritualist, to hold a séance. As a result of the séance, the spirit of Charles's first wife, Elvira, has been brought back. Because Charles is the only one who can see her, he is constantly trying to convince his present wife, Ruth, that he is not crazy or being deliberately rude to her. In the following scene, Elvira has once again popped up, and Charles once again tries to cope with two wives — one a spirit and one very, very real.

(ELVIRA comes in from the garden, carrying an armful of roses. The roses are as grey as the rest of her.)

ELVIRA   You've absolutely ruined that border by the sundial — it looks like a mixed salad.

CHARLES   Oh my God!

RUTH   What's the matter now?

CHARLES   She's here again!

RUTH   What do you mean? Who's here again?

CHARLES   Elvira.

RUTH   Pull yourself together and don't be absurd.

ELVIRA   It's all those nasturtiums — they're so vulgar.

CHARLES   I like nasturtiums.

RUTH   You like what?

ELVIRA   *(Putting her grey roses into a vase)* They're all right in moderation but in a mass like that they look beastly.

CHARLES   Help me, Ruth — you've got to help me —

RUTH   *(Rises)* What did you mean about nasturtiums?

CHARLES   Never mind about that now — I tell you she's here again.

ELVIRA   You have been having a nice scene, haven't you? I could hear you right down the garden.

CHARLES   Please mind your own business.

RUTH   If your behaving like a lunatic isn't my business nothing is.

ELVIRA   I expect it was about me, wasn't it? I know I ought to feel sorry but I'm not — I'm delighted.

CHARLES   How can you be so inconsiderate?

RUTH   *(Shrilly)* Inconsiderate — I like that, I must say —

CHARLES   Ruth — darling — please . . .

RUTH   I've done everything I can to help — I've controlled myself admirably — I should like to say here and now that I don't believe a word about your damned hallucinations — you're up to something. Charles — there's been a certain furtiveness in your manner for weeks — Why don't you be honest and tell me what it is?

CHARLES   You're wrong — you're dead wrong — I haven't been in the least furtive — I —

RUTH   You're trying to upset me — for some obscure reason you're trying to goad me into doing something that I might regret — I won't stand for it any more — You're making me utterly miserable — *(She bursts into tears and collapses on sofa.)*

CHARLES   Ruth — please — *(Sits on sofa beside* RUTH*)*

RUTH   Don't come near me —

ELVIRA   Let her have a nice cry — it'll do her good.

CHARLES   You're utterly heartless!

RUTH   Heartless!

CHARLES   *(Wildly)* I was not talking to you — I was talking to Elvira.

RUTH   Go on talking to her then, talk to her until you're blue in the face but don't talk to me —

CHARLES   Help me, Elvira —

ELVIRA   How?

CHARLES   Make her see you or something.

ELVIRA   I'm afraid I couldn't manage that — it's technically the most difficult business — frightfully complicated, you know it takes years of study —

CHARLES   You are here, aren't you? You're not an illusion?

ELVIRA   I may be an illusion but I'm most definitely here.

CHARLES   How did you get here?

ELVIRA   I told you last night — I don't exactly know —

CHARLES   Well, you must make me a promise that in future you only come and talk to me when I'm alone —

ELVIRA   *(Pouting)* How unkind you are — making me feel so unwanted. I've never been treated so rudely —

CHARLES   I don't mean to be rude but you must see —

ELVIRA   It's all your own fault for having married a woman who is incapable of seeing beyond the nose on her face — if she had a grain of real sympathy or real affection for you she'd believe what you tell her.

CHARLES   How could you expect anybody to believe this?

ELVIRA   You'd be surprised how gullible people are — we often laugh about it on the other side.

*(*RUTH, *who has stopped crying and been staring at* CHARLES *in horror, suddenly gets up)*

RUTH   *(Gently)* Charles —

CHARLES   *(Surprised at her tone)* Yes, dear —

RUTH   I'm awfully sorry I was cross —

CHARLES   But, my dear —

RUTH   I understand everything now, I do really —

CHARLES   You do?

RUTH   *(Patting his arm reassuringly)* Of course I do.

ELVIRA   Look out — she's up to something —

CHARLES   Will you please be quiet?

RUTH   Of course, darling — we'll all be quiet, won't we? We'll be as quiet as little mice.

Liliom
by Ferenc Molnar

Liliom is the drama on which the musical Carousel *is based. Liliom is a merry-go-round barker at an amusement park. Julie and Marie are both maids. They are still young, innocent teenagers. Liliom has just been fired by the carousel owner, Mrs. Muskat, after he insulted her. In the following scene, Marie and Julie are waiting for Liliom's return because he has offered to take them out.*

MARIE   Are you sorry for him?

JULIE   Are you?

MARIE   Yes, a little. Why are you looking after him in that funny way?

JULIE   *(Sits down)* Nothing — except I'm sorry he lost his job.

MARIE   *(With a touch of pride)* It was on our account he lost his job. Because he's fallen in love with you.

JULIE   He hasn't at all.

MARIE   *(Confidently)* Oh, yes! he is in love with you. *(Hesitantly, romantically)* There is someone in love with me, too.

JULIE   There is? Who?

MARIE   I — I never mentioned it before, because you hadn't a lover of your own — but now you have — and I'm free to speak. *(Very grandiloquently)* My heart has found its mate.

JULIE   You're only making it up.

MARIE   No, it's true — my heart's true love ——

JULIE   Who! Who is he?

MARIE   A soldier.

JULIE   What kind of a soldier?

MARIE   I don't know. Just a soldier. Are there different kinds?

JULIE   Many different kinds. There are hussars, artillerymen, engineers, infantry — that's the kind that walks — and ——

MARIE   How can you tell which is which?

JULIE   By their uniforms.

MARIE   *(After trying to puzzle it out)* The conductors on the streetcars — are they soldiers?

JULIE   Certainly not. They're conductors.

MARIE   Well, they have uniforms.

JULIE   But they don't carry swords or guns.

MARIE   Oh! *(Thinks it over again; then)* Well, policemen — are they?

JULIE   *(With a touch of exasperation)* Are they what?

MARIE   Soldiers.

JULIE   Certainly not. They're just policemen.

MARIE   *(Triumphantly)* But they have uniforms — and they carry weapons, too.

JULIE   You're just as dumb as you can be. You don't go by their uniforms.

MARIE   But you said ——

JULIE   No, I didn't. A letter-carrier wears a uniform, too, but that doesn't make him a soldier.

MARIE   But if he carried a gun or a sword, would he be ——

JULIE   No, he'd still be a letter-carrier. You can't go by guns or swords, either.

MARIE   Well, if you don't go by the uniforms or the weapons, what *do* you go by?

JULIE   By —— *(Tries to put it into words; fails; then breaks off suddenly)* Oh, you'll get to know when you've lived in the city long enough. You're nothing but a country girl. When you've lived in the city a year, like I have, you'll know all about it.

MARIE   *(Half angrily)* Well, how *do* you know when *you* see a real soldier?

JULIE   By one thing.

MARIE   What?

JULIE   One thing —— *(She pauses.* MARIE *starts to cry.)* Oh, what are you crying about?

MARIE   Because you're making fun of me. . . . You're a city girl, and I'm just fresh from the country . . . and how am I expected to know a soldier when I see one? . . . You, you ought to tell me, instead of making fun of me ——

JULIE   All right. Listen then, cry baby. There's only one way to tell a soldier: by his salute! That's the only way.

The Diary of Anne Frank
by Frances Goodrich and Albert Hackett

The Franks and the Van Daans, two Jewish families, are in hiding in a secret attic above a warehouse in Amsterdam during World War II. They are hoping to escape Nazi capture and the inevitable imprisonment in a German concentration camp. In the following scene, both families celebrate Hanukkah, also called the "Feast of Lights," a Jewish ceremony.

ANNE   *(Singing)* "Oh, Hanukkah! Oh, Hanukkah! The sweet celebration."

MR. FRANK   *(Rising)* I think we should first blow out the candle; then we'll have something for tomorrow night.

MARGOT   But, Father, you're supposed to let it burn itself out.

MR. FRANK   I'm sure that God understands shortages. *(Before blowing it out)* "Praised be Thou, oh Lord our God, who hath sustained us and permitted us to celebrate this joyous festival."

(He is about to blow out the candle when suddenly there is a crash of something falling below. They all freeze in horror, motionless. For a few seconds there is complete silence. MR. FRANK *slips off his shoes. The others noiselessly follow his example.* MR. FRANK *turns out a light near him. He motions to* PETER *to turn off the center lamp.* PETER *tries to reach it, realizes he cannot and gets up on a chair. Just as he is touching the lamp he loses his balance. The chair goes out from under him. He falls. The iron lamp shade crashes to the floor. There is a sound of feet below, running down the stairs.)*

MR. VAN DAAN   *(Under his breath)* God Almighty! *(The only light left comes from the Hanukkah candle.* DUSSEL *comes from his room.* MR. FRANK *creeps over to the stairwell and stands listening. The dog is heard barking excitedly.)* Do you hear anything?

MR. FRANK   *(In a whisper)* No. I think they've gone.

MRS. VAN DAAN   It's the Green Police. They've found us.

MR. FRANK   If they had, they wouldn't have left. They'd be up here by now.

MRS. VAN DAAN   I know it's the Green Police.

They've gone to get help. That's all. They'll be back!

MR. VAN DAAN   Or it may have been the Gestapo, looking for papers.

MR. FRANK   *(Interrupting)* Or a thief, looking for money.

MRS. VAN DAAN   We've got to do something — Quick! Quick! Before they come back.

MR. VAN DAAN   There isn't anything to do. Just wait. *(MR. FRANK holds up his hand for them to be quiet. He is listening intently. There is complete silence as they all strain to hear any sound from below. Suddenly ANNE begins to sway. With a low cry she falls to the floor in a faint. MRS. FRANK goes to her quickly, sitting beside her on the floor and taking her in her arms.)*

MRS. FRANK   Get some water, please! Get some water! *(MARGOT starts for the sink.)*

MR. VAN DAAN   *(Grabbing MARGOT)* No! No! No one's going to run water!

MR. FRANK   If they've found us, they've found us. Get the water. *(MARGOT starts again for the sink. MR. FRANK, getting a flashlight)* I'm going down. *(MARGOT rushes to him, clinging to him. ANNE struggles to consciousness.)*

MARGOT   No, Father, no! There may be someone there waiting. It may be a trap!

MR. FRANK   This is Saturday. There is no way for us to know what has happened until Miep or Mr. Kraler comes on Monday morning. We cannot live with this uncertainty.

MARGOT   Don't go, Father!

MRS. FRANK   Hush, darling, hush. *(MR. FRANK slips quietly out, down the steps and out through the door below.)* Margot! Stay close to me. *(MARGOT goes to her mother.)*

MR. VAN DAAN   Slush! Slush! *(MRS. FRANK whispers to MARGOT to get the water. MARGOT goes for it.)*

MRS. VAN DAAN   Putti, where's our money? Get our money. I hear you can buy the Green Police off, so much a head. Go upstairs quick! Get the money!

MR. VAN DAAN   Keep still!

MRS. VAN DAAN   *(Kneeling before him, pleading)* Do you want to be dragged off to a concentration camp? Are you going to stand there and wait for them to come up and get you? Do something, I tell you!

MR. VAN DAAN   *(Pushing her aside)* Will you keep still? *(He goes over to the stairwell to listen. PETER goes to his mother, helping her up onto the sofa. There is a second of silence, then ANNE can stand it no longer.)*

ANNE   Someone go after Father! Make Father come back!

PETER   *(Starting for the door)* I'll go.

MR. VAN DAAN   Haven't you done enough? *(He pushes PETER roughly away. In his anger against his father PETER grabs a chair as if to hit him with it, then puts it down, burying his face in his hands. MRS. FRANK begins to pray softly.)*

ANNE   Please, please, Mr. Van Daan. Get Father.

MR. VAN DAAN   Quiet! Quiet! *(ANNE is shocked into silence. MRS. FRANK pulls her closer, holding her protectively in her arms.)*

MRS. FRANK   *(Softly, praying)* "I lift up mine eyes unto the mountains, from whence cometh my help. My help cometh from the Lord who made heaven and earth. He will not suffer thy foot to be moved. He that keepeth thee will not slumber . . . " *(She stops as she hears someone coming. They all watch the door tensely. MR. FRANK comes quietly in.* ANNE *rushes to him, holding him tight.)*

MR. FRANK   It was a thief. The noise must have scared him away.

MRS. VAN DAAN   Thank God.

A Raisin in the Sun
by Lorraine Hansberry

Walter is struggling to retain his self-esteem in the face of family and financial obstacles. He lives in a small apartment with his wife, Ruth, their son, Travis, his sister, Beneatha, and his mother. The close quarters and the money problems create tensions and conflicts among the family members. In the following scene, Walter is trying to assert himself by attacking his sister's ambition to be a doctor.

BENEATHA   *(Her face is in her hands — she is still fighting the urge to go back to bed. Sits R. of table.)* Really — would you suggest dawn? Where's the paper?

WALTER   *(Senselessly.)* How is school coming?

BENEATHA   *(In the same spirit.)* Lovely. Lovely. And you know, Biology is the greatest. *(Looking up at him.)* I dissected something that looked just like you yesterday.

WALTER   I just wondered if you've made up your mind and everything.

BENEATHA   *(Gaining in sharpness and impatience prematurely.)* And what did I answer yesterday morning — and the day before that — ?

RUTH   *(Crossing back to ironing board R., like someone disinterested and old.)* Don't be so nasty, Bennie.

BENEATHA   *(Still to her brother.)* And the day before that and the day before that!

WALTER   *(Defensively.)* I'm interested in you. Something wrong with that? Ain't many girls who decide —

WALTER and BENEATHA   *(In unison.)* — "to be a doctor." *(Silence.)*

WALTER   Have we figured out yet just exactly how much medical school is going to cost?

BENEATHA   *(Rises, exits to bathroom. Knocks on the door.)* Come on out of there, please! *(Re-enters.)*

RUTH   Walter Lee, why don't you leave that girl alone and get out of here to work?

WALTER   *(Looking at his sister intently.)* You know the check is coming tomorrow.

BENEATHA   *(Turning on him with a sharpness all her own. She crosses D.R. and sprawls on sofa.)* That money belongs to Mama, Walter, and it's for her to decide how she wants to use it. I don't care if she wants to buy a house or a rocket ship or just nail it up somewhere and look at it — it's hers. Not ours — hers.

WALTER   *(Bitterly.)* Now ain't that fine! You just got your mother's interests at heart, ain't you, girl? You such a nice girl — but if Mama got that money she can always take a few thousand and help you through school too — can't she?

BENEATHA   I have never asked anyone around here to do anything for me!

WALTER   No! But the line between asking and just accepting when the time comes is big and wide — ain't it!

BENEATHA   *(With fury.)* What do you want from me, Brother — that I quit school or just drop dead, which!

WALTER   (*Rises, crosses down back of sofa.*) I don't want nothing but for you to stop acting holy around here — me and Ruth done made some sacrifices for you — why can't you do something for the family?

RUTH   Walter, don't be dragging me in it.

WALTER   You are in it — Don't you get up and go work in somebody's kitchen for the last three years to help put clothes on her back —?

(BENEATHA *rises, crosses, sits armchair D.R.*)

RUTH   Oh, Walter — that's not fair —

WALTER   It ain't that nobody expects you to get on your knees and say thank you, Brother; thank you, Ruth; thank you, Mama — and thank you, Travis, for wearing the same pair of shoes for two semesters —

BENEATHA   (*In front of sofa, falls on her knees.*) WELL — I DO — ALL RIGHT? THANK EVERY-BODY — AND FORGIVE ME FOR EVER WANTING TO BE ANYTHING AT ALL — FORGIVE ME, FOR-GIVE ME! (*She rises, crosses D.R. to armchair.*)

RUTH   Please stop it! Your Mama'll hear you.

WALTER   (*Crosses U.C. to kitchen table. Ties shoes at chair R. of table.*) — Who . . . told you you had to be a doctor? If you so crazy 'bout messing around with sick people — then go be a nurse like other women — or just get married and be quiet —

BENEATHA   (*Crossing toward L. end of sofa.*) Well — you finally got it said — It took you three years but you finally got it said. Walter, give up; leave me alone — it's Mama's money.

WALTER   HE WAS MY FATHER, TOO!

BENEATHA   So what? He was mine, too — and Travis' grandfather — BUT the insurance money belongs to Mama. Picking on me is not going to make her give it to you to invest in any liquor stores — (*Sits armchair D.R. Under her breath.*) And I for one say, God bless Mama for that!

(On BENEATHA's *line* RUTH *crosses U.L. to closet.*)

WALTER   (*To* RUTH.) See — did you hear? — Did you hear!

RUTH   (*Crosses D.C. to* WALTER *with* WALTER'S *jacket from the closet.*) Honey, please go to work.

WALTER   (*Back of sofa, crosses U.C. to door.*) No-body in this house is ever going to understand me.

BENEATHA   Because you're a nut.

WALTER   (*Stops, turns D.C.*) Who's a nut?

BENEATHA   You — you are a nut. Thee is mad, boy.

WALTER   (*Looking at his wife and sister from the door, very sadly.*) The world's most backward race of people and that's a fact. (*Exits C.*)

BENEATHA   (*Turning slowly in her chair.*) And then there are all those prophets who would lead us out of the wilderness — (*Rises, crosses U.C. to chair R. of kitchen table, sits.* WALTER *slams out of the house.*) Into the swamps!

RUTH   Bennie, why you always gotta be pickin' on your brother? Can't you be a little sweeter some-times?

(*Door opens.* WALTER *walks in.*)

WALTER   (*To* RUTH.) I need some money for carfare.

RUTH   (*Looks at him, then warms, teasing, but ten-derly.*) Fifty cents? (*She crosses D.L. front of ta-ble, gets her purse from handbag.*) Here, take a taxi.

Arsenic and Old Lace
by Joseph Kesselring

Mortimer has just discovered that his sweet old aunts have murdered several old gentlemen.

MORTIMER   TWELVE!

MARTHA   Yes, Abby thinks we ought to count the first one and that makes twelve. *(She goes back to sideboard.)*

MORTIMER   *(Placing a chair; then takes* MARTHA's *hand, leads her to chair and sets her in it.)* All right — now — who was the first one?

ABBY   *(Crossing from above table to* MORTIMER*)* Mr. Midgely. He was a Baptist.

MARTHA   Of course, I still think we can't claim full credit for him because he just died.

ABBY   Martha means without any help from us. You see, Mr. Midgely came here looking for a room —

MARTHA   It was right after you moved to New York.

ABBY   And it didn't seem right for that lovely room to be going to waste when there were so many people who needed it —

MARTHA   He was such a lonely old man. . . .

ABBY   All his kith and kin were dead and it left him so forlorn and unhappy —

MARTHA   We felt so sorry for him.

ABBY   And then when his heart attack came — and he sat dead in that chair *(Pointing to armchair)* looking so peaceful — remember, Martha — we

made up our minds then and there that if we could help other lonely old men to that same peace — we would!

MORTIMER   *(All ears)* He dropped dead right in that chair! How awful for you!

MARTHA   Oh, no, dear. Why, it was rather like old times. Your grandfather always used to have a cadaver or two around the house. You see, Teddy had been digging in Panama and he thought Mr. Midgely was a yellow fever victim.

ABBY   That meant he had to be buried immediately.

MARTHA   So we all took him down to Panama and put him in the lock. *(She rises, puts her arm around* ABBY.*)* Now that's why we told you not to worry about it because we know exactly what's to be done.

MORTIMER   And that's how all this started — that man walking in here and dropping dead.

ABBY   Of course, we realized we couldn't depend on that happening again. So —

MARTHA   *(Crosses to* MORTIMER*)* You remember those jars of poison that have been up on the shelves in Grandfather's laboratory all these years —?

ABBY   You know your Aunt Martha's knack for mixing things. You've eaten enough of her piccalilli.

MARTHA   Well, dear, for a gallon of elderberry wine I take one teaspoonful of arsenic, then add a half teaspoonful of strychnine and then just a pinch of cyanide.

MORTIMER   *(Appraisingly)* Should have quite a kick.

ABBY   Yes! As a matter of fact one of our gentlemen found time to say "How delicious!"

MARTHA   Well, I'll have to get things started in the kitchen.

ABBY   *(To* MORTIMER*)* I wish you could stay for dinner.

MARTHA   I'm trying out a new recipe.

MORTIMER   I couldn't eat a thing.

Impromptu
by Tad Mosel

The scene is a nondescript room, the walls of which are not very high. They are set at peculiar angles to one another. There is a distorted doorway rear center. The furniture consists of a sofa, a chair, and perhaps a small table. Beyond the entrance and surrounding the room there is nothing but blackness.

The stage is dark. Nothing is visible but the glow of Winifred's cigarette. There is a pause, and then the actors speak out of the darkness.

WINIFRED   Well, we're here. Somebody say something.

TONY   Is the curtain up?

WINIFRED   Yes.

TONY   But we can't see anything. It's like the end instead of the beginning. What's wrong?

ERNEST   That fool stage manager has forgotten to bring up the lights.

WINIFRED   Oh, no, Ernest, he didn't forget. There's something deliberate about this. I don't trust him.

LORA   You've got him wrong, Winifred. He was very nice. He wouldn't play tricks on us. Not him.

ERNEST   Just leave everything to me. I'll go out and talk to him.

TONY   But you can't!

ERNEST   Why not?

TONY   Don't you remember what he said? We're not to leave the stage until we have acted out the play.

ERNEST   He was just trying to be impressive. I've met his kind before. It's time he learned that actors are more important than stage managers.

TONY   He said it as if it were a law.

ERNEST   Well, I won't stand here in the dark. *(Shouting)* Lights! Hey, you, out there — lights! *(There is a pause.)*

LORA   Maybe we're not as important as you think, Ernest. Let's just be quiet and wait.

TONY   Is there an audience out there?

WINIFRED   Yes, I can hear them soughing.

ERNEST   You can hear them what?

WINIFRED   Soughing, dear. Breathing heavily, as in sleep.

TONY   I feel as if I'm asleep, too.

WINIFRED   If everybody's going to feel things, we won't get anywhere at all. *(Pause)*

TONY   Yes. Asleep and dreaming. I'm a child again. I can see myself being led into a room full of people. They laugh and tell me to dance. I don't know what to do. I can't dance. So I hop up and down on one foot. Up and down, up and down. Now they're applauding. I'm a great success. Why do I want to cry? *(There is a pause. The lights come on.)*

ERNEST   That's more like it!

LORA   I knew he'd take care of us! I knew it!

WINIFRED   The stage manager said, "Let there be light," and there was light.

TONY   But the lights won't stand still. They seem to be changing! It's worse than it was before.

WINIFRED   Why don't you go off in a corner and have that cry? *(TONY looks at her.)*

ERNEST   And look, Winifred, you were right. There is an audience!

WINIFRED   So there is!

LORA   Isn't it wonderful? Do you see them, Tony?

TONY   Yes, I see them.

ERNEST   They're waiting for us to begin.

TONY   Do they know what we're going to do? Has it been explained to them?

WINIFRED   I defy you to explain anything that is happening on this stage.

TONY   I was just asking a question.

LORA   Don't ask questions, Tony. You'll only make yourself unhappy. Ernest says they're waiting for us to begin. Well, let's begin!

ERNEST   Wait a minute, Lora. Tony may have a point there. I wonder if they do know what we're doing.

TONY   Maybe we ought to tell them.

WINIFRED   All right, then, tell them!

TONY   Me?

WINIFRED   Certainly. It's your bright idea.

ERNEST   I'm sure I could explain everything very lucidly.

WINIFRED   You probably could, Ernest. That's why I want him to do it.

TONY   I wouldn't know what to say.

WINIFRED   I know you wouldn't.

TONY   *(Naively, inquiringly)* Are you making fun of me, Winifred?

WINIFRED   Whatever gave you that idea? *(She laughs lightly.* TONY *looks at her a moment, then he steps down to the edge of the stage and addresses the audience.)*

TONY   Ladies and gentlemen, we are here to — they say every actor has a dream — a recurring dream — and he's on a stage and there's an audience, and — he doesn't know what the play is or what his lines are. That's the way it is with us. This afternoon. Maybe we are dreaming — maybe we're not really here —I don't know —

WINIFRED   You can stop right there! I know that I'm here, thank you. Irrevocably, unwillingly, disgustingly here.

ERNEST   *(With great tolerance)* You'd better let me do it, Tony. *(To the audience)* Ladies and gentlemen, an hour ago each of us received a message to report to this theater; there were jobs waiting for us. When we arrived, the stage manager told us we were to go on stage immediately, before an audience, and improvise a play — which we are about to do. *(To* TONY*)* You see how easy it is?

TONY   Yes, it's easy to say what happened. You didn't say what it means. Who are we? Why are we here? That's the important thing.

WINIFRED   That young man has rocks in his head.

LORA   Would it help if we told them our names, Tony?

ERNEST   An excellent suggestion, Lora. I was about to think of it myself. *(He turns to the audience.)*

WINIFRED   Here we go!

ERNEST   *(To the audience)* You have no programs, so you know nothing about us. My name is Ernest. I am returning to the stage after several successful seasons on the West Coast, where I scored personal successes in more than two-score films. Born of a theatrical family, I was reared in stage dressing rooms. At the age of five, I scored a personal success in —

TONY   Ernest, you're not explaining anything!

ERNEST   I'm telling them who I am!

TONY   But it's more than that!

LORA   Be quiet, Tony. This is very interesting. I love hearing about other people.

TONY   All right. I'll be quiet.

LORA   Go on, Ernest.

(ERNEST begins to speak.)

WINIFRED   *(Quickly)* Why don't you be quiet, too, Ernest?

ERNEST   I haven't finished.

WINNIFRED   Surely they know all about you — an actor of your standing. You don't want to bore them by telling them things they know, do you?

ERNEST   Well — no.

WINIFRED   Then sit down. *(He does so.)*

LORA   It's your turn, Winifred.

WINIFRED   *(Shrugs her shoulders, moves down to the edge of the stage, and addresses the audi-ence)* I'm Winifred. I have had rather a cloudy career as an actress. You may have seen me, but you won't remember. I usually play the leading lady's best friend. I don't like the theater because you can't trust it. This is an example of what I mean. Next. *(Indicating LORA)*

LORA   *(After thinking a moment)* My name used to be Loralee, but somebody said a long stage name is bad luck, so I shortened it to Lora. It hasn't helped me much, but I don't really mind. Perhaps I wasn't meant to be an actress. I think that's all. *(She steps back.)*

WINIFRED   Hold tight, everybody. *(With mock seriousness)* Your turn, Tony.

TONY   I have nothing to say.

LORA   But, Tony, you've got to tell them something about yourself.

TONY   Why? None of you did. It's all so unreal. *(To the audience)* Who are you? Why are you here? Did you come for escape, for enlightenment, for curiosity? Or were you, too, commanded?

ERNEST   We weren't any of us commanded!

TONY   Then what are we doing here? It's the only explanation! You're a celebrity — surely this is beneath you. Lora wasn't meant to be an actress. Winifred hates the stage.

WINIFRED   *(Cuttingly)* And you're afraid, aren't you?

TONY   Yes, I'm afraid! There — I've told them something about myself!

WINIFRED   If that's all you've got to say, sit down. You were amusing for a while, but no longer. Soul-searching is the lowest form of entertainment.

ERNEST   I don't see why you're afraid, Tony. You ask what we're doing here, and the answer is simple.

We are here to please the audience, and they are here to be pleased.

WINIFRED   Why can't you be like Ernest, Tony? He knows everything.

LORA   The stage manager's not going to like it if we don't do something soon.

ERNEST   Of course, Lora. *(To the audience)* I hope you will be patient with outbursts of this sort, ladies and gentlemen. Naturally, some of us are a little confused. But don't worry, we're going to begin our play as soon as we've made a few preparations. You see, the stage manager gave us instructions —

WINIFRED   He wrote upon the table the words of the Covenant —

ERNEST   Shut up, Winifred. *(To the audience)* And I think it only fair to let you know what they are. First of all, our play will not end until he is completely satisfied with our performance.

WINIFRED   That's a cheerful thing to tell them. *(To the audience)* He's one of those sour little men who never like anything.

LORA   You'd better stop talking that way about him, Winifred. He's right over there behind that wall; he can hear you. You might offend him.

WINIFRED   That's nothing compared to what he's done to me.

LORA   But he's so important, and — good. I think he's been very kind to me. I have great faith in him.

ERNEST   I thought you wanted to begin, Lora.

LORA   Oh — I'm sorry, Ernest.

ERNEST   *(To the audience)* Secondly, we are not permitted to leave the stage until the play has ended. And last of all, our play is to be an imitation of life.

TONY   No, that's wrong! (ERNEST *looks at him annoyed.)* Well, it is. He didn't say that.

LORA   Are you sure, Tony?

TONY   I listened very carefully. He didn't say it was to be an imitation of life. It's supposed to *be* life.

Saint Joan
by Bernard Shaw

According to legend, Joan of Arc was an illiterate girl who heard voices and led soldiers into battle. In Shaw's Saint Joan, Joan is portrayed as an independent, courageous visionary who wanted to lead a man's life. In the following monologue, Joan is addressing her inquisitors, who have just sentenced her to life imprisonment instead of to burning at the stake.

JOAN   *(Rising in consternation and terrible anger)* Perpetual imprisonment! Am I not then to be set free?

. . .

Give me that writing. *(She rushes to the table; snatches up the paper; and tears it into fragments)* Light your fire; do you think I dread it as much as the life of a rat in a hole? My voices were right.

. . .

Yes; they told me you were fools *(The word gives great offense.)*, and that I was not to listen to your fine words nor trust to your charity. You promised me my life; but you lied *(Indignant exclamations)* You think that life is nothing but not being stone dead. It is not the bread and water I fear: I can live on bread: when have I asked for more? It is not hardship to drink water if the water be clean. Bread has no sorrow for me, and water no affliction. But to shut me from the light of the sky and the sight of the fields and flowers; to chain my feet so that I can never again ride with the soldiers nor climb the hills; to make me breathe foul damp darkness, and keep from me everything that brings me back to the love of God when your wickedness and foolishness tempt me to hate Him; all this is worse than the furnace in the Bible that was heated seven times. I could do without my warhorse; I could drag about in a skirt; I could let the banners and the trumpets and the knights and soldiers pass me and leave me behind as they leave the other women, if only I could still hear the wind in the trees, the larks in the sunshine, the young lambs crying through the healthy frost, and the blessed blessed church bells that send my angel voices floating to me in the wind. But without these things I cannot live; and by your wanting to take them away from me, or from any human creature, I know that your counsel is of the devil, and that mine is of God.

. . .

His ways are not your ways. He wills that I go through the fire to His bosom; for I am His child, and you are not fit that I should live among you. That is my last word to you.

The Belle of Amherst
by William Luce

The Belle of Amherst is a one-character play about Emily Dickinson. In this opening monologue of the play, Emily sets the stage for the evening's entertainment. She gives glimpses of her past and recalls her independent nature.

EMILY   *(She enters, carrying the teapot. She calls back over her shoulder.)* Yes, Vinnie, I have the tea, dear!

(She places the tea on the tea cart, then looks up wide-eyed at the AUDIENCE. *Slowly she picks up a plate with slices of dark cake on it, walks shyly downstage, and extends it to the* AUDIENCE*)*

This is my introduction. Black cake. My own special recipe.

Forgive me if I'm frightened. I never see strangers and hardly know what I say. My sister, Lavinia — she's younger than I — she says I tend to wander back and forth in time. So you must bear with me. I was born December tenth, eighteen thirty, which makes me — *fifty-three?*

Welcome to Amherst. My name is Emily Elizabeth Dickinson. Elizabeth is for my Aunt Elisabeth Currier. She's father's sister. Oh, how the trees stand up straight when they hear Aunt Libbie's little boots come thumping into Amherst! She's the only male relative on the female side.

Dear Aunt Libbie.

But I don't use my middle name anymore — since I became a *poet*.

Professor Higginson, the literary critic, doesn't think my poems are — no matter. I've had seven poems published — anonymously, to be sure. So you see why I prefer to introduce myself to you as a poet.

Here in Amherst, I'm known as Squire Edward Dickinson's half-cracked daughter. Well, I am! The neighbors can't figure me out. I don't cross my father's ground to any house or town. I haven't left the house for years.

The soul selects her own society —
then — shuts the door. Why
should I socialize with village gossips?

(EMILY turns to the window, still holding the cake.)

There goes one of them now — Henrietta Sweetser — everyone knows Henny. She'd even intimidate the anti-Christ. Look at her! She's strolling by the house, trying to catch a glimpse of me. Would *you* like that?

So I give them something to talk about. I dress in white all year around, even in winter. "Bridal white," Henny calls it.

(She mimics back-fence gossips.)

"Dear, dear! Dresses in bridal white, she does, every day of the blessed year. Year in, year out. Disappointed in love as a girl, so I hear. Poor creature. All so very sad. And her sister Lavinia, a spinster too. Didn't you know? Oh, yes. Stayed unmarried just to be at home and take care of Miss Emily. Two old maids in that big house. What a lonely life, to shut yourself away from good people like us."

Indeed!

You should see them come to the door, bearing gifts, craning their necks, trying to see over Vinnie's shoulder. But I'm too fast for them. I've already run upstairs two steps at a time. And I hide there until they leave. You can imagine what they make of that!

One old lady came to the door the other day to get a peek inside. I surprised her by answering the door myself. She stammered something about looking for a house to buy.

(Mischievously)

To spare the expense of moving, I directed her to the cemetery.

A Raisin in the Sun
by Lorraine Hansberry

Mama's son, Walter, has accused her of not trusting his judgment in handling money. In the following monologue, Mama admits that she has misjudged her son and will hand over to him the insurance money given to her on her husband's death.

MAMA *(Crosses R. to* WALTER.*)* Listen to me now. I say I been wrong, son. That I been doing to you what the rest of the world been doing to you. *(She turns off radio.)* Walter — *(She stops and he looks up slowly at her and she meets his eyes evenly.)* what you ain't never understood is that I ain't got nothing, don't own nothing, ain't really wanted nothing that wasn't for you. There ain't nothing as precious to me — there ain't nothing worth holding on to, money, dreams, nothing else — if it means — if it means it's going to destroy my boy. *(Crosses U.R.C. to buffet for her pocketbook and money. He watches her without speaking or moving.)* I paid the man thirty-five hundred dollars down on the house. That leaves sixty-five hundred dollars. Monday morning I want you to take this money and take three thousand dollars and put it in a savings account for Beneatha's medical schooling.

(WALTER rises, crosses U.C.)

The rest you put in a checking account — with your name on it. And from now on any penny that comes out of it or that go in it is for you to look after. For you to decide. *(Puts money on coffee table and drops her hands a little helplessly.)* It ain't much, but it's all I got in the world and I'm putting it in your hands. I'm telling you to be the head of this family from now on like you supposed to be.

A Member of the Wedding
by Carson McCullers

Frankie's brother is getting married and Frankie is having difficulty adjusting to the idea. In the following monologue, Frankie comes up with her solution to the problem of her brother's marriage and her fears of separation.

FRANKIE Don't bother me, John Henry. I'm thinking.

. . .

About the wedding. About my brother and the bride. Everything's been so sudden today. I never believed before about the fact that the earth turns at the rate of about a thousand miles a day. I didn't understand why it was that if you jumped up in the air you wouldn't land in Selma or Fairview or somewhere else instead of the same back yard. But now it seems to me I feel the world going around very fast. (FRANKIE *begins turning around in circles with arms outstretched . . .)* I feel it turning and it makes me dizzy. . . . *(Suddenly stopping her turning)* I just now thought of something.

. . .

I know where I'm going.

(There are sounds of children playing in the distance)

I tell you I know where I'm going. It's like I've known it all my life. Tomorrow I will tell everybody.

. . .

(Dreamily) After the wedding I'm going with them to Winter Hill. I'm going off with them after the wedding.

. . .

Just now I realized something. The trouble with me is that for a long time I have been just an "I" person. All other people can say "we." When Berenice says "we" she means her lodge and church and colored people. Soldiers can say "we" and mean the army. All people belong to a "we" except me.

. . .

Not to belong to a "we" makes you too lonesome. Until this afternoon I didn't have a "we," but now after seeing Janice and Jarvis I suddenly realize something.

. . .

I know that the bride and my brother are the "we" of me. So I'm going with them, and joining with the wedding. This coming Sunday when my brother and the bride leave this town, I'm going with the two of them to Winter Hill. And after that to whatever place that they will ever go. *(There is a pause.)* I love the two of them so much and we belong to be together. I love the two of them so much because they are the *we* of me.

Spoon River Anthology
adapted by Charles Aidman from
Edgar Lee Masters

Lucinda Matlock "rests" in the cemetery in Spoon River with fond memories and with no regrets for her long life of marriage, child rearing, and hard work.

LUCINDA MATLOCK I went to the dances at
    Chandlerville,
And played snap-out at Winchester.
One time we changed partners,
Driving home in the moonlight of middle June,
And then I found Davis.
We were married and lived together for seventy
    years,
Enjoying, working, raising the twelve children,
Eight of whom we lost
Ere I had reached the age of sixty.
I spun, I wove, I kept the house, I nursed the sick.
I made the garden, and for holiday
Rambled over the fields where sang the larks,
And by Spoon River gathering many a shell,
And many a flower and medicinal weed —
Shouting to the wooded hills, winging to the
    green valleys.
At ninety-six I had lived enough, that is all,
And passed to a sweet repose.
What is this I hear of sorrow and weariness,
Anger, discontent and drooping hopes?
Degenerate sons and daughters,
Life is too strong for you —
It takes life to love life.

Joan of Lorraine
by Maxwell Anderson

*Joan of Arc, the simple country girl who led the
French army against the English, has self-doubts
about her visions. Having yielded to the pressures
of the trial and the educated religious leaders, she
"confessed" that she could not prove the voices she
heard were from heaven. In this scene, she prays to
God, thinking she will live, but finds little happiness
in this thought.*
(In her cell, JOAN *is kneeling in prayer.)*

JOAN King of Heaven, the night is over. My jailors
    have worn themselves out with tormenting me,
    and have gone to sleep. And I should sleep — I
    could sleep safely now — but the bishop's ques-
tions come back to me over and over. What if I
were wrong? How do I know my visions were
good? I stare wide awake at the dawn in the window and I cannot find an answer.

    So many things they said were true. It is true
the king we crowned at Rheims is not wise nor
just nor honest. It is true that his realm is not well
governed. It is true that I am alone, that my
friends have forgotten me, both the king and the
nobles who fought beside me. There is no word
from them, no offer of ransom.

    And I am doubly alone, for I have denied my
visions, and they will come to me no more. I believe my visions to be good, but I do not know
how to defend them. When I am brought into a
court, and must prove what I believe, how can I
prove that they are good and not evil?

    Yes, and I ask myself whether I have been
honest always, for when I went among men, I
acted my part. It was not only that I wore boy's
clothes — I stood as my brother stood and spoke
heartily as he spoke, and put challenges in the
words he would have spoken. When I spoke with
my own voice, nobody listened, nobody heard
me, yet was it honest to assume ways that were
not my own? I know there's to be no answer.

    I can expect no answer now, after I have be-
trayed and denied my saints. They will not burn
me now because I admitted that I could not
prove my Voices good — and I submitted to the
church. And now, when I am to live, when I have
done what they say is right, I am more unhappy
than when they said I was wrong and must die.

The Effects of Gamma Rays on Man-in-the-Moon Marigolds
by Paul Zindel

*Beatrice Hunsdorfer, a nervous, single mother, is
calling her daughter Ruth's teacher, Mr. Goodman,
to question a science project he has assigned.
Beatrice is standing at the telephone, waiting for
her party to answer.*

BEATRICE Mr. Goodman please. *(Pause.)* How would I know if he's got a class? *(She finds a cigarette next to the hot plate.)* Hello, Mr. Goodman? Are you Mr. Goodman? Oh, I beg your pardon, Miss Torgersen. Yes, I'll wait. *(She lights her cigarette.)* Couldn't you find him, Miss Torgersen? *(Pause.)* Oh! Excuse me, Mr. Goodman, how are you? I'll bet you'll never guess who this is . . . It's Mrs. Hunsdorfer — remember the frozen foods? You know, Ruth tells me she's your new secretary and I certainly think that's a delight. *(She picks up the phone, crosses to* u. *of the kitchen table, puts the phone on the table, and sits.)* You were paying so much attention to Matilda that I'll bet Ruth just got jealous. She does things like that, you know. I hope she works hard for you, although I can't imagine what kind of work Ruth could be doing in that great big science office. She's a terrible snoop . . . *(Pause.)* The attendance? Isn't that charming. And the cut cards! Imagine. You trust her with . . . Why I didn't know she could type *at all* . . . imagine. *(Pause.)* Of course, too much work isn't good for anybody, either. No wonder she's failing everything. I mean, I never heard of a girl who failed absolutely everything regardless of what she was suffering from. I suppose I should say recovering from . . . *(Pause.)* Oh, I'll tell you why I'm calling. It's about those seeds you gave Matilda. She's had them in the house for a while now and they're starting to grow. Now she tells me they had been exposed to radioactivity and I hear such terrible things about radioactivity that I naturally associate radioactivity with sterility, and it positively horrifies me to have those seeds in my living room. Couldn't she just grow plain marigolds like everyone else? *(Pause.)* Oh . . . *(Pause.)* It does sound like an interesting project . . . *(Pause.)* No, I'm afraid that at this very moment I don't know what a *mutation* is. *(Pause.)* Mr. Goodman . . . Mr. Goodman! I don't want you to think I'm not interested but please spare me definitions over the phone. I'll get down to the library next week and pick me out some little book on science and then I'll know all about mutations . . . *(Pause.)*

No, you didn't insult me, but I just want you to know I'm not stupid . . . I just thought prevention was better than a tragedy, Mr. Goodman. I mean, Matilda has enough to worry about without sterility. *(She rises, picks up the phone, crosses* R *and returns the phone to its shelf.)* Well, I was just concerned, but you've put my poor mother's heart at ease. You know, really, our high schools need more exciting young men like you, I really mean that. Really, I do. Goodbye, Mr. Goodman. *(She hangs up the phone, and then turns front.)*

The Star-Spangled Girl
by Neil Simon

Sophie, an All-American young woman from the South, has moved into the same apartment building as Norman Cornell. She feels that Norman has become too attentive and decides she must put an end to it.

SOPHIE Mr. Cornell, Ah have tried to be neighborly, Ah have tried to be friendly and Ah have tried to be cordial . . . Ah don't know what it is that you're tryin' to be. That first night Ah was appreciative that you carried mah trunk up the stairs . . . The fact that it slipped and fell five flights and smashed to pieces was not your fault . . . Ah didn't even mind that personal message you painted on the stairs. Ah thought it was crazy, but sorta sweet. However, things have now gone too far . . . Ah cannot accept gifts from a man Ah hardly know . . . Especially canned goods. And Ah read your little note. Ah can guess the gist of it even though Ah don't speak Italian. This has got to stop, Mr. Cornell. Ah can do very well without you leavin' little chocolate-almond Hershey bars in mah mailbox — they melted yesterday, and now Ah got three gooey letters from home with nuts in 'em — and Ah can do without you sneakin' into mah room after Ah go to work and paintin' mah balcony without tellin' me about it. Ah stepped out there yesteday and mah slippers are still glued to the floor. And Ah can do without you tying big bottles of eau de cologne to mah cat's tail. The poor thing kept swishin' it yesterday and nearly beat herself to death . . . And most of all, Ah can certainly do without you watchin' me get on the bus every day through that high-powered telescope. You got me so nervous the other day Ah got on the wrong bus. In short, Mr. Cornell, and Ah don't want to have to say this again, *leave me ay-lone!*

I Remember Mama[1]
John Van Druten

Katrin, a writer in her early twenties, begins reminiscing about her childhood.

KATRIN   *(Reading)* "For as long as I could remember, the house on Streiner Street had been home.

Papa and Mama had both been born in Norway, but they came to San Francisco because Mama's sisters were here. All of us were born here. Nels, the oldest and the only boy — my sister Christine — and the littlest sister, Dagmar." *(She puts down her manuscript and looks out front.)* It's funny, but when I look back, I always see Nels and Christine and myself looking almost as we do today. I guess that's because the people you see all the time stay the same age in your head. Dagmar's different. She was always the baby — so I see her as a baby. Even Mama — it's funny, but I always see Mama as around forty. She couldn't *always* have been forty. *(She puts out her cigarette, picks up her manuscript, and starts to read again.)* "Besides us, there was our boarder, Mr. Hyde. Mr. Hyde was an Englishman who had once been an actor, and Mama was very impressed by his flowery talk and courtly manners. He used to read aloud to us in the evenings. But first and foremost, I remember Mama."

Cyrano de Bergerac
by Edmond Rostand
translated by Brian Hooker

Cyrano, a seventeenth-century poet, swordsman, and philosopher, is charming, witty, and bold. However, his huge nose often makes him the object of ridicule. In this speech, he sadly tells a friend that he knows no woman can ever love him.

CYRANO   My old friend — look at me,
    And tell me how much hope remains for me
    With this protuberance! Oh I have no more
    Illusions! Now and then — bah! I may grow
    Tender, walking alone in the blue cool
    Of evening, through some garden fresh with
      flowers
    After the benediction of the rain;
    My poor big devil of a nose inhales
    April . . . and so I follow with my eyes
    Where some boy, with a girl upon his arm,
    Passes a patch of silver . . . and I feel
    Somehow, I wish I had a woman too,
    Walking with little steps under the moon,
    And holding my arm so, and smiling. Then
    I dream — and I forget . . . And then I see
    The shadow of my profile on the wall!

Talley's Folly
by Lanford Wilson

It is July 4, 1944, in the early evening. Matt Friedman is outside the boathouse on the Talley place in Lebanon, Missouri. He has come to persuade Sally Talley to marry him. Matt's opening monologue ends as Sally calls from outside the boathouse.

A Victorian boathouse constructed of louvers, lattice in decorative panels, and a good deal of Gothic Revival gingerbread. The riverside is open to the audience. The interior and exterior walls have faded to a pale gray. The boathouse is covered by a heavy canopy of maple and surrounded by almost waist-high weeds and the slender, perfectly vertical limbs of a weeping willow. Lighting and sound should be very romantic: the sunset at the opening, later the moonlight, slant through gaps in the ceiling and walls reflecting the river in lambent ripples across the inside of the room.

The boathouse contains two boats, one turned upside down, buckets, boxes, no conventional seating. Overhead is a lattice-work attic in which is stored creels, bamboo poles, nets, seines, minnow buckets, traps, floats, etc., all long past use.

At opening: All this is seen in a blank white work light; the artificiality of the theatrical set quite apparent. The houselights are up.

MATT   *(Enters in front of the stage. MATT FRIEDMAN is forty-two, dark, and rather large. Warm and unhurried, he has a definite talent for mimicry. In his voice there is still a trace of a German-Jewish accent, of which he is probably unaware. He speaks to the audience.)* They tell me that we have ninety-seven minutes here tonight — without intermission. So if that means anything to anybody; if you think you'll need a drink of water or anything . . .

I'll just point out some of the facilities till everybody gets settled in. If everything goes well for me tonight, this should be a waltz, one-two-three, one-two-three; a no-holds-barred romantic story, and since I'm not a romantic type, I'm going to need the whole valentine here to help me: the woods, the willows, the vines, the moonlight, the band — there's a band that plays tonight, over in the park. The trees, the berries, the breeze, the sounds: water and crickets, frogs, dogs, the light, the bees, working all night.

Did you know that? Bees work — worker bees — work around the clock. Never stop. Collecting nectar, or pollen, whatever a bee collects. Of course their life expectancy is twenty days. Or, in a bee's case, twenty days and twenty nights.

Or possibly "expectancy" is wrong in the case of a bee. Who knows what a bee expects. But whatever time there is in a life is a lifetime, and I imagine after twenty days and twenty nights a bee is more or less ready to tuck it in.

(In a craggy, Western, "Old-Timer" voice) "I been flyin' now, young sprout, nigh-on to nineteen days an' nineteen nights."

(Imitating a young bee) "Really, Grandpa Worker Bee?"

(Old-Timer) "An' I'm 'bout ready to tuck it in."

(Slight pause. Reflectively) Work. Work is very much to the point. *(Showing the set)* We have everything to help me here. There's a rotating gismo in the footlights (do you believe footlights) because we needed the moon out there on the water. The water runs right through here, so you're all out in the river — sorry about that.

Now I know what you're thinking. You're saying if I'd known it was going to be like this, I wouldn't have come. Or if I'd known it was going to be like this, I would have listened. But don't worry, we're going to do this first part all over again for the latecomers. I want to give you and me both every opportunity. So. Okeydokey. *(Checks pocket watch)* Oh, boy, this has gotta be fast. So: *(Deep breath, then all in a run)* They tell me that we have ninety-seven minutes here tonight without intermission so if that means anything to anybody if you think you'll need a drink of water or anything I'll just point out some of the facilities till everybody gets settled in if everything goes well for me tonight this should be a waltz one-two-three, one-two-three a no-holds-barred romantic story and since I'm not a romantic type I'm going to need the whole shmeer here to help me the woods the willows the vines the moonlight the band there's a band that plays tonight over in the park the trees the berries the breeze the sounds water and crickets frogs dogs the light the bees . . . *(Pauses. With a slight hill accent)* Frogs, dogs . . . *(To stage manager in sound booth)* Could we have a dog? I'd like a dog. *(He listens a second. Nothing. Then a furious, yapping, tiny terrier is heard.)* Fellas! Fellas! A *dog!* *(Beat. Then a low, distant woof-woof-*

woof *that continues until* SALLY's *entrance.* MATT *listens a beat, pleased.)*

Oh, yeah. Old man Barnette kicked out Blackie and called in the kids, and about now the entire family is sitting down to supper. Even Blackie, out by the smokehouse. But a car pulled off the road about a mile downstream, and someone got out. And at this hour it begins to be difficult to see, the chickens have started to go to bed, and noises carry up the river as though there was someone there in the barnyard. And Blackie wants to let everybody know the Barnette farm is well guarded. *(Beat. Then back to run-on narration)*

Working all night did you know that bees work worker bees work around the clock never stop collecting nectar or pollen or whatever a bee collects of course their life expectancy is twenty days or in a bee's case twenty days and twenty nights or possibly expectancy is wrong in the case of a bee who knows what a bee expects but whatever time there is in a life is a lifetime and I imagine after twenty days and . . .

Wine in the Wilderness
by Alice Childress

Bill Jameson is an artist preparing his culminating work, a triptych (three paintings that make up one work). What he is seeking is a female model to represent the third part of the triptych, the lost and abandoned black woman of today. In the following monologue, Bill is talking on the phone to his agent.

BILL . . . *(Phone rings. He finds an African throw-cloth and hands it to her.)* Put this on. Relax, don't go way mad, and all the rest-a that jazz. Change, will you? I apologize. I'm sorry. *(He picks up the phone.)* Hello, survivor of a riot speaking. Who's calling? *(*TOMMY *retires behind the screen with the throw. During the conversation she undresses and wraps the throw around her. We see* TOMMY *and* BILL, *but they can't see* *each other.)* Sure, told you not to worry. I'll be ready for the exhibit. If you don't dig it, don't show it. Not time for you to see it yet. Yeah, yeah, next week. You just make sure your exhibition room is big enough to hold the crowds that's gonna congregate to see this fine chick I got here. *(This perks* TOMMY's *ears up.)* You ought to see her. The finest black woman in the world . . . No, . . . the finest *any* woman in the world . . . This gorgeous satin chick is . . . is . . . black velvet moonlight . . . an ebony queen of the universe . . . *(*TOMMY *can hardly believe her ears.)* One look at her and you go back to Spice Islands . . . She's Mother Africa . . . You flip, double flip. She has come through everything that has been put on her . . . *(He unveils the gorgeous woman he has painted . . . "Wine in the Wilderness."* TOMMY *believes he is talking about her.)* Regal . . . grand . . . magnificent, fantastic . . . You would vote her the woman you'd most like to meet on a desert island, or around the corner from anywhere. She's here with me now . . . and I don't know if I want to show her to you or anybody else . . . I'm beginnin' to have this deep attachment . . . She sparkles, man, Harriet Tubman, Queen of the Nile . . . sweetheart, wife, mother, sister, friend. . . . The night . . . a black diamond . . . A dark, beautiful dream . . . A cloud with a silvery lining . . . Her wrath is a storm over the Bahamas. "Wine in the Wilderness" . . . The memory of Africa . . . the *now* of things . . . but best of all and most important . . . She's tomorrow . . . she's my tomorrow. . .

You're a Good Man, Charlie Brown
by Clark Gesner, based on the comic strip *Peanuts* by Charles M. Schulz

Charlie Brown is alone in the school yard during lunchtime. He is feeling very sorry for himself because he is always alone. During the following monologue, he wonders how a young girl also sitting alone would react if he joined her for lunch.

CHARLIE BROWN I think lunchtime is about the worst time of the day for me. Always having to sit here alone. Of course, sometimes mornings aren't so pleasant, either — waking up and wondering if anyone would really miss me if I never got out of bed. Then there's the night, too — lying there and thinking about all the stupid things I've done during the day. And all those hours in between — when I do all those stupid things. Well, lunchtime is *among* the worst times of the day for me.

Well, I guess I'd better see what I've got *(He opens the bag, unwraps a sandwich, and looks inside.)* Peanut butter. *(He bites and chews.)* Some psychiatrists say that people who eat peanut butter sandwiches are lonely. I guess they're right. And if you're really lonely, the peanut butter sticks to the roof of your mouth. *(He munches quietly, idly fingering the bench.)* Boy, the PTA sure did a good job of painting these benches. *(He looks off to one side.)* There's that cute little redheaded girl eating her lunch over there. I wonder what she'd do if I went over and asked her if I could sit and have lunch with her. She'd probably laugh right in my face. It's hard on a face when it gets laughed in. There's an empty place next to her on the bench. There's no reason why I couldn't just go over and sit there. I could do that right now. All I have to do is stand up. *(He stands.)* I'm standing up. *(He sits.)* I'm sitting down. I'm a coward. I'm so much of a coward she wouldn't even think of looking at me. She hardly ever *does* look at me. In fact, I can't remember her ever looking at me. Why shouldn't she look at me? Is there any reason in the world why she shouldn't look at me? Is she so great and am I so small that she couldn't spare one little moment just to . . . *(He freezes.)* She's looking at me. *(In terror he looks one way, then another.)* She's *looking* at me.

(His head looks all around, frantically trying to find something else to notice. His teeth clench. Tension builds. Then, with one motion, he pops the paper bag over his head.)

Amen Corner
by James Baldwin

David is a brilliant young jazz musician. In the following monologue, he decides to leave his home and reject his mother's goal for his future. He decides to go out into the world and become his own man.

DAVID   And if I listened — what would happen? What do you think would happen if I listened? You want me to stay here, getting older, getting sicker — hating you? You think I want to hate you, Mama? You think it don't tear me to pieces to have to lie to you all the time. Yes, because I been lying to you, Mama, for a long time now! I don't want to tell no more lies. I don't want to keep feeling so bad inside that I have to go running down them alleys you was talking about — that alley right outside this door! — to find something to help me hide — to hide — from what I'm feeling. Mama, I want to be a man. It's time you let me be a man. You got to let me go. *(A pause)* If I stayed here — I'd end up worse than Daddy — because I wouldn't be doing what I know I got to do — I *got* to do! I've seen your life — and now I see Daddy — and I love you, I love you both! — but I've got my work to do, something's happening in the world out there, I got to go! I know you think I don't know what's happening, but I'm beginning to see — something. Every time I play, every time I listen, I see Daddy's face and yours, and so many faces — who's going to speak for all that, Mama? Who's going to speak for all of us? I can't stay home. Maybe I can say something — one day — maybe I can say something in music that's never been said before. Mama — *you* knew this day was coming.

A Thousand Clowns
by Herb Gardner

Murray has quit his job in protest against the stagnation and conformity of the business world. He is a "rebel with a cause" who tries to sort out what power a person has to effect change. In this scene, he starts off a typical day in his garden-level apartment by conversing with a recorded weather report and commenting on the quality of garbage in the alley outside his window.

MURRAY   *(Picks up phone and speaks immediately into it)* Is this somebody with good news or money? No? Good-bye. *(He hangs up.)* It's always voices like that you hear at eight A.M. Maniacs. *(He pulls up the shade to see what kind of day it is outside. As usual the lighting of the room changes not at all with the shade up; as before, he sees nothing but the blank, grayish wall opposite.)* Crap. *(With a sigh of resignation, he picks up the phone, dials, listens.)* Hello, Weather Lady. I am fine, how are you? What is the weather? Uh-huh — uh-huh — uh-huh — very nice. Only a *chance* of showers? Well, what exactly does that — ? Aw, there she goes again. *(He hangs up.)* Chance of showers. *(Phone rings. He picks it up, speaks immediately into it.)* United States Weather Bureau forecast for New York City and vicinity: eight A.M. temperature, sixty-five degrees, somewhat cooler in the suburbs, cloudy later today with a chance of — *(Looks incredulously at phone)* He hung up. Fool. Probably the most informative phone call he'll make all day. *(He stands, opens the window, leans out, raising his voice, shouting out the window.)* This is your neighbor speaking! Something must be done about your garbage cans in the alley here. It is definitely second-rate garbage! By next week I want to see a better class of garbage, more empty champagne bottles and caviar cans! So let's *snap* it up and get on the ball!

A Thousand Clowns
by Herb Gardner

Upset by the rat race of the media world, Murray confronts his brother, Ernie, who he considers a prize example of a total conformist.

MURRAY   Oh, Arnie, you don't understand any more. You got that wide stare that people stick in their eyes so nobody'll know their head's asleep. You got to be a shuffler, a moaner. You want me to come sit and eat fruit with you and watch the clock run out. You start to drag and stumble with the rotten weight of all the people who should have been told off, all the things you should have said, all the specifications that aren't yours. The only thing you got left to reject is your food in a restaurant if they do it wrong and you can send it back and make a big fuss with the waiter. *(MURRAY turns away from* ARNOLD, *goes to window seat, sits down.)* Arnold, five months ago I forgot what *day* it was. I'm on the subway on my way to work and I didn't know what day it was and it scared the hell out of me. *(Quietly)* I was sitting in the express looking out the window same as every morning watching the local stops go by in the dark with an empty head and my arms folded, not feeling great and not feeling rotten, just not feeling, and for a minute I couldn't remember, I didn't know, unless I really concentrated, whether it was a Tuesday or a Thursday — or a — for a minute it could have been *any* day, Arnie — sitting in the train going through any day — in the dark through any year — Arnie, it scared the hell out of me. *(Stands up)* You got to know what day it is. You got to know what's the name of the game and what the rules are with nobody else telling you. You have to own your days and name them, each one of them, every one of them, or else the years go right by and none of them belong to you.

The Teahouse of the August Moon
by John Patrick

During World War II, the United States Marines captured the Japanese-held island of Okinawa. Sakini, an Okinawan interpreter, greets the audience with his whimsical bits of Oriental philosophy.

SAKINI   Tootie Fruitie. *(He takes the gum out of his mouth and, wrapping it carefully in a piece of paper, puts it in a matchbox and restores it to pocket in shirt.)*
Most generous gift of American soldier.
Lovely ladies and gentlemen: Please to introduce myself.
Sakini by name. Interpretor by profession.
Educated by ancient dictionary.

Okinawan by whim of gods. History of Okinawa reveal distinguished record of conquerors. We have honor to be subjugated in fourth century by Chinese pirates. In sixteenth century by English missionaries. In eighteenth century by Japanese war lords. And in twentieth century by American Marines. Okinawa very fortunate. Culture brought to us. . . . Not have to leave for it. Learn many things. Most important that rest of world not like Okinawa. World filled with delightful variation. Illustration. In Okinawa. . . . no lock on doors. Bad manners not to trust neighbors. In America. . . . lock and key big industry. Conclusion? Bad manners good business. In Okinawa. . . . wash self in public bath with nude lady quite proper. Picture of nude lady in private home quite improper. In America — statue of nude lady in park win prize. But lady in flesh in park win penalty. Conclusion? Pornography question of geography. But Okinawans most eager to be educated by conquerors. Deep desire to improve friction. Not easy to learn. Sometimes painful. But pain makes man think. Thought makes man wise. Wisdom makes life endurable.

The Glass Menagerie
by Tennessee Williams

Man of La Mancha
by Dale Wasserman

Tom Wingfield supported his outspoken Southern mother, Amanda, and his handicapped sister, Laura, from the time their father abandoned them. He too had to leave, however, and in this closing speech of the play he reflects on his departure.

Miguel de Cervantes is the creator of Don Quixote, the idealistic knight-errant whom everyone thinks is mad. In this speech, Cervantes muses about what madness actually is.

TOM   I didn't go to the moon, I went much further — for time is the longest distance between two places — Not long after that I was fired for writing a poem on the lid of a shoe-box. I left Saint Louis. I descended the steps of this fire-escape for a last time and followed, from then on, in my father's footsteps, attempting to find in motion what was lost in space — I traveled around a great deal. The cities swept about me like dead leaves, leaves that were brightly colored but torn away from the branches. I would have stopped, but I was pursued by something. It always came upon me unawares, taking me altogether by surprise. Perhaps it was a familiar bit of music. Perhaps it was only a piece of transparent glass — Perhaps I am walking along a street at night, in some strange city, before I have found companions. I pass the lighted window of a shop where perfume is sold. The window is filled with pieces of colored glass, tiny transparent bottles in delicate colors, like bits of a shattered rainbow. Then all at once my sister touches my shoulder. I turn around and look into her eyes . . . Oh, Laura, Laura, I tried to leave you behind me, but I am more faithful than I intended to be! I reach for a cigarette, I cross the street, I run into the movies or a bar, I buy a drink, I speak to the nearest stranger — anything that can blow your candles out! *(LAURA bends over the candles.)* — for nowadays the world is lit by lightning! Blow out your candles, Laura — and so good-bye. . . .

CERVANTES   I have lived nearly fifty years, and I have seen life as it is. Pain, misery, hunger . . . cruelty beyond belief. I have heard the singing from taverns and the moans from bundles of filth on the streets. I have been a soldier and seen my comrades fall in battle . . . or die more slowly under the lash in Africa. I have held them in my arms at the final moment. These were men who saw life as it is, yet they died despairing. No glory, no gallant last words . . . only their eyes filled with confusion, whimpering the question: "Why?" I do not think they asked why they were dying, but why they had lived. *(He rises, and through the following speech moves into the character of* DON QUIXOTE*)* When life itself seems lunatic, who knows where madness lies? Perhaps to be too practical is madness. To surrender dreams—this may be madness. To seek treasure where there is only trash. Too much sanity may be madness. And maddest of all, to see life as it is and not as it should be.

• Part Three •

Appreciating the Drama

Chapter 6

. . . .

The Structure of Drama

You Will Learn

What are the four narrative essentials of a written play.

What influence Aristotle had on drama.

How the structure of plays has changed in modern times.

What happens in the exposition of a play.

What the parts of plot structure are.

How playwrights create characters.

What the theme of a play is.

How playwrights use dialogue, action, and situation.

Vocabulary

protagonist	preliminary situation	crisis	theme
exposition	initial incident	catastrophe	dialogue
mood	rising action	denouement	action
atmosphere	climax	soliloquies	situations
plot	falling action		

*I*n the historic world of Western drama, "the play's the thing." Brought to life by the actors; expressed through the mediums of color, light, and movement against the background of stage and scenery; and unified by the creative vision of the director, the play itself is the nucleus around which the art of the theater is centered.

The only true test of the success of a production is the emotional response it arouses in the audience. A good play can fail to arouse that response because it is inadequately produced. A poor play may be so effectively acted and staged that it is reasonably successful. The great dramas of the world have survived, however, because the plays themselves are fine enough to rise above inadequate production or can be effectively adapted to changing tastes.

Drama is the most thrilling form of literature because through it we recognize ourselves in the experience of others. We sorrow or rejoice in their defeats or triumphs because the characters have become living human beings to us. The dramatist is dependent for both character portrayal and plot development solely upon dialogue that must be concise and can build action swiftly. The play's action unfolds before our eyes in a closely related series of events that reach a dramatic climax, work out to a logical conclusion, and bring out a definite idea. In other words, a play has the four narrative essentials — *exposition, plot, character,* and *theme* — presented by means of dialogue and action, in which the elements of conflict and suspense arouse a definite emotional response on the part of the spectators. To build a drama, then, the dramatist must arrange the presentation of these four narrative essentials. This "arrangement" is the *structure* of the play.

Tradition and the Changing Scene

Since the middle of the twentieth century, playwrights have broken away from traditional rules, and many of them have modified play structure to a lesser or greater degree. For example, there was a tradition for many years that divided a play into three or five acts. The climax came at the end of the second act in three-act plays and at the end of the third act in five-act plays. Minor plots were frequently introduced and the resolution of the plot lengthened. Now plays are more often separated into two parts or several scenes with a single intermission or, on occasion, no intermission at all. The assumption is that fewer breaks in the action encourage more concentrated attention. This change affected plot structure.

Today the dramatist must adapt the play structure to fit the theater structure, for the open stage has come into increasing use. Unlike the proscenium arch, which strictly separates the audience from the actors, the open stages — the arena, the theater-in-the-round, and the thrust stage — eliminate the principle of aesthetic distance, the reminder that a play is a play and not reality. The resulting intimacy and lack of realistic sets and stage curtains affect the play-wright's style. Play structure must now accommodate the growing use of im-provisation and action in place of written dialogue.

However, since you are now studying the art of the theater, it is necessary for you to understand the structure of the traditional drama, which still dom-inates the theatrical scene.

In a well-written play or movie, one of the satisfactions is seeing how the actions of people we are deeply interested in are carried to a logical conclu-sion. We seldom see such results in life itself, where even intimate friends drift out of our lives, and we never find out what happened to them. In a well-constructed play, we see how the lives of human beings end in success or failure as the result of their own actions during crucial events. Out of their experiences, we are shown a fundamental truth that inspires and uplifts us or deepens our insights into the human experience.

The traditions that established these principles were originally expressed by the world's first literary critic, the great Greek philosopher Aristotle (384–322 B.C.). His principles have usually been applied in the great dramas of most periods. When Aristotle discussed tragedy in his *Poetics,* he stressed that drama is an imitation of life, that humankind learns through imitation, and that learning something is the greatest pleasure of life. He pointed out that all human happiness or misery takes the form of action. Therefore, he places plot first in his list of the parts of a play, which include plot, character, diction (language), thought, spectacle, and melody.

In Aristotle's discussion of plot, he maintains that the action must be com-plete in itself, with a beginning, a middle, and an end. The incidents must follow each other in logical order and reach a plausible conclusion. Out of the complications of the plot, the main character, called the **protagonist,**

Caesar, played by Robert Christie, is stopped by a soothsayer who warns him to "beware the Ides of March" (initial incident in Julius Caesar*). This was a 1955 production at the Stratford, Ontario, Festival Theatre.*

does and says the things that are consistent with the protagonist's personality. Therefore, failure or success is the result of the protagonist's inherent nature. The characters must imitate reality in that they are true to life. And they must experience happiness or misery as a result of their reactions to the situations of the plot. The resolution of the action in a serious play should purge the emotions through pity and fear and bring out a universal truth.

Aristotle said that there should be unity of time and action, emphasizing that the drama be restricted to one basic idea dependent upon a single incident taking place within one day, "a single circuit of the sun." The French and Italian neoclassicists of the sixteenth century misinterpreted Aristotle and set up rules which they felt followed the ancient dramatic traditions. These rules in turn have been applied down through the years by many leading dramatists in famous plays. They require the use of three unities — time, action, and place — verse forms in five acts, one series of events without subplots, characters of nobility and power, and exalted themes. The rules also prohibit the showing of scenes of violence on the stage. The audience learns about such events in great detail from long speeches by some person who has witnessed them.

The traditions and principles, then, that have most affected playwrights down to our time have come to us from ancient Greek drama, from Aristotle's *Poetics,* from the refinements and misinterpretation of Aristotle by the French and Italian neoclassicists, and from the formula for "the well-made play" put forth by the French playwright, Eugene Scribe, in the early nineteenth century. If contemporary playwrights are departing from a tradition, it is this tradition, or elements of it, that they are reacting against. Now let us look more closely at the four essential narrative elements as they have been employed traditionally in Western drama.

The Exposition

As soon as possible after the play begins, the audience must know what kind of play is being presented, where and when it is taking place, who the leading characters are, and in what situations and conflicts they find themselves. These facts constitute the literary setting. The process of putting them before the audience is called the **exposition.** A skillfully written exposition is brief and unobtrusive. It tells us the *where, when, why,* and *who* without our realizing that we have been told anything.

Exposition of the Setting

Today the time and place are usually printed clearly on the program, but the script should describe the complete setting in detail. Sometimes the author merely states the facts. Shakespeare did this many times because he had no scenery to show the place and no programs to supply the information. For example, in *Twelfth Night,* the captain says to Viola, "This is Illyria, lady," and the entire scene that follows (Act 1, Scene 2) describes what has happened to the leading characters before the play begins.

Mood and Atmosphere

The exposition also establishes the mood and atmosphere of the play. **Mood** is the emotional feeling of the play. The characters, setting, lighting, time of day, and dialogue all help to bring out the mood. The audience should identify the mood at the start of the play.

Atmosphere is the environment of the play. Atmosphere is largely created by staging and lighting. But the tempo of speech and movement and the choice of language, which helps to identify the country and class of society that make up the background for the play, also contribute to the atmosphere. The atmosphere helps to bring out the feelings that form the mood.

Preliminary Situation

The most important part of the exposition is the **preliminary situation,** sometimes called the *antecedent action.* This is a clearly defined explanation

The mood and atmosphere of Julius Caesar *is furthered in Act II, scene I when Portia urges Brutus to share his troubled thoughts.*
. . . .

of the events that have occurred in the lives of the leading characters before the action of the play itself begins. These events place them in the situation in which we find them.

Playwrights use all sorts of devices to handle the exposition of the preliminary situation. The most common is to have minor characters bring the audience up-to-date. More original methods are the use of prologues, telephone conversations, narrators, and ingenious scenic effects. In *The Caine Mutiny Court Martial,* a drama about a military court trial, front curtains are not used. So the audience becomes a part of the action while clerks, attorneys, and attendants casually explain the case. In *The Diary of Anne Frank* and *I Remember Mama,* the audience sees the young heroines writing about themselves in their journals at the opening of the plays and between scenes.

Plot

The **plot** of the play is the series of related events that take place before the audience. It is the working out of the major conflict. A well-constructed play can be diagrammed by steps of varying heights going up to a turning point, which is then followed by steps going down. There is always a problem facing the protagonist and in the conflict between the protagonist and the antagonist arising from the problem. The conflict need not be physical as in many plays of violence, particularly in motion pictures and television. It can be a clash of wills or wits. It can be a psychological struggle between phases of the protagonist's personality and the environment. It can be a battle between a group of ideological antagonisms. Whether physical, mental, or emotional, the conflicting elements must give rise to suspense.

The Initial Incident

The **initial incident** opens the play. It is the first important event that sets the plot moving, and it is the point from which the rest of the plot develops. The initial incident makes the audience want to know what will happen next. For example, the first scene of *Julius Caesar,* in which the people and the members of noble families are discussing the war between Caesar and Pompey, presents the situation in Rome. The initial incident comes when the soothsayer cries out to Caesar, "Beware the Ides of March." That cry foreshadows the danger to Caesar.

The Rising Action

The **rising action** is the series of events following the initial incident. These events take place on the stage. Each situation developing out of the conflict

On the steps of the Senate House, the conspirators stab Caesar to death (rising action in Julius Caesar). The actors are Max Helpmann, Joseph Shaw as Caesar, Dan MacDonald, and Peter Donat at the Stratford, Ontario, Festival Theatre.
. . . .

In Act III, scene I, Antony stands over the body of the slain leader and speaks, "O mighty Caesar! Dost thou lie so low? Are all thy conquests, glories, triumphs, spoils, shrunk to this little pleasure."
. . . .

Julius Caesar.

between the protagonist and the antagonist lifts the action to a higher level of interest and suspense.

In *Julius Caesar,* the rising action moves from Caesar's refusal to listen to the soothsayer into the scenes in which Cassius works upon Brutus to join a conspiracy to assassinate Caesar. Cassius plays upon Brutus's democratic ideals and loyalty to the citizens of Rome. Then Cassius stirs others to join the conspiracy. Important steps include Brutus's decision to join the conspiracy; his resolution not to kill Antony; his wife, Portia's, plea to share in whatever he is undertaking; the effort Calpurnia, the wife of Caesar, makes to prevent Caesar's going to the Senate and the conspirators' persuading him to go; the assassination; the permission to Antony to deliver the funeral address; the brief remarks of Brutus calming the citizens; and the beginning of the address by Mark Antony.

The Climax

The **climax** is the turning point of the play toward which the rising action leads. It is the moment that determines what the outcome of the conflict will be. The dramatist often makes this event a thrilling one, and the director must arrange the action to arouse the most intense interest in the audience.

There must be several important events before and after the climax to sustain the suspense and keep the interest of the audience to the end. However, the climax must be the crucial event of the play as a whole. The dramatist must build up to it in the lines and situations, and the director must use every appropriate stage technique to emphasize it. In *Julius Caesar,* the climax comes at the close of Mark Antony's funeral address, when the citizens rush away to burn the houses of the conspirators with the burning pieces of wood from Caesar's pyre.

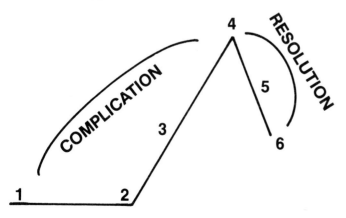

1. Preliminary Situation
2. Initial Incident
3. Rising Action
4. Climax
5. Falling Action
6. Conclusion

PLOT STRUCTURE

The Falling Action

The **falling action** is the series of events following the climax. It is usually shorter than the rising action, but the incidents must be of real significance and of keen interest. In *Julius Caesar,* the mob murder of Cinna the poet and the meeting of the Triumvirate precede the final events: the quarrel between Brutus and Cassius and the decision to face battle at Philippi. The appearance of the ghost of Caesar to Brutus in his tent on the night before the battle leads into the fighting and the suicides of Cassius and of Brutus.

There are two additional elements that can be found in the rising or falling action. The first of these is the **crisis,** a moment of decision for the protagonist. There are usually several crises in a play. The second element is the **catastrophe,** an unlucky event that may strike the protagonist or one of the other major characters in the play.

The Conclusion

The end of the play must be the logical outcome of all that has gone before. The success or failure, happiness, or sorrow of the characters must be the result of their inherent natures or their actual deeds. The fate of the characters should not be the result of an outside force previously unrelated to them nor a matter of luck, chance, or happy accident. In *Julius Caesar,* the famous tribute of Antony above the body of Brutus is a fitting conclusion.

When the plot of a play consists of a mystery to be solved or a complicated series of interrelated events involving the leading characters, another element in the plot — a **denouement** — may be added to the falling action or to the actual conclusion. The denouement is a solution of the mystery and/or the explanation of the outcome.

After a funeral oration, Robert Stephens as Mark Antony shows the crowd the body of the murdered Caesar. He turns the people of Rome against Brutus and the other conspirators (climax in Julius Caesar*).*

Brutus meditates on the coming battle with the forces of Mark Antony and Octavius (falling action in Julius Caesar*). Lorne Greene is Brutus and William Shatner is Lucius at the Stratford, Ontario, Festival Theatre.*

Characters

Nothing in the world is as interesting as people. The characters in a play should be compelling people who hold the center of interest throughout the drama. In a well-written play, even the most minor characters are living, individual personalities. Occasionally a dramatist may resort to using stage "types," characters every audience will accept without thought. Shakespeare holds his position as the world's finest dramatist because even his minor characters are individually developed.

Characters in a play must be vivid and varied in personality, with their dominant traits clearly brought out in their speeches and actions. The success or failure of the characters must be the logical result of their own actions or the situation in which they are placed.

Methods of Characterization

The playwright develops characters mostly by making them act and speak. The characters' actions must suit their position in life and their past experiences. The playwright also reveals characters by what they say about each other. Sometimes playwrights use **soliloquies** to reveal character. Soliloquies are speeches in which actors talk alone — think aloud — about themselves and their motives or other people and situations. Soliloquies were accepted as a vital part of drama until the realistic play became prevalent. In real life, people do not talk aloud to themselves very often. However, the soliloquy is such a simple way to reveal inner reactions and characters that modern playwrights still use it effectively. Thornton Wilder does this in *Our Town,* and Tennessee Williams does it in *The Glass Menagerie.* Usually today's tendency is for dramatists to avoid direct descriptions as much as possible and have their characters reveal themselves rather unconsciously through action and speech.

Motivation of Action

As you read or see a play, you must be able to ask why a character did something and find a logical answer in the nature of the person as brought out by the play. The most important phase of characterization is thus the motivation of action. Every action of a character must have a reason behind it, which in turn must be the result of both the character's personality and the situation of the moment.

Therefore, the playwright should constantly ask such questions as the following regarding each of the characters in his or her play: Where did they come from and why (on their entrances)? Where are they going and why (on their exits)? Why did they make certain statements?

Theme

The **theme** is the basic idea of a play, which the author dramatizes through the conflicts of characters with one another or with life events. Sometimes the playwright states the theme in words spoken by a character, but often it is left to the interpretation of the spectator or reader. The theme is the specific idea that gives unity and purpose to everything that happens in the play. It should be an interesting phase of the particular problem, rather than a general principle that could apply to dozens of plays.

You may find it difficult to determine the theme of a play as you read or see it, but you should enjoy analyzing the plot and characters and finding what the author has expressed through them. Remember that there may be many good ideas presented in a play, but do not be misled into mistaking a minor truth for the theme of the play as a whole. The theme is the specific idea that gives unity and purpose to everything that happens.

Do not confuse the theme with a moral. Many plays have no moral. They are written to show how a certain type of individual would react under certain circumstances or to portray an interesting phase of life.

Most theatergoers like a definite statement of the theme to help them arrive

Brutus encounters the ghost of Caesar: "I think it is the weakness of my eyes that shapes this monstrous apparition" (Act IV, scene III).
. . . .

at the dramatist's reason for writing the play. Sometimes, therefore, the writer states the theme in the title as in *Whose Life Is It, Anyway? You Can't Take it With You,* and *She Stoops to Conquer.* At other times, the theme is actually stated in a key line, definitely emphasized or expressed by the leading character as a personal philosophy of life, and then carried out in the situations resulting from this philosophy. For example, in *The Man of La Mancha,* Cervantes says, "Too much sanity may be madness, but the maddest of all is to see life as it is and not as it should be."

Dialogue, Action, and Situation

The success of a play depends upon the writer's skillful use of dialogue and action, since they are the sole means by which the playwright can portray character, set forth theme, and develop plot.

In writing the **dialogue** or lines of the play, the dramatist must make characters speak as the women and men of the class, community, and experience they represent would speak in real life. At the same time, the playwright must advance the plot, motivate the actions of the characters, and place the characters in exciting or amusing situations. The playwright must often sacrifice beauty of language to naturalness of speech, yet the characters cannot talk aimlessly as people do in real life, for every word must develop the play.

Mark Antony pays tribute to the dead Brutus: "This was the noblest Roman of them all" (conclusion in Julius Caesar*). Actors in this New York Shakespeare Festival production are Garnett Smith, Richard Roat, Jack Granino, and Leonard Hicks.*

Clever lines in themselves are valuable in a comedy, but they should be consistent with the character of the person speaking them. Sparkling dialogue may actually hurt the play if it is not in harmony with the overall aim of the playwright. We can hardly speak of dialogue apart from action and situation. When we refer to a playwright's style, then, we mean the cleverness or beauty of the lines in relation to the mood and characterizations in the play.

Action is the lifeblood of drama; something must happen constantly to hold the undivided interest of the onlookers. Events must not only be talked about, they must also occur on the stage. Action is the natural result of conflict.

As you attend films and plays, note how the **situations** are always presented in dialogue and action. The characters may be placed in embarrassing predicaments, moments of great danger, tense emotional upheavals, or other combinations of circumstances. We must see the characters solve one difficult situation after another.

The ability to place characters in exciting, tragic, comic, or pathetic situations is what makes a playwright successful. Occasionally one situation alone can be so striking that it helps make the play a hit. The next time you are at the theater, watch especially for the opening situation, the climax, and the closing event. Georges Polti, in his book *The Thirty-Six Dramatic Situations,* discusses the situations on which all drama is based (see page 247).

Whatever the future structure of drama may be, plays must maintain the universal appeal they have had through the centuries. In the long run, dramatists whose plays will survive will continue to reveal the heights and depths of human experience and be an uplifting and creative force in civilization. Those playwrights whose plays are carelessly constructed and tasteless will not exert an influence beyond their own generation.

THE THIRTY-SIX DRAMATIC SITUATIONS
Georges Polti

1. Supplication
2. Deliverance
3. Crime pursued by vengeance
4. Vengeance taken for kindred upon kindred
5. Pursuit
6. Disaster
7. Falling prey to cruelty or misfortune
8. Revolt
9. Daring enterprise
10. Abduction
11. The enigma
12. Obtaining
13. Enmity of kinsmen
14. Rivalry of kinsmen
15. Murderous adultery
16. Madness
17. Fatal imprudence
18. Involuntary crimes of love
19. Slaying of a kinsman unrecognized
20. Self-sacrificing for an ideal
21. Self-sacrifice for kindred
22. All sacrificed for a passion
23. Necessity of sacrificing loved ones
24. Rivalry of superior and inferior
25. Adultery
26. Crimes of love
27. Discovery of the dishonor of a loved one
28. Obstacles to love
29. An enemy loved
30. Ambition
31. Conflict with a god
32. Mistaken jealousy
33. Erroneous judgment
34. Remorse
35. Recovery of a lost one
36. Loss of loved ones

The One-Act Play

Dramatists today feel that a play should be as long as the central idea demands for full expression. As a result, both very long and very short plays have become common. The current short play has aroused renewed interest in the one-act play.

The one-act play is a major structural form, and justifiably so. It demands careful writing of a compact plot centered about one dramatic incident with vividly presented characters and condensed, rapidly moving dialogue. The one main idea is today considered of paramount value, so it must be brought out without confusing sidelights. Usually the exposition is brief and the rising action short, with the climax becoming the focus of the play very near the end.

One-act plays offer an ideal medium in the dramatics classroom to study the structure of drama, to see plays in class, and to give all members an opportunity to appear in a good part and to share in the actual production of a play. They also serve as a means of interesting young people seldom or never exposed to live plays.

Recalling Ideas

1. Name and define each of the four narrative essentials of a play.

2. In what ways have twentieth-century playwrights broken away from tradition?

3. Who first expressed the principles of traditional drama?

4. How does mood differ from atmosphere?

5. List the five major parts of plot structure that follow the preliminary situation.

6. Describe three methods of characterization available to playwrights.

7. How does a theme differ from a moral?

8. Describe the structure of a one-act play.

Discussing Ideas

1. Why is it satisfying to see the actions of characters in a play carried to a logical conclusion? How do you feel after watching a play or movie that does not have a logical ending?

2. Twentieth-century playwrights often break the traditional rules of drama. Describe some of the rules that are broken. Read either Samuel Beckett's *Waiting for Godot* or Eugene Ionesco's *The Chairs*. Discuss their lack of conventional plot, theme, and characters.

3. Select a popular motion picture or television play. Identify the initial incident and the climax. How were suspense and interest maintained during the rising and falling action? Did the drama end as you suspected it would? What was the problem presented? How was the conflict presented? State the theme in one sentence.

4. Describe a play or movie that made you think deeply about its theme.

Careers

Playwrights write plays for the theater. They may also write scripts for motion pictures and plays produced for radio or television. They may work for an employer, such as a motion picture or television studio, but are often freelancers who are self-employed and write for various clients. Because of the high cost of producing a play, most find it difficult to find a **producer** for their work. In addition to plays, they may write short stories, articles, and novels.

Most playwrights have at least a bachelor's degree from a 4-year college. A broad background in literature, history, philosophy, and social science is helpful.

Some people combine their interests in writing and the theater by pursuing a career as a **Publicity Director.** Publicity directors are responsible for free publicity, paid advertising, and subscription campaigns. They gather facts about the play and biographical information about the cast. They send out news releases and public service announcements to reviewers, newspapers, and radio and television stations. They make mailings to interested people. They urge **reporters** to cover the play and **critics** to review it. They produce display ads, posters, flyers, and other items needed to keep the theater and its productions in the public eye.

Publicity directors often have a bachelor or higher degree in English, communications, or journalism from a 4-year college or university. Some courses in theater as well as English, creative writing, advertising, and public relations are helpful. So too is experience with school publications, radio and television stations, and advertising agencies.

Chapter 7

Varieties of Drama

You Will Learn

What tragedy is.

What comedy is.

What the various types of comedy are.

What makes people laugh.

What the many styles of theater are.

Vocabulary

tragedy

catharsis

pathos

comedy

exaggeration

incongruity

grotesqueness

unnatural

unnatural
  sounds

twist

reversal

irrelevant

anticipation

ambiguity

recognition

protection factor

relief

low comedy

farce

aside

burlesque

middle comedy

humor

romantic comedy

fantasy

sentimental comedy

melodrama

social drama

high comedy

comedy of manners

satire

style

representational

presentational

romanticism

realism	constructivism	stylization
naturalism	epic theater	theater of involvement
symbolic	existential theater	theater of the absurd
allegory	expressionism	theatricalism
avant-garde	impressionism	total theater

*T*he more plays you see and read, the more you will find yourself reacting differently to each writer's style, basic themes, characters, and dialogue. You will also soon recognize that plays fall into types or categories and that your response to each kind will vary accordingly.

Tragedy and comedy are the two chief divisions of drama. In the broad sense, all plays may arbitrarily be placed within the definitions of *tragedy* and *comedy*. Although tragedies are among the earliest of recorded dramas, most plays — fantasy, melodrama, farce, comedy of manners, sentimental comedy, and social drama — fall within the definition of comedy. None of these divisions is absolute or entirely separate, and overlapping is quite common. Some plays that have the qualities of both tragedy and comedy are called *tragicomedies*. Some serious plays that do not fit the qualifications of tragedy but are serious in nature are simply called *dramas*.

Classification is further complicated by a consideration of the styles in which a play may be written. The most commonly recognized literary styles are classicism, romanticism, realism, naturalism, symbolism, expressionism, and impressionism. In addition, there are period styles determined by theater conventions of historical eras, such as the ritualistic formalism of the Greek theater, the madcap antics of the commedia dell'arte, and the powdered wigs, fans, and coquetry of the Restoration period.

Remember that the classification of plays is rather arbitrary. Still, the following introduction to types should challenge your critical faculties and imagination and give you some knowledge of the terms used to describe plays.

Tragedy

The greatest plays of all time have been tragedies. In fact, tragedy has been considered by many critics as humanity's highest literary achievement because only through suffering and sacrifice can human beings achieve true nobility. A **tragedy** is a play in which the protagonist fails to achieve desired goals or is overcome by opposing forces. The action usually ends with the

According to Aristotle, the tragic protagonist is a "better than average person" guilty of hamartia. Shakespeare's Othello is one of the most famous tragic characters.

protagonist's death, but in some plays, this main character lives on, crushed in spirit and will.

Tragedy Is Emotional

Tragedies are based on profound emotions that, in their universal appeal, transcend time and place. Strong emotions, such as love, hate, ambition, jealousy, and revenge, move the audience to empathize with tragic figures. Since emotions are the true expressions of humanness, it is neither necessary nor desirable to intellectualize tragedy. Instead, you should be struck by an emotional bolt of lightning that leaps through the storm of conflict. Comedies, on the other hand, often depend upon local, regional, or topical situations. They seem entertaining when the audience's cultural background, temperament, and past experience relate to the comic events or when the characters go beyond their particular situations and can be related to something or someone familiar to an audience.

The most important basis for judgment of tragedy is found in a critical essay, the *Poetics,* by the Greek critic-philosopher Aristotle. According to Aristotle, the tragic protagonist is a "better than average person" guilty of hamartia. *Hamartia* is an error in judgment or a shortcoming. The most common form of hamartia is hubris, an act of excessive pride. However, it is quite wrong to look for a "flaw" in every tragic hero, for the greatest tragic characters do not possess a real flaw. They more frequently fail because of costly errors in judgment, or even because of their own almost too-virtuous nature. Through suffering, the tragic protagonist usually acquires a sense of awareness — of truth, of self, or of others. During this time of struggle, the protagonist becomes alienated and isolated from society. Human beings seem capable of seeing clearly only when under great stress.

When a person of stature, struggling mightily against dynamic forces, finally falls, the audience experiences what Aristotle termed **catharsis,** a purging or cleansing that comes as a result of emotional release. The most forceful catharsis is experienced when an audience realizes that the doomed protagonist has seen life more perceptively than most humans could ever hope to. Aristotle said that the catharsis comes through pity and terror — pity for the protagonist that such a great person should fall, and terror aroused by the fear that we could easily have made the same error in judgment and paid the same price.

To heighten the impact, Aristotle said writers of tragedy would use scenes of recognition and of reversal. There are usually two kinds of scenes of recognition. In one, the protagonist achieves an inner awareness as a result of great personal suffering. In the second kind, the protagonist identifies a loved one, kinfolk, or friend from a birthmark, scar, or some other means. In a scene of reversal, there is an ironic twist in which an action produces an effect opposite to what would at first seem probable.

The student of drama will observe certain other characteristics in tragedy apart from Aristotle's theories. The essential quality of a tragic character is suffering. This suffering occurs in most instances because of a rebellion against some divine or human authority or against society. Most tragedies have a ritualistic nature, and the protagonist assumes the role of a sacrifice or scapegoat. Oedipus died for Thebes; Hamlet, for Denmark; and Willie Loman, for his dreams and for his son Biff.

Another characteristic of tragedy is inevitability. What is going to happen will happen. There is no way to prevent the protagonist's tragic fall. For example, in *Romeo and Juliet* the chorus informs us that Romeo and Juliet are "star-crossed lovers." From this point, their fate is sealed.

Pathos is another characteristic of tragedy. **Pathos** is the power to arouse feelings of pity and compassion in an audience. It is through these feelings that the tragic impact of events is intensified. Still, by the time the tragedy is over, the pathos has been purged.

Tragedies are sober, thoughtful examinations of life dealing quite often with laws of the gods and laws of humanity, social conflict, or the identity and sanctity of self. In all cases, a struggle exists — a struggle of dignity and value. The higher the goals toward which the protagonist reaches, the greater may be the fall and the greater the catharsis for the audience. If the character is not noble in rank or stature, there must be something that elevates that character above the average. Willie Loman in *Death of a Salesman* has his dreams; the weavers in Hauptmann's play *The Weavers* have a hope for a better life.

Great tragic characters all have five characteristics in common: (1) they know what they stand for and do not swerve from that stand; (2) they make no apology for their actions; (3) they set goals based on their dogmatism; (4) they know that almost everything worth having demands some sacrifice; and (5) they are willing to make the sacrifice themselves, never asking another to do what they alone can do.

A Definition of Tragedy

Probably one of the finest descriptions of tragedy since Aristotle's is found in a speech by the Chorus in Jean Anouilh's *Antigone*.

"The spring is wound up tight. It will uncoil of itself. That is what is so convenient in tragedy. The least little turn of the wrist will do the job. Anything will set it going: a glance at a girl who happens to be lifting her arms to her hair as you go by; a feeling when you wake up on a fine morning that you'd like a little respect paid to you today, as if it were as easy to order as a second cup of coffee; one question too many, idly thrown out over a friendly drink — and the tragedy is on.

"The rest is automatic. You don't need to lift a finger. The machine is in perfect order; it has been oiled ever since time began, and it runs without friction. Death, treason, and sorrow are on the march; and they move in the wake of storm, of tears, of stillness. Every kind of stillness. The hush when the executioner's ax goes up at the end of the last act. The unbreathable silence when, at the beginning of the play, the two lovers, their hearts bared, their bodies naked, stand for the first time face to face in the darkened room, afraid to stir. The silence inside you when the roaring crowd acclaims the winner — so that you think of a film without a sound track, mouths agape and no sound coming out of them, a clamor that is no more than a picture; and you, the victor, already vanquished, alone in the desert of your silence. That is tragedy.

"Tragedy is clean, it is restful, it is flawless. It has nothing to do with melodrama — with wicked villains, persecuted maidens, avengers, sudden revelations, and eleventh-hour repentances. Death, in a melodrama, is really horrible because it is never inevitable. The dear old father might so easily have been saved; the honest young man might so easily have brought in the police five minutes earlier.

"In a tragedy, nothing is in doubt and everyone's destiny is known. That makes for tranquility. There is a sort of fellow-feeling among characters in a tragedy: he who kills is as innocent as he who gets killed: it's all a matter of what part you are playing. Tragedy is restful; and the reason is that hope, that foul, deceitful thing, has no part in it. There isn't any hope. You're trapped. The whole sky has fallen on you, and all you can do about it is to shout.

"Don't mistake me: I said 'shout': I did not say groan, whimper, complain. That, you cannot do. But you can shout aloud; you can get all those things said that you never thought you'd be able to say — or never even knew you had it in you to say. And you don't say these things because it will do any good to say them: you know better than that. You say them for their own sake; you say them because you learn a lot from them.

"In melodrama you argue and struggle in the hope of escape. That is vulgar; it's practical. But in tragedy, where there is no temptation to try to escape, argument is gratuitous: it's kingly."

Tragedy vs. Comedy

Tragedy	Comedy
Inevitable — no way to change or stop	Predictably "unpredictable" — can expect the unlikely to occur
Universal in theme and audience appeal	Time-place oriented
Emotional	Intellectual
Protagonist fails to achieve goals	Protagonist achieves goals
Protagonist alienated from society	Societal; protagonist often becomes "head" of new society; even villain accepted
Protagonist average or better	Protagonist less than average in some way
Protagonist falls from leadership, losing respect, dreams, position	Protagonist achieves success, even leadership, often as a result of own mistakes or shortcoming

Comedy

The word **comedy** is derived from a Greek word, *komos,* meaning "festival or revelry." Comedies are usually light, written with clever dialogue, and peopled with amusing characters who are involved in funny situations that they solve by their wit, their charm, and sometimes by sheer good fortune. Comedies are usually "societal," meaning that all the characters come together at the end of the play. Even the villains rejoin the group.

Throughout the history of the theater, the greatest and most enduring comedies have taken situations and characters from life. They therefore contain certain timeless human truths. Molière, Shakespeare, and Shaw are considered three of the world's great writers of comedy. Their comedies have had lasting appeal because they are based on universal human experience.

Comedy does not always make you laugh, but most comedy will amuse, delight, or please you. In comedy, the protagonist overcomes opposing forces, achieves desired goals, or perhaps accomplishes both those things. The protagonist is most often a "less than average person" in some way. The comic protagonist may be an idealist, a romantic, an extreme pragmatist, a blunderer, a dreamer, or a rogue.

The last scene fantasy of Shakespeare's Merry Wives of Windsor *is set in Windsor Park. It is here that Falstaff, dressed as a buck, gets his "come-uppance." Mistresses Page and Fora repay him for sending them identical love letters in hopes of controlling their family money.*

Comedy is built around character, situations, or dialogue. A strange character bumbling along through life like a Don Quixote provokes laughter. The pleasure-loving but cowardly Falstaff, the linguistically confused Mrs. Malaprop, and the female-masquerading Fancourt Babberly become natural causes for mirth. Involved predicaments that seem insurmountable or improbable provide a "situation." Mistaken identities, rash promises, or a series of events where everything seems to go wrong focus audience attention on the solving of the problem. Trying to live one life in town and another in the country makes the situation in *The Importance of Being Earnest* ripe for amusing farce. In Noel Coward's *Blithe Spirit,* the ghost of Charles's first wife tries to murder her former husband in order that he might join her "on the other side," but by accident it is the second wife who drives off in the sabotaged car, and the hapless Charles finds himself plagued by two spirit-spouses.

It seems strange to many students of the drama that almost all comedy has its basic appeal to the intellect rather than to the emotions. However, this is the reason for the question "Did the audience 'catch on'?" There are several types of comedy, some causing great belly laughs, some bringing laughter to the point of tears, and some causing only inner smiles or chuckles.

The Causes of Laughter

It is difficult to determine what makes people laugh. Some laugh at very strange things — the exaggerated, the grotesque, even the horrifying. Others laugh out of embarrassment, sometimes to save themselves from tears and sometimes, it seems, for no reason at all. Partly because of this unpredictable audience response, comic plays are more difficult to perform successfully than serious plays. Laughter is fickle and oriented to a particular time and place. What is funny today may not be funny tomorrow. What is humorous in New York City might not be amusing in London or Paris. However, it is possible to identify seven causes of laughter.

Exaggeration

The most noticeable characteristic of anything comic is probably **exaggeration.** Almost every character, line, or situation must be at least slightly exaggerated in order to be funny. One form of exaggeration is the overstatement, or hyperbole. "I can lick you with both hands tied behind my back" is an example of hyperbole. The opposite of overstatement is understatement. "Elementary, my dear Watson" says Sherlock Holmes of his amazing feats of detection.

Exaggeration may also be applied to physical characteristics, such as a

bulbous nose or buck teeth; to mannerisms, such as a strange walk or a twitching eye; to mental characteristics, such as the almost-too-brilliant child prodigy, or the incredibly-too-stupid person; or to personality characteristics, such as miserliness, prissiness, or fanciful romanticism.

Another form of exaggeration stems from the "humours" of Shakespeare's time. The humours are personality determiners that make people giggly, care-free, happy-go-lucky (air); moody, philosophical, love-sick (earth); impatient, hot-headed, passionate (fire); and dull, lazy, sluggish (water). Each of these personality types is such an exaggeration from the normal that people cannot help responding with laughter or tears.

Incongruity

Anything that seems out of place, out of time, or out of character is an example of **incongruity.** Human beings have a built-in system of order, and if what they expect does not occur, they laugh. Someone waltzing to a rhumba beat, the hulking fullback who quotes Shelley and Keats, and the "harmless little fellow" who is as brave as an army are examples of incongruities audiences find amusing. **Grotesqueness** is another incongruity. In theater, grotesqueness means an unusual or distorted feature. The grotesque can become a subject for pathos or comedy depending upon the point of view. Cyrano de Bergerac's nose speech is humorous because he jests at his own features.

However, we are compassionate when we realize how painful his physical features are to him. Missing teeth, an exaggerated limp that becomes a hippety-hop, or drooping eyelids may produce laughter mainly because we do not wish to cry.

Incongruity is also found in action that is **unnatural** or machine-like. This is often accomplished by machinelike or puppetlike behavior. A person who moves about like a windup toy makes us laugh. We find it amusing to see people behave like animals or animal characters behave like people. Ben Jonson's *Volpone* has human beings with animal personalities — a fox, a fly, a parrot, a vulture, a crow, and a raven. The cowardly lion of *The Wizard of Oz* seems hilariously like his faint-hearted human counterpart. Long sweeps about the stage, seven-league strides, grandiose gestures, almost too-flowing movements, or a walk with some part of the body seeming to advance or trail unnaturally have always been good for a laugh.

Unnatural sounds — such as a brayish laugh as piercing as that of a hyena, severely trilled *r*'s that pound like a jackhammer, or an undulating pitch that soars up and down like a slide trombone — are sure to draw laughter from the audience. We will even discover that certain words are comic, not merely because they seem odd, but because the sound is incongruously funny to the ears — we laugh at "Piscataway," but not at "Schenectady."

The **twist** or the unexpected provides another form of incongruity, since

In The Wizard of Oz, *the Scarecrow's transformation into a living being is not without its problems. The comic element is set up as the sagging Scarecrow, already suffering the effects of having lost a considerable amount of straw, tries to stand up.*
● ● ● ● ● ● ● ● ● ● ● ● ● ● ● ● ● ●

the logical completion of a pattern is turned inside out or upside down by a strange turn of events. One kind of twist is based on what the audience knows the character is really like as opposed to what he or she pretends to be. Abby and Martha, the sweet old ladies of *Arsenic and Old Lace,* have convinced the community that they are the epitome of kindness and generosity. But the audience discovers they have poisoned twelve old gentlemen, eleven of whom are buried in the cellar.

Reversal is a kind of incongruity that enables the audience to enjoy seeing the tables turned. Reversal often involves the weak overcoming the strong, the servant overpowering the master, and the underdog beating the favorite, as well as a change from unhappiness to happiness, poverty to prosperity, or lowliness to prestige.

The **irrelevant** or unimportant is a final form of incongruity. This is especially true when the treatment of a lofty subject is involved. All forms of burlesque humor, which will be discussed later in this chapter, exaggerate the unimportant.

Anticipation

The key to many laughs is **anticipation**, or the looking forward to a potential laugh. The strength of the laugh is determined by how much the audience is "in the know." We wait for the characters of mistaken identity to meet and booby traps to ensnare innocent victims. After Teddy charged up "San Juan Hill," for the first time, the audience watching *Arsenic and Old Lace* anticipates his next exit upstairs, holds its breath as he stops on the landing to draw his imaginary sword, and convulses in laughter as he roars "CHARGE! Charge the blockhouse!"

The old gag of the banana peel on the sidewalk is an excellent example of anticipation. The observer will start to laugh even before the clown takes that disastrous step.

Many times anticipation is created by the *plant* — an idea, a line, or an action emphasized early in the play that is used later for a laugh. It must be remembered that it usually takes at least three exposures to an idea to provoke a laugh: one to plant, a second to establish, and the third to clinch, or bring out a response. From then on, the gag should be good for a laugh until it is milked dry.

Incompletion is another form of anticipation. Here people's sense of order is appealed to. A line or a bit of action is started but never finished. The audience completes the thought with laughter.

A third type of anticipation is what is called the *anticlimax* or letdown. The excitement over something is built up to great proportions, and then, like a bursting bubble, there is nothing. The follow-through is never equal to the preparation. An example of this is what is called the *flat line*, a line delivered with either a drop in pitch or with little or no expression in the voice.

Ambiguity

Double meaning, or **ambiguity,** is the heart of many humorous lines. Puns and word play depend upon the audience's recognizing the possible interpretations and, almost always, selecting the one least likely. Even names like Lydia Languish, Lady Teazle, or Sir Fopling Flutter provide comic clues to personality as well as identification of characters. Mistaken identities, lines meant for one person but "accepted" by another, and ruses and disguises are other ways to create double meaning.

Recognition

Discovering hidden or obscure meanings is called **recognition.** "Solving the puzzle," especially in a line or passage of wit where the audience must think twice, is the basis of high comedy and satire. We find it humorous when we recognize the inner motivation of a character. The motivation may be implied by a subtle act, such as the sly wink of a coquette as she hides behind her fan and asks, "Why, Sir, were you addressing me?" We are also amused when we discover what is going to happen just before it does. The *take* — the "mouth-agape freeze" of farce — has always brought down the house. The character sees or hears something that apparently does not sink in, takes a step or two, and then "Pow!" the meaning hits.

Protection

One of the most important elements of comedy is called the **protection factor.** Cruel, violent, grotesque, and abusive actions and events often cause laughter when the audience is under the protection of knowing these things are not really happening. The secret of the cartoon in which a character runs off a cliff is this protection factor. The character falls 100 feet to apparent "doom," but amazingly reappears in the next frame. The old slapstick of pies in the face and beatings with water-filled rubber bags is another example; it made considerable noise but hurt no one. We are truly amused when we are certain that no one is really being injured, and we can accept the illusion as being real, for then we laugh because it is not happening to us.

Relief

The **relief** of pressure, such as comic relief in a tragedy or in a situation that builds up to a point where the audience feels it can take no more, is humorous when the pent-up emotions are allowed to explode in a laugh. When your emotions suddenly erupt, you often explain: "I couldn't hold it in any longer." Good comedies build up pressures and release them, as you can see in the following example, which shows how some of these causes of laughter work together.

Good comedy is like a powder keg (plant) with a lighted fuse (anticipation). When the fuse fizzles (unexpected) at just the moment of expected explosion (anticlimax), the audience may laugh. They will probably snicker when the too-curious buffoon approaches the keg to see why it did not go off. But, as the audience could have predicted (recognition), the keg then blows up in the buffoon's face (protection). When the victim emerges ragged and soot-covered (incongruity), the audience roars even louder (relief).

Types of Comedy

The traditional classification of comedies is important, for each kind demands a special kind of staging. There are three levels of comedy: low, middle, and high.

Low Comedy

What we call **low comedy** is quite physical, is sometimes vulgar, and produces a knee-slapping guffaw or belly laugh. Low comedy is highly exaggerated in style and performance. The situation is outlandish, if not ridiculous, and the characters are not at all like anyone you might meet on the street. Low comedy includes farce and burlesque.

Farce

Almost everything done strictly for laughs — clowning, practical jokes, and improbable characters and situations involve **farce.** Farce frequently features a considerable amount of assault and battery: ears are pulled, shins are kicked, and pies are shoved into faces. Many of these actions come within the term *slapstick,* which is derived from an old stage prop consisting of two thin boards hinged together. The slapstick made a loud but harmless crack when applied to the backside of a performer.

The more unbelievable the situation, the riper it is for farce. A young man from Oxford University tries to pass himself off as a wealthy woman of charm from Brazil *(Charley's Aunt).* An unusual family encourages its members to do whatever they please, whenever they please: take ballet lessons, play the xylophone, write novels, make fireworks in the basement, refuse to pay income tax *(You Can't Take It with You)*. Two sweet old ladies poison elderly gentlemen by putting arsenic in elderberry wine *(Arsenic and Old Lace)*.

Farces usually have chase scenes — through gardens or houses, around furniture, or in and out-of-doors. *Charley's Aunt* has a hilarious chase scene through the Oxford gardens.

Farces may also have *screen scenes.* In a screen scene, some of the actors hide from the others onstage — behind doors, inside closets, or behind bushes. The concealed characters always overhear the onstage dialogue and may pop out to say something, talk to each other, or make asides — all unheard by the other characters onstage. An **aside** is a line spoken directly to the audience. The hidden characters in a screen scene may change position from one hiding spot to another. An unusual screen situation is found in much of the play *Blithe Spirit.* The ghost of Charles Condomine's first wife is onstage, but only Charles can see and hear her. So she moves about and makes witty comments that are not heard by Ruth, Charles's second wife.

Chases and screen scenes are sometimes combined. The sidesplitting hat shop scene from *Hello, Dolly!* has Barnaby and Cornelius popping in and out of closets, hiding under tables, even marching onstage, right behind Horace Vandergelder.

In Joseph Kesselring's Arsenic and Old Lace, *two eccentric old ladies murder a lonely old man. The unbelievability of the situation creates a sense of comedy.*

Elements such as exaggerated mannerisms and stereotypical gangster characterizations in the farce, Archangels Don't Play Pinball, *demonstrates how burlesque pokes fun at seriousness.*
• •

Burlesque

A common form of low comedy that is seen most frequently in skits on television and in performances by stand-up comedians is **burlesque.** It is a broad kind of comedy that pokes fun at people, at society's foibles, and even at other forms of theater.

One kind of burlesque is *travesty,* which pokes fun at revered and lofty subjects. A noble thought, a noble individual, or a dream is made to appear ludicrous. For example, in *The Man of La Mancha,* a scarecrow-like old man sets out on a noble quest as a knight-errant 300 years too late. He fights his first battle with a windmill. The incongruous mixture of the nobility of the knight-errant tradition and a feeble old man's dream makes us laugh.

A second kind of burlesque is the *mock heroic* or *mock epic.* In this form of low comedy, a person or subject that is not of heroic proportions is humorously elevated. Shaw's *Androcles and the Lion* does just this: Androcles, the timid Greek tailor, survived the lion-feeding time in the Roman arena. Androcles became a folk hero that day. The lion, instead of eating Androcles, nuzzled up against him, wanting to be petted. Earlier that day, before the lion was captured in the woods, Androcles had removed a thorn from the lion's foot.

A third kind of burlesque is *parody.* A parody is an imitation of a work of literature. One kind of parody is the parody of form, in which words of the original are readily identified by the audience. Another kind of parody is the parody of idea, in which an entire subject is held up to ridicule. Soap operas, western movies, and musicals are frequent sources of parody. In *How to Succeed in Business Without Really Trying,* a college song and cheer are parodied. In *No Time for Sergeants,* psychological examinations are parodied.

Caricature is a fourth kind of burlesque. A caricature is like a political cartoon that overdraws a physical feature or personality trait. A caricature does not try to show a real personality but exaggerates an unusual manner of speaking, a strange posture, or a peculiar walk. This is the type of thing done by impressionists who do imitations of famous people. Children's plays often feature caricatures, such as the wicked witch, the evil adviser to the king, and so on.

The most common forms of burlesque in full-length stage productions are *spoofs* or *takeoffs*. These are imitations of types of stage presentations. For example, *Little Mary Sunshine* is a takeoff on old movie musicals that starred a well-known musical pair, and *The Boy Friend* is a spoof on the 1920s.

Middle Comedy

What we call humor includes **middle comedy. Humor** involves an appeal to the heart, where the audience can gently feel love, tenderness, pity, or compassion. Humor is tied firmly to an emotional empathy, although the

In Shakespeare's romantic comedy Much Ado About Nothing, *Alfred Drake plays the bachelor, Benedick, and Katherine Hepburn takes the part of the merry and independent Beatrice.*

laughter itself comes from the thinking process. No one has to tell an actor who has studied people carefully how closely related laughter and tears may be. The closeness of happiness to sorrow, bitterness to sweetness, and hopefulness to futility increases comic effect because the leap from one extreme to the other prompts an emotional response. Some types of middle comedy are romantic comedy, sentimental comedy, melodrama, and social drama.

Romantic Comedy

A **romantic comedy** presents life as we would like it to be. Romantic comedies usually are set in some far-off locale with an exotic name. Romantic comedies do not necessarily involve romance, but the "good" characters are recognizably *good,* and the "evil" characters are obviously *evil.* Romantic comedies are sometimes referred to as costume dramas because they so often take place in a time and location requiring the actors to wear lavish costumes.

Most of Shakespeare's comedies are of this type. Among them are *Twelfth Night, As You Like It, The Tempest,* and *A Midsummer Night's Dream.* Another classic romantic comedy is *Cyrano de Bergerac.* Cyrano stands out as one of the great protagonists of romantic comedy.

Fantasy

Largely a form of romantic drama but frequently introduced into sequences in realistic plays, **fantasy** deals with unreal characters in dreams and scenes imaginary in time and place. The land of make-believe forms the background — inhabited by spirits with supernatural powers, gods from another world, and the eternal personalities of Pierrot and Pierrette, witches, and will-o-the-wisps. Some of the most popular adult productions are Shakespeare's *A Midsummer Night's Dream* and *The Tempest,* and such modern plays as Maxwell Anderson's *High Tor* and *Star-Wagon,* Paul Osborn's *On Borrowed Time,* and J. M. Barrie's *Peter Pan.* Such musicals as *Brigadoon, Finian's Rainbow,* and *Cats* have strong elements of fantasy in them.

Sentimental Comedy

Sentimental comedy is one of the most popular forms of drama. It tugs at our hearts as it makes us smile and laugh. Based on themes of personal relationships, self-sacrifice, patriotism, lost affection, mother love, and youthful romance, these plays at their best meet the universal need of average people to have faith in others and to lose themselves in the lives of others like themselves.

Shakespeare's The Tempest *has its romantic plot set within Prospero's fantasy of a magic island and his own magical powers.*

There are many good sentimental comedies that high school groups often produce. Among the most appealing are Mary Chase's *Harvey*, John Van Druten's *I Remember Mama*, and the many plays of Neil Simon, including *Barefoot in the Park* and *The Odd Couple*. At their worst, sentimental comedies include soap operas seen so often on television.

Melodrama

A **melodrama** is a serious play written to arouse intense emotion by blood-curdling events, terrific suspense, and horrifying details centering on murders, greed, and revenge. Motivation and logical explanations are not so important in a melodrama. Therefore, we do not question why things turn out as they do. Some melodramas you might enjoy are *Ten Little Indians*, *Witness for the Prosecution*, *Dial M for Murder*, *Dracula*, *Deathtrap*, and *Sleuth*. Movie and television melodramas include western, courtroom, law-enforcement, and hospital dramas.

A mystery play is a melodrama of the "whodunit" class. The plot centers on tracking down a criminal. Agatha Christie's *The Mousetrap*, a mystery play, holds the all-time record for the continuous run of a play.

Social Drama

Sometimes called the problem play, **social drama** will always exist in one form or another as dramatists seek to right the wrongs of society. These plays are frequently comedies in the sense that they offer a solution for the problems they present. Many are tragedies because the protagonist loses the battle against evil, sometimes even dying.

Some famous social dramas are Ibsen's *An Enemy of the People*, which shows how a man from a small town stands for civic integrity against all the

Whose Life Is It Anyway? by Brian Clark is a social drama of the 1980s. Richard Dreyfuss plays Ken Harrison, who is paralyzed from the neck down as the result of an automobile accident.

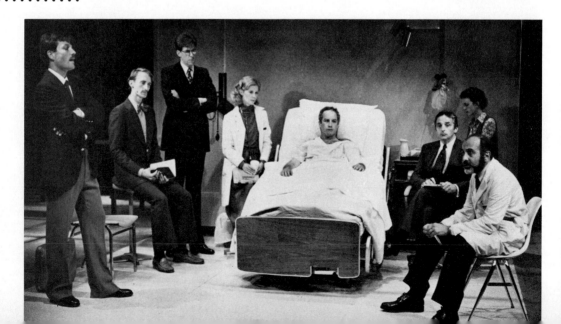

citizens of his community; Bertolt Brecht's *The Caucasian Chalk Circle,* which attacks the selfishness of the elite; and Lorraine Hansberry's *A Raisin in the Sun,* which shows a black family struggling to escape the ghetto.

High Comedy

Humor that appeals to the head is called **high comedy.** The audience must be on its toes in order to catch the clever lines, word play, and allusions. High comedy often appeals only to well-educated, sophisticated theater-goers. High comedy includes comedy of manners and satire.

Comedy of Manners

The **comedy of manners** laughs at the foolish thoughts, actions, and pretenses of a particular segment of society — usually the upper class. Built on clever use of language, the wit of comedy of manners includes puns, paradoxes, epigrams, and ironies. The dialogue is razor-sharp conversation between clever people, often attacking the socially accepted standards of the day.

Restoration drama, written in the seventeenth century, represents the masterpieces of comedy of manners. Such plays as Wycherley's *The Country Wife,* Congreve's *The Way of the World,* Goldsmith's *She Stoops to Conquer,* and Sheridan's *The School for Scandal* and *The Rivals* are examples of this genre. These plays are frequently produced in repertory theaters across the country.

Satire

Satire holds human frailty up to ridicule. The comedy of satire is a humorous attack on accepted conventions of society or a humorous observation on the foibles and follies of humanity. Nothing is exempt from the barbs of the satirist — politics, education, religion, philosophy, and other revered topics are subject to attack.

Oscar Wilde and George Bernard Shaw will probably remain unsurpassed in the field of satire. Twentieth-century dramatists of expert comedies of this kind include Noel Coward, Tom Stoppard, Peter Shaffer, and Alan Ayckbourn.

Styles

The term **style** refers to the way in which a play is written, acted, and produced. Dramatists adopt the language and action they feel best express their ideas. Directors and scenic artists present the play in a form that they feel suits the script.

The Madwoman of Chaillot is a classic of wit, charm, and fantasy that is supported by the graceful use of language.

Classification of plays today is complicated by the fact that many modern playwrights and directors are breaking away from historical styles. They ignore or combine these styles to suit themselves. Following is a description of the major styles of plays you are likely to perform, see, or read.

Representational and Presentational

All plays are either **representational** or **presentational** in style. Most plays that you will see are representational. Sometimes this style is called "fourth wall" theater. The play is performed as if the audience is watching the action through an imaginary fourth wall. The characters on stage are not aware of the audience. The presentational style acknowledges that an audience is present. Characters may even speak to the audience, and some action may take place in the seating area, as in *Our Town.*

Romanticism

The style of romantic comedies is often **romanticism.** Romanticism shows life as we would like it to be. The setting is in a faraway place or an ideal spot of great beauty. The language is lofty and poetic. The protagonist seeks a noble goal and may face an antagonist who has great power, magic, or knowl-edge. *Androcles and the Lion, The Madwoman of Chaillot, Cyrano de Bergerac,* and Shakespearean comedies are written in this style. Modern play-wrights using the romantic style include Robert Bolt and Jean Giraudoux.

Realism and Naturalism

The dominant style of the twentieth century is **realism.** Realistic plays present life as it actually is — often unpleasant and unhappy, but not necessarily so. Realistic plays can sometimes be quite positive and amusing. The characters talk and act as people in ordinary life do in whatever social group they belong. The outcome of the play is what it would logically be in the real world. Selec-tive realism — using selected scenes to typify reality — became the primary style of stage, screen, and television in this century. The Norwegian playwright Henrik Ibsen has been called the "father of realism," as well as the "father of modern drama." He introduced realism in *A Doll's House* in 1879.

The style called **naturalism** grew out of realism but became exaggerated in the early years of this century. Naturalism is often sordid and shocking. "Life as it is with no holds barred" is its central topic. Naturalistic protagonists

No Place To Be Somebody *is a realistic play whose action is set in the 1960s. The dialogue and staging make this moment in time come alive.*
. . . .

Godspell is presented as if the young actors are a group of friends who have casually gathered together and are passing the time by telling each other stories. The stories of the friends are in actuality a retelling of biblical parables. The symbolism of the John the Baptist and Jesus of Nazareth dramatizations is apparent.

are often weak, misguided, and unheroic, such as Willie Loman in *Death of a Salesman* and Keller in *All My Sons.*

Symbolism

In a **symbolic** play, the dramatist emphasizes the theme by having characters, props, even sets, stand for something else. In *Death of a Salesman,* Willie Loman is the symbol of the "person in-between." He is a man caught between changing eras. The mortgage on his house and his insurance policy both suggest that life is often "used up" before it is paid for. In the *Miracle Worker,* the well symbolizes Helen Keller's soul and the key dropped in the well is the key to language. In *The Glass Menagerie,* the audience is told directly that Laura's glass animals, her menagerie, represent her own delicate beauty and inability to cope with a harsh world.

Allegory

A powerful form of symbolism is **allegory.** The characters in an allegory definitely represent abstract qualities like Truth, Justice, and Love or personalities like Death, God, and Humanity as characters in a play that has as its goal the teaching of moral concepts. It has been a popular form of storytelling throughout the history of humanity.

The greatest allegory of them all is *Everyman.* Everyman is suddenly summoned to meet Death. He must appear before God and seek salvation. In his desperate need, all his friends — Five Wits, Fellowship, Kindred, Discretion, Beauty, Strength, and Knowledge — fail him. Only his Good Deeds, enchained and feeble, will go with him. *J.B.* by Archibald MacLeish, the modern version of the Book of Job, is a fine contemporary allegory. Thornton Wilder's *Our Town,* which shows how typical human beings in a modern small town are failing to realize the beauty of daily life, has many characteristics of the allegorical play.

The Avant-Garde Theater

The term **avant-garde** is used to identify whatever the new and experimental styles of any art form happen to be at the time. Many techniques accepted today as general theater practices were considered avant-garde at their beginning. In the United States, much of the new experimentation takes place off-Broadway and off-off-Broadway. While many of the avant-garde movements quickly die off, a few become part of the continuing theater. However, once a style is accepted, it is no longer avant-garde.

Other Twentieth-Century Theater Styles

This century has seen many changes in theatrical trends. These changes continue every season. How much they will affect the drama of the future cannot be estimated at the present time, but they will undoubtedly be exciting for theatergoers.

Constructivism

The style referred to as **constructivism** originated in the first quarter of the twentieth century by Vsevolod Meyerhold. It was in direct contrast with the far more widely renowned realism of Stanislavski. Meyerhold did not present productions based on real life on a picture-frame stage. Instead, he constructed backgrounds of mechanical skeletons on various levels connected by arches, ramps, ladders, and platforms. On these, actors were trained to move with precise symbolic movements that were to take the place of language. Today, the acting style associated with constructivism has faded, but similar sets and skeletal frameworks are used to suggest location and feeling.

Gloria Foster is Mother Courage in the Bertolt Brecht epic drama Mother Courage and Her Children. *Brecht's piece is about war, the followers of armies, as well as human profiteering and powerlessness.*

The Epic Theater

The **epic theater** is a journalistic, nonemotional style that was first developed by Bertolt Brecht. It uses signs, projections, films, and loudspeakers to present events in an episodic form.

The epic theater is a reaction against emotionalism, naturalism, and the "well-made play." For example, Brecht's plays do not involve the spectators in the problems and feelings of the characters as most plays do, and entertainment is a secondary goal. The plays objectively set forth events in episodic form, using broad phases of human experience rather than individual relationships. Brecht's plays include *Mother Courage and Her Children, The Good Women of Setzuan, The Caucasian Chalk Circle,* and *The Threepenny Opera.*

Existential Theater

Basically, the **existential theater** supports the philosophy of the existentialists. They believe that human beings do not really begin to live until they define their existence. Only after existence is defined can humanity discover the true meaning of life.

Jean Paul Sartre's *No Exit* has three characters who find themselves in a room without doors or windows. As the play develops, one character discovers her real identity, only to find that she and her companions are in hell.

Tom Stoppard's *Rosencrantz and Guildenstern Are Dead* is another existential play. It is a lesson in existential frustration. All that Rosencrantz and Guildenstern know is that "they were sent for." They spend the entire play trying to find out what they are supposed to do. But before they discover the answer to what they were sent for, their time onstage is over.

Expressionism

In **expressionism,** the dramatist has a theme, usually centered on ideas of justice, social relationships, and the evils of the machine age. The qualities and thoughts of the characters are expressed against highly imaginative symbolic sets.

The first such play to become a hit in the United States was *Beggar on Horseback,* produced in the twenties and revived in 1970. The hero, a young musician, is on the verge of marrying the daughter of a big businessman. In a dream, the hero experiences the horrors of an industrial career, an unhappy marriage, and in-law troubles in an exaggerated and amusing nightmare. Incidents are all accompanied by jazz rhythms from a nearby orchestra, the last thing he heard before going to sleep. Georg Kaiser's *From Morn to Midnight* and O'Neill's *The Hairy Ape* are expressionistic plays.

Performance Art is a recently coined term used to describe a unique form of drama that may include many different elements of performance juxtaposed in a novel way.

Impressionism

In using **impressionism,** the dramatist gives the audience the inner reactions of characters under great stress. The drumbeat heard in Eugene O'Neill's *The Emperor Jones* is an excellent example of impressionism. The drums begin beating at 70 beats a minute, the normal rate at which the human heart beats. By the end of the play, the drumbeats may increase to 200 beats a minute, reflecting the growing fear of Emperor Jones.

Stylization

A blending of script and production, achieved in stylized drama, is called **stylization.** Stylized productions bear the stamp of the personality and individual point of view of the director-designer. Stylized productions have included characters dressed like the animals they resemble in spirit or Shakespearean characters dressed in modern garb. Other stylized productions have made good use of the constructivistic sets mentioned previously.

Theater of Involvement

The participation of the members of the audience in the action of the performance is the keynote of the **theater of involvement.** *Paradise Now* was one of the first productions staged by the Living Theater. Theatergoers declared themselves bored, annoyed, intrigued, flattered, and disgusted when they found themselves involved with members of the cast in arguments, physical attacks, and invitations to actually take part in the proceedings. Critics wrote cynical and amusing reviews of the episodes of "liberation, mysteries, and rites" that made up the evening's activities.

The theater of involvement works well with children's theater. It has also been successful, however, in productions such as *Cats.* In this play, the performers go into the audience and play directly to individuals.

Theater of the Absurd

The **theater of the absurd** says that human beings are absurd creatures living in an absurd world, making an absurd attempt to find meaning in absurdity. There is many times no plot or characterization, and the theme, if any, is often hidden in confusion. Some absurdists go so far as to show the language breaking down into meaningless patter. At its best, absurdist drama offers a challenge to the cast and audience alike. *Waiting for Godot, Rhinoceros, The Bald Soprano, The Lesson, Endgame,* and *The Sand Box* are examples of the theater of the absurd.

Theatricalism and Total Theater

The style of **theatricalism** simply says: "This is the theater. Accept it for what it is, as it is." The cardboard moon, wooden-dowel swords, and the mute wall of *The Fantasticks* are illustrations of theatricalism.

The concept of **total theater** attempts to fuse all the performing arts into one presentation. At its best, it combines a strong plot with impassioned characters, well-written dialogue, and first-class acting. These are enhanced by delineative dancing and mime, atmospheric music with inspirational lyrics, and creative costuming and staging, capitalizing on the wonders of today's audiovisual special effects.

Special Styles

There are three special styles that have an important place in contemporary theater: one-person shows, children's theater, and puppet theater.

One-Person Shows

At one time, the monodrama was a favorite vehicle for personal appearances. The supreme example was *Before Breakfast,* the Eugene O'Neill tragedy in which a nagging wife drives her husband into committing suicide offstage. Today the one-person show has taken its place in the theater, and a number of actors and actresses have become famous with their arrangements of the life stories and literary works of well-known actors. Witness Hal Holbrook's presentations of Mark Twain and Charles Dickens.

Other performers, such as Lily Tomlin, present an evening of loosely structured monologues.

In recent years, several actors and actresses have presented one-person shows. Among the most highly acclaimed productions are James Whitmore as Harry Truman, Julie Harris as Emily Dickinson, Henry Fonda as Clarence Darrow, and Vincent Price as Oscar Wilde.

You will be seeing more and more of these one-person shows. You may want to work some up for yourself, for they are a most appealing form of easily produced theater. The structure is loose, but the presentation should have interesting incidents, with natural conversation, depicting events in the life story of a well-known personality.

Children's Theater

A large part of contemporary theater is devoted to what is called children's theater — theater written, designed, and performed for children. Most high school drama groups produce at least one children's play each season. Regional, civic, and professional theater groups often include children's theater as part of their seasons. Some even run a separate children's theater schedule. Many original scripts and new adaptations are available for production. No longer are producing groups limited to a handful of the old fairy-tale adaptations. The popularity of Story Theater has opened new doors to this style.

Puppet Theater

Puppets have long been a part of theater the world over. However, in recent years, television programs such as the *Muppets* and *Sesame Street* have prompted a new interest in puppets.

There are several types of puppets that have been used in theater: (1) the marionette, a puppet operated by strings from above the puppet; (2) the stick puppet, operated by sticks from below the puppet; (3) shadow puppets, silhouette puppets operated by sticks from behind the puppet; (4) hand puppets, operated by the fingers and hand; (5) "life-size" puppets, operated from inside, behind, or below; and (6) mechanized puppets, operated by motors, electronic controls, or other mechanical means.

Hand puppets have become the most popular. Three-finger hand puppets allow the operation of a head and two hands. Two-finger puppets, as they are called, usually operate only the mouth of a glove or sock puppet. This type of puppet evolved into the Muppet so well known today. The puppet-muppets of *Little Shop of Horrors* have delighted and horrified audiences all across the country.

Recalling Ideas

1. Does each of the following statements refer to tragedy or to comedy?

   a. The protagonist is less than average in some way.

   b. The protagonist may be guilty of *hamartia.*

   c. There are frequently scenes of recognition and reversal.

   d. These plays are usually societal.

2. What should an audience feel at the end of a tragedy?

3. List and describe seven causes of laughter.

4. Describe four types of middle comedy.

5. Define *style* and describe three different styles of drama.

Discussing Ideas

1. What is the appeal of tragedy for an audience? What makes the roles of tragic protagonists so challenging for actors?

2. Tragedy is universal; comedy is rooted in a particular time or place. Discuss this statement. Cite examples of plays or movies you have seen.

3. Think of a play or movie you have seen with a particular style, such as a romantic fantasy. Discuss the sources of the production's style. How did the script, set, lighting, costumes, and actors' diction and gestures contribute to the style?

4. What risks do spectators at experimental drama take? What are the possible rewards of that risk?

Careers

In the theater, **musical directors** audition and select vocal and instrumental talent for shows, then direct the musicians during rehearsals and performances. They may also work in motion pictures, radio, and television, where they select music suitable to the program, motion picture, or entertainer. They assign and review the work of the staff in scoring, arranging, music copying, lyric writing, and vocal coaching.

Most musical directors are graduates of theater arts, professional, or music schools and are experienced performers.

Over 1,000 colleges, universities, conservatories, and specialty schools teach music-related subjects. **Singers** with that training perform in operas or operettas, in nightclubs, with orchestras, at concerts, and in musical plays. They often begin in small clubs, working with a **vocal coach** familiar with the needs of nightclubs and cabarets.

Other music graduates become **composers** or **arrangers.** Composers write music; arrangers adapt musical composition to a style for which it was not originally written. When writing for a Broadway show, a composer usually works with a **lyricist,** who writes the words, as well as an **arranger,** who writes the music for the various instruments in the orchestra.

Instrumentalists are other music graduates who play one or more instruments. Many come to the pit orchestra of the theater from an opera or symphony orchestra. Some earn their living by playing with one orchestra, while others play small club dates or teach to supplement their income. Some eventually become **conductors** of orchestras.

To get recognition, performers often make demonstration records or video cassettes of their work. Some hire a hall and give a debut recital for critics and art managers.

Chapter 8

. . . .

Evaluation of Drama

You Will Learn

What some rules of theater etiquette are.

What to judge in a play.

What to consider when evaluating the directing, acting, and staging.

How to evaluate avant-garde theater.

Vocabulary

critic   etiquette

$\mathcal{S}$ince the days of ancient Greece, people have enjoyed watching plays. But never before have so many people seen so many plays of so many varieties. You can see plays at performing arts centers, local theaters, repertory theaters, and experimental playhouses. You can see plays on television or videos. You may be able to see road shows or summer stock productions. What plays you watch depends entirely upon your own judgment as to how you wish to use your leisure hours.

You and the Drama

Perhaps the biggest bonus of dramatics class is the ability you will develop to watch plays with intelligence and with emotional and aesthetic sensitivity. Your study of plays and their production will help you to evaluate dramatic literature and its interpretation onstage.

Most Americans still view Broadway as the epitome of this country's theater experience. The Shubert Theatre is one of Broadway's most famous.
· · · · · · · · · · · ·

You should learn to judge what good theater is to enjoy what it has to offer you. A person who is a specialist in judging plays is called a **critic.** A critic may discuss new productions in reviews in newspapers, in magazines, or on television. However, a good critic does not go to a play looking for things to criticize. The most highly trained theatergoers are often the most enthusiastic, because they understand the art of the playwright, the director, and the actors. When you have studied all the phases of the drama and then been enthralled by a fine production, you will experience the same satisfaction that comes to an artist standing before a superb painting or to a musician at a splendid concert.

Theater Etiquette

As you study drama, you should see as many productions as possible and discuss them in class. Therefore, as a student of the theater, you should know some of the basic rules of theater **etiquette,** or proper behavior.

Theatergoers should always know the curtain time and arrive early enough to obtain tickets and be seated before the lights dim. Many theaters will not seat patrons once the first act has begun, until the intermission. A courteous audience does not talk during the production. This applies to the overture of a musical which is part of the performance.

It is customary to applaud as the conductor approaches the podium. When the curtain opens and the set pleases you, it is a compliment to the scenery designer and crew to applaud. An especially fine scene or individual performance may bring applause in a rare "show-stopper." The curtain call is usually the time that the audience shows with its applause how much it enjoyed the show. Standing ovations should be reserved for truly outstanding performances. Remember, the play is not over until the last bow has been taken. It is poor theater manners to leave before the houselights come up.

Playgoers should only leave the theater during a performance out of necessity or emergency. It is wise to remember that first acts are long, especially in musicals.

In American theater, presentations of flowers, gifts, or recognitions are usually made offstage, not before the audience. Exceptions should have the approval of the director or stage manager.

In this country, food and drink are usually not permitted in the theater. Whatever the rules of the particular theater you are visiting, be sure that your crackling wrappers do not disturb your neighbors.

Above all, come to enjoy — to learn and to grow! Despite their mechanical perfections and marvelous special effects, television and movies can never create that intangible, magnetic quality that passes from actor to audience in a live play. Movies and television can never become the unity of light and color, voice and movement, imagination and reality that is a play produced by living actors before a living audience.

To fully appreciate any type of drama and to judge it fairly, you must consider the play itself, its interpretation by the actors, its staging, and its reception by the audience. Your personal preferences, your state of mind, your background, and your knowledge of the theater will naturally influence your judgment.

Judging the Play

The type of play you see must color your attitude toward it. You cannot judge a light social satire by the same standards as a romantic drama in blank verse. You cannot judge a tragedy and a farce by the same standards, nor can an avant-garde production be judged by the standards of a traditional production.

Theme

Your first consideration in evaluating a play should be the theme. Determine for yourself the playwright's purpose. You might follow Goethe's example and ask "What did the author try to do? Did the author do it? Was it worth doing?"

Plot

The plot should hold your intense interest. If the play is any good at all, you will be wondering most of the time "what is going to happen next." If you do not care, focus on whether the events are plausible and the situations interesting in themselves. Decide whether there is a convincing climax, which stirs you emotionally, and a logical conclusion, which satisfies you intellectually.

Dialogue

The dramatist's style is revealed through dialogue. Your appreciation of dialogue will increase as you see many plays. Clever repartee (the swift give and take of conversation), apt figures of speech that are natural to the characters, and the turn of phrase that only the character speaking would use are all aspects of good dialogue.

Characterization

Dialogue serves to bring out the characterization. The individual characterizations you see in a performance frequently result from careful analysis and discussion among the director and the actors.

Children of a Lesser God *by Mark Medoff was the outstanding Tony Award winning play in the 1980 New York City theater season. Phyliss Frelich and John Rubinstein won Best Actress and Best Actor awards. Mark Medoff, the playwright, won the award for best play.*

This a relaxed and soft grouping appropriate for Mornings at Seven, *Paul Osborn's comedy about the elderly in a small midwestern town in 1922.*

Judging the Acting

Of all the aspects of a play, the acting generally arouses the keenest response from the audience. One result of theatrical training is skill at appraising the work of performers. Even a short time in a dramatics class should help you appreciate the discipline and skill that go into a fine piece of acting. A good actor creates a role that is constantly convincing because it is always an integral part of the action. Good actors avoid attracting attention to themselves. By speaking and listening in character, an actor builds up a personality in which you can believe. The actor must be natural and spontaneous while remaining true to the period and spirit of the play. Further, the spectators in the very last row of the theater should be able to hear each actor clearly.

Appreciating the Production

Audiences today are more knowledgeable about the details of play production than ever before. This is largely because so many of today's theatergoers have studied drama and have had actual backstage experience. Your study of drama will help you understand all phases of a play and appreciate the methods of its presentation.

The Director

The director is the most important factor in the ultimate success of a production, because the director is personally responsible for every phase of the play. You will get real enjoyment from noting how the director develops contrast in casting, costuming, and interpretation; how he or she works out interesting stage pictures that emphasize the center of interest; and how the actors, lighting, setting, and costumes create the proper atmosphere.

Set Design

The setting determines the atmosphere of the play. The scenic artist works closely with the director, stage manager, and backstage crew to create the proper effects with sets and lighting.

The goals of scenic art are to create the atmosphere, establish a center of interest, and help carry out the fundamental purpose of the play through the setting itself. The magic of modern lighting and mechanical and electronic effects plays a vital part in this. Simplicity, naturalness, and effectiveness are the principles behind modern staging. More and more, for many reasons — the expense of labor in handling sets, the kind of stage in use, the available lighting equipment and mechanical devices — elaborate scenery is giving way to bare stages or screen projections, or to scenic units that can be easily rearranged.

The Audience Reaction

The reaction of the audience may or may not be a fair criterion in judging the ultimate success of a performance. However, a play is written for an audience, and if it does not satisfy playgoers, then something must be wrong somewhere. Usually the fault lies with the play or with its production, for the average audience is eager to be pleased.

Of course, all plays are not suitable for all audiences. Local politics or religious views, for example, may affect an audience's response to a play. Nevertheless, if a drama deals with fundamental human reactions, presents a definite phase of a universal theme, and is produced in an adequate manner, it is certain to hold the interest of the playgoer.

Judging the Avant-Garde Theater

It is difficult to judge avant-garde theater because the novelty often impresses audiences more than the lasting contribution the new approach might be making to the dramatic arts. Human beings like to experiment, yet at the same

Innovation may take its form in production decisions. Sam Shepard's A
Killer's Head, *a monologue of a man's last moments before electrocution,
was performed every hour, twelve hours a day, behind glass. The
audience listened to the actor through an audio hook-up.*

time, they want to hold on to the traditional and familiar. Especially when the
innovation seems too extreme, too unnatural, or too "new," the observers demand a return to the kind of theater they are used to.

As a student of the drama, you should want to evaluate the merits of experimental theater. A critic must evaluate these experiments from certain "traditional" criteria. First of all, theater is illusion, and illusion, not reality, is one
of its major strengths. Shakespeare said the role of theater is "to hold, as
'twere the mirror up to nature." A mirror shows a reflection of life, never life
itself. Therefore, if the events presented in a play appear to be a newscast, the
audience is not really observing "theater."

Second, whenever you judge a work of literature, you should strip away all
shock, all spectacle, all obscenity in language and action. If what remains has
something to say, provides a clever or entertaining situation, or affords insight
into interesting characters, the play may stand as "good" drama. But if the
work has no theme, no plot, no situation, no characterization, no effective use
of meaningful language, it must be rejected as a poor work of art and unworthy
of the term *theater.*

Third, the ability of such a play to survive time, socioeconomic changes,
people, and nations is very important. Universality is a prime requisite of great
words of literature and art.

Evaluation of a piece in performance is often enhanced by prestudy which in turn may compel further examination. In this production of Samuel Beckett's Waiting for Godot, *John Bottoms is Estragon and Mark Linn-Baker is Vladimir.*

Evaluating a Play

Real theater enthusiasts free their imagination and emotions while watching a play. At the same time, they use their intelligence and discrimination to heighten their appreciation of what they are seeing. The following questions may help you evaluate the plays you attend, the television dramas you watch, and the movies you see.

Theme

1. Is the fundamental idea underlying the play true or false in its concept of life?

2. Does seeing the play add something positive to your understanding and experience?

3. Is the theme consistent with the setting, plot, and characters presented in the play?

Plot

1. Does the play have a clear-cut sequence of events?

2. Does it rise to a strong climax?

3. Does the suspense hold until the end?

4. Was the play emotionally stirring?

5. Are you satisfied by the final outcome?

Characterization

1. Are the characters true to life?

2. Do the characters seem to fit into the social and geographical background of the play?

3. Do they definitely arouse such feelings as sympathy, affection, amusement, disgust, admiration, or hatred on the part of the audience?

4. Are the characters' actions in keeping with their motives?

5. Are the situations at the climax and conclusion the result of their inherent natures?

Style

1. Is the dialogue brilliant and entertaining in itself?

2. Is the dialogue consistent with the characters and setting?

3. Is the dialogue an end in itself, or is it an adequate means of plot advancement and characterization?

4. After seeing the play, do you remember the lines because of their significance or beauty?

5. Is the power of expression worthy of the ideas expressed?

6. Do sound, electronic effects, and staging take the place of words?

Acting

1. Is the interpretation of any given role correct from the standpoint of the play itself?

2. Does the actor make the character a living individual?

3. Are you conscious of the methods of getting effects?

4. Does the actor grip you emotionally? Do you weep, laugh, suffer, and exult?

5. Is the actor's voice pleasing?

6. Does the actor have a magnetic charm?

7. Is use of dialect correct in every detail?

8. Does the actor keep in character every moment?

9. Do you think of the actor as the character depicted or as himself or herself?

10. Does the actor apparently cooperate with the other actors, the director, and the author in interpreting the play by knowing lines, helping to focus the attention on the center of interest, and becoming one with the role?

11. Does the actor become an acceptable part of the style of the production?

Staging

1. Is the setting in keeping with the play itself?

2. Is it beautiful and artistic in itself?

3. Is the setting conducive to the proper emotional reaction to the play?

4. Are the costumes and properties in harmony with the background?

5. Does the setting add to or detract from enjoyment of the play?

6. Is the interest centered on the total effect or on the details?

Audience Reaction

1. Is the audience attentive, involved, or restless during the performance?

2. Is there a definite response of tears, laughter, or applause?

3. Is there an immediate appreciation of clever lines, dramatic situations, and skillful acting?

4. Is the applause spontaneous and wholehearted, or is it merely polite?

5. To what types of people does the play seem to appeal?

Recalling Ideas

1. What does a drama critic do?

2. When does an audience customarily applaud during a musical?

3. What is the first consideration in evaluating a play? Why?

4. What are three characteristics of a good actor?

5. What are three principles behind modern staging?

6. Name three criteria for evaluating avant-garde drama.

Discussing Ideas

1. Compare the experience of a former high-school gymnastics champion watching the Olympic gymnastics competition to the experience of an active high-school drama club member at the opening night of a Broadway play. How do the training of a gymnast and a drama student enhance their viewing of events in their fields.

2. Collect reviews of one new play from several newspapers and magazines. Make a chart comparing the various reviewers' comments on the play's theme, plot, characterization, dialogue, acting, direction, and set design. Would you like to see the play, considering its reviews?

3. Sometimes live theater productions are shown on television. Why is it difficult to evaluate such productions? What is different about a live theatrical experience and a televised play?

4. Why is it possible to enjoy seeing the same play in a number of different productions?

5. In a review of a recent play, drama critic Mimi Kramer comments that the lighting "deftly steers us away from taking the action of the play too literally." What is Ms. Kramer praising about the lighting? Why is that quality desirable?

Careers

Critics are employed by newspapers, magazines, wire services, and radio and television stations to review movies, musical and literary works, and the performing arts. They attend theater performances and special events, such as awards ceremonies, and report their impressions and recommendations to the public. Critics often determine the financial success or failure of a play.

Critics may seem to live a glamorous life: prestige, free tickets, high pay. But they often work under extreme deadline pressure, often on the night shift, in fast-paced, noisy surroundings.

Critics often come from the ranks of reporters. They need a bachelor's or master's degree in journalism or communications, as well as sound knowledge of the theater arts.

Visual artists and **photographers** may also work in newspaper or theater related careers. Visual artists design, paste up illustrations and copy, and sometimes oversee printing of display and hand-out materials.

Photographers also play an important role in producing the publicity for a theater production. They take pictures of costumed actors for press kits and releases, public service announcements, posters, and display ads. Enlargements of photos taken during performances are often hung in the lobby as a chronicle of a theater's offerings.

For artists and photographers, a portfolio is probably more pertinent than a college degree. They may train in a college or university, junior or community college, school of design, or specialty school. Job leads may come through school contacts, part-time work, or internship programs.

Chapter 9

. . . .

History of the Drama

You Will Learn

How drama began.

About the development of drama in ancient Greece.

About the ways drama changed during the Middle Ages and Renaissance.

About some of the great Elizabethan playwrights, including Shakespeare.

How English drama has changed since the time of Shakespeare.

About drama in other parts of the world.

How drama has developed in the United States since colonial times.

Vocabulary

closet dramas	Morality play	Kabuki
Miracle and Mystery plays	commedia dell'arte	regional theaters
mansions	Nō (Noh)	repertory theater
cycle	Bunraku	

*T*he history of the drama is closely related to the history of humanity. When the first hunters recounted their adventures by means of vivid pantomime, when the first storytellers told their tales in rhythmic chants, and when the first organized groups of people found expression in the pantomime of hunting, war, and love dances, the dramatic impulse showed itself. Later the primitive actor hid behind a mask to become a god or an animal. The key to people's dramatic action seems to be a desire to imitate. As civilization developed, drama took definite form in the worship of heavenly gods and the glorification of earthly rulers. The Book of Job and the Song of Solomon of the Old Testament are written in dramatic form. Then tales were told of noble characters engaged in mighty conflicts and humorous types bumbling along through their comic paces. And, at last, the tales produced dramatic presentations, ultimately to be written and acted in concrete form.

The Origins of Western Drama

The earliest record of a theatrical performance comes from Egypt, the birthplace of much of the world's art. Carved on a stone tablet some 4,000 years ago, this account tells how I-Kher-Wofret of Abydos arranged and played the leading role in a three-day pageant made up of actual battles, boat processions, and elaborate ceremonies that told the story of the murder, dismemberment, and resurrection of the great god Osiris.

Greek Drama

Drama as we know it began in Greece in the sixth century B.C., as part of the worship of Dionysus, god of wine and fertility. To commemorate the god's death, a group of chanters, called the chorus, danced around an altar upon which a goat was sacrificed. This chorus was called the "goat-singers," and their ritualistic chant was called the *tragos,* or goat-song. From this term the word *tragedy* came. These ceremonies in honor of Dionysus evolved into dramatic contests, the first of which was won by Thespis. In 534 B.C., he stepped from the chorus and engaged in a dialogue between the chorus and himself, thus becoming the first actor. The term *thespian* has been given to actors ever since. This actor-playwright is also credited with introducing masks into the Greek plays.

The dramatic contests were part of a festival that lasted five or six days. On each of the last three days a different playwright would present four plays. The first three plays were tragedies, often a trilogy — three plays related in theme, myth, or characters. The fourth play mixed both tragic and comic elements. We call such plays *tragicomedies.* Playwrights competed fiercely for the honor of winning the laurel wreath at the contests.

Production in the Greek theater was a highly complex art form that used many clever mechanical devices. The performances were at first held in the open hillsides surrounding a circular area called the *orchestra,* where the

Scenery was originally a temporary unit behind the orchestra. This engraving of the Athenian Theatre of Dionysus is based on the more permanent structures that appeared later.

chorus danced. Wooden and then stone seats were added to form the theater. Originally the theater was only for men, both as performers and spectators. Women did not attend the theater until the fourth century B.C. It is believed that some theaters seated over 17,000 patrons.

Originally, at the rear of the acting area, was a small hut called the *skene*, where the actors changed masks and costumes. After a time, the skene was enlarged into a stone building. A second story and wings were added, and scenery was painted on the front. On the roof was the god-walk, from which the gods delivered their monologues.

Another device used in Greek plays was the *machina,* a cranelike hoist that permitted actors to appear above the stage as if flying. The machina could also lower actors from the roof of the skene to the orchestra. The machina was heavy enough to carry a chariot and horses or several persons. Most frequently the character lowered represented a god from Mount Olympus who came to Earth to settle the affairs of human beings — and the problems of a playwright who could not resolve the conflict satisfactorily. From the use of this contrivance came the term *deus ex machina* (god from the machine), which is still used today to indicate some device an author introduces late in a play to resolve plot difficulties. Examples are the unknown relative who

The Theatre of Dionysus is shown as it appears today, after approximately twenty-four centuries of use. Productions of the Greek classics are given here each summer.

leaves a legacy, a long-lost letter, or the discovery of a relative given up for dead. Usually such a plot resolution weakens the play and works out acceptably only in farce, melodrama, or fantasy.

Greek tragic actors wore masks, padded costumes, and boots with thick soles called cothurni, or *buskins,* in Latin. Comic actors wore rather grotesque masks, costumes with exaggerated padding, and a type of sandal called a *sock.*

The chorus, however, was an integral part of the early Greek theater. It served to explain the situation, to bring the audience up-to-date, to make a commentary on the action from the point of view of established ideas or the group it represented, and to engage in dialogue with the actors. Although, with time, the responsibilities of the chorus diminished as the actors took over key roles, vestiges of the Greek chorus are found in theater even today: the chorus in Anouilh's *Antigone,* the Stage Manager in *Our Town,* and El Gallo in *The Fantasticks* are three well-known examples of a modern chorus.

Greek Tragedy

The main conflicts of the Greek tragedies evolved from the clash between the will of the gods and the ambitions and desires of humanity. The plays showed how useless were human efforts to change fate. The greatest writers of Greek tragedy were Aeschylus (525–456 B.C.), Sophocles (497–405 B.C.), and Euripides (485–406 B.C.).

Aeschylus was a warrior-playwright who held firmly to the Greek religion of his day. He added the second actor and reduced the chorus to twelve. He is noted for the elevation and majesty of his language, which has never been surpassed. Many critics refer to him as the "father of tragedy." Of his seventy to ninety plays, only seven remain. Aeschylus also left us the Greek trilogy, the *Oresteia.* It tells the story of the murder of Agamemnon, the revenge taken by his children, and the punishment and final acquittal of his son.

The greatest of the Greek tragedians, ranked with Shakespeare as one of the greatest playwrights of all time, was Sophocles. This writer of perfectly crafted plays added the third actor and introduced dramatic action leading to a definite plot structure of unity and beauty. He achieved an amazing balance between the power of the gods and the importance of humanity, believing that human beings have a little of the divinity in them that elevates their struggles against fate. Questioning, yet reverent, Sophocles allowed his characters to ask "Why?" within the framework of their acceptance of the will of the gods and fate. As a result, his characters are among the strongest ever to walk upon the stage. He wrote at least 110 plays, of which only seven have survived. However, we do know that Sophocles won the first prize eighteen times.

Sophocles' *Oedipus Tyrannus* stands as one of the world's most powerful plays of dramatic irony. Aristotle described it as the ideal tragedy. It is the story of a man in search of Truth. His fate, to unwittingly kill his own father and marry his mother, has been preordained by the gods. It is not until he gouges out his eyes that Oedipus perceives the Truth he could not see.

Sophocles' *Antigone* is also one of the world's great tragedies. Antigone is Oedipus's daughter. Her two brothers, Eteocles and Polynices, disagreeing about who should rule, slay each other. Their uncle, Creon, takes over the throne and decrees that Polynices was wrong and, consequently, must remain unburied. The Greeks believed that desecration of the dead was offensive to the gods and that the soul of a body not given proper burial was doomed to wander eternally. Antigone defies Creon's decree in order to fulfill her higher loyalties to family and gods. She attempts to bury Polynices, is caught, and is placed in a cave to die. It is not until his own world crumbles about him that Creon realizes that human laws cannot supplant the laws of the gods. A modern version of *Antigone* by Jean Anouilh has been widely produced in colleges and high schools.

The playwright Euripides seriously questioned life. He became more interested in human lives than in the religious views of his day. He emphasized human relationships and became a master of pathos, human sorrow and compassion. One of his plays, *The Trojan Women,* is one of literature's strongest indictments against war. His play *Medea* is the tragedy of a woman who seeks revenge on her husband, even by killing her own sons. Antigone and Medea still rank among the most poignant portrayals of women in dramatic literature.

Greek Comedy

The outstanding author of Greek comedy was Aristophanes (450–380 B.C.), who contributed forty plays, eleven of which still remain. Aristophanes was a skilled satirist and a keen observer of humanity. He considered nothing sacred. His barbed wit mocked the leaders of Athens and the gods themselves. Three of his best-known plays are *The Frogs*, a writer's contest between Aeschylus and Euripides in Hades judged by Dionysus himself; *The Clouds*, a travesty on Socrates and Greek education; and *Lysistrata,* a scathing attack on war.

Aristophanes was the chief writer of "Old Comedy." Many of the Roman and Renaissance writers were influenced by the "New Comedy," whose best-known author was Menander (342–291 B.C.). Only one complete script, *The Curmudgeon,* is known, and only three fragments remain of his other plays. Menander's comedies seem gentle compared to those of Aristophanes. The satire of Aristophanes gave way to sentimental comedy based on a love story. By this time, the chorus had disappeared and stock characters had made their appearance upon the stage.

Roman Theater

Roman drama was a decadent imitation of Greek drama. It deteriorated at last into sensual interpretative dances called pantomimes, vulgar farces called mimes, and colossal gladiatorial contests in which the slaughter of human beings and beasts became the emotional delight of the audience. The Roman theater at first resembled the Greek, with a heightened skene elaborately decorated with arches and statues of varying sizes. Gradually the theater was

This bas-relief of a Roman comedy is from Pompeii. Note the double flutes accompanying the dramatic action as well as the masks and costumes of fixed characterization.
· · · · · · · · · · · ·

extended into a circular arena surrounded by towering tiers of seats. Strangely enough, when Rome had no theaters, two writers of comedy stood out — Plautus and Terence. Two hundred years later, when Rome had constructed huge amphitheaters, only Seneca, a writer of bombastic tragedies, attempted anything like a play. Seneca's plays are usually referred to as **closet dramas** — plays meant to be read rather than acted. Although these three playwrights offered little compared to their Greek predecessors, their plays did influence later writers, including Shakespeare.

As the Roman Empire grew, the cultural life of Rome began to decay. The emperors amused the citizens with spectacles such as chariot races and battles among gladiators. Romans would only watch the most vulgar sorts of plays.

In 476 A.D., Rome finally fell to invading Germanic tribes. In Europe, the centuries that followed the fall of Rome are called the Middle Ages. In the early Middle Ages, few people could read or write. Much Greek and Roman literature was lost completely or ignored for centuries. Only wandering players and minstrels kept the drama alive with their dancing, singing, juggling, acrobatics, and marionette shows. From 400 B.C. to the Elizabethan Age of England nearly 2,000 years later, not a single great play was written.

Medieval Drama

During the period extending roughly from the fifth to the fifteenth centuries, drama developed along slightly different lines in various European nations. In each case, however, its rebirth came about through the Christian church. Gradually, liturgical chants became part of the mass to teach the many people who could not read about the great events in Biblical history.

Slowly these church plays evolved into elaborate productions that had to move outdoors to accommodate the crowds. Latin was used, as in the mass, and the performers were priests, nuns, and choirboys.

Gradually church drama expanded. Plays were translated from the Latin, and little by little, lay members of the parishes took part in the performances. The **Miracle and Mystery plays** were based on the lives of the saints and on stories in the Bible. The *Passion Play*, which is concerned with the last week in the life of Christ, is an example of these medieval church dramas. It still is given in Europe at Oberammergau, Germany, by the citizens of the Bavarian village where it was first performed in 1634. It has been produced every ten years since 1760.

The early Miracle and Mystery plays were performed with **mansions,** a series of acting stations placed in a line. The mansions, or houses, were Biblical localities such as Heaven, Pilate's House, Jerusalem, and Hell's Mouth.

Peasant social life in the late 16th century centered around the marketplace. This engraving by Pieter Brueghel was drawn around the year 1565. It depicts the temporary stages that were often used.
• • • • • • • • • • •

Hell's Mouth was a strange contraption that delighted medieval audiences. It breathed fire and smoke, its jaws opened and closed, and as the wicked were pushed in, their pitiful cries could be heard.

By the twelfth century, the medieval trade unions, or *guilds*, had taken over the presentation of most of the plays during a celebration called the festival of Corpus Christi. Each guild, according to the craft of its members, presented one part of the story. The bakers presented *The Last Supper;* the goldsmiths, *The Three Wise Men,* the shipwrights, *The Construction of the Ark.*

Each guild had its own pageant wagon, or stage on wheels. The pageant wagon was divided into two levels. The upper level was a platform stage, and the lower level, curtained off, served as a dressing room. The wagons traveled from town to town in a procession. The audience could remain in one spot while the pageant wagons moved through town one by one. The entire sequence of plays was called a **cycle.** The guilds competed with one another to see which could stage the most elaborate production.

Gradually, an increasing amount of secular material, especially humorous incidents, crept into performances. For example, *The Second Shepherd's Play* is 90 percent secular burlesque focused upon a clever rogue named Mak, who steals a sheep, hides it in a crib, and passes it off as his son.

Groups of strolling players began presenting the Miracle and Mystery plays,

A scene from the Passion Play, *given every ten years at Oberammergau, Germany.*

but they drew criticism from the Church and the number of their performances declined. These wandering troupes, however, were the first acting companies, which later came under the patronage of the nobility.

The **Morality play** followed the themes of the Miracle and Mystery plays. But the Morality play was primarily ethical in purpose, dealing with the principles of right and wrong. The plays usually took the form of allegories dramatized by symbolic characters who represented abstract qualities. The most important surviving Morality play is *Everyman,* described in Chapter 6.

Other dramatic forms developed in the fifteenth century. They included interludes, short humorous sketches performed between serious plays; chronicle plays, based on historical events; and masques, highly artistic spectacles written and performed for the glorification of the nobility. The backgrounds for the masques were designed by renowned artists like Leonardo da Vinci.

The Renaissance and Drama

The Renaissance (meaning "rebirth") began in Italy in the early fourteenth century. Painting, sculpture, and architecture flourished, but drama did not.

The Renaissance in Italy

Italy did develop theater architecture and stage equipment, introducing sets with perspective and colored light. Among Italy's architectural contributions to theater were the Teatre Farnese at Parma and the famous Teatro Olimpico, still preserved at Vicenza.

The early offerings of Italian playwrights, however, were only weak imitations of classical plays, cheap obscenities, or poorly constructed scripts.

The **commedia dell'arte** provided much of the new interest in the theater. The commedia was professional improvised comedy. These troupes had mastered the art of playing out their comic *scenarios,* plot outlines posted backstage before each performance. There were no fully composed play scripts as we know them. Instead, the scenarios were quite detailed plot outlines that included *lazzi* and certain memorized lines. The *lazzi* were special humorous bits of stage business, usually set apart from the main action. A well-known *lazzi* was one in which the stage action continued while a comic actor laboriously caught a fly. Actors memorized set speeches, such as declarations of love, hate, and madness. The troupes also learned comments on extraneous matters that could be used wherever convenient, and stock jokes, proverbs, songs, and exit speeches.

This contemporary performance of Carlo Grossi's King Stag *is a direct descendant of the commedia dell'arte that was known during the Italian Renaissance.*

. . . .

A manager who usually was the company's author led each troupe. The plots were almost always comic intrigue involving fathers who put obstacles in the way of their children's romances. Servants were very important characters, often successfully completing the matchmaking.

All the characters of the commedia were stock types identified by their costumes and their masks. There were usually two young male lovers, the innamorate, and their female counterparts, the innamorata. All four were beautifully dressed and spoke in refined language. The lovers did not wear masks.

The only other character to perform unmasked was the *fontesca,* a serving maid. She appears in many plays as Columbina, a clever and high-spirited flirt. The *fontesca* was the forerunner of the witty soubrette of musical comedy, such as Ado Annie in *Oklahoma!*

The *zanni* were clever male servants, excellent at ad-libbing and acrobatics. Most *zanni* belong to the same character-type as Mak — the rogue or clever rascal. It is difficult to categorize them by name, but there were basically two kinds of *zanni;* the clever prankster, agile in mind and body; and the dullard, blundering in thought and action. Of the first type, Arlecchino was probably the most popular. He is more commonly known to us by his French name, Harlequin. Little pantomimes and playlets based on the style of the commedia are often called Harlequinades. However, the diamond-patterned costume people associate with Harlequin, came late in the history of the commedia.

Opposite Arlecchino was Brighella — slow, dishonest, cruel, and vulgar. Another name used for a servant was Pulchinello. This malicious character with his hooked nose and high-peaked hat was the ancestor of Punch of the Punch and Judy shows. Still another of the male servants was Pedrolino, who later became known as Pierrot, the moonstruck eternal lover — melancholy and gentle, but always too romantic and too sad. Later, a sincerely devoted sweetheart, Pierrette, was paired with him, and they became the eternal lovers. To this duo, the temptress Columbina was added to form the eternal triangle. One other variation of the *zanni* must be mentioned — Pagliacci, the man who must make others laugh while his own heart breaks.

Pantalone was an old man — the father competing romantically against his own son, the husband deceived by a young wife, or an overly protective father zealously guarding his young daughter from suitors. His costume consisted of a black coat with flowing sleeves, a red vest, and the breeches from which we have taken the words *pantaloon* and *pants.* The Pantalone is a common character in later drama. For example, we see him as Polonius in *Hamlet.*

The last character important to recognize was the Capitano, a mustached, boastful, but cowardly Spaniard who quaked at his own shadow. He is often considered the ancestor of the villain of the Victorian melodramas. The great "save-your-own-skin" death speech is typical of the "brave" Capitano.

The Renaissance Elsewhere on the Continent

Written drama evolved in Spain, where Cervantes (1547–1616), Lope de Vega (1562–1635), and Calderón (1600–1681) contributed to the mounting interest in theater. *The Man of La Mancha* is a musical adaptation by Dale Wasserman of Cervantes' famed *Don Quixote.*

Many rulers of this period, encouraged the production of great spectacles. Many stage hands were needed to change the parallel wings of scenery that were an innovation of the 17th century.

••••••••••••

France developed the professional theater under the patronage of the state with such great plays as *The Cid* by Corneille (1606–1684), *The Miser, The Misanthrope,* and *The Imaginary Invalid* by Molière (1622–1673), and *Phaedra* by Racine (1639–1699).

Strolling players kept the drama alive during this period, appearing before the public in village squares and before the nobility in their castles. They created melodramatic history plays, rowdy comedies, and romantic love stories that were the origins of the great dramas of later generations.

The Renaissance in England

The climax of the dramatic renaissance came during the Elizabethan age in England. This was a period in which the drama was the expression of the soul of a nation, and the theater became a vital force in the lives of the people.

The first English comedy was *Ralph Roister Doister* produced in 1553, which the author, Nicholas Udall (1504–1556), modeled on Plautus's plays. The first true English tragedy was *Gorboduc,* which was performed in 1561. Among the many writers in this period were John Webster (1580–1625) *(The Duchess of Malfi),* Thomas Heywood (1570–1641) *(A Woman Killed with Kindness),* Thomas Kyd (1557–1594) *(The Spanish Tragedy),* and Francis Beaumont (1584–1616) and John Fletcher (1579–1625) *(The Knight of the Burning Pestle* and *The Maid's Tragedy).*

Three Monumental Elizabethan Dramatists

Towering above all the other brilliant actor-playwrights responsible for the glory of the period, three men — Marlowe, Jonson, and Shakespeare — produced plays that have never lost their appeal.

Christopher Marlowe (1564–1593) introduced the first important use of blank verse, the "mighty line" of English poetic drama. Combining extraordinary use of language and the excitement of melodramatic plots, he wrote *Tamburlaine the Great, The Jew of Malta,* and *Edward II.* These plays present the glory and the horror of the age. However, it is *Doctor Faustus*, the story of a man who sells his soul for 24 hours of damning knowledge, that brilliantly bridges the gap between the medieval age and the Renaissance.

Ben Jonson (1573–1637) was the first master of English comedy. He wrote *Volpone, The Alchemist,* and *Every Man in His Humour.*

To the Elizabethan, the word *humour,* as used in the phrase "He's in a good humour," did not refer to an attitude of amusement. The Renaissance was a period in which anatomical study, as well as the arts, developed. Physicians were amazed by the amounts of fluids (humour) found in the human body. Scholars believed that all matter was made up of four elements — air, earth, fire, and water. It was also assumed that the human body was composed of these same four elements, each having its own effect on the personality. Air was identified with blood and caused the *sanguine* humour — light-hearted, airy, happy-go-lucky. Fire was associated with bile and brought about the *choleric* humour — angry, hot-tempered, impetuous. Water was identified with phlegm and caused the *phlegmatic* humour — dull, listless, lethargic.

The humour of most interest in Elizabethan plays is that of black bile, identified with earth, which resulted in the melancholy humour. The melancholy character fell into three main types: the lover, the malcontent, and the intellectual. Hamlet is an excellent example of the intellectual melancholy humour. Although most stage figures have a predominating humour, a balanced personality was the most desirable. This is evidenced by Antony's tribute to Brutus in *Julius Caesar:* " . . . the elements [were] so mixed in him that Nature might stand up and say to all the world, this was a man."

Jonson widened the scope of the humours to include any strong personality trait, especially a weakness, foible, or folly that could make a character a cause of laughter.

William Shakespeare (1564–1616) was the greatest Elizabethan dramatist as well as the greatest dramatist of all time. Not only is Shakespeare the towering literary figure of all the ages, but his characterizations, beautiful poetry, and never-to-be-forgotten lines echo a majesty best expressed by his friendly rival, Ben Jonson, who said that Shakespeare "was not of an age but for all time."

Shakespeare's Plays

The ideal way to become acquainted with Shakespeare is to see his plays, not merely to read them or read about them. The plays were written by a practical man of the theater who wrote them to be seen — not read — by a loud, boisterous audience accustomed to shouting its approval or hissing its displeasure. A play had to be exciting, moving, and violent, filled with fury, humor, and truth, in order to keep such an audience interested. Shakespeare's characters felt emotions — love, jealousy, ambition, joy, and grief — that are as universal today as they were 400 years ago.

The characters form the center of the interest of Shakespeare's plays. Note exactly how each is introduced and how well defined the personality becomes immediately. Shakespeare used the soliloquy and accurate descriptions by other actors to delineate his characters, for there were no programs to provide any explanations. A soliloquy is a speech delivered by an actor alone on the stage which reveals the character's innermost thoughts aloud.

The stage of Shakespeare's time evolved from the interior courtyards of inns. The majority of the audience would stand in the pit or balconies to watch the action taking place on the stage before them.

The Elizabethan Playhouse

The first English public playhouse, the Theatre, was built across the Thames River from London in 1576 by James Burbage. He was the manager of the company later housed in the famous Globe Theatre, with which Shakespeare was associated as actor-playwright. The theaters were modeled after medieval inn yards and *animal pits,* which were circular arenas where bears and ponies were teased and tormented for entertainment. The inns had open courtyards where the audience could stand around a platform stage or sit in the galleries surrounding the courtyard.

The playhouses were round or octagonal in shape and had two to three tiers of galleries. The stage has been called an "unlocalized platform stage" because this 5- to 6-foot high acting area used little scenery to indicate locale. A sign or an actor's line was usually enough to inform the audience of geographical locations. The area surrounding the stage was called the *pit,* and the playgoers who paid a modest fee to stand there, were called *groundlings.* The groundlings were, for the most part, apprentices, soldiers, sailors, and country folk. In some of his plays, Shakespeare commented sharply on the lack of discernment in the fickle mob that reeked of garlic and body odor, ate and drank during the performances, and reacted loudly to what they liked or disliked. The more refined audience occupied the gallery seats, for which an additional fee was charged. The most expensive seats were on the stage itself.

Over the stage was the Heavens, a roof supported by two 2- or 3-story columns. The underneath side of the Heavens was painted blue, with a golden sun in the center surrounded by stars and the signs of the zodiac. An actor who spoke of the heavens and earth, had only to point to the roof overhead and the stage floor beneath to create the illusion of a microcosmic universe. The "back wall" of the stage looked like the outside of a multistoried building.

The area backstage was called the tiring house. In the center rear was a curtained recess called the inner below, or study. This area could be used for "reveal" scenes, such as a bedroom or the tent of Antony. There were second-floor acting areas also: a central area consisting of the shallow balcony; the tarras, separated by a curtain called the arras from a recess called the chamber. On either side of the chamber were the window boxes, probably used for such settings as the balcony scene of *Romeo and Juliet.* A third level could be used for acting when necessary, but seems to have served primarily as the musicians' gallery. In all these acting levels, there were trapdoors, some mechanically operated. They were used in scenes like that of the grave diggers in *Hamlet.*

Over the third level was what appeared to be a small house, which was appropriately called the scenery hut. This structure housed stage machinery and a cannon. From the peak of the roof a flag was flown to inform the resi-

Burgher women and a country woman as they might have appeared in Shakespeare's The Merry Wives of Windsor.

dents of London when a play was to be given. Since there was no artificial lighting, plays were presented in the afternoon, which accounts for the description of the Globe as a "wooden O" — a circular building open to the sky.

Specially trained boys played all female roles. Wealthy patrons sponsored the acting companies and competed with one another for the success of their troupes. Patrons donated castoff clothes for costumes. Of course, this meant that although costumes were often quite luxurious, little attempt was made at historical accuracy. Roman citizens in *Julius Caesar* appeared in the gorgeous satins, velvets, and plumes of the sixteenth century. The audiences loved color, sound, and pageantry. A march of armies garbed in royal colors, the ringing of the alarm bell, and the firing of cannon heightened the action on the stage.

Later Drama in England

The American stage has its origins in British theater. Therefore, you should know about the history of drama in Great Britain in order to better understand drama in the United States.

Restoration Drama

Following the Elizabethan era, England plunged into the political upheaval of the Puritan Rebellion (1642–1660). For eighteen years the theater was banned. It was not until Charles II returned to the throne in the period known as the *Restoration* that the theater became legal again.

Important innovations were made in drama during the Restoration. With the English Royal Patent of 1662, women appeared as players for the first time. The patent said that "all women's parts should be performed by women" and said also that plays and acting should be considered "not only harmless delights but useful and instructive representations of human life." Only two playhouses had official sanction. Their names are still famous: the Drury Lane Theater and the Covent Garden. From these two theaters came the term *legitimate theater*, which we now use to refer to professional stage plays.

During the Restoration theater buildings closed to the sky were built. Audiences were seated on level floors. So they could see the stage, the stage floor was raked, that is, sloped upwards away from the viewers. The actors, therefore, moved "up" and "down" the stage. This is where we received the terms *upstage* and *downstage* which we use today. During the Restoration elaborate scenery and mechanical equipment came into use.

Among the Restoration dramatists are a few whose plays have survived until today. William Wycherley (1640–1716), in *The Country Wife*, started the fashionable trend in comedies. William Congreve (1670–1729) ranks as one of the great masters of comedy. The brilliant art and pace of his *Love for Love* and *The Way of the World* set a standard for later comedies of manners. George Farquhar (1678–1707), in his *The Beaux' Stratagem*, brought a refreshing breath of the country into the dissolute city life depicted on the stage.

Eighteenth- and Nineteenth-Century English Drama

The eighteenth century produced only two outstanding playwrights. Richard Brinsley Sheridan (1751–1816) wrote two social comedies: *The School for Scandal* and *The Rivals*, which features the immortal Mrs. Malaprop, the world's greatest misuser of words. Oliver Goldsmith (1728–1774) was a dramatist whose fame rests on one play, *She Stoops to Conquer*.

In the 1700s, professional stage plays were presented in London, England, at the Drury Lane Theater, one of the first "legitimate" theaters in the world.

． ． ． ． ． ． ． ． ． ． ．

The London stage of the nineteenth century established the trends that have given it the prestige it holds today. Gilbert and Sullivan created their clever comic operas, such as *The Mikado, H.M.S. Pinafore,* and *The Pirates of Penzance.* Oscar Wilde, with his genius for epigrams and brilliant dialogue, wrote *The Importance of Being Earnest.*

George Bernard Shaw (1856–1950) ranks as the greatest playwright next to Shakespeare among English dramatists. Although he is primarily a philosopher frankly declaiming his theories, his satiric humor and fascinating characters keep alive such plays as *Saint Joan, Candida, Man and Superman, Caesar and Cleopatra, Pygmalion, Androcles and the Lion,* and *Arms and the Man.*

Shaw stressed two concepts in his plays. The first of these was what he called the Life Force — the belief that humanity will improve and strengthen in spite of itself. Shaw stated this philosophy strongly in the third act of *Man and Superman* in a dream sequence often presented alone as "Don Juan in Hell." The second idea is called the "Thinking Person's Society." Shaw said that of every 1,000 people, there are 700 people who do not think, 299 idealists, and one thinking person. Shaw hoped to turn the idealists into thinkers.

Drama in England Today

England is a center of the world for theater lovers today. They flock to London to the National Theatre, the Barbican, and the West End where they can choose from any number of productions of all types. They are assured of versatile and superlative acting at reasonable prices.

English summer theater festivals are flourishing. Of these the Royal Shakespeare Memorial Theater at Stratford-upon-Avon, the Edinburgh International Festival, and the Malvern Festival offer the most varied and exciting fare.

Drama students may be familiar with the works of such modern British playwrights as John Osborne, who introduced the "angry young men," in *Look Back in Anger;* J.B. Priestley *(An Inspector Calls);* T.S. Eliot *(Murder in the Cathedral);* Harold Pinter *(The Caretaker);* Tom Stoppard *(Rosencrantz and Guildenstern Are Dead);* Anthony Shaffer *(Sleuth);* Peter Shaffer *(Amadeus);* and Alan Ayckbourn *(Absurd Person Singular).*

Drama in Ireland

Drama in southern Ireland has had a brief but brilliant history, starting with the plays of William Butler Yeats and Lady Gregory at the turn of the century. Yeats was dedicated to poetic drama retelling the ancient tales of Ireland. His *At the Hawk's Well* beautifully combined myth, dance, and poetry. John Millington Synge is considered by many to be the finest of the Irish dramatists. His *The Playboy of the Western World* and *Riders to the Sea* are frequently produced today. Sean O'Casey, with *Juno and the Paycock, Within the Gates,* and *The Plough and the Stars,* was the prominent mid-century voice of the Irish theater.

Drama on the Continent

Drama has flourished throughout Europe for three centuries. The chief contributions of the European dramatists has been in initiating trends that have been followed in all countries. No longer can we divide any discussion into the drama of the various countries, because today they are interrelated.

Notable Dramatists

In France, Molière, Voltaire, Victor Hugo, and Alexandre Dumas broke away from classical traditions and produced exciting drama. Edmund Rostand wrote *Cyrano de Bergerac,* the romance of the poet-swordsman with the huge nose. The story is world-famous, and several movies have retold the tale. Jean Giraudoux *(Tiger at the Gates, The Madwoman of Chaillot)* and Jean Anouilh *(The Lark, Antigone, Becket)* have also been popular in the United States. Their plays have been translated by such dramatists as Christopher Fry and Lillian Hellman. Jean-Paul Sartre's *No Exit* and *The Flies* reflect his existentialist outlook.

In Germany, the colossal figure of Goethe towers above all others with his *Faust.* His poetic drama, telling the tragedy of the man who sold himself to the Devil to get all worldly desires in a new-lived youth, was written in glorious verse and has inspired three grand operas as well as literary works in other languages.

Gerhart Hauptmann in the nineties began the new era of realism in the German theater. His work culminated in *The Weavers,* one of the great dramas setting forth a social issue built around a "group protagonist." Bertolt Brecht developed epic theater. *Mother Courage, The Caucasian Chalk Circle,* and *The*

Moliere's troup was one of 12 or 15 theater troupes touring France in the 17th century. An invitation, by the King of France's brother, to perform at the court, assured Moliere's fortunes.

The plays of Moliere, Voltaire, Victor Hugo, and Alexander Dumas would have played at the Varietes Amusantes (now called the Theatre-Francais), shown as it appeared in 1789.
· · · · · · · · · · · ·

Good Woman of Setzuan are among his plays most often produced in the United States.

In Czechoslovakia, the Capek brothers achieved fame working together and separately on expressionistic plays of social impact, such as *R.U.R.*, the theme of which is robots taking over humanity.

In Spain, after the great early period, José Echegaray was the only dramatist whose plays were acted abroad until Jacinto Benavente won the Nobel Prize for Literature for *The Passion Flower*. Symbolist playwright Federico García Lorca's *Blood Wedding* is frequently seen in university theaters.

From Italy comes Luigi Pirandello, whose conviction that people are not what they appear to be is described in his "naked masks" theory. His plays are exceedingly complicated and difficult on the whole. However, *Six Characters in Search of an Author* and *Henry IV* are frequently produced.

Henrik Ibsen of Norway, sometimes called the "father of modern drama" and the "father of realism," introduced realism in conversation and presentation. His chief theme — that society must protect and develop the individual rights of each person — had a special appeal for Americans. Ibsen wrote two magnificent poetic dramas in the Romantic style, *Peer Gynt* and *Brand*, but it is his realistic dramas—*A Doll's House, Ghosts, Hedda Gabler, An Enemy of the People,* and *The Master Builder*—that account for his world influence.

A Russian who had major influence in the United States was Konstantin Stanislavski. His "Method" established the acting theory centered on the inner understanding of a role plus the perfecting of physical response when presenting the role to the audience. The Moscow Art Theater, which he founded and directed, became the finest in the world from the viewpoint of ensemble acting and realistic production. The greatest of all Russian dramatists was the early realist Anton Chekhov who wrote *The Sea Gull, The Three Sisters, Uncle Vanya* and *The Cherry Orchard.*

Drama in Asia

To the Westerner, the appeal of the drama of the Far East lies largely in the gorgeous costumes that are complemented by masks or elaborate makeup, in the brilliant color, and in the grotesque and expressive pantomime. Asian drama is presented in a highly traditional manner inherited from the distant past. The subject matter deals with historical and religious legends not easily understood by a foreigner. The length of the performance, the high-pitched voices, and the discordant music are often difficult for Westerners, but there is an exotic charm in every program.

The Chinese theater, using the same symbolism and techniques as it has for centuries, can still be seen in Hong Kong and occasionally in Honolulu. Historical plays featuring the actions of generals, long journeys by characters, and many battle scenes predominate.

All forms of the drama of Japan have been brought to the United States in the last few years and shown on stage and television. There are three forms of drama distinctly Japanese: The **Nō** (Noh), the **Bunraku** or Doll Theater, and the **Kabuki.**

The Nō theater is the oldest form of drama to be preserved in its exact form, with words, dance, and music rhythmically coordinated as they were in productions 600 years ago. The traditional forms have been handed down by generations of actors strictly trained from childhood in what is practically isolation. The special theater is like a temple, with the 18-foot square stage extending into the audience and supported by four wooden pillars that form a part of the action. The characters — all of whom are played by men — include an old man, an old woman, a young man, a child, a monster, a formidable god, a gentle god, and an animal. The essence of Nō lies in creating beauty of motion and speech. The plots are short and very simple, and the language is intricate. The spectators follow the libretto closely.

To the Westerner, the appeal of the drama of the Far East lies largely in the gorgeous costumes, which are complemented by masks or elaborate makeup, and in the expressive pantomime. This scene is from the Chinese theater spectacle The Sun and Moon.

The Bunraku features marionettes about 4 feet tall, carved in wood and gorgeously costumed. They are so realistic that they move their fingers, mouths, eyes, and eyebrows with lifelike expressiveness. Each doll is manipulated by three attendants who are dressed in black and wear gauze masks to symbolize their invisibility. Amazingly they soon seem to disappear. The dialogue is read in turn by five narrators in elaborate costumes. This form of theater was brought from Korea to Japan in the sixth century.

The Kabuki came into being in the sixteenth century and was originally an imitation of both the Doll Theater and the Nō drama. Women first produced and acted the plays, but today only men are the players. The actors spend their lives in the theater. They begin as children and continue to act in plays and dance-dramas until they are in their seventies. The infinitely detailed pantomime and the superlative acting, enhanced by elaborate costuming and makeup painted with brushes, are true theater.

Drama in the United States

The theater in America, because of its British origins, has naturally been strongly influenced by the dramatists and actors of England from Colonial days to the present.

As settlers moved westward into the newly opened territories, the American theater followed. New plays, as well as the classics, were performed.

Early American Drama

The first theater in America was built in Williamsburg, Virginia, in 1716, but all traces of it had disappeared by the time the entire city was restored in the 1920s.

The first American dramas were produced by the American Company, managed by David Douglass. The first play was *The Prince of Parthia* by Thomas Godfrey, given on April 24, 1767, in Philadelphia. It was strictly an imitation of British blank-verse tragedies and had only one performance. *The Contrast* by Royall Tyler opened at the John Street Theater on April 16, 1787, and was an instant success. It was a comedy and introduced Jonathan, the original typical Yankee — shrewd, wholesome, and humorous — who has appeared in many guises ever since. However, *Fashion* by Anna Cora Mowatt, produced in 1845, is considered our first native comedy on the same theme — poking fun at social pretenders.

The first actors were English professional troupes who presented popular London plays. The legendary family that links the early American stage with the modern is the Barrymores. John Drew was an Irish actor who came to America in 1846; he married Louise Lane, our first distinguished actress-manager. They had three children: John Drew, Sidney, and Georgiana, who married

Maurice Barrymore, a dashing Irish actor. The Barrymores were the parents of Lionel, Ethel, and John Barrymore, who were for years America's leading actors.

Edwin Booth (1833–1893) was one of the greatest romantic actors America has produced. His illustrious career nearly suffered an eclipse when he retired after his brother, John Wilkes Booth, also a well-known actor, assassinated Abraham Lincoln. Edwin Booth later returned to the stage but never appeared again in Washington.

Modern American Drama

The American theater continued to be an imitation of European theater until the 1920s when several playwrights emerged whose plays were uniquely American. The first of these was Eugene O'Neill who led the way with his powerful non-Aristotelian tragedies. *Ah, Wilderness!, The Emperor Jones, The Iceman Cometh, Mourning Becomes Electra, Anna Christie, The Hairy Ape,* and *A Long Day's Journey Into Night* are but a few of his gripping dramas. O'Neill, Clifford Odets *(Waiting for Lefty, Country Girl)* and William Saroyan *(The Time of Your Life)* opened the door for the many fine American dramatists who followed. Of these, four stand out.

Arthur Miller wrote of the American family and the tragedy of the common person in *The Crucible, All My Sons,* and the play that has been called the great American tragedy, *Death of a Salesman.*

Thornton Wilder contributed three outstanding plays: a farce, *The Matchmaker,* from which the musical *Hello, Dolly* was adapted; an offbeat comedy about the struggle for human existence, *The Skin of Our Teeth;* and the American play of all American plays, *Our Town.*

Tennessee Williams combined a poetic quality with intriguing characters in plays that reached even broader audiences through their film versions. Among Williams' many intense dramas are: *The Glass Menagerie, Cat on a Hot Tin Roof, A Streetcar Named Desire,* and *Night of the Iguana.*

Neil Simon has become the most successful American playwright in history by bringing to the stage a special warmth of humor that is both personal and universal. *Barefoot in the Park, The Odd Couple, Come Blow Your Horn, The Star-Spangled Girl, Chapter Two, Brighton Beach Memoirs, Biloxi Blues,* and *Broadway Bound* are just some of his amusing comedies.

A number of outstanding women playwrights have enriched the modern American stage. Among them are Lillian Hellman *(The Little Foxes),* Susan Glaspell *(Trifles),* Lorraine Hansberry *(A Raisin in the Sun)* and Beth Henley *(Crimes of the Heart).* Alice Childress *(Wine in the Wilderness)* and Elizabeth Swados *(Runaways)* have received critical acclaim for their presentations of modern themes.

Regional theater companies, such as the American Repertory Theatre, continue to support new playwrights as well as revivals such as The School for Scandal.

Regional and Repertory Theaters

Off-Broadway plays became in the fifties a new source of inspiration for the American theater, with creative producers, actors, and backstage artists bringing fresh talent to reviving our great plays and encouraging new ones to be written. Greenwich Village has been the center for progressive artists since the early twenties, so it was naturally the first area where less expensive, more original, and interesting presentations found a satisfactory environment. By the sixties, off-Broadway theaters had opened all over New York City in any available building — cafés, churches, lecture halls, lofts.

The hope of the American theater lies in the growth of the regional and repertory theaters. **Regional theaters** present any type of play for as long as they wish and can repeat a play when and if they think it wise. **Repertory theaters** set up a definite number of productions, which they repeat at regular intervals or rotate as advertised at the beginning of each season. Both are known as resident theaters when guest stars are not used, and they specialize in ensemble acting. They both usually have subscription memberships. Individual admissions, at higher cost per performance than the memberships, may or may not be sold.

The first regional theater to be built was the Tyrone Guthrie Theater, which opened in Minneapolis in 1963. The Guthrie was one of the first theaters to feature a thrust stage. Since the opening of the Guthrie, regional theaters have sprung up in cities across America.

Another development in regional theater is the growth of dinner theater. Offering a package price for a meal and a professional play, dinner theaters have captured a suburban audience that might not have ventured into a city to see a play. In addition, the emergence of dinner theater has provided a new place for actors, designers, and technicians to work at their art.

In many areas, theater production groups bring a wide variety of performances to a larger audience. Some of these theaters are able to supplement local talent with professional actors.

The Amateur Theater

Amateur means "one who loves." In America, the number of amateurs who give hours and hours of their leisure time to putting on plays is a national fact of importance. If you really want to enjoy acting in, directing, or staging plays, you will become involved in the amateur field.

The little theaters were a part of the life of almost every city and town in the twenties and thirties. They were usually formed by people who loved the theater and wanted to bring the best Broadway plays to their communities. The one-act play came into prominence in the twenties, largely because tournaments where only one-act plays could be entered were held in many states.

Community theaters gradually superseded the little theaters. They are more democratic, drawing players from all sections of cities and catering to larger and more varied audiences. In many places where no professional theaters are located, community theaters serve as the principal contact of legitimate theater.

University Theater

Some of the finest theater buildings in the world are located on the campuses of American colleges and universities, and their drama departments cover every field of drama. Each year thousands of teachers of dramatics enter the high school and elementary fields. Professional aspirants can get practical experience in every type of play — period, classical, contemporary, and children's theater.

Guest stars have become resident instructors and actors under special arrangements made through the Extension Department of Equity. Thus drama majors get firsthand instruction and information from guest stars.

Theater of the Future

What form the productions of the future will take will depend on the taste of the public. The commercial theater in many cities is losing some of its hold, and nonprofit theater of some sort is growing. With the increasing spread of regional theaters all over free Europe, England, and America and the interchange of plays in festivals and conferences growing more frequent every season, there is justifiable hope that drama of the world will hold the best of the past, will safely survive the changes of the present, and will create ever-expanding means of expressing the dreams of humanity.

It is impossible to determine the future. Never have young people had more need for a firm foundation of knowledge on which to base their judgment of what they choose to see in the theater. You are fortunate in being introduced to the world of the theater in a dramatics class where you can become familiar with great dramas and learn to distinguish between the best and the worst theatrical practices of today.

Recalling Ideas

1. How did drama probably originate? Where were the first known performances?

2. What was the function of the Greek chorus?

3. Name the three most important Greek tragedians.

4. What were the Mystery plays?

5. Describe some of the characters of the commedia dell'arte.

6. Describe the Elizabethan playhouse.

7. What is the essence of Nō theater?

8. Identify each of the following playwrights: Goethe, Shaw, Marlowe, Pirandello, Ibsen, Miller.

Discussing Ideas

1. If you could choose one period in the history of the theater to be an actor, which would it be? Why?

2. Shakespeare was an actor as well as a playwright. How do you think his stage experience affected his writing? Why do you think Shakespeare's plays are still successful?

3. Discuss what makes a play "American." Cite as many examples as you can from the American theater.

4. Explore the regional, repertory, university, and amateur theater in your community. Discuss some of the kinds of plays you can see and the kinds of productions mounted.

5. Shakespeare said "all the world's a stage." How does the theater affect the world?

Careers

There are a number of managerial positions in the theater. **House managers** oversee the box office staff. They take reservations, hire and instruct **ushers,** greet people at the door, see that patrons get into and out of the theater safely, control the temperature, and guard the halls during performances. They complete the box office statement at the end of each performance, recording attendance, reservations, no-shows, off-street tickets, and other helpful information. They lock up the evening's receipts, keep the halls quiet, and follow the director's guidelines for admitting latecomers.

Ushers sweep the house before and after performances, take and tear tickets, distribute programs, and handle special seating arrangements.

Ushers may begin in small theaters and work part-time. They may go on to become house managers, who need a business background and the ability to handle emergencies quickly.

Program Managers work with the **Publicity Director** and other crew members to produce, print, and record the cost of the program. They write program notes, include the names of performers and staff, acknowledge public funding, and thank financial contributors.

Program managers need training and experience in writing. Communication courses in 2- or 4-year institutions are helpful.

Ticket Managers are responsible for the design, sale, and distribution of tickets. They and their crews often handle large sums of money.

A 2- or 4-year program in business is needed for this position. Knowledge of theater arts is helpful but not essential.

Part Four

Producing the Drama

Chapter 10

Fundamentals of Play Production

You Will Learn

Who the members of a production staff are.

What the responsibilities of each staff member are.

What makes up a master production schedule check list.

How to prepare a budget.

How to make a promptbook.

How to conduct and participate in an audition.

How to prepare a resumé.

What types of rehearsals there are.

How to make up a rehearsal schedule.

What the acting areas of a stage are.

About dress rehearsals, the performance, and curtain calls.

Vocabulary

producer	scenic artist or designer	stage manager
director		grips
assistant director	technical director	property chief
prompter		business manager

publicity manager   prepared audition   blocking rehearsal

house manager   textual tryout   working rehearsal

promptbook   cold reading   polishing rehearsals

audition   improvisational audition rhythm

resumé   callbacks   technical rehearsals

open audition   reading rehearsal   curtain calls

closed audition

*P*lay production offers many opportunities that you may well find more stimulating and exciting than acting. All the activities involved in the design and construction of sets and costumes, the handling of lighting equipment, and the managing of affairs backstage and in the front of the house are of absorbing interest once the preparation for a play gets underway.

At present, your main interest probably centers on the plays given by your own school. School stages may range from simple ones in classrooms to theaters having a computerized lighting console, sophisticated recording and sound equipment, fine dressing rooms, and ample work and storage space. If your school does not have all these facilities, do not be dismayed. A small stage, crowded backstage area, and the minimum of stage lights are limitations that may challenge your imagination and ingenuity. As a result, your productions may well be superior to those presented more easily with extensive physical equipment. Whatever the size and equipment of your theater, having a share in a big public production is a rewarding experience.

Putting on a public production of a long play means several weeks of intensive work by a large group of people. Before that period, much preliminary planning and preparation must be done. To get the most from the experience, follow all the activities from the beginning, carrying out your own special duties with enthusiasm and responsibility.

In school dramatics, the director usually plans the production in accordance with the schedule for school events and often works with a student executive committee in the selection of individual production staff members and their assistants. The director and this executive committee also set up special committees to assist in all, or some of, the following production procedures: play reading and selection, casting, costuming, properties, publicity, business management, and stage crew work. All the people chosen should be dependable and enthusiastic, since a great deal of the authority in production rests with them. The number of people on the production staff will be determined by the size of the production, the availability of capable people, and the needs of the individual school or class.

The Production Staff

The Producer

The director is usually the **producer** of a high school production. In the professional theater, the producer agrees to back a show by finding financial investors called "angels." The producer also hires the director and the production staff, sets the budget, and pays the bills.

The Director

The dramatics teacher is usually the **director** of the public productions in high school. Many high schools today have a trained, and frequently professionally experienced, teacher-director.

In the professional theater, the director is usually credited with the play's success or failure. Actors also seek out fine directors under whom to work. Actors take minor parts frequently for the privilege of sharing the experience of creating the perfect performance of a play — the ideal of every dedicated person involved in theater.

The ideal director inspires actors with confidence in their abilities and intelligence in building their roles, molding all phases of production into a unified whole. Concentrated attention to every detail maintains enthusiasm and dedication on the part of every individual involved in each situation and eliminates distracting and nerve-racking crises. The director is responsible for onstage empathies and backstage morale. The director's objective at all times must be to produce the playwright's intentions as faithfully as possible by an intensive study of the script, including the author's style, the play's theme, and the characters' relationships. The director is responsible for the overall interpretation of the play, its style, and its theme. The director must approve all designs and any changes in design. The director should be a person who can "see" the areas of needed improvement and have the ability and personality to communicate the means by which improvement can take place. This communication is accomplished in rehearsal and through oral, written, or taped notes called *critiques*. The director's word is law, for only the director has visualized the production as it should be performed.

In high school productions, the students usually have a much larger input, and the director is a teacher-director. Therefore, putting on a play can be a cooperative, delightful experience of a team working together in an exciting game. You are fortunate to be having the companionship and excitement of high school dramatics as your introduction to theater.

Andrei Serban directing King Stag *at the American Repertory Theater.*

The Assistant Director

In the school theater, the position of **assistant director** (AD) is held by a capable student. This must be a person whom the director finds dependable and whom the students respect. The AD will serve as a liaison between the

---

MASTER PRODUCTION SCHEDULE CHECKLIST

1. Production budget established
2. Play-reading committee selected
3. Committee reports
4. Final selection of play
5. Staff organized
6. Research
7. Production rights obtained
8. Scripts ordered
9. Meeting of director, technical director, and stage manager
10. Promptbook prepared
11. Floor plan designed
12. Basic design presented— scenery, lights, costumes
13. Tryouts
14. Cast selected
15. Stage and costume crews recruited
16. First publicity release
17. Costume measurements taken
18. Light plot prepared
19. Floor plan laid out on rehearsal floor
20. Blocking rehearsals begun
21. Tickets ordered
22. Publicity committee organized
23. Scenery begun
24. Program prepared for printing
25. Working rehearsals
26. First costume fittings
27. Arrangements made for publicity photos
28. Props secured
29. Second publicity release
30. Tickets placed on sale

director, cast, and crew, taking charge of rehearsals in the absence of the director. This is a position you must aspire to if you are interested in all phases of the theater.

---

31. Construction of scenery completed

32. Special effects (recordings and the like) secured

33. Lighting, cue sheets, and prop plots completed

34. Tickets distributed and/or racked

35. Rental or purchase of costumes and accessories arranged

36. Second costume fitting

37. First lighting check

38. Polish rehearsal and rehearsal timed

39. Rehearsal with props

40. Set completed

41. Major press releases

42. Technical rehearsals

43. Costume parade

44. Final set touches

45. Dress rehearsals

46. Performances

47. Costume and prop check-in

48. Bills paid and tickets audited

49. **a.** Scenery struck and stored

  b. Props put away

  c. Borrowed items, such as furniture and the like, returned

  d. Rented costumes packed and returned

  e. Own costumes cleaned and stored

  f. Dressing rooms cleaned

  g. Thank-you letters sent

50. Final financial statement drawn

The Prompter

This position should also be held by a dependable student who will attend every rehearsal. During rehearsals, the **prompter,** or holder of the book, keeps the director's promptbook and makes penciled notes on interpretation, movement, and business, light and sound cues, and warning signals. This is done under the supervision of the director.

A numbering system is recommended for marking the blocking — the movements, positions, and crosses. In this system, each movement on each page is given a number of easy reference by actors and director. Sound and light cues and other special effects are numbered in different colors. By using floor-plan sketches in the promptbook, the prompter can clarify any questions concerning stage groupings, crosses, and changes.

The prompter must mark every pause so that an unnecessary prompt will not be given. During the performance, the prompter can often save the show if emergencies arise by giving correct cues and lines. If the cast starts to skip passages, the prompter can feed the vital lines to keep the meaning clear for the audience. If the prompter fails at these crucial times, the entire production can be ruined. Audiences will often remember and laugh about one moment of confusion after they have forgotten all the fine points of a production.

Some directors do not use the prompter during the performance, preferring to have the actors know they are on their own. Others feel that a skilled prompter is essential. If your school does use a prompter, this is a position from which you may learn a great deal. It is a job that requires both reliability and intelligence.

The Scenic Artist and the Technical Director

The **scenic artist,** or the **designer,** usually designs the settings but in many cases may also design the costumes, the makeup, and the lighting. Though these designs may be simple or complex, they must always give the play visual dimensions in harmony with the aims of the director.

The work of the **technical director** (TD) is also vitally important. It is the TD who executes the designs of the scenic artist, with the assistance of a crew for building sets, painting drops, creating costumes, and hanging lights. In some cases, the scenic artist and the technical director are the same person. Though their functions are different, they both aim at serving the director's intentions as effectively, simply, and beautifully as possible to achieve a unified production.

The Stage Manager

Aided by the stage crew, the **stage manager** (SM) takes complete charge backstage during rehearsals and performances. In some cases, the SM and the crew act as both the stage carpenters who build the set and the **grips** who change the scenery. The stage manager also keeps a promptbook containing all cues and effects. The SM makes up cue sheets or charts containing the cues for lights, sound, and curtain. For the stage crew, the SM makes up a chart of set and prop changes to guide them through the play. During the performance, the stage manager usually sits at a prompt table in the stage right wing just upstage of the proscenium. From that vantage point, the SM gives all cues (lights, sound, curtain) to the technical crew. In addition, the stage manager must handle any and all emergencies that arise during the performance. A good stage manager is essential to a smooth production.

In the professional theater, the stage manager has to be versatile and experienced in all phases of theater production. The SM not only runs the show backstage but also acts as a director for brush-up rehearsals, breaking in new cast members, and keeping the production fresh and sharp.

The Backstage Assistants

The **property chief** and property assistants get the furniture and props the designer has planned, store them backstage, arrange them, prepare a prop table, and give the hand props to the actors backstage just before entrances. These hand props should be kept on the side of the stage where the actors who use these props will make entrances. Props are returned to the prop table after use and never touched. The wardrobe person and makeup crew serve under the stage manager. The efficiency, ingenuity, and dependability of these backstage assistants during long hours of hard work are determining factors in a successful production. Without them, the play cannot go on.

The Business Manager

The **business manager** is responsible for the financial arrangements of the production. In accordance with school policy, the business manager may be in charge of all funds, pay all bills, and handle the printing and selling of tickets. The business manager and the director should gauge probable receipts and achieve a reasonable profit by watching production and publicity expenses.

In the school theater, the business manager has the difficult task of issuing tickets to many salespersons and checking on sales. The business manager should give out all passes to the show with the permission of the director and should issue stage-door slips to those working backstage. It is most important that people who do not have specific duties in the dressing rooms or backstage area not be admitted during performances. (If stage-door slips are not used, a list of the staff may be substituted. A responsible person may use it to check entrances and exits at the stage door.)

The business manager is also in charge of printing the programs, which should be designed in harmony with the production. The cast is usually listed in order of appearance. The business manager should be accurate in listing names of cast members, production staff, committee chairpersons, backstage crew, and acknowledgments for favors and assistance from businesses and individuals. Selling advertising to pay for the program is usually a matter determined by school authorities. If advertising is used, the business manager supervises it.

BUDGET

John Adams High School Drama

Production: _____

Dates: _____

Projected Income:

Tickets sold _____ @ $ _____ = $ _____

_____ @ $ _____ = $ _____

Other income:

Concessions $ _____

Program ads _____

Total Projected Income: $ _____

Projected Expenses

Royalty $ _____

Play books _____

Tickets _____

Programs _____

Advertising _____

Scenery _____

Properties _____

Costumes _____

Makeup _____

Miscellaneous:

Custodial fees $ _____

Police department _____

Fire department _____

Ushers _____

Box-office staff _____

Total Projected Production Costs $ _____

Projected Net Income (Total income less total production costs) $ _____

The Publicity Manager

The person who promotes the show in the school and community is the **publicity manager.** Good publicity is vital to the success of the play. If they are properly approached, the public press, newspapers published at other schools, local radio and television stations, and church publications will give space and time to notices about public school productions. In these days of broadcasting systems, tape recordings, and other devices in many high schools, there are almost limitless possibilities for promoting a play.

The publicity manager and assistants have a real opportunity to make original and artistic contributions to the success of a production. The advertising staff would do well to consult the art department of the school. With serious dramas, advertising in keeping with the spirit of the play may include well-designed individual notices sent to all drama enthusiasts in the community. For comedies, cartoons of the cast and humorous items about the funniest rehearsal situations can be featured, possibly with lively quotations from the play. The title of the play itself, the author, the skill or prominence of the performers, the past achievements of the director, and striking scenic effects can also furnish material for publicity.

The House Manager

The person responsible for the seating and comfort of the audience, the competence and training of the ushers, and the distribution of the programs is the **house manager.** Ushers in uniform, evening dress, or appropriate costumes can add to the pleasure of the audience.

Other Personnel

School productions frequently involve still more people. Fire fighters and police officers are often required. In some communities, they will be on hand if they are notified when a production is scheduled; otherwise, they must be hired. In some schools, members of the faculty are required to be in attendance for supervision, and they often take or sell tickets out front.

A crew member may be in charge of furnishing recorded music for the curtain raiser or intermissions. If so, the selections should be approved by the director far in advance, and they should be properly rehearsed. Music should also be in keeping with the production and subordinate to it, not added as a special feature. Be sure that any permissions required for the use of music are secured well in advance.

1. In your school, what are some of the special problems connected with putting on a play? Are they being solved? Is the entire student body interested in them? Are the people in the community interested?

2. Discuss the school plays you have attended or assisted with, and note the part the backstage people had in their success or failure.

3. For what purpose are the proceeds of your dramatic productions used? Are they used exclusively for improving the stage and its equipment, as a means of raising money for other school activities, or for charity? How do you think they ought to be used?

4. Discuss possible difficulties that might arise during a performance. Show how the prompter and/or the stage manager might avoid or overcome them.

Prerehearsal Activities

After the director and the executive committee have set up the special committees and after individual production staff members have been selected, the next step is to choose a play. This is usually done by the reading committee and the director. Before, or immediately after play selection, a tentative budget should be prepared. If production costs will be a determining factor, the budget should be established first.

Choosing a Play

Choosing the play is the first decision to be made. The right choice has everything to do with the level of success of the production. Before the choice can be made, many plays must be read. The producing group must know the purpose of the proposed production. Is it primarily a school project, recognized as an important group activity? Or is it to raise funds for a specific purpose or organization? A play must be found that will fulfill its designated purpose, appeal to its particular audience, and be adaptable to the ability of the actors, the size and equipment of the stage, and the limits of the budget. Whatever the purpose, it is important to select the best play possible as far as script quality, strength of parts, and entertainment value are concerned.

Rather than compromise the quality of a script, it is better to present classics (most of which require no royalty) or cut production expenses sufficiently to pay the royalty of a first-class contemporary play. Remember that there are many classics that the other students and the parents will thoroughly enjoy. There are also many plays of the last century, now released from royalty charges, that your audience would enjoy. Try to avoid plays that a large portion of your audience may have seen recently, and try to provide variety in the annual programs of your school.

The size of the cast requires attention in the choice of a play. When the cast is large, more students receive the benefits of training and experience. However, large casts make for difficult rehearsals and staging. Ability to create the necessary stage settings and the possibility of adequate interpretation by available actors must be considered.

Securing Production Rights

Before a play is finally selected, the director or some authorized person should write to the publisher controlling the acting rights of the play. The director should state the dates and number of performances planned and request authorization to present the play. There are many regulations restricting the presentation of plays by amateurs, especially in larger cities where stock and road companies appear. Therefore, full permission should be obtained for a public performance before preparations start.

Planning the Production

If the budget has not been established, it must be set before proceeding further. The director must estimate the probable size of the audience and take into account sets and props that may be obtained without expense. The director should set up a master production schedule such as the one on pages 328 — 329. Careful scheduling is often the difference between a smoothly run production and a chaotic one.

Early in a production, scenery must be visualized. This process may be aided by a scale model of the set and the theater.
● ● ● ● ● ● ● ● ● ● ● ●

The director must first study the play from every angle to determine the style and atmosphere to be carried out in the sets and costumes. The director must understand the theme and decide how best to express it, decide how to emphasize the conflict, suspense, and climax of the plot, and analyze the characters and their relationships with one another. For a period play, the director must study the historical background, social conditions, and attitudes of the people represented, as well as the costumes, furnishings, and manner of speech and movement.

After studying the play, the director makes a floor plan. This is an overhead view of the set and helps the director plan the action that will take place on the stage. During this early period, the director should have frequent conferences with the scenic artist and stage manager concerning many aspects of the production. Problems of handling the show backstage must be discussed.

The entrances and exits must be practical and logical. The location and size of the furniture should be planned to create helpful, meaningful units for definite bits of action and to form effective and balanced stage pictures. The light sources must be considered and marked on the floor plan. Windows provide daytime light; lamps, fireplaces, and perhaps chandeliers give light at night. Sufficient backing for windows and doors must be considered in planning the action, and the director must make these needs clear to the scenic artist. The backstage storage areas for furniture, props, and sets must be diagrammed. After the director, the scenic artist, and the stage manager have made overall plans, the director will visualize important scenes carefully and plan for effective grouping. Unimportant characters can be momentarily emphasized by being placed upstage or apart from the others.

Making the Promptbook

The backbone of a production is the **promptbook,** started by the director during the planning period and containing the entire play script. Into this book go the director's plans as well as the telephone numbers and addresses of all the people involved in the production. The easiest way to make a promptbook is to paste the pages of the play in a large loose-leaf notebook. This system requires two copies of the play. If there is only one copy available for this purpose, page-size windows can be cut in the sheets of the notebook, and each page of the script can be fastened with cellophane tape or glue into these windows.

Large margins around the script are essential for the sketches, cues, and notes, first made by the director in the preliminary planning and then added to and changed during rehearsals. The marginal notes show script cuttings, stage directions, and markings of difficult passages for pauses, phrasing, and emphasis. The sketches or diagrams of floor plans and sets show positions of furniture and actors in every scene. Stage groupings of actors can be drawn

Stress 7 mirror lines and actions *

Ent Jack (Enter JACK.)

¹GWENDOLEN. (*Catching sight of him.*) Ernest! My own
Ernest!

x's her w/ open arms

²JACK. Gwendolen! Darling! (*Offers to kiss her.*)*1

strikes melodramatic pose of indignation

warn:
Alg-ENT
#4

³GWENDOLEN. (*Drawing back.*) A moment! May I ask if
you are engaged to be married to this young lady? (*Points
to* CECILY.)*2

"forced" — *w/fan*

Play up little's

⁴JACK. (*Laughing.*) To dear ⓛittle Cecily! Of course not!
What could have put such an idea into your pretty ⓛittle
head? *as if "Just as I thought" — Jack kisses her (#5) and keeps arm around waist*

⁵GWENDOLEN. Ⓣhank you. You may. (*Offers her
cheek.*)

⁶CECILY. (*Very sweetly.*) I knew there must be some mis-
understanding, Miss Fairfax. The gentleman whose arm
is at present around your waist is my dear guardian, Mr.
John Worthing. *(X DL) #6*

Jack runs finger nervously around inside of collar

⁷GWENDOLEN. I beg your pardon?

⁸CECILY. This is Uncle Jack.

Melodramatic shock pose — back of hand to forehead — flutters fan

⁹GWENDOLEN. (*Receding.*) Jack! Oh! *7 *x's DR Turns back on G.*

Ent Algy (Enter ALGERNON.)

¹⁰CECILY. Here is Ernest. *G and J — "Jake"*

¹¹ALGERNON. (*Goes straight over to* CECILY *without noticing anyone else.*) My own love! (*Offers to kiss her.*)
*1 *x's to her w/open arms — mirror of Jack*

¹²CECILY. (*Drawing back.*) A moment, Ernest! May I ask *2
you—are you engaged to be married to this young
lady?

Points w/fan

"Jake"

¹³ALGERNON. (*Looking round.*) To what young lady? Good
heavens! Gwendolen!

15

Sample promptbook page

with the initials of the characters' names marked in little circles. Most directors like to sketch important crosses and countercrosses in the promptbook and mark actors' movements with symbols. For example, "XR from C" means that the actor moves to the right from a position in stage center. "Enter UL, exit DR" means that the actor comes in from the farthest upstage entrance on the left and crosses the stage diagonally, going out nearest the audience on the right.

Cues marked in the margin include those for lights, sound effects, curtains, and other effects both on and off the stage. As rehearsals progress, individual cue sheets are made from the book by the stage manager. These sheets are given to the electrician, the wardrobe people, the prop committee, the sound technician, and others whose tasks require written directions. When marking the promptbook, pencil rather than pen should be used so that changes may be made when necessary. It is advisable to use different colors for particular types of cues and warning signals, such as red for lights, blue for curtain, and green for entrances and exits. Most directors and stage managers want *warn* cues marked in the promptbook. A warn cue advises the stage manager of an entrance, sound effect, or lighting change before it is to take place. For example: WARN: phone 2. This says that the phone is to ring two pages from that point in the script. A sample promptbook page appears on page 337.

When a play is finished, the promptbook should be completed with a copy of the program and photographs of the production. Frequently a school play is repeated in five or six years without much duplication in the audience. Although every production has a new promptbook, the original can be most useful for reference purposes.

Casting the Play

Few phases of production are more important to the ultimate success or failure of a play than the choice of the cast. Casting demands tact, sincerity, fairness, and sound judgment. Those planning to audition should fill out an audition form, such as the one found opposite. The director must cast, not solely on the tryout, but upon past experience with the individual and especially upon a projection of what that actor will be able to do after weeks of rehearsal and direction. This ability to look ahead is possessed by only a few directors and goes hand in hand with a director's ability to visualize the final production even before the first rehearsal. A successful production demands that actors be equipped physically, mentally, and temperamentally to give convincing interpretations of the roles assigned to them. Personality development belongs in classroom dramatic work, not in public productions.

TRYOUT INFORMATION CARD

NAME (LAST NAME FIRST)	CLASS	AGE	PHONE
ADDRESS	SEX	HEIGHT	WEIGHT

PREVIOUS ACTING EXPERIENCE

WHAT VOCAL PART
DO YOU SING?
  S   A   T   B

WHAT MUSICAL INSTRUMENT DO YOU PLAY?

EXPERIENCE:

WHAT DANCE TRAINING HAVE YOU HAD?

LIST YOUR CLASS SCHEDULE:

1	4	7
2	5	8
3	6	9

WILL YOU BE ABLE TO ATTEND ALL REHEARSALS?   YES_____   NO_____
IF NOT, WHAT CONFLICTS ARE THERE?

ARE YOU INTERESTED IN WORKING ON ANY OF THE FOLLOWING COMMITTEES?

MAKEUP	PROPERTIES	SCENERY CONST.
PUBLICITY	COSTUMES	STAGE CREW

ARE YOU INTERESTED IN BEING STUDENT DIRECTOR?

PROMPTER?   TECHNICAL DIRECTOR?   STAGE MANAGER?

DIRECTOR'S COMMENTS:
  VOICE: PHYSICAL APPEARANCE:

  QUALITY: IMAGINATION:

  PITCH: ANIMATION:

  VARIETY: STAGE PRESENCE:

PARTS CONSIDERED FOR:

Auditions

One of the most important experiences for an actor is the **audition.** Some of the most talented actors fail to get parts because they give poor auditions. Many stage hopefuls find themselves on the other side of the footlights because they choke at their audition.

Those of you wanting to pursue acting as a professional career should have a **resumé,** such as the one found opposite, and a portfolio. Your resumé includes an 8×10 inch headshot photograph of you as you appear offstage, not as a character in costume. The resumé also includes all the important information a casting director wants to know: name, address, phone number, type of voice (if you sing), vital statistics, experience, education and professional training, and special skills. Since all actors are typed by class of performer, include at the top of the resumé your type classification. For example, if acting is your strongest skill, followed by dancing, followed by singing, your classification would be actor-dancer-singer. Similarly, there are dancer-singer-actors, singer-actor-dancers, actor-singer-dancers, and so on.

The portfolio you present at an audition should include other photographs of you as you appeared in specific roles. If possible, select roles that show you to have a range of abilities from drama to comedy to musical theater. Include reviews of your performances and sample programs of the plays in which you appeared.

In some public schools, auditions are limited to drama or speech students. In others, they are open to all students. This is a matter to be decided by the director or by the individual school. Perhaps the director will want to use a point system of stage experience and service to help determine eligibility for an important role. In some schools, scholastic standing in other departments and good citizenship are considered before an applicant is allowed to try out. In any case, eligible applicants must be made to understand that casting is usually probationary until the director has been able to determine the actor's ability to take direction, willingness to work, and understanding of the task.

Every possible means of publicizing the roles to be filled should be used prior to the tryouts. Posters, articles in the school paper, and posted descriptions of the characters are all good ways of circulating the information. If possible, the director will place a copy of the play on reserve in the school library for all applicants to read or will make the play available in some other way.

The tryout arrangements must be determined by the number of people who wish to read for the play, the length of time that can be devoted to casting, and the kind of play to be presented. It is always preferable to hold tryouts in the auditorium or theater in which the play is to be performed. Sometimes, however, this is not possible.

When the applicants have assembled, the director can explain all details of the tryouts, discuss the play briefly, and describe the characters. Applicants should be asked to fill out cards giving name, address, phone number, height, weight, past experience in school plays, and any previous commitments that might interfere with attendance at rehearsals. Complete *all* requested information honestly. Do not leave blanks or give false information, particularly in areas such as age, height, weight, and special training.

Methods of conducting auditions vary with directors. Auditions can be

---

```
JOYCE JACKSON                ACTRESS-SINGER-DANCER          HOME PHONE: (209) 658-7028
4950 Cove Road                                              SER. PHONE: (209) 799-9190
Stamford, CT 06904           Legit. Soprano: low G-high C

Age Range: 16-30    Height: 5'6"    Weight: 108    Hair: Blonde, long   Eyes: Blue   Dress: 7/8
```

EXPERIENCE

HANSEL AND GRETEL	Wicked Witch	Courtyard Playhouse, N.Y.C.
GUYS AND DOLLS	Sarah Brown	Rochester, Minn., Civic Theatre
110 IN THE SHADE	Lizzie	Highland Summer Theatre, Minn.
THE FANTASTICKS	Luisa	Highland Summer Theatre
DARK AT THE TOP OF THE STAIRS	Flirt Conroy	Highland Summer Theatre
DIRTY WORK AT THE CROSSROADS	Nellie Lovelace	Ohio Valley Summer Theatre
NAUGHTY MARIETTA	Marietta	Ohio Valley Summer Theatre
THE SOUND OF MUSIC	Maria	Mosby Dinner Theatre, Virginia
OKLAHOMA!	Understudy for Laurey and Dancing Laurey (played by Kathleen Conry of Broadway's NO, NO, NANETTE)	Mosby Dinner Theatre
ANYTHING GOES	Hope Harcourt	Club Bone Dinner Theatre, N.J.
LIL ABNER	Daisy Mae	Club Bone Dinner Theatre
MARY POPPINS	Mary Poppins	Club Bone Dinner Theatre
LAUGHING GAS (original musical)	Mrs. Krause	Cavalier Productions, Virginia
RUMPELSTILTSKIN	Maiden Queen/Mother	National Parks and Planning Commission, Washington, D.C.
HAPPY BIRTHDAY, AMERICA!	Voice-overs	Library Theatre, Washington, D.C.
AMAHL AND THE NIGHT VISITORS	Mother	Kenyon, Minnesota
MAN OF LA MANCHA	Antonia & Housekeeper	Boulder, Colorado

NIGHTCLUB AND CABARET

HOLIDAY INN	"Rooftop Revival" singing group show	Denver, Colorado
	Featured singing duo, musical comedy, operetta and popular	Washington, D.C.
INN OF TRENTON and PRINCETON UNIVERSITY	"Broadway Showstoppers" Revue	

EDUCATION AND TRAINING

DEGREE: Bachelor of Music Ed. in Voice, University of Colorado
GRADUATE   Acting- Mankato State College, Minn., under Dr. C. Ron Olauson
STUDY: Ohio University under Robert Winters
                Private study with Richard G. Holmes (Senator Dawes in Broadway's INDIANS), Washington, D.C.
DANCE: Ballet- 8 years   Modern- 2 years   Tap- 1 year
SINGING: 8 years classical and musical comedy training, some belting
MODELING: J.C. PENNEY CO., 3 years floor modeling and fashion shows - Denver, Colorado
            Print and promotional work in Colorado for Wells, Rich, Green Inc. of N.Y.C.
            First Runner-up, JANTZEN SMILE GIRL, Colorado Region
OTHER   Subject of prize-winning photos in Eastman-Kodak's National Photographic Contest
SKILLS: Play piano; Teach piano and voice; Sing in Italian, German, Spanish, French
            Accents: Norwegian, Swedish, Cockney, Irish, Southern
            Excellent snow skier and swimmer
            Own and drive a car
            Public elementary school teacher

either open or closed. To a professional, an **open audition** is for nonunion actors; a **closed audition** is open only to union members. In the high school, an open audition means that anyone in the student body is eligible to try out. A closed audition means that only certain students may try out — members of the drama club or the senior class, for example. A second classification of auditions is prepared or cold. A **prepared audition** permits the actor to bring in material that has been thoroughly worked out, including memorization and action. A prepared tryout is sometimes called a **textual tryout** because the audition material comes from a manuscript or printed play. Textual tryouts may be either monologues or scenes. A **cold reading** is one in which the actor is given material never seen before. The actor is expected to read the unfamiliar material with imagination, feeling, and confidence. Unless the casting director summarizes the situation and the characters, the actor is usually not penalized for making errors in interpretation. If the cold tryout uses a scene, the actor has the disadvantage of playing with another actor whose acting skills are unknown. On the other hand, the actors have the advantage of having someone to play against. Sometimes a cold tryout is not textual, but improvisational. In an **improvisational audition,** the actor is assigned a character and given a brief description of a situation. Then the actor must improvise a scene around the assigned character and situation.

Some directors like to combine audition formats. This is especially true of tryouts for musicals. In musicals, the actors very often have to be able to act, sing, and dance.

Callbacks

After the best possibilities for all roles have been selected, second or perhaps third **callbacks** should be held for final selection of the candidates who might work together in regard to physical appearance, voice, and personality. By this time, any problems concerning rehearsal attendance, dependability, responsiveness to suggestions, and general attitudes should be determined as far as possible.

Perhaps the most important aspect of auditions is that they be conducted in a friendly and relaxed atmosphere. Each student who tries out must know that she or he is being given a fair chance. Good auditions can set morale at a high level for the rest of the production.

You and Your Audition

In order to have the best audition possible, the first thing you must know well is yourself. You must be honest in your self-appraisal, neither conceited nor overly modest. Know what kind of actor you are and what kinds of roles you can play. You may aspire to play every great role ever written, but if you are

Chorus Line is a play about the "drama" of an audition, about the anxiety that must be mastered, and the ability to relax and just be yourself.

truly objective, you know that you are best suited for certain roles. The director will be looking for certain vocal and physical attributes. Know how your voice sounds to an audience. Listen to a recording of your voice to hear how you sound to others. Look in the mirror and be objective about what you see. Bear in mind that auditioning is a selling job, and you are the product that must be sold. This selling process begins when the director first sees you.

Dress appropriately for the audition. Correct dress shows you off to your best advantage. Line, color, and style are important. Avoid wearing offbeat clothes, jewelry, or shoes. They tend to be distracting, drawing attention away from you. If you know the play, you can help the director visualize you in a part if your auditioning clothes suggest the part you desire. However, be careful that you do not overdo the suggestion. Girls should wear a dress or skirt and shoes with low heels. Young men are better off wearing a shirt and slacks. Avoid auditioning in jeans.

Observe the time limits that you are given. Contrary to inexperienced actors' beliefs, most directors know within the first fifteen seconds whether or not an actor is right for a part. Length is not necessarily strength in an audition.

Know the play that you are auditioning for whenever possible. Know the character or characters you really believe you can play and want to play. If you bring a prepared audition, select a monologue or single-character scene that suits the play and character for which you are auditioning. A comic monologue is inappropriate for a drama. A contemporary drama monologue is inappropriate for classical tragedy.

If you are asked to do both comedy and drama, do your strongest selection first. If you are permitted, prepare a series of short monologues rather than one long one. Work up at least ten to twelve auditioning pieces that last a few seconds to a minute each. Be certain there is enough of each to really show what you can do. In this way, you can show a director in five minutes your range of acting abilities. This is especially important in casting for a whole season or for a repertory group. Do not accompany yourself on the piano or guitar. When you have a vocal audition, use the accompanist provided or bring your own. Sing show music, not contemporary pop music.

Play to, but not up to, the director. Do not avert your eyes from nor stare at the person evaluating you. Walk to your auditioning position with a show of confidence — even if you are petrified. Pause for a moment when finished and leave the stage with poise. Should you be cut off, smile. Do not appear hurt or flustered. Show the director only your positive side.

Finally, develop a good audition attitude. Look forward to auditioning. Shake off the nervousness. Show a little hunger for the part. Be ready, willing, and eager to take a part, whatever part is offered to you. But also learn to take rejection. For one reason or another, you may be turned down. If you have the talent and the desire, bounce back to audition again and again. If the message you are receiving is saying that you may not have what it takes, accept that reality.

Rehearsing

If you are wise, you will attend every rehearsal, whether you are due on stage or not, in order to become a part of the play as a whole, appreciate the director's motivation for movements and tempos, and sense the satisfactory empathies being sought, to which the audience will respond later. You can also profit by the director's suggestions to the other actors and thus avoid their mistakes and profit by their achievements. One of the advantages of a school production is that the director has often had many of the actors in dramatics class and knows what to expect of them in regard to stage techniques. Much time is saved in avoiding explanations of stage terms. As an onlooker, you can become conscious of the importance of developing a scene without needless interruptions by members of the cast who bring up personal problems of interpretation onstage. All discussion and arguments should be offstage during rehearsal breaks. Remember, practice and rehearsal are not synonymous. Practice, for the most part, is what you do on your own time; rehearsal is what you do in the presence of the director and the other members of the cast.

Reading Rehearsals

The first rehearsal is most important. At it, the director should expect all members — cast, stage manager, and crew, all understudies, the technical director; and the chairpersons of committees involved in the backstage activities — to

Lewis Merkin and Valerie Curtin in a reading rehearsal of Children of a Lesser God *by Mark Medoff presented at the Mark Taper Forum in Los Angeles. This award-winning play was praised not only as a fine piece of dramatic literature but also for the outstanding performances by the leading actors—Phyllis Frelich and Lewis Merkin—who are both deaf.*

be present. The director should make it clear that the pleasure of play production lies in the efficient, happy, conscientious working together of everyone toward the objective of putting on the best production of that particular play with that particular group under the particular stage circumstances. The director should point out the factors that make a fine performance. These factors are perfect timing, excellent individual characterizations, and careful coordination of onstage and backstage activities. It is through this working together of cast and crew that the play's theme is brought out, and the play's spirit is maintained.

At this first rehearsal, called a **reading rehearsal,** some directors prefer to read the play themselves, thus setting at once the interpretation of the entire play and of individual roles. Others prefer to give the cast the opportunity to suggest their own characterizations by reading the parts assigned, while the director merely points out important details of phrasing, timing, and inflections. Whatever the method, the rehearsal should build up a clear-cut conception of the play and of conduct during rehearsals. All present should take careful notes in pencil.

In the first hours of work on the play, the director can sense the actor's ability to understand lines and project personality. The director can also judge the actors' willingness to respond to direction and to what extent they pay attention. If there is ample time, a number of reading rehearsals can "set" the characters and the lines. More reading rehearsals are necessary when dialects or stage diction are required. In any case, a number of reading rehearsals makes actors feel more secure about interpretation when rehearsing on the stage.

Rehearsal Schedules

A time schedule for the entire rehearsal period should be worked out and copies made for participants to give their parents. This procedure helps parents understand how much time will be involved in the production. When making this rehearsal schedule, the director considers the time allotted for preparing the production, the length and difficulty of the play, and the availability of the cast. For instance, if the audition-rehearsal-performance period has been set at seven weeks, after-school rehearsals should probably be planned for two to three hours a day, five days a week. The individual director can adjust the schedule to fit the particular situation.

In such a schedule, the first week should complete the tryouts and the reading rehearsals. The second week includes blocking and business rehearsals and a line check for the first and second acts. The third week should complete blocking and business rehearsals for the third act, full line check, and initial run-throughs. The fourth and fifth weeks constitute working rehearsals of the entire play.

If the auditorium has not been available previously, a long Saturday rehearsal should be held at the end of the fourth week. At this time, whatever is technically difficult should be rehearsed. All available sounds, lights, props, scenery, furniture, and costumes should be used. The sixth week is for polishing rehearsals, including stage crew rehearsals and run-throughs with props and at least some costumes.

The dress rehearsals with full stage crew and the performances take place in the seventh week. On Monday of this last week, the staff should hold its last rehearsal in which interruptions can be made, problems discussed, final costumes and props checked, and all details settled.

At least two dress rehearsals are recommended. However, if there is only one dress rehearsal, it should come on the Wednesday or Thursday before a Friday night performance. Tuesday may be spent in a final run-through. It is wise to invite a few people to a dress rehearsal to accustom the cast to playing before an audience. Many directors leave the night before the performance free for final adjustments. Others feel that a continuous flow right up to the opening night is desirable.

Sample 7-Week Audition-Rehearsal Schedule

Week 1: Auditions and first rehearsal (3 hours each)
- Monday   Auditions
- Tuesday   Auditions
- Wednesday   Callbacks (if necessary)
- Thursday   Cast posted
- Friday   Reading rehearsal

Week 2: Blocking and line-check rehearsals (2½–3 hours)
- Monday   Blocking Act I
- Tuesday   Rehearse Act I
- Wednesday   Line-check Act I
- Thursday   Blocking Act II
- Friday   Rehearse Act II

Week 3: Blocking and line-check rehearsals (2½–3 hours)
- Monday   Line-check Act II
- Tuesday   Run through Acts I and II
- Wednesday   Blocking Act III
- Thursday   Line-check Act III
- Friday   First run-through

Week 4:	Working rehearsals (3 hours)
Monday ⎫	Special scenes — chase, fight, and so on — rehearsed
Tuesday ⎭	privately
Wednesday	Act I concentrated
Thursday	Act II concentrated
Friday	Act III concentrated
Week 5:	Working rehearsals (full stage crew present — 3 hours)
Monday	Acts I, II, III in sequence
Tuesday	Acts II, III, I — in that order
Wednesday	Acts III, I, II — in that order
Thursday	Problem scenes only
Friday	Final working run-through
Week 6:	Polishing rehearsals (all crews present — 3 hours)
Monday	Run-through and dress parade
Tuesday	Run-through with lights
Wednesday	Run-through with scenery
Thursday	Run-through with lights and scenery
Friday	First complete run-through
Week 7:	Polishing rehearsals and performances (4–5 hours)
Monday	Second complete run-through
Tuesday	Final run-through
Wednesday	First dress rehearsal
Thursday	Final dress rehearsal
Friday	Performance
Saturday	Performance

Students involved in a production should be urged not to be absent from school because of their participation in a play. Much discrediting of school dramatics results from unnecessary cutting of classes and requests for special consideration when a play is being produced. With wise management and administrative cooperation, a big production can be put on without complicating the daily schedule. The auditorium should be closed to all other activities during the last three weeks, and enough time must be given the technical director and crew to "hang the set."

Blocking Rehearsals

Blocking the movement and planning stage business follow the reading rehearsals. The major blocking areas of the traditional and the arena stages are

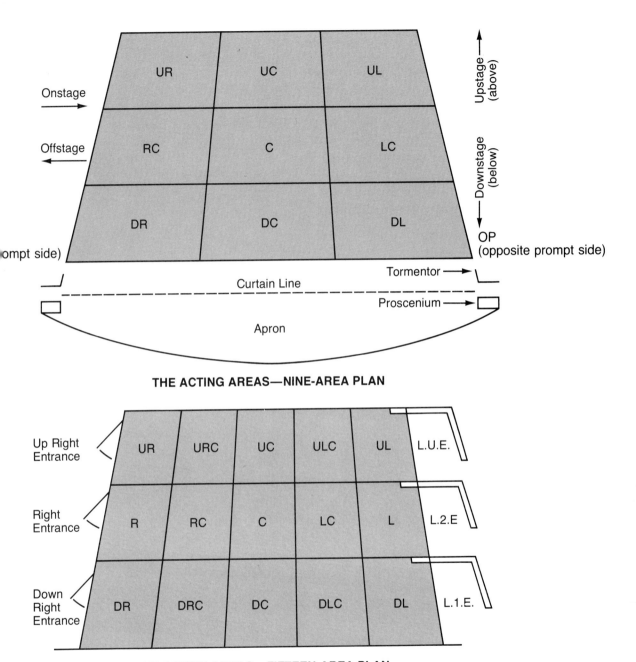

THE ACTING AREAS—NINE-AREA PLAN

THE ACTING AREAS—FIFTEEN-AREA PLAN

The upper diagram also indicates directions from the actor's point of view. The lower diagram shows entrance positions used with the old wing setting—L.1.E. (left first entrance), etc.—and early box sets—down right entrance, etc. These symbols are still used with many musical plays.

shown on page 349. Work on the interpretation of lines should be delayed while attention is focused on movement and stage groupings. The director will have already worked out plans for using the stage area, emphasizing important groupings, and keeping effective stage pictures. However, in the early rehearsals, most directors are willing to discuss possible changes and incorporate spontaneous reactions of the actors. When the fundamental blocking of the first act has been set, the blocking of the second act should follow. The two acts can then be put together at a combined **blocking rehearsal.** Following this, the third act should be set, and the first and second reviewed. As soon as the business of the first act is clarified, the lines and blocking may be memorized.

When planning stage business, the director must be sure that all gestures and movements are meaningful. In order to avoid later delay, the director should try to eliminate tendencies of the actors to fidget, shift weight, and gesture ineffectively. If the actors have studied dramatics, they should understand that every gesture and cross must be motivated and definite and that the center of interest should be accentuated at all times. The director must adhere to fundamental directions when dealing with inexperienced people to avoid confusing them with too much detail.

If blocking rehearsals cannot be held in the auditorium, the assistant director should arrange a rehearsal area that has exactly the same dimensions as the stage. The assistant director should then indicate the entrances and exits with chalk or tape and obtain furniture that resembles the pieces that will eventually be used. If rehearsal furniture cannot be obtained, or is not of the same size or shape, the floor should be marked to the correct dimensions to facilitate proper blocking.

During this period, a feeling of comradeship should develop. Both the actors and crew members should feel free to approach the director with their problems and suggestions and receive considerate attention and advice. If the director remains poised and pleasant, many of the complications that attend school dramatics may be avoided. The director is largely responsible for establishing morale, because his or her methods will be copied unconsciously by the cast and the crew.

The artistic principles prompting the director's planning for unity, proportion, and balance in the grouping of characters and furniture against the intended setting should be made clear to the actors at this time. It is often difficult to have them make the necessary movements an intrinsic part of the dialogue. Many directors then "give the actors the stage" and let them read their lines and move about as they please, and frequently their instinctive reactions are the right ones. Other directors have the actors improvise the scene without the script in their hands, and their natural reactions are often both pleasing and effective and can be incorporated into the planning. Such methods avoid the puppetlike following of directions, not felt necessary by actors, which ruins the immediacy of a scene.

Working Rehearsals

After all the action has been blocked out, the most creative part of rehearsing begins. At the **working rehearsal,** interpretation is developed, and words and action are put together. All the acting techniques previously discussed are brought into play and are coordinated with the director's carefully thought-out plans. Some directors use the terms *essential* and *accessory* to describe action. The former is set by the director; the latter is worked out as a means of character delineation by the actor.

The interpretations of the roles are set during the working rehearsals. The influence of the Stanislavski Method has complicated this phase of early rehearsals, for some Method actors get too deeply involved in their own inner reactions. Always keep in mind that the director is in absolute control of the production, for the director alone has planned the stage settings, action, tempo, and rhythm to create an artistic whole of which the actors are only one part. The director is also privileged to change his or her mind without question. However, individual and group discussions should be arranged, or encouraged informally offstage, where ideas can be exchanged and questions

As early in the schedule as possible, it is important to have platform levels for rehearsals that will be part of the final set design.

answered. Actors might find that writing character sketches of their roles before such discussions helps clarify their thinking.

After the stage business has been blocked for the whole play, memorization should be nearly completed. Usually a date is set after which no scripts can appear onstage. Only then can real characterization begin. At this point, actors should be left relatively free to move and speak, for spontaneous physical and vocal responses frequently improve a scene. In fact, actors should be left as free as possible in their interpretation of lines, but they must not be permitted to fix a false inflection or swallow important words and phrases. Having the actor rewrite a passage often will help that actor appreciate the exact meaning of the lines. It is sometimes helpful if the director stops the actor suddenly and says, "Wait a minute. Where are you going after this scene? What were you doing just before this entrance? What are you saying? What is happening to your character in this scene?" Only as a last resort should the director read the lines.

Speeding up or slowing down words and action to attain a certain mood or meaning is often difficult for amateurs. It is during the working rehearsals that the actors must develop tempo — learn to pick up cues rapidly, listen effectively, hold for a laugh or a pause, point lines, break up long speeches with action, and use appropriate body movement.

This phase of interpretation is especially critical. There is a tendency to return to first inclinations under the pressure of performance, so no false inflections or moves, especially gestures, must become set. With troublesome lines, sometimes bridging is helpful. *Bridging* is adding words before or after the difficult ones. Beginners must be helped to help each other by feeding cues properly, by listening effectively but not conspicuously, or by taking themselves out of a scene when necessary. Most amateurs have trouble giving sufficient time on pauses. Here it is frequently helpful to have them count, usually from one to three beats or even longer, for a desired effect. Restraining bodily movements in order to give a telling gesture or a glance a chance to register is very important.

The location of the director is crucial during working rehearsals. Most directors sit on the stage beside the prompter during early rehearsals and quietly interrupt to ask relevant questions and to give directions. Other directors place the prompter on one side of the stage and seat themselves about halfway back in the auditorium in order to check the entire stage area. Usually a combination of methods is preferable. When sitting too near the actors, the director does not get a good perspective of the stage pictures, the sense of unity of the action as a whole, and the clear and harmonious blending of the voices. On the other hand, if the director is near, the intimate question-and-answer procedure can be used to inspire the actor in trouble to think out a problem. A good procedure is to work intimately with a scene, bringing out details and correcting mistakes, and then retire to a distance and watch the entire action from different vantage points, while checking the clarity of key lines and words, the spacing of the actors, and the continuing effect of stage pictures. The director can then have the difficult bits of action repeated correctly until they are set.

Especially in period and stylized plays, mock costumes and props should be used as soon as possible. Usually the assistant director is responsible for obtaining long skirts, hoops, proper shoes, coats, swords, hats, cups and saucers, cigarette cases — whatever the play requires — and for storing them after rehearsals.

In addition to the general rehearsal schedule, a second, specialized schedule should be worked out for actors who are together in a number of scenes. These scenes or fragments of scenes can be rehearsed separately by the assistant director. This schedule of simultaneous rehearsals avoids long waits and the resulting boredom and restlessness. Important roles can often be rehearsed separately. Love scenes and other intensely emotional scenes should always be directed privately until the action is crystallized and the responses are natural and convincing.

Projection of lines is the means by which the play is heard and understood and is an absolute necessity, frequently disregarded by actors today. If you have taken seriously the exercises found in the chapter on voice and diction and have been practicing regularly, you should understand the fundamental

Each element of a richly stylized scene should be worked into the performance before the final rehearsals. The longer the actors have to work with period costumes, props, and specific furniture, the better.

principles. Your work now is to correlate the physical processes of correct breathing and articulation with the psychological consciousness of speaking to everyone in the audience. Remembering the last person at the farthest point in the auditorium, and at the same time considering everyone else as well, will enable you to project key words and sentences clearly. You should by this time be breathing correctly and relaxing your inner throat muscles from force of habit, while at the same time you are clarifying the important words with flexible lips and tongue.

Speaking intelligibly, not necessarily loudly, depends, of course, upon the exact meaning of what you are saying. From the first rehearsal, you should have begun marking the words and phrases that must be stressed and taking your breath in pauses to emphasize meanings. These pauses should also be marked while you are working out your characterization. The most common fault of amateurs is to drop the last words of every sentence instead of breathing between thought groups, for often the most vital words are at the end and must be heard.

Unless you are specifically told by the director to speak upstage, it is wise to speak front or diagonally front (three-quarter front), turning your head toward the person you are addressing on sentences of little consequence. Remember also that many small words, such as articles, prepositions, *be* verbs, and minor adjectives and adverbs, can be "thrown away," just as are the unaccented vowel sounds in many words. Too precise pronunciation of all words is a fatal mistake and should be used only in caricature for a definite effect.

Polishing Rehearsals

The real joys of directing and acting are experienced in the **polishing rehearsals.** These rehearsals must be characterized by complete concentration, sustained discipline, and joyous participation on the part of all persons concerned. With lines memorized and action set, all phases of the production can be brought together in an artistic whole.

From the standpoint of the actor, these rehearsals should bring the creative satisfaction of developing the subtle shades of vocal inflection and pantomime that make the character live for both the actor and the audience. Mannerisms of movement, distinctive physical attitudes, and subtle coloring of lines can develop through identification with the role only when the actor feels perfectly at ease in the environment of the setting.

Approximate costumes and accessories, such as wigs and body padding, should be worn at polishing rehearsals. The essential elements of the production should be in place. Exits and entrances, windows, staircases, fireplaces, and basic furniture should be onstage. Telephones and lamps should be in position, and sound effects necessary for cues should be set. Only then can the actors find themselves in the environment of the play and become a part of it. Once the mechanics of fitting themselves into the sets have been mastered, the actors can complete their search for identity with their roles in relation to the play as a whole.

It is in these final rehearsals that subtle touches of improvisation perfectly in accord with the entire production creep into both acting and directing to enhance its appeal. These must be absorbed and not lost by overrehearsing. Overrehearsing occasionally results in a whole company's going stale. The director must establish the tempo of the production as a whole, speeding up cues, eliminating irrelevant action, clarifying speech while assisting the cast to point their lines and hold their pauses. Voices, color, and lights must be blended harmoniously. Even the music between acts, if there is any, should be in accord with the type, mood, and period of the play.

If the play is dragging because of pauses between sentences, it is helpful to have a rapid-fire line rehearsal, with the actors conversationally running through the play without any action or dramatic effects. To pace the timing and to make sure of clarity, some directors listen to difficult scenes without watching them.

To a director, the most important element in play production is **rhythm.** The rhythm of a play is the overall blending of tempo, action, and dialogue. It is during the polishing rehearsals that the rhythm of the play is set and maintained. Sound and light cues must be carefully timed. Telephones, lamps, fireplaces, and sound effects should function smoothly. A single

Pirandellos's play, Tonight We Improvise, *involved sophisticated equipment that necessitated rehearsals that emphasized precision. (*Tonight We Improvise *was directed by Robert Brustein, left, with video sequences by Frederick Wiseman, right.)*
● ● ● ● ● ● ● ● ● ● ● ●

extraneous sound, a slight motion, an unmotivated gesture, or a poorly timed sound cue can destroy the effect of a scene. The director must scrutinize every stage picture from all parts of the auditorium.

About ten days before the first performance, the complete play must be put together in rehearsal. When the actors make their proper entrances and exits, wear costumes, and use props, the director can see exactly what is still needed to make the play a success. From this time on, the rehearsals should be by acts, played through without interruption as much as possible. Separate rehearsals for difficult scenes can be held as needed, however.

In the polishing process, some scenes are built up by having the lines top preceding ones, some are speeded up by rapid picking up of cues, and some are slowed down by effective pauses. It is possible to err in any of these directions. Members of the prop committee should have all props ready, and the wardrobe committee should have all costumes and accessories finished and on hand during polishing rehearsals. Curtain calls must be rehearsed, intermission time checked, and time allowances made for costume changes.

Technical Rehearsals

During the weeks of rehearsal, the scenic artist and stage manager have designed and constructed the sets and planned the lighting. Fundamental scenic units should be onstage as soon as possible in order for necessary adjustments to be made. Ideally the stage should be available for the 3 weeks before the performance, with entrances, exits, stairways, functional windows, doorways, doorbells, and practical sources of light all ready for use. As soon as possible, the cast and backstage crews should be working together so that costumes, makeup, scenery, properties, and furniture can be considered simultaneously from the standpoint of color, light, and form.

Stage plots must be made by the stage manager for each scene, showing exact positions and angles of flats and furniture. Each piece should be numbered and stagehands appointed to place and remove it and store it backstage properly.

Crew rehearsals must establish a sequence of action that must be carefully rehearsed so that changes can be made in seconds rather than minutes. The same members of the crew should always handle the curtain, lights, and props, because exact timing must be established for every scene. Mistakes are disastrous and can ruin a whole performance.

Special lighting rehearsals are imperative, for only experimentation can assure the most effective results. Stage lighting today is an art in itself. Light often replaces paint for rapidly changing effects. It takes hours of adjustment before shadows are removed, special areas are highlighted, artificial sources

Technical rehearsals are crucial to the success of any production, especially one in which special effects are important. In this opening scene from Peter Pan *by J.M. Barrie, the actors must learn to feel comfortable as they are whisked about the stage on overhead wires.*

of lighting are made to appear natural, and exact moods are established. Light must not be allowed to leak through flats, reflect from mirrors onstage, or splash on the proscenium, apron, or orchestra pit.

Only a standby cast need be called to help in the experimentation. Usually the crew can act as stand-ins for lighting placement and adjustment. School lighting equipment is often inflexible, and the regulations concerning its use are quite stringent. If there is any question of overloading the circuits, it should be settled before a lighting rehearsal begins.

Dressing the stage is too often neglected in the later rehearsals when it should be done. It is often difficult to obtain the correct pictures, hangings, props, and household effects and to arrange them so that the stage looks "lived in" but not cluttered. It may take a week or more to locate just one article.

Securing curtains of the right color and texture is always a problem, but a good stage design demands that they be well chosen and properly draped. Backing for windows and doorways must be carefully planned. Often shrubbery, garden walls, and skylines seen through the stage windows must be properly lighted to show the time of day and to create the mood. It also may be necessary to have backstage floodlights to kill any shadows that might precede the actors onstage. Ample space must be allowed for the cast to get on and off the stage in character. The cast must learn a safe means of using any stage stairways and balconies, even in the dark.

Evita, the award-winning rock opera, relies a great deal on special effects and dramatic lighting. Whenever screens and film clips are part of a live theater production, timing is essential. The screen must lower, and the film must appear at precisely the right moment. It takes many hours of technical rehearsals to perfect the timing.

• • • • • • • • • • • •

These matters must be settled before the dress rehearsals. However, the planning is worth the effort if it avoids hectic dress rehearsals and a slipshod performance. "Eventually, why not now?" is an excellent motto for everyone connected with a play to keep in mind, for it is easier to attend to the inevitable details beforehand than on the day of performance.

Technical rehearsals are the first rehearsals on the stage with complete stage equipment. They are not always possible to arrange, and the group sometimes has to go directly from the polishing to the dress rehearsals. Far too often the auditorium is not available until the final week before the first performance.

The first time the cast and technical crew work together with the set there is likely to be chaos. There will probably be confusion and delays in getting lamps to work, doors to open, curtains to come down exactly on time, and props to be in the right place at the right time. During these technical rehearsals, the grips, fly operators, wardrobe people, and property crew must get their performance duties clearly in mind and their materials organized. Actors should be trained to return props to the appointed tables backstage.

A long technical rehearsal on Saturday of the week before the performance is invaluable. All details of setting, costume, and makeup will not be ready, but the essentials should be. A run-through of the whole play with changing of costumes, coordination of all effects, and curtain calls should begin fairly early in the morning. The assistant director, stage manager, and prompter work together to keep things going smoothly onstage. The director should move through the auditorium checking sight lines, acoustics, and total effects and taking notes to share with the cast after the final curtain. Every person involved will write down the director's suggestions.

In the afternoon, weak scenes can be redone, important scenes restaged, and all loose ends and details settled. If possible, photographs should be taken for the press at this time, with the leads in costume and makeup.

Dress Rehearsals

If possible, three dress rehearsals should be held, the last with an invited audience so that the cast can learn to point lines and hold the action for laughter and applause. An audience at the last dress rehearsal provides an occasion, too, for the house manager and ushers to learn their duties and familiarize themselves with the seating arrangement.

Usually photographs of the cast in various scenes are taken at a dress rehearsal. The picture-taking should be done either before or after the rehearsal so that the timing of the production and the establishment of moods are not interrupted. Every person involved in the dress rehearsals should have an instruction sheet listing the time actors are due for makeup; responsibilities for props, costumes, and stage equipment; and backstage regulations about outsiders who may wish to call or deliver flowers.

The final dress rehearsal should begin on time and go straight to the end without interruption. The cast and crew should be instructed not to correct mistakes obviously, but to go right along adjusting whatever is seriously wrong as best they can while the action continues. The main consideration is to avoid awkward pauses and the repetition of lines or action.

Backstage organization must be efficient. There must be a chain of command from the director down so that everyone has specific responsibilities. The director is the final authority, checking the makeup, costumes, props, lights, and stage before going out front. Then the assistant director takes over backstage, receiving suggestions from, or sending questions to, the director concerning the lights, furniture, and other matters. Next in command is the stage manager (SM), who has full responsibility for the backstage area. The SM checks the lights and stage before the curtain goes up, sees that the cast is ready, gets the crew members in their places, and gives the signals for lights, curtain, and sound effects. Once the show opens, the stage manager is the only backstage authority.

The prompter should not be interrupted once the curtain is up because he or she must remain alert every instant that the play is in progress. Prompting should be for the actors, not for the audience. The prompter should be not only inaudible but also invisible to the spectators.

When the final dress rehearsal is finished, the actors should leave the dressing rooms in perfect order, put away their makeup, and hang their costumes neatly. The wardrobe crew can then check to see if any pressing or mending is needed.

During final rehearsals, some directors sit at the back of the house and dictate notes, which are written on separate sheets of paper for each performer. As these are given out, the director explains the correction and may ask the actor to run through the line or business. Other directors prefer that the cast write down the comments and remember them. Both cast and crew

Galileo by Bertolt Brecht presented by Catholic University. Dress rehearsals are real performances. The actors may or may not present their dress rehearsals before an audience.

should feel encouraged and confident after a dress rehearsal. If there is continued cooperation, a good dress rehearsal should ensure a satisfactory performance.

Curtain Calls

As part of the production, **curtain calls** should be rehearsed and should never be considered as an add-on. The last impression that an audience has of a play is of its curtain call. It is really the final scene of the performance. Therefore, the finishing touch of a good production is a polished curtain call.

The form of a curtain call is determined by the director and by the style of the show. It is important to keep in mind that curtain calls are largely a matter of time. An audience will clap a certain length of time, depending on the quality of the production and the number of characters. A curtain call should be executed quickly and efficiently. Do not expect or desire standing ovations. The "everybody on their feet" attitude seen in so many high schools has robbed many students of the rare thrill of a true standing ovation.

The Performance

On the night of the performance, the actors, crew, and ushers need to arrive promptly. The actors should be in costume and makeup at least 15 minutes before curtain, even earlier if relaxation exercises and vocal warm-ups are scheduled after makeup. Most directors, especially on opening night, want to meet with the cast five minutes before curtain. Once the stage manager calls "Places!" the only cast members allowed in the wings should be those awaiting entrances or helping with scene shifts.

When each performance is over, actors should return all personal props to the prop chief and remove all costumes and makeup. The crews should check the scenery and lighting fixtures for any reparable damage, touching up, burnt out lamps, faded gel, and so on.

After the final performance, all props should be returned to their owners or to the prop room. Costumes should be returned to the rental firm or sent out to be cleaned, repaired, catalogued, and stored for future use. The set must be carefully struck and stored.

Remember: A production is never over until every bill is paid and every prop, costume, and scenic piece is stored in its proper place.

Recalling Ideas

1. What determines the number of people on a production staff?

2. Explain what *critiques* are and what the director does with them.

3. What production job should you aspire to if you are interested in all aspects of theater? Why?

4. Briefly explain the responsibilities of the following: prompter, technical director, stage manager, property chief, business manager, publicity manager, house manager.

5. When should a production budget be prepared? Why?

6. Why is the promptbook "the backbone of a production"?

7. Define the following terms: open audition, closed audition, prepared audition, cold reading, improvisational audition, and textual tryout.

8. What is the difference between practice and rehearsal?

9. Explain the differences between a blocking rehearsal, a working rehearsal, a polishing rehearsal, a technical rehearsal, and a dress rehearsal.

Discussing Ideas

1. Considering the production facilities available at your school, discuss the kinds of productions that would probably be most successful for you.

2. Discuss the effect that limited facilities might have on a production. How can such limitations actually lead to more successful play productions?

3. Discuss the role of the director in casting. Why is the director's ability to look ahead of crucial importance?

Careers

Sound designers analyze a play to determine the need for sound. Sound includes music, noises of no recognizable origin, and realistic effects such as thunder. Sound sets the mood and style and helps tell the story. Such sounds as rain and the lonely wailing of a foghorn create atmosphere for a scene. Offstage gunshots, the clopping of horses' hooves, the rumble of traffic, and the ringing of doorbells tell the audience what is happening.

Sound designers work with the **technical director** and the **director** to determine the effects and placement of sounds. Sound is live, created fresh for each performance, or recorded. The sounds of planes, traffic, and crowds may be recordings.

Sound designers are responsible for both sound effects and amplification. Most small and noncommercial theaters use only sound effects, but commercial theaters often equip actors with portable microphones so their lines may be clearly heard.

Amplification is needed because some actors, used to television and movie studios where their voices are caught by nearby microphones, cannot project their voices well. Also, with today's louder, rock-inspired music, actors' lines often cannot be heard well above the amplified instruments.

The **sound crew,** who reports to the sound designer, maintains and operates all sound equipment. Because that equipment is expensive, they must be careful of its security.

Sound designers need some theater arts background, plus technical knowledge that can be acquired through professional or technical schools. Experience on a sound crew is helpful.

Chapter 11

Producing the Musical Play

You Will Learn

About different forms of musical theater.

About the challenges of planning a musical play.

About the special concerns of the director of a musical play.

Six techniques that the cast of a musical should know.

About the staging needs of a musical play.

Vocabulary

opera	crossovers	hanging
operetta	spoofs	plot
comic opera	satires	backlighting
musical comedy	concept	reversibles
musical play	musicals	coordinates

*M*usical theater includes several forms. The oldest form is the **opera.** Since the voice and the orchestra are the only media of performance, opera is "total music." Even conversations are sung, not spoken as in other forms of musical theater. The **operetta** is another type of musical. Operetta music is lighter than operatic music, and the singer/actor speaks lines rather

Ain't Misbehavin'
is essentially a
musical revue. It
is a collection of
Fats Waller songs,
performed by a
cast of five. The
production
contains very little
dialogue.

than sings them. Operettas are usually built on flimsy plots that serve only to connect one song with another. Plot, character, and acting are incidental to the music. The music must be well written, and the performers must be accomplished singers. Some popular operettas are *The Student Prince, Babes in Toyland,* and *The Merry Widow.* An off-shoot of the straight operetta is **comic opera,** humorous or satirical operettas. For many years, the comic operas of Gilbert and Sullivan have been very popular as high school shows. Among the favorites are *The Mikado, H. M. S. Pinafore,* and *The Pirates of Penzance.* Another form of musical theater is the *musical revue,* a loosely connected series of production numbers. The Ziegfield Follies was the most famous of these lavish extravaganzas. *Ain't Misbehavin* is a recent example.

A **musical comedy** combines some elements from the musical revue and the operetta. Music remains the most important element, and the plot still tends to be weak. However, the characters are more believable, and the dialogue is clever. Some of the musical comedies presented by high schools are *Anything Goes; No, No, Nanette; Annie Get Your Gun; Guys and Dolls;* and *The Pajama Game.*

The Musical Play

Show Boat is the musical that bridged the gap between the operetta, musical comedy, and today's musical play. The score of *Show Boat* is much like that of an operetta and the staging is like that of a musical comedy, but the story line and character development are very like that of the musical play.

Oklahoma! created the **musical play,** a form of musical theater character- ized by an increased emphasis on real people in real situations. In the musical play, acting and choreography are an integral part of the production. Because a well-written musical play contains a good story, clever dialogue, interesting characters, well-designed choreography, bouncy tunes, and meaningful bal- lads woven into a sparkling package of color and spectacle that provides excellent opportunities for showmanship and talent, it has replaced many operettas and variety shows in the high school theater repertoire.

The musical play has become a major part of high school theater for other reasons. The sophistication of contemporary audiences demands more than a stage full of people in a simple review of pretty songs loosely tied together. In addition to greater audience appeal, a musical play involves many students on the stage, in the orchestra pit, and behind the scenes. It is a form of live theater that can pull people away from their television sets. Because the mu- sical play is a total theater experience involving young people in all the facets of play production — singing, dancing, acting, stagecraft, and costuming — students are highly motivated to participate in such a play.

Musical Play Terminology

book: The script of a musical.
choreographer: A person who designs dance for the stage.
choreography: The dances designed for a production.
chorus: The singers other than the principals.
composer: A person who writes music.
conductor: A person who directs the orchestra.
entr'acte: Music that precedes the second act curtain.
librettist: A person who writes the book (script).
libretto: The book, including lines and lyrics.
lyricist: A person who writes words to music.
lyrics: The words to a song.
overture: The music, usually a medley of the show's songs, played at the beginning of the show.

principals: The named characters in a musical play.

production number: A large-scale musical number involving many performers in lavish costumes. Frequently a production number is a dance number.

recitative: Singing style that is closer to speaking than singing.

score: The music of a show as composed.

segue: A music term which means the music continues on to the next number without stopping.

sides: Booklets containing half sheets of paper on which are written the cues and lines for one character.

soubrette: A secondary female lead, usually a comic role.

underscore: Music played to accompany dialogue.

vamp: To repeat measures of music until a singer or scene is ready to begin.

Producing the Musical Play

Staffing a musical play is considerably more difficult than staffing a straight play. A musical play usually calls for a play director, a vocal director, an instrumental director, a technical director, and a choreographer. In addition, there is a need for a costumer, a business manager, and a publicity director. However, only one person must be the director, and all the participants must recognize the director as being in charge of the entire production.

To direct a musical play, an individual must know all aspects of musical theater: acting, singing, dancing, orchestrating, and set designing. This does not mean that the director needs to be an expert in all these areas. However, she or he must be aware of all the components of the musical play.

Choreography has become such an essential part of the modern musical play that some of the most successful directors on Broadway started out as choreographers — Jerome Robbins, Gower Champion, and Bob Fosse, for example. With the emergence of such directors, musical plays have been created around dance and choreographic movement. *West Side Story* is an outstanding example. However, the choreography for a Broadway musical is designed for experienced professionals, not for high school performers with limited dance skills. Nevertheless, excellent and exciting dance numbers can be presented if the dances are suited to the abilities of the performers.

After the staff has been chosen, a budget must be prepared. The total expenses are considerably more for a musical than for a straight play (two to ten times as much). These expenses include costs not associated with the production elements of the play. For instance, royalty and script costs are significantly more complicated. Before producing a musical play, the publisher of the work must be contacted to grant permission to hold public performances of that play. Every publisher has a different formula for calculating royalty costs, which may include or exclude certain rehearsal material in the fee quoted.

A royalty fee is normally based on the number of seats sold and the ticket prices charged. The number of seats reported should represent what you determine your "house" to be. Otherwise, you will be charged for all your empty seats. For example, if you have an auditorium seating 1,500 but you plan to use only the front section seating 500, report your capacity as 500. Have tickets printed for 500 seats only. Do not sell more than those 500 seats unless you contact the publisher of the play and make the necessary royalty adjustments for the additional seats you intend to sell. Some royalty fees include music rental for one month; some charge music rental separately. An additional fee is charged for a longer rehearsal time. Most schools need the music

Choreography has become an important part of the modern musical. In the musical Pippin *(Ben Vereen center), the dance ensemble is the chorus as well.*
• • • • • • • • • • • •

When Chorus Line *broke the longevity record for most continuous performances of a Broadway play, a spectacular extravaganza was staged to commemorate the occasion. Touring companies from all over the United States were brought together for a production that was a feat of directorial organization.*
· · · · · · · · · · · ·

for at least two months. Be sure you understand the script policies of each firm. Does the fee include vocal scores, librettos, two piano scores?

Once the show has been selected and the rights to produce it obtained, the play must be cast. Under the best of circumstances, a musical play is much more difficult to cast than a straight play. Not only must acting ability be judged, but singing and dancing abilities must also be considered. Some shows require that the leads be skilled in all three of these areas; other shows require skills in only one or two of these areas. Too often a musical play is chosen that is too complex for a particular school to do well. It may require more strong characters than can be cast. The vocal requirements may be too demanding for high school voices. There may not be sufficient time to train students in the special skills the show requires, such as tap dancing. All too often and too late it is discovered that the best actor has "two left feet" or the individual with the finest voice cannot act. Another often-forgotten factor in putting on a musical is the effect interpersonal relationships can have on a production. Since there are usually more cast members in a musical than in a straight play, there are more interpersonal relationships to consider when casting. Be aware of the personality mixture. Many potentially fine shows have been marred by squabbling among temperamental cast members.

In summary, when selecting a musical play for production, consider these questions:

Are the production costs within our budget limits?

Do we have the staff to direct this show?

Do we have the acting, musical, and technical abilities this show requires?

Do we have the time required to prepare this show?

Is this a musical play that will please both performers and audience?

Is the musical play suitable for high school production?

Once the casting is completed, a rehearsal schedule must be planned. Obviously the size and scope of a musical play is greater than that of a straight play. Therefore, more rehearsal time will be needed. Most directors want a minimum of 8 weeks of rehearsal. For the first few weeks, it is more efficient to rehearse several groups simultaneously. The orchestra can rehearse by itself. The dancers can rehearse with the choreographer to piano accompaniment or a rehearsal tape of the orchestra. The chorus can rehearse with the vocal director. If possible, it is best to stagger rehearsal schedules so that the chorus members do not have to sit through an entire rehearsal just to sing one or two songs. The principals can rehearse with the play's director. Step by step, the separate elements are combined. Rehearsals of the vocal and dance numbers begin with the orchestra, the vocal numbers are rehearsed in the context of entire scenes, and finally, all the groups join to rehearse the entire show.

Plan for at least 2 weeks of rehearsal with the entire cast. Schedule a minimum of 4 days of dress rehearsal: 1 day for each of the two acts and two complete dress rehearsals. This may seem like too many dress rehearsals, but a musical play has so many elements to coordinate that anything short of three times through in costume with complete technical support will probably result in the opening night being the final dress rehearsal.

Directing a Musical Play

Directing a musical play is a very complex task. First, the director must consider the construction of this type of play. Most have two acts. A few shorter shows are written as one act. In musical plays and some musical comedies the song lyrics are important in developing action, theme, and character.

The songs in operettas, on the other hand, are entities in themselves. The plot, such as it is, continues "around" the song. Not so in musical plays. If members of the audience miss some of the lyrics, there will be gaps in their understanding and appreciation of the entire show. Rodgers and Hammerstein often used a song to state the theme of a show: "Climb Every Mountain," "You'll Never Walk Alone," and "Something Wonderful."

Musical plays usually have many scenes (ten to thirty or more). This means that some scenes must be played in front of a curtain or a drop on a shallow segment of the stage while scenery is being changed behind the curtain. This is called playing a scene "in one." A scene played "in one" takes place on that portion of the stage which is 8 to 10 feet deep and upstage of the curtain line or on the apron of the stage. Musical theater stages are usually divided into three depths, each 8 to 10 feet deep. Performers may enter *one, two,* or *three* right or left. The terms go back to the days of the wing stage, when the wing spaces were called first, second, and third wings. Some "in one" scenes consist of characters walking across the stage together or entering from opposite

The staging of Alan Jay Lerner and Frederick Loewe's Brigadoon *involved gracefully choreographing the placement of townspeople in a mystical village.*

The choreography/ direction of the skaters in **Starlight Express** *was complex due to the ramps and runways built around the audience and the balcony.*
• • • • • • • • • • • •

sides and meeting on stage. Such scenes are called **crossovers.** Crossovers may also be played on the apron of the stage in front of the act curtain. Some librettists consider the length of scenery changes and write crossover scenes. Others make no allowances for scenery changes, assuming that a scene can be changed within the 7 seconds that is the usual time limit for professional scene shifts. Since few high school stages are equipped like those on Broadway, scenery changes often take longer. A director must work with the technical director to determine the exact scenery shift time so that the smoothness and rhythm of the production is not lost. The conductor may vamp the change music (the music played to cover the sound of scenery changes) if it becomes apparent that a shift cannot be completed quickly.

Stage positions are extremely important in directing a musical play. Center, down center, and down right are the locations for most solos. Down right is a very strong solo position. Since we are a left-to-right-oriented society, an audience always turns back to its left when there is a large open stage, as there usually is in musical plays. The chorus must be blocked in groups to avoid solid lines that look like a school chorus on stage. Groups should consist of one, two, three, four, five, or seven people. However, odd-number groupings are preferable. The asymmetrical look of odd-number groups provides a dynamic sight line, while the symmetrical look of even-number groups provides a static sight line. Getting these groups of chorus members on and off the stage presents a real traffic problem for the director. She or he must rehearse extensively on chorus entrances and exits so that these comings and goings are smooth and inconspicuous.

The chorus must learn to "turn scenes in" to or direct the audience's attention to the soloists. The chorus accomplishes this in various ways: by turning the shoulder closest to the soloist upstage, by dropping the downstage shoulder slightly, by getting into a bent-knee or semi-crouch position, by kneeling on the downstage knee, and even by reclining on the floor with the head toward the soloist. There is a tendency for the downstage end of a large chorus to "creep" too far downstage, shutting off the audience's view of the soloist. Choruses must guard against this and maintain their groupings and positions. Otherwise, they will drift together into one large mass.

Another difficulty in directing a musical play is teaching the performers to project over the underscore. Actors sometimes feel shut off by the orchestra. If the actors cannot project over the orchestra pit, the director may have to ask the orchestra to play more softly. Often the best solution is to delete the underscore entirely.

A director may choose to have a performer recite lyrics rather than sing them for a couple of reasons. Sometimes reciting lyrics is more effective than singing them. Other times a performer may have difficulty reaching high notes, so reciting the lyrics is easier. This style is called recitative. Recitatives can bring interest and variety to musical numbers.

The cast should know which musical numbers are *melodic* and which are *rhythmic.* Melodic songs are those with pleasing sound combinations combined with moving lyrics, such as ballads and "theme" songs. "The Impossible Dream," "Tomorrow," and "Some Enchanted Evening" are melodic. Rhythmic numbers focus on tempo, musical style, beat, and orchestration, such as "Easy Street," "Trouble," and "Belly up to the Bar, Boys."

Techniques for the Musical Play

There are six simple techniques that the director should point out over and over to the cast of a musical play: (1) attack the first beat of each measure; (2) sing "through the eyes"; (3) play out to the audience; (4) be "alive in character"; (5) play in a "state of action"; (6) look as if you are enjoying yourself.

One of the secrets of putting life into a musical play is placing a strong vocal attack on the first beat of each measure. Most show tunes are lively, bouncy, driving numbers, and the stress words come on the first beat. When there is a rest on the first beat, the mood of the song is usually gentle, unsure, questioning.

Singers, especially those with trained voices, tend to swell and hold vowel sounds. For crispness, singers should attack the initial consonant instead of sliding into the vowel. Also, singers must learn not to hold a note too long when the number is light, bright, or upbeat.

A second technique that adds sparkle to a musical number is to sing "through the eyes" or through the "mask of the face." A well-trained singer strives to focus the voice properly so that it projects clearly and forcefully, but without straining, over the orchestra pit.

A third technique for all members of the cast to remember is to play out to the audience. This is especially true when performing in a musical play where more theatrical conventions are common. The sense of intimacy of the straight play is not so much a part of a musical play, since most songs and dances are staged to be played directly to the audience rather than to other members of the cast.

42nd Street was director-choreographer Gower Champion's last show. Here you can see a well-disciplined chorus "alive in character," playing out to the audience.
● ● ● ● ● ● ● ● ● ● ● ●

A fourth technique directors try to instill in cast members is to be "alive in character." This is especially difficult for chorus members, who often do not realize their importance to the total production. They may take an "I'm just a member of the chorus" attitude, which can kill a show. The director must stress the need for each chorus member to develop a well-defined character. "Just a chorus member" must become "Sam Tilsbury, owner of the corner drugstore in River City, whose wife, Martha Mae, just bought their son, Freddie, a double-belled euphonium from that fast talking two-bit swindler, Harold Hill." When there are twenty to sixty people onstage, it is easy for a few individuals to lose their concentration. The chorus must remember that an audience sweeps its eyes over the entire cast looking for someone really "alive" or really "dead." Alive is better. One dead chorus member can spoil an entire scene.

A fifth technique is that characters — principals and chorus — should play most of the time in a "state of action." Standing erect and motionless may be appropriate for a choir or some opera choruses, but it is usually boring in a musical. Singing while moving or doing something is always stronger. Principals can learn to deliver their lines in an even more active state than they would in a straight play. They "set" their actions by momentarily freezing a gesture, pose, or movement before continuing on the line or business. This is particularly effective when the "lead-in" line is delivered just before the song is to be sung. Chorus members rarely stand straight and tall: they lean, crouch, bend their knees, gesture, move, and dance.

The final technique that the director should teach to the cast is to enjoy, enjoy, enjoy. Excitement, pleasure, and energy are contagious. An audience is eager to be drawn into the spirit of a play. When a cast appears to have fun, the audience, too, shares the enthusiasm.

Directing Different Types of Musicals

Some types of musical plays are particularly difficult to direct. A spoof is such a play. **Spoofs** are farcical and poke fun at certain subjects or time eras. For example, *Little Mary Sunshine* pokes fun at a style of musical film; *Once Upon a Mattress* laughs at fairy tales; *The Boy Friend* ridicules the 1920s practices of love and romance. If spoofs are overacted, they are absurd. If they are played straight, they are tediously outdated. **Satires** are also difficult. To direct a satire effectively, the director must make sure that the audience clearly understands what aspects of human behavior or human society are being held up to criticism. The director must pace a musical satire expertly so that the comic moments and the serious moments stand out at the appropriate times.

Cab Calloway and Pearl Bailey in Hello, Dolly!*, the long-running musical hit.*

How to Succeed in Business Without Really Trying satirizes the shenanigans of getting ahead in the business world.

Concept musicals are built around a single theatrical idea. Plot, if any, is secondary to situation. The production is usually a series of independent scenes loosely tied together. The director's main concern is how the show is handled, not what it has to say. It is sometimes difficult to break away from the traditions of the musical play to make the "concept" of a production the focus. *A Chorus Line, Cats,* and *Starlight Express* are concept musicals.

Some musical plays are controversial, and unless the director interprets such a work carefully, the audience may not be prepared for some of the disturbing elements portrayed through character, plot, song, and dance. *Cabaret* is such a play. Because it is rather moralistic for a musical, there is a temptation to stress the surface aspects of the play depicted quite vividly in the cabaret scenes. By emphasizing the frivolous, titillating, and bawdy side of *Cabaret*, the director will turn the audience away from the play's serious commentary on the destruction of human lives and values during that time just prior to the rise of Nazi Germany. Some musicals are "pace" shows, requiring a brisk tempo. *George M* is a pace musical. Other musicals, such as *Man of La Mancha* are "heart" shows. They require special sensitivity without sentimentality. *Hello, Dolly!* is an example of a "splash" musical, one calling for large production numbers. Few directors can handle each of these kinds of musicals with equal skill. Therefore, choose carefully.

Staging a Musical Play

There are many staging decisions associated with musical plays. The director's first decision will be to determine the number of *sets* needed for the production. Few high schools can build as many sets as the script calls for, and it may be necessary to combine, eliminate, or reuse some scenery. Often the only choice is to play a scene in front of a traveler or the act curtain. After determining the number of scenes and set changes required, the director must decide which scenes will use drops, which scenes will use wagons, which scenes will use set pieces, and which scenes will be played in front of a curtain. (See Chapter 12 for a full discussion of stage sets.)

Professional theaters often have sixty or more counterweight lines on which to hang scenery. Few high schools have more than one third that number, and many schools have no fly system at all for hanging drops. Of those schools that have some kind of system for hanging drops, some do not have counterweighted or electric winch systems and the only way to raise and lower scenery is manually.

Broadway shows often use a combination of portals and backdrops. Portals are drops looking much like tunnel portals with a teaserlike piece of cloth across the top and leglike extensions that come to the floor at each end. The portals solve the need to mask the wings, always a problem in musicals, by making a solid set that can be changed in seconds.

Another way to handle scenery is by using revolving and jackknife wagon stages. These stages are especially effective when a scene calls for a lot of furniture or set pieces and, with scenery mounted on them, they allow for quick scene changes. Wagons can also be mounted with walls that are hinged so that the flats can be flipped over, revealing the other side. Unfortunately, wagons take up considerable wing space, and many schools have limited side stage areas.

These fly space and wing area limitations force many schools to use other means of set changing. Prism sets *(periaktoi)* are alternatives for schools with no fly space and limited wing areas. Scenery can be painted on all three sides

HANGING PLOT FOR ___WILD SONG___

LINE NO.		USE	DISTANCE FROM CURTAIN LINE
16	～	Cyc _ _ _ _ _ _ _ _ _ _ _ _ _ _ _ _ _ _ _	24'
15	—	Countryside drop _ _ _ _ _ _ _ _ _ _ _ _	26'6"
14	—	Gymnasium interior _ _ _ _ _ _ _ _ _ _ _	21'8"
13	—	Ballet drop _ _ _ _ _ _ _ _ _ _ _ _ _ _ _	20'
12	E	4ᵗʰ electric (3ʳᵈ border) _ _ _ _ _ _ _ _	18'6"
11	⤴-	Leg #2 (strike) garden drop _ _ _ _ _ _ _	17'
10	～	Teaser #3 _ _ _ _ _ _ _ _ _ _ _ _ _ _ _	16'
9	～	Scrim _ _ _ _ _ _ _ _ _ _ _ _ _ _ _ _ _	14'6"
8	～	Traveler _ _ _ _ _ _ _ _ _ _ _ _ _ _ _	13'
7	E	3ʳᵈ electric (2ⁿᵈ border) _ _ _ _ _ _ _ _	11'6"
6	～	Teaser #2 _ _ _ _ _ _ _ _ _ _ _ _ _ _	10'
5	～	Garden portal _ _ _ _ _ _ _ _ _ _ _ _ _	9'3"
4	⤴-	Leg #1 (strike) town hall exterior _ _ _ _ _	8'
3	E	2ⁿᵈ electric (1ˢᵗ border) _ _ _ _ _ _ _ _	6'
2	⤴-	Teaser #1 (strike) show curtain _ _ _ _ _	4'6"
1	E	1ˢᵗ electric — X-ray—500 watt presnels _ _ _	1'6"
0	～	Act curtain _ _ _ _ _ _ _ _ _ _ _ _ _ _	0

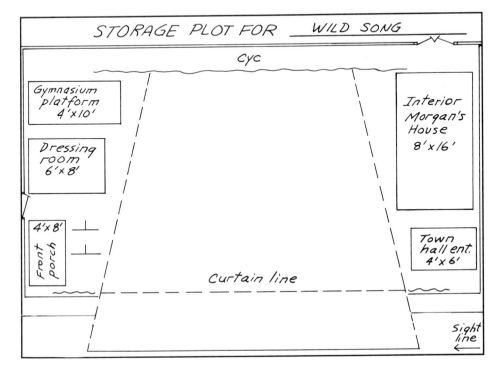

STORAGE PLOT FOR ___WILD SONG___

Cyc

Gymnasium platform 4'x10'

Dressing room 6'x8'

Interior Morgan's House 8'x16'

4'x8'

Front porch

Town hall ent. 4'x6'

Curtain line

Sight line

of the prisms and used in different combinations, as seen on page 402. Wagons with double-covered flats (flats with muslin on both sides) can be turned around to show a different scene on the reverse side. The plywood on the reverse side causes slight bulges, but they are not too noticeable, and the saving of construction and the weight of a double wall of flats is well worth the aesthetic sacrifice. Double-covering is a good way to use the muslin from old drops.

There are often special scenic demands that are difficult to handle on any stage; for example, fog or mist, flying apparatus, carousels, Wells Fargo wagons, automobiles, and surreys. Sometimes it is better to work around such problems if you cannot treat them adequately on your stage. Rather than try too many poor substitutes, it may ultimately be better to try another show.

Once all the scenery decisions are made, the technical director or the stage manager makes a hanging plot and a storage plot for the play. **A hanging plot** shows all the fly lines and what is on each. A storage plot shows the wing areas and how the scenic units are to be stored during the show. Refer to page 377 for an example of a hanging plot and a storage plot.

Lighting a musical play calls for more equipment than needed for a straight play. There is usually a greater likelihood of shadows appearing on the stage in a musical because a limited number of instruments with a limited lighting range may have to be used to cover more stage areas. If the instruments are available, backlighting soloists and one-character and two-character scenes is quite effective. **Backlighting** throws light on the performer from above and slightly upstage. This causes a glow, or halo effect, that makes the actor stand out from the background or chorus. Backlighting should be used only with actors who have a strong stage presence, because the radiant glow can easily swallow up weak performers.

A *follow spot* can create another lighting effect. High school directors often have mixed feelings about their use. These spots do make the soloists stand out. However, they are an obvious artificial light source that can do strange things to the drop behind the performer — and if the chorus is behind the soloist, the spot may cut off the heads of the chorus members. Most directors dim the stage lights during a solo if a follow spot is used, then bring them back up after the applause. The audience recognizes this dimming as an acceptable theatrical convention. Normally, white or flesh pink follow spots are preferred. Avoid ambers and primaries (red, blue, green) that will turn costumes and makeup purplish or black.

Makeup and *costumes* for musical plays should be stronger and more exaggerated than those used in straight plays, since the many lights used in a musical play can deaden an actor's appearance. Costumes are more colorful and more highly stylized. Most musicals are bright, lively productions, and costume colors that would appear gawdy and unbelievable in a straight play seem totally acceptable in a musical play. Costumes for a musical may be quite elaborate, so it might be wise to consider renting them.

Dance costumes, especially for shows with several large production numbers, should be reversibles and coordinates. **Reversibles** are such clothing as vests, scarves, belts, and skirts that are made double-faced so that by reversing one or more of these articles of clothing, the illusion of a different costume is created. **Coordinates,** which can also be reversible, are separates or interchangeables. Costume coordinates such as hats, scarves, ties, vests, jackets, blouses, shirts, skirts, gloves, belts, spats, and shoes can be used in varied combinations.

The director and costumer should select or approve all costumes. This will prevent embarrassing situations that can occur when costumes are not in balance. A chorus member in a wonderful homemade costume may outshine all the other people on stage, or a principal's costume may be too drab for the role.

One last note about costumes: do not try to costume everyone in every scene as done on Broadway. In a Broadway show, nearly every time a character comes onstage, he or she wears a new outfit. This is too costly, in time and money, for a high school production. One well-made, well-designed costume is far better than several mediocre ones.

The Orchestra

Although musical plays can be presented with piano accompaniment alone, an orchestra can greatly enhance the quality and impact of a production. Most musical plays open with an overture that features a medley of the show's total score. A similar, but briefer, orchestral piece, *the entr'acte,* precedes the second-act curtain. Unfortunately, orchestras often play too loudly, drowning out lines and lyrics, since few high school voices are strong enough to be heard over a "full pit." Good rapport must exist between the conductor and the director so that the priorities of the production can be met without creating animosity.

One of the most critical problems facing a high school musical production is the limited vocal range of young voices. Rewriting the music or transposing it is normally a last resort. There is so much involved in rewriting the music for an entire orchestra that the time taken for this task is not well spent. Also, using just a piano for a particular number rewritten in a transposed key weakens that number when the rest of the show is fully orchestrated. The best way

In Dream Girls *it was essential that the actresses performed as a well coordinated singing group both among themselves and in relationship to the orchestra.*

• • • • • • • • • • •

to handle the vocal restraints of high school singers is to choose a musical with a limited vocal range.

Acoustical problems are common to high school musical productions. Many schools do not have a recessed orchestra pit, so sound tends to attack the audience. Other schools have tile, brick, or masonry on the auditorium floor and the apron of the stage. Such hard surfaces act as reflectors, and sound cannonades into the audience with deafening loudness. It sometimes helps balance sound to put carpeting on the floor of the orchestra pit, if there is one, and to drape sheets of acoustical material or old stage curtains over the front rows of seats. Some high schools solve their sound problems by building a shell around the orchestra so that the sound is slightly contained.

Communication between the pit and the stage is important. The conductor of the show, usually the instrumental director, must give clear signals to the performers on the stage. These signals must not be confused with those meant for the orchestra. Most conductors lead the orchestra with the right hand and cue the stage with the left. Whatever cuing system the conductor wishes to use, it should be made clear to the cast in early rehearsals. Giving the pitch to the stage performers is also quite vital in pit-to-stage communication. Remember, the conductor is in charge of the pit *and* of the performers on stage once he or she raises the baton.

What Can You Do?

The experience of presenting a musical play can be very rewarding. It is unfortunate that many schools feel they are too small or cannot afford the production costs. There are several shows that have small casts, require simple scenery and costumes, and can be done with minimum accompaniment. Among these shows are *The Fantasticks* and *You're a Good Man, Charlie Brown*. There are also some musical plays with large casts that can be staged more economically than others. These include *Carnival, Once Upon a Mattress, The Pajama Game, Damn Yankees,* and *How to Succeed in Business Without Really Trying.*

One of the real problems facing all high schools today is the fact that very few shows that have come off Broadway in recent years are suitable for high school production. School administrators, boards of education, teachers, and students must look very carefully at the available musical plays and decide which shows are fitting in subject matter and community taste and values.

Musical Plays for High School Production

Annotations: A = acting demanding; B = book difficult; C = choreography needed; CH = children needed; COS = costumes complex or numerous; D = dialect; LA = limited appeal; M = music difficult; NM = predominantly male cast; PC = production costs high; S = scenery complex; SC = small cast; SM = mature subject matter; SP = spoof or satire; ST = staging complex; V = vocal demands difficult.

Annie (CH, SC)
Annie Get Your Gun (COS, D, SC)
Anything Goes (C, SC)
Barnum (COS, S, SC, V)
Big River (D, NM, SC, ST, V)

The Boy Friend (C, SP)
Brigadoon (C, D, M, ST, V)
Camelot (A, B, COS, M, PC, SC, V)
Carnival (SC, V)
The Fantasticks (NM, SC)
Fiddler on the Roof (A, D, ST)
Flower Drum Song (COS, D)
Funny Girl (A, D, SC, V)

Gilbert and Sullivan's The Mikado *is an operetta with beautiful but complex vocal demands.*

George M (C, SC)
Guys and Dolls (D, NM, SC)
Gypsy (A, SM)
Hello, Dolly! (A, C, ST, V)
How to Succeed in Business Without Really Trying (M, SP)
Joseph and the Amazing Technicolor Dreamcoat (COS, SC, SP)
The King and I (COS, D, M, PC, SC, V)
Kiss Me Kate (COS, V)
L'il Abner (D)
Little Mary Sunshine (COS, LA, SP)
Little Shop of Horrors (D, PC, SC, SP, S)
Mame (A, COS, PC, SC)
The Man of La Mancha (A, ST, V)
Me and My Gal (C, COS, D, PC)
The Music Man (A, C, SC, ST)
My Fair Lady (A, B, D, PC, SC, ST)
The Mystery of Edwin Drood (COS, SC, SP, ST, V)
No, No, Nanette (C, COS, ST)
Oklahoma! (B, V)
Oliver! (A, CH, D, SC, V)
Once upon a Mattress (COS, SP)
Paint Your Wagon (SM, ST)
The Pajama Game (B, SC, ST)
Peter Pan (CH, COS, NM, PC, ST)
Pippin (COS, SM, SP)
Pirates of Penzance (Papp version) (C, COS, D, NM, PC, S, SP, V)
The Roar of the Greasepaint, the Smell of the Crowd (LA, NM, SC)
1776 (A, COS, D, NM, V)
Something's Afoot (D, SC, SP, ST)
The Sound of Music (CH, D, SC, V)
South Pacific (CH, D, NM, V)
Stop the World, I Want to Get Off (LA, SC)
The Unsinkable Molly Brown (A, B, SC, ST)
West Side Story (C, M, ST)
The Wiz (COS, PC, ST)
You're a Good Man, Charlie Brown (SC)

Recalling Ideas

1. What are the differences between an opera and an operetta? How does a musical play differ from a musical comedy?

2. What are three considerations in casting a musical play?

3. What are two problems in grouping the chorus of a musical on stage?

4. What are the six techniques that the cast of a musical should know?

5. Describe each of the following types of musical play: spoofs, satires, concept musicals.

6. Describe each of the following types of sets: portals and drapes, wagon sets, prism sets. Which of the three types is best for a stage with no fly space and limited wing area?

7. What is backlighting? What problems can a follow spot cause?

Discussing Ideas

1. What is the ideal relationship among the following participants in a musical play: actor, conductor, choreographer, director? Discuss why the director of a musical must be tactful and good with people.

2. As you have learned, producing a musical play is very difficult. Why are musicals so popular?

3. Listen to records or tapes of several Broadway musicals. Discuss numbers where you think singers are attacking the downbeat and singing "through the eyes."

4. In what ways do the director and technical director of a high school musical play need to be creative and imaginative? Why are these skills essential?

5. Discuss the biggest pitfalls in producing a musical play. What effect can each have upon the production?

Careers

Choreographers direct dancing for television, movies, and the stage. They stage dances in variety shows, vaudeville, industrial shows, ice skating and roller skating shows, and musical comedies. Few choreographers get rich in ballet, an area of dance which often finds it difficult to enlist financial support, but commercial stage and motion picture choreographers have become millionaires.

Most choreographers come from the ranks of energetic, creative **dancers.** Dancers perform in classical ballet or modern dance. They perform folk, ethnic, jazz, and other popular kinds of dances. They may appear in opera, in musical comedy, or on television.

Dancers, who often begin their training between the ages of 7 and 12, must endure exhausting rehearsals, performances, and travel, often late at night and on weekends. For dancers, formal education is less important than professional instruction and practice. Because dancing is strenuous, many dancers in their thirties are ready to find other work, so they turn to choreography.

Others decide to become choreographers in their late teens or twenties. Most are self-taught. Choreographers need a rich background in music, cameras, lighting, drama, stage dimensions, and the limits of human endurance, as well as dance.

Chapter 12

Stage Settings

You Will Learn

About the purposes and effects of scenery.

About the development of scenic design from the Renaissance through modern times.

About some of the types of sets.

Some of the basic principles and considerations of set design.

How to construct and erect a set and how to paint and build scenery.

How to shift and set scenery.

Some tips for backstage safety.

Vocabulary

ground row	unity	hue	spattering
box set	emphasis	value	rag rolling
unit sets	proportion	tints	stippling
permanent set	balance	shades	featherdusting
screens	central axis	intensity	gridding
profile sets	line	saturation	
prisms or *periaktoi*	mass	size	
curtain sets	shape	floor block	
rendering	hues	scumble	

*A*n appreciation of the significance and beauty of stage settings should be one of the rewards of your study of the theater. Scenery and lighting are an integral part of contemporary play writing and production. No longer is the "set" a platform with a nondescript background or a drop with a poorly painted perspective of a locale totally unrelated to the play.

All students of drama should have a basic knowledge of stagecraft and design for four reasons: (1) to develop an appreciation of the importance of scenery to fine productions; (2) to better understand the relationship of each element of production to total theater; (3) to learn about another realm of the dramatic arts; and (4) to provide knowledge that may enable you to share in further theater activities in college and community life. Wishing to act without knowing your theater environment is like wishing to sail without knowing the bow of a boat from the stern.

Even if you do not feel artistically inclined, you will find there are many things to be done backstage by those with a little knowledge, a lot of enthusiasm, and a willingness to learn. It takes many workers behind the scenes — stagehands, property people, carpenters, costume and set designers, tailors, painters, and lighting technicians, to name a few — to make possible the bows of a few performers at curtain call. Backstage theater experience may bring you the satisfaction of knowing that you have played a part in making a successful show possible and help you discover talents and acquire skills that will be useful to you beyond your theater experience.

Stage Terminology

To understand the various phases of scenic design and the kinds of stage equipment that have been developed in the last 350 years, you should be familiar with the following terms.

act curtain: The curtain, hung just upstage of the proscenium, that opens or closes each act or scene.
acting area: The portion of the stage used by the actors during the play.

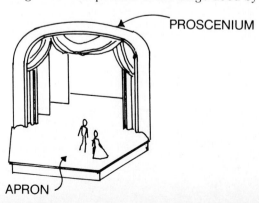

apron: The section of the stage in front of the curtain.

asbestos or *fire curtain*: A fireproof curtain closing off the stage from the auditorium.

auditorium: Where the audience sits.

backdrop (drop): A large piece of cloth upon which scenery is painted, fastened at top and bottom to battens, and hung at the back of the stage setting.

backing (masking): Flats or drops behind scenery openings to mask the backstage area.

backstage: That part of the stage — left, right, and rear — that is not seen by the audience; also the dressing rooms, greenroom, prop room, shops, and storage areas.

batten: A long piece of wood or pipe from which scenery, lights, and curtains are suspended; also used at top and bottom of a drop.

book: To hinge two or three flats together so that they will stand free or fold up; also the script in a musical play.

border: A short curtain hung across the stage above the acting area to mask the overhead lights from the audience; also refers to overhead strip lights.

box set: A two-wall or three-wall set composed of flats representing an interior of a room, often covered by a ceiling.

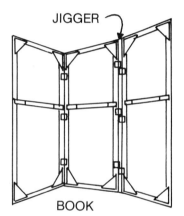

JIGGER

BOOK

brace: An adjustable, polelike support for flats.

clout nail: A special, soft, self-clinching nail used in flat construction.

counterweight system: A system of lines and weights that gives mechanical advantage to the raising and lowering of scenery.

CURTAIN: Playbook instruction to close the curtain.

curtain line: The imaginary floor line the curtain touches when closed.

cyclorama or *cyc*: A background curtain hung around the three sides of the stage.

dutchman: A canvas strip 4 to 5 inches wide to cover the gap between flats.

elevation: An eye-level-view drawing showing the flats arranged in a continuous row to be used in a set, or any front or rear head-on 2-dimensional drawing.

false proscenium: A frame built inside the proscenium to reduce the size of the stage opening.

flat: A wooden frame covered with cloth used as the basic unit of structure of a box set.

flies or *loft*: The area above the stage in which scenery is hung.

floor plan: A drawing of the overhead view of a set showing the exact location of all entrances, walls, and furniture.

fly: To raise or lower scenery.

gauze or *scrim*: A drop, usually seamless, made of special fabric that seems almost opaque when lit from the front and semitransparent when lit from behind.

grand drape: A curtain at the top of the proscenium, usually made of the same material as the act curtain, used to lower the height of the proscenium opening.

gridiron or *grid*: A series of heavy beams or metal framework just under the roof of the stage to which are attached the pulleys or blocks through which lines pass to raise or lower scenery.

grip: A stagehand who moves scenery.

ground cloth or *floor cloth*: A canvas covering for the floor of the acting area.

ground row: A low profile of scenery that can stand by itself, used to mask the bottom of the cyc or backdrop.

jack: A triangular brace for supporting scenery.

jigger: A board used as a spacer in three-fold booked flats.

jog: A narrow flat, usually less than 2 feet in width, used to form such things as alcoves and bay windows.

lash line: Rope used for lashing flats together.

legs: Pieces of cloth, usually hung in pairs, stage left and stage right, to mask the backstage area.

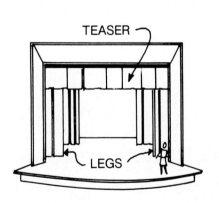

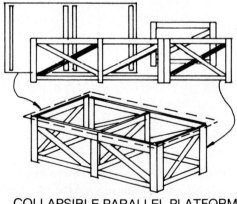

COLLAPSIBLE PARALLEL PLATFORM

permanent setting: A setting that remains the same throughout a play, regardless of change of locale.

perspective: A head-on view of a set having the illusion of depth.

pit: The part of the auditorium where the orchestra may be located — often an area below floor level.

plastic: A three-dimensional article or structure.

portal: A drop that has its lower middle section removed so that the drop will mask only the top and sides of the stage. A portal may be built with flats.

practical: A term applied to such parts of the set as doors and windows that must open and shut during the action, a rock that can bear a person's weight, and lamps that can be turned on.

profile (cut-out): A two-dimensional piece of scenery, such as a hedge or bush.

proscenium: The arch or frame enclosing the visible stage, the opening between the stage and the auditorium.

rake: To slant or set at an angle. A raked stage is inclined from the footlights to the rear of the stage.

ramp: A sloping platform connecting the stage floor to a higher level.

PROFILE

returns: Flats placed at the downstage edges of the set extending into the wings right and left.

reveal: A thickness piece placed in door, window, and arch openings to give the illusion of the third dimension to walls.

set pieces: Individual pieces of scenery, such as trees, rocks, and walls, that stand by themselves.

sight line: A line for the side walls and elevation of the set established by taking a sighting from the front corners and upper balcony seats.

sky cyc: Smooth cloth hung at the back and sides of the stage and painted to give the illusion of the sky.

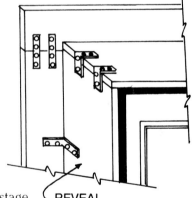

REVEAL

strike: The stage manager's order to remove an object or objects from the stage or to take down the set.

stop cleat: A piece of metal or wood attached to the back or corner of a flat to keep adjacent flat flush.

tab: A narrow drop.

teaser: A curtain or set of flats hung just upstage of the act curtain, used to adjust the height of the stage opening.

theater: A building used for the presentation of plays.

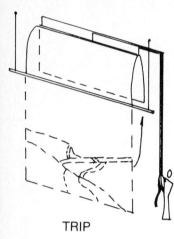

TRIP

tormentors: Side pieces — flats or drapes — just back of the proscenium, used to narrow the opening.

traveler: A stage curtain upstage of the act curtain that opens to the right and left rather than moving up and down.

trip: To double a drop for raising when there is insufficient fly space.

wagons: Low platforms on casters.

wing setting: A set made with pairs of wings on both sides of the stage, used with a matching backdrop.

wings: The offstage areas to the right and left of the set; also one or more flats, usually hinged at an angle but sometimes parallel to the footlights, used as entrances but which conceal backstage areas.

working drawing: A detailed drawing showing how a piece of scenery is to be constructed.

Purposes of Scenery

The most important function of scenery is to provide a place to act. The set should define the time of the play: the historical period, the time of day, the season of the year, and the changes in time that may occur during the play. The set should define the place: the climate and geographical conditions, the socioeconomic situation, the cultural background, or the political-governmental system of the area. It should also indicate whether the setting is interior or exterior, rural or urban, real or imaginary.

A set should help inform the audience about the effects of the environment upon the characters, and how, in turn, the characters' personality traits affect the surroundings. In *You Can't Take It with You,* the strange conglomeration of mismatched objects found in the family living room indicates the let-one-do-as-one-pleases attitude of the Sycamores.

A set often reveals the interrelationships between people, their rank, station, influence, or position in the family, office, or community. Scenery can provide a means for focusing audience attention on the actor. Elevating the actor on stairways and platforms provides a strong stage position. Furniture and actors may be arranged to facilitate triangular blocking with the key actor at the point of the triangle. Well-placed doorways can dramatically frame the actor.

In *Our Town,* Thornton Wilder focused attention on action and lines with a set design that most audiences have felt has "no design." *Our Town* has inaccurately been called "the play without scenery," but there *is* scenery — the scenery that Wilder felt necessary for the universality he sought. In fact, he used the most effective designer: the imagination of the audience. *Our Town* has been a popular play for high school productions, not because of its beauty and greatness, but because it doesn't take any scenery. Many directors and their casts have failed to recognize that such a stage design demands an even stronger interpretation of the roles by the actors than do plays with conventional scenery.

Scenery should indicate the style of the production. Of course, stage settings are not totally realistic, especially when presented on a proscenium stage. Theater conventions determine general positions for set pieces and entrance areas. For example, all, or nearly all, furniture faces the audience. Exterior doors are usually off stage right; most interior doors are stage left or upstage. Fireplaces tend to be placed on stage right walls. French doors are usually stage left. Living room and dining room furniture often appear in the same area. These are only a few of the staging conventions used in the theater.

Another important function of scenery is to create mood and atmosphere. The reaction of the audience to the actors and the script may be determined to a great extent by the "mental framework" a set may create. For example, if the set is painted in bright yellows, oranges, and pinks, the audience will expect the play to be correspondingly light and cheery. On the other hand, if

A scene from Death of a Salesman. In designing this set, Jo Mielziner selected details that would create the atmosphere of the Loman home but that would not distract attention from the play itself.

a set is painted in violets, dark blues and greens, grays and black, the audience will expect the play to be heavy and serious. The scenic designer utilizes the known psychological effects of color and design to arouse a subconscious emotional reaction from the audience. However, sets should be aesthetically satisfying, even when an atmosphere of fear, chaos, or mystery is to be created.

Scenic Design

Scenery must be in keeping with the author's intent and the director's interpretation. It must always serve the actor, never dominate. Scenery must not clash with costumes or become an obstacle course when blocking. It should never be distracting or inconsistent. In addition, a set must aid the action of the play, never hinder it. It must fit the needs of the play, yet maintain simplicity in design, construction, and shifting. A basic rule for all aspects of theater from acting to stagecraft is "use the least to say the most."

Proper design adds color and life to a production that makes theater an exciting experience. Costumes seem more appropriate and attractive against a fitting background. A careful selection of stage furnishings makes the set and its people seem complete and correct. However, the scenic artists must always remember that a design can only be as elaborate or difficult as the crew can handle.

Scenic Design and the Student of Drama

The basic high school drama course is concerned more with the principles of design and scenic construction than with the actual building of sets. However, some knowledge of scenic design is valuable whether or not you plan to take a course in stagecraft. You may want to work on backstage crews or committees. Every performer needs to know the role of the director, scenic designer or technical director, and the stage manager and the stage crew in order to appreciate the contribution each makes and to achieve the spirit of cooperation essential to successful productions.

In bringing a play to life, the scenic designer is next to the director in importance. The aim of both is to create the proper atmosphere to express the meaning of the play. The scenic designer does not build real rooms, houses, or mountaintops but uses painted canvas, creative lighting, and special effects to stir the imagination of the audience so that the playwright's dream seems a reality. The scenic designer works with the four areas of scenery, lighting, makeup, and costumes to create satisfying empathetic illusions. The more satisfying the empathies that are established, the better the production.

The Development of Scenic Design

From primitive campfires to the modern theater house, devoted theater technicians have improved scenery and light design in the desire to convey meanings through visual sensations. The first important step was the "skene" building, which the Romans subsequently enlarged. Later came the "stations" of the Miracle plays, with the special mechanical effect of Hell's Mouth.

Renaissance Designs

Stage design as we know it came into being in Italy in 1508 at the royal court of the Duke of Ferrara. The Teatro Olimpico, perfectly preserved in Vicenza,

The proscenium was introduced to the English stage by the architect Inigo Jones. This 1673 engraving details an extravagant set used for The Emperest of Morocco.
. . . .

was modeled after the ancient Roman theaters, solidly built and heavily decorated with elaborate niches, columns, and statues. Behind the entrances appeared streets in perspective from stucco and paintings. Buildings covered with statues of diminishing size lined the streets. The amazing effect is that of a city stretching into the distance.

The proscenium arch developed from the large central entrance of the Teatro Olimpico. The first real proscenium was in the Farnese Theater of Parma, where an elaborate architectural structure surrounded a frame with a curtain. Behind this frame, the actors performed against painted scenes. To facilitate scenery changes, *periaktoi* like the revolving prisms of the Greek theater were sometimes used.

Another Renaissance invention, which spread to England and was still used in London early in this century, was the raked stage. In a further attempt to make false perspective complete, the stage floor was slanted upwards toward the back of the stage. From this the terms *upstage* and *downstage* came into being; the actor was actually walking up or down the stage.

The tiring house facade of the Elizabethan playhouse emphasized simplicity and used a minimum of scenic effects, but Renaissance masques, elaborate musical and dramatic productions of the sixteenth and seventeenth centuries, were famous for their beautiful scenery. Backdrops became very popular, and large theaters were built to accommodate the extensive rigging needed to raise and lower the scenery. Wing settings were a continuation of the attempt to achieve perspective. The demand for many scenic backgrounds brought the introduction of shutters — flats that moved back and forth on tracks or grooves — and nested wings — several wings placed one behind the other to allow quick scene changes. Even revolving stages were tried during Renaissance stage experimentations.

Restoration Stages

The Restoration period in England found most of the acting taking place on raked aprons, with little action behind the proscenium "in" the scenery. The proscenium at this time was a very thick wall compared to our picture frame stages — so thick that one or two doors were placed in each side wall of the proscenium to enable the actors to enter on the apron rather than in back of the frame.

The Nineteenth Century

In the nineteenth century, an effort was made to suit the scenery to the play. However, typical interior sets were still made of canvas drops and wings painted to represent walls, windows, curtains, furniture, potted palms, mir-

rors, and all the other details of a conservatory or a parlor. Exterior scenes were also painted. For example, the conventional garden and forests consisted of painted trees, shrubs, fountains, gates, and pathways. Street scenes had painted buildings, store windows, signs, and street lamps. Entrances were made through wings parallel to the back wall. These were often painted like the backdrop, with furniture and draperies for interiors and cut-out greenery for exteriors. Some of these sets are still used in isolated "opery" houses, and imitations are made for revivals of the old-fashioned melodramas.

A notable change in the mid nineteenth-century theaters was the gradual shrinking of the apron and the addition of orchestra seats in the space formerly occupied by the stage. In addition, the flapping canvas wings and backdrops with their painted doors and windows and illogical shadows no longer satisfied the designers, who sought greater accuracy in historical and realistic representation. The wings gradually "closed," forming "real" left and right walls on the stage. Thus, the box set came into being, and the beginnings of realism took root.

The Twentieth Century

The cry for realism was answered in France by André Antoine and in the United States by David Belasco. Their stage sets were so photographically accurate that their style of design was called naturalism. Many stories have been told of Belasco's stress on accuracy, including individual selection of books and what-nots for shelves and the dismantling and reconstructing of real rooms. Belasco was so concerned with exact detail that his scenery distracted the audiences from the action of the play. However, the naturalists were important because their ultrarealistic sets worked toward making the realistic drama ring true.

Most realistic stage sets today are designed with *selective realism*. This modified form of realism developed because the many details of naturalism confused the audience. An impression of actuality is better theatrically and artistically. The designer selects scenic elements that convey the idea of the locale and does not attempt to create an exact replica.

The modern realistic interior set in a proscenium theater has all essential entrances, doorways, windows, and so on, placed in a two-sided or three-sided room. The room is usually placed off-center and at an angle instead of

*Realistic details in architecture, set dressing, and lighting fixtures and props add to a performance's texture. (*The Front Page *at the Williamstown Theatre Festival.)*

squarely on the stage in the old-fashioned manner. The fourth wall is imaginary, of course, and its presence is only suggested. Furniture usually faces that fourth invisible wall, through which the audience observes the action. There have been attempts to treat the fourth wall as a wall by placing a sofa with its back to the audience or by having an actor look out an imaginary window. However, the selective realists for the most part have agreed that "a set is a set," and the audience must accept it as a room. Natural sources of light — windows, lamps, skylights — have helped establish the illusion of reality.

The properly designed stage set can be an ideal background for the author's theme, as well as a pleasing picture for the audience. In addition, it represents the actual living quarters of people, disclosing their tastes, financial status, cultural level, and habits.

Exterior sets are at best only suggestive. Plastics (three-dimensional structures) and cut-outs (two-dimensional profiles) are placed against a drop or sky cyc. A low cut-out called a **ground row** is used to break the line between the floor and the drop and to give the illusion of distance.

The twentieth century has seen many experiments in scenic design. Two European designers of symbolic sets rebelled against ultrarealism. Adolphe Appia concentrated on three-dimensional forms, which he contended were essential for the performance of the three-dimensional actor. Appia emphasized the importance of the actor and used dramatic lighting innovations to focus attention on the performer. Gordon Craig believed the essential message of a play could be conveyed most effectively by the scenic designer. He even suggested eliminating the actors and replacing them with super-marionettes.

The revolutionary ideas of Appia and Craig were carried out in this country in a modified form, especially in productions of the plays of Eugene O'Neill. Flexible sets were made of screens, platforms, columns, and stairs. Lighting and color schemes expressed the spirit and mood of the plays. The staging was in direct contrast to the physical detail of the realistic style.

Types of Sets

The Box Set

The most common type of interior set has been the **box set** since it replaced the old wings and drops of the nineteenth century, although it, too, has been replaced by other forms in recent years. The box set consists of two or three walls built of flats and often covered by a ceiling.

Perspective of a Box Set

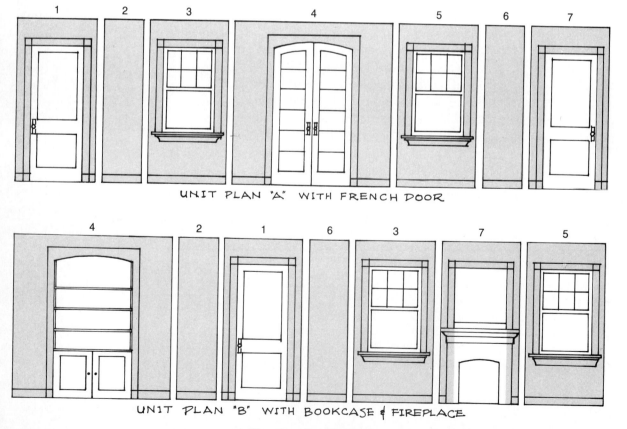

UNIT PLAN "A" WITH FRENCH DOOR

UNIT PLAN "B" WITH BOOKCASE & FIREPLACE

Elevation of a Unit Set

Permanent set (Elizabethan)

The Unit Set

Certain basic structural units called **unit sets** are utilized to create several settings. Unit sets are quite practical for schools that wish to present multiset plays or a program of one-act plays, or to build units for a little theater that can be arranged to fit the needs of almost any play. There are several kinds of unit sets. One type uses door or window flat units, which may be completely rearranged for each scene change. There are usually two door flats, one or two window-bookcase flats, and sometimes a wall with an arch-French door opening. These openings may be interchanged or may be "booked" together to form four-unit or five-unit walls; this allows for a variety of combinations.

A second important type of unit set consists of many openings, some of which are quite large. Once the set is erected for a play, it is not struck, but doors, windows, arches, curtains, and backing units are placed within or behind the openings to simulate scene changes.

A third type of unit set uses scenic units mounted on movable platforms. These may be shifted from one area of the stage to another, turned to different positions, or modified with simple set decorations, such as railings, or drapes.

The Permanent Set

Another type of staging is the use of the **permanent set,** one that never changes during the play except in some instances when a set piece, stairway, or flown unit may be brought in. Most high schools use a single permanent set for straight plays. Formalism can be very effective in permanent sets. A simple doorway can be either an interior or exterior entrance, a gate or a passageway; a platform may become a porch, a boudoir, a garden, or a sofa. Controlled light helps to determine the locale.

A modification of the permanent set is the multiple set, which has several distinct acting areas, each representing one or several locations. See-through walls, semipartitions, railings, and platforms can serve as dividers between acting areas. These strong dividers provide the main distinction between the permanent set and the multiple set. Flexible, controlled lighting equipment is necessary.

The Profile Set

Further opportunities for scenic variations are provided by using **screens** and **profile sets,** sometimes called *cut-down* or *minimum* sets. Screens consist of two-fold and three-fold flats, which are used either to form walls against a

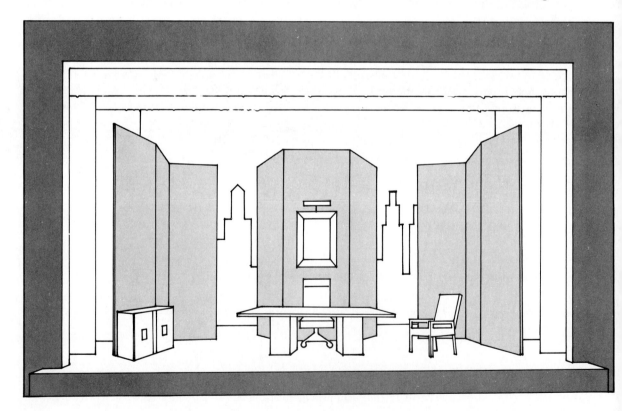

Screen set

drapery background or to cover openings or furnishings as a quick means of changing scenes. Screens may be almost any height and width, but a height of 8 to 10 feet is usually the most satisfactory. Although screens may be hinged or lashed together to form solid walls, that is seldom necessary, since two-fold and three-fold units are freestanding.

Cut-down scenery may be constructed of screens, but the chief difference between the two is that the cut-down set is more like the box set in that it forms the entire perimeter of the setting. Its height may vary from a mere 2 feet to 8 feet, depending upon the stage openings and furniture. Colors suggesting changing moods and emotions may be aimed against the background cyc to bring about a strong identification with the action.

The Prism Set

When fast changes with a minimum of equipment and space are needed **prisms** or **periaktoi** are used. The prisms are usually equilateral or isosceles triangles mounted to a wheeled carriage, which can be pivoted. Each *periaktos* is made up of three 6-foot flats or of two 4-foot flats and one 6-foot flat. At least four *periaktoi* are needed, but for more variety in combination and position and for more set possibilities, six or eight prisms may be used. Doorways may be created in several ways. The simplest method is to merely use a space between two prisms. Another method is to hook a normal door flat between two prisms. A third method uses inserts, sometimes called plugs, that may be hung between two *periaktoi.* The plugs may be shaped like ordinary doors or may be arched according to various architectural or stylistic designs. Window, bookcase, and fireplace flats may be used as one side of the *periaktos.* The prisms are especially valuable for schools that lack fly space, have trouble masking the sides of the stage, or need quick changes but have limited equipment.

Curtain (Drapery) Set

Set designers have frequently used **curtain sets** as substitutes for constructed scenery. A curtain set is simply the use of curtains as a backdrop for a play. The typical school cyclorama rarely provides an adequate background for a play, but sometimes space, equipment, and budget force the director to use a modified curtain set. There are, however, many ways to use curtains. A formalistic set with ramps, platforms, columns, and so on, may be at its best against a curtain set. The placing of a few flats, such as doorways, windows, and fireplaces, between curtains can often turn a "plain curtain set" into an acceptable theatrical set. Nevertheless, curtains can never be transposed into convincing realistic sets. One of the disadvantages of a cyclorama is that the

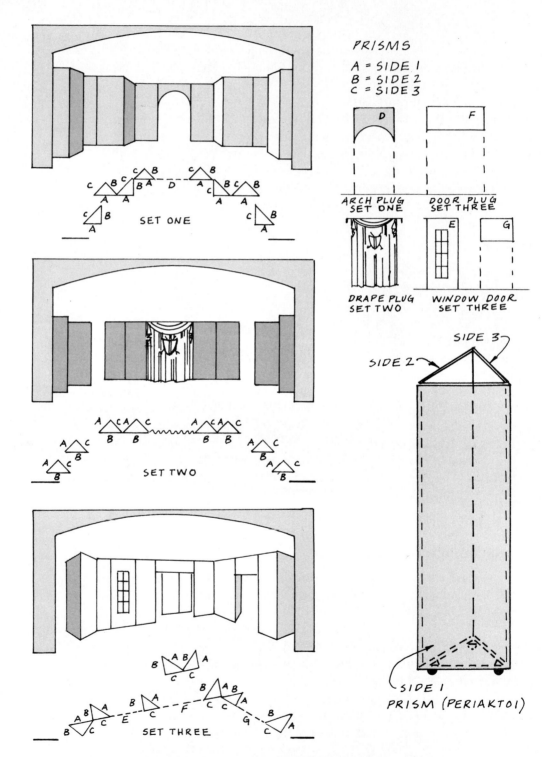

Prism Set—Rotating 8 Prisms to Create Three Different Sets

but one of the most effective innovations is the floating screen or multiple plane set. This technique employs single flats or narrow drops 6 feet or less in width that are placed at various depths parallel to the front of the stage. These floating screens provide concealed entrances for actors and suggest a locale.

Arena staging (theater-in-the-round) uses a different approach. Since the audience completely surrounds the stage, scenery may block the view of the spectators. Objects normally placed on walls, such as pictures, are often casually laid on tables or suspended by thin wire. For example, a mirror may be simply an open frame suspended from above. A set of andirons and a grate may serve as a fireplace. What furniture is used may be placed in natural groupings but must allow the actors to move constantly in "S" and circular patterns.

Procedures in Scenic Design

The basic goal of scenic design is to enhance the production by creating a functional background for the action that does not intrude on that action. A set may have aesthetic appeal, establish tone and atmosphere, convey symbolism, and even aid in the expression of the theme. However, if the set does not provide the actors with a workable environment in which to move, it has failed in its primary function.

Before making any plan, the designer reads the play carefully several times and discusses the play and its style of production with the director. The director will provide a foundation for design, including a basic floor plan. The designer then makes a pencil sketch or watercolor, called a **rendering,** that scenically expresses the meaning and spirit of the play. After considering available equipment, funds, and material the designer enlarges this sketch into a perspective drawing.

Next, the scenic designer works out a detailed floor plan — an exact diagram showing the position and size of entrances, windows, fireplaces, stairways, the backing for all doors and windows, and any pieces of plastic scenery or ground rows to be used. The furniture may be included in the original floor plan or in one made after rehearsals have started. At this point, many directors and scenic designers build model sets as a basis for blocking and for a three-dimensional study of the design. Some directors have a model set viewer, often complete with simple lighting, in which the model can be tested. The final step in design is the drafting of an elevation and working drawings, which are detailed construction illustrations or blueprints.

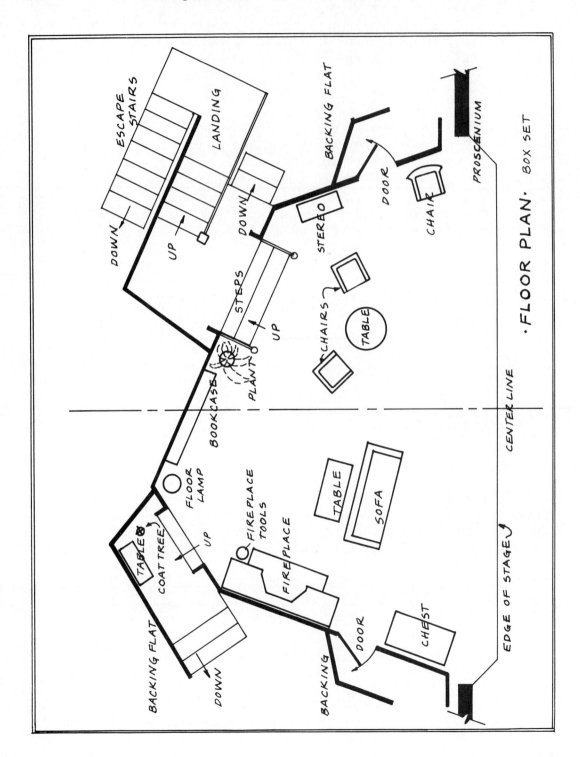

· FLOOR PLAN · BOX SET

Predesign Considerations

Before designing a set, the scenic designer must obtain certain important in-formation. First of all, the designer should know the size and shape of the auditorium, whether the floor is raked, and the type of seating arrangement. This is especially important in gymnasium-auditorium combinations and little theaters. Next, the designer must determine what space, including storage areas, will be available for the production; the dimensions of the apron and wings and the amount of fly space; and what equipment is available or can be obtained for use on this particular stage.

If there is fly space, the designer must know if the flies are high enough to handle a drop without tripping and whether the system is manual, sand-bagged, or counterweighted. In most school situations, the designer should determine how many flats are available, their height and widths, and how many drops and scrims are ready for use. In addition, it is important to know how many special units, such as platforms, ramps, and staircases, are already constructed. And finally, the designer must consider lighting equipment and its flexibility before designing the set.

The budget for the production may greatly affect the design as well as the number and kinds of sets to be used. When several sets are called for, the

Drops may be painted or rented for various shows and then hung upstage as a backdrop. In theaters with full drop height fly space and available pipes, many drops may be easily shifted for different scenes.
• • • • • • • • • • • •

designer must always plan for the weight and mobility of scenic units and the availability of a traveler or apron space for acting during scene changes. Time and sound are two important factors to consider whenever a shift in scenery takes place. An audience can become distracted during a long wait while scenery is shifted. Equally disconcerting is the amount of noise too often heard coming from the stage during a scenery change.

Basic Principles

The first consideration of scenic design is the play itself — its theme, type, and style. The designer must be aware of important scenes and special effects essential to that particular play, including lighting needs. The functional aspects of the set provide the information necessary for a preliminary design — location of doors, windows, fireplaces, elevated areas, essential props, and so on. Since a set is the background for actors, their experience, ages, sizes, costumes, and makeup must be considered. A stage designer must plan a set with and without people: How will the set look with the maximum number of performers on stage and with the fewest number of actors that ever occupy the set?

Naturally, the designer must also consider the audience. Since the spectators must see all important action, the designer must take sight lines from the front corner seats and the highest balcony seats that may be sold. This means that the side walls must be raked (set at an angle) so that each person in the audience can see each entrance. Likewise, the designer must position elevated upstage platforms so that the upper balcony audience will not see "headless" actors. Second-story levels are often raked toward the audience. The designer may "cheat down" the height of a second story and even lower the heights of doors and bannister rails.

Artistic Considerations

Unity and emphasis are the two most important design principles to keep in mind when designing a set. **Unity** demands that all elements of the set form a perfect whole, centering around the main idea of the play. All furniture and properties must be in keeping with the background and, if possible, be a part of the stage design in period and composition. **Emphasis** focuses audience attention on some part of the stage (a hallway or a staircase), a piece of furniture (a piano or a desk), or an object on the set (a moose head or a rifle rack). A good set design emphasizes this center of interest by placing it in a prominent position, by painting it a color that makes it stand out from all else, by making it the focus of all lines of interest, or by playing light upon it. Everything else on the stage should be subordinated to the center of interest.

Proportion and **balance** are also important artistic principles to be observed. Proportion takes the human being as the unit of measurement. In realistic plays, all scenic elements are scaled to a person 6 feet tall. Nonrealistic sets may make people appear dwarfed or engulfed by rocks, huge columns, or towering buildings. Except in stylized settings, asymmetrical or informal balance is preferable to perfect symmetry.

In any case, the central axis must not be forgotten. The **central axis** is the focal point in the design, usually the deepest point just off-center. The "halves" of the stage on either side of this axis should be balanced but not exactly alike. The director and the scenic designer must work closely together because the position, number, and importance of people on stage form an intrinsic part of the scenic pattern.

For example, a strong character, who is to exemplify spiritual leadership and be the center of interest in a scene, can be placed on a height to one side against tall columns, a high arched doorway, or long drapes, with the other characters, perhaps a large crowd, below. The emphasis of the strong character's influence in the minds of the audience will offset the size of the crowd, and the stage picture will balance.

The next three artistic values are those of **line, mass,** and **shape.** The use of lines alters the sense of proportion and affects the observer psychologically. Long vertical lines in draperies, columns, or costumes suggest dignity, elevation, hope, or spirituality and may be used for temples and solemn places. Horizontal lines are emotional levelers, bringing about calm, evenness, and tranquility. Diagonal lines may suggest a driving force, strife, uncertainty, or concentration. Curved lines may give the impression of ease, wealth, and expanse. Curves and angles, usually combined with strongly contrasted colors, give a sense of intense excitement. Crooked or jagged lines suggest chaos, shattered dreams, injustice, or pain.

Mass takes into consideration the concepts of bulk and weight, both of which are difficult to determine without testing under the lights. Dark-colored objects usually appear heavier than light objects. Shape often influences both the concept of mass and the psychological reaction to objects on the stage. Remember that shape is outline, but mass is three-dimensional. Shapes may be geometric or free-form, natural or stylized, realistic or impressionistic. A circle may seem infinite, eternal, or feminine; a square or cube may appear staid or unimaginative; a triangle may seem uplifting or securely founded; a diamond may seem calming and restful.

The Use of Color

Color is one of the most important elements of staging, for the various colors and their combinations produce very different emotional effects. The relationship between characters or scenes and the colors used may be factors in a play's success. On the stage, color effects are achieved by playing colored lights on the pigments used in sets, costumes, and stage furnishings. Because colored light makes very definite and often surprising changes in the appearance of pigment, it is necessary to experiment with both to get the desired result. Though this may be a long and involved process, it is fascinating to see what happens to fabrics and painted surfaces under different lighting.

Color almost always arouses an emotional response, which can help establish the mood and atmosphere for each scene as well as for the whole play. Sets and costumes may be color-coded for both identification and emotional response. Color coding means identifying the emotional tone of a scene by its color dominance; for example, a "pink scene" may be that of romantic fantasy; a "red scene" may be one of anger and passion. Characters, too, may be color-coded in stylized productions. Costume colors may identify romantic pairings, members of the same family, an ideological group, or personality types of the characters.

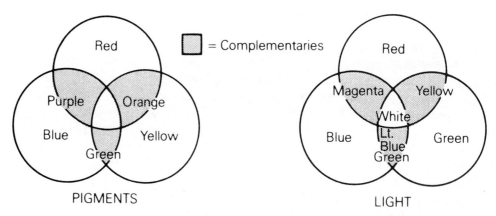

PIGMENTS

LIGHT

In pigment, the primary colors are red, yellow, and blue. The secondary colors are orange, green, and violet. When dealing with light, the primary colors are red, green, and blue, and the secondary colors are yellow, cyan (a light blue-green), and magenta.

Colors differ from each other in **hue, value,** and **intensity. Hues** are the various colors seen in the spectrum of a beam of light that passes through a prism. **Hue** indicates the purity of color — the redness, blueness, and so on. Black is the absence of light and therefore is the absence of color. White is the fusion of all the spectral colors. As light falls on different surfaces, the colors are absorbed or reflected. A surface that absorbs all colors and reflects none is black. A surface that absorbs all the hues except green appears to be green because it reflects only that color.

The **value** of a color — its lightness or darkness — is determined by the amount of black or white mixed with it. **Tints** (light or pastel colors) contain a good deal of white. **Shades** (dark or deep colors) contain more black. The light colors generally suggest youth, comedy, and informality. Dark colors suggest dignity, seriousness, and repose. Each color is said to have a value scale, running from white at one end to black at the other. If a costume or prop is to be emphasized, it should be placed against a background of different value or hue. If it is to be made inconspicuous, it should be shown against a background of its own value or hue so that, in effect, it disappears.

Intensity is the brightness or dullness of a color, often referred to as **saturation.** You can usually intensify a color by casting on it light of the same color. Intensity will be lessened if you add gray to the pigment or use a light or a complementary color. The complementary color for any one of the primary colors is achieved by mixing together the other two primaries. Thus, violet is the complement of yellow; orange, of blue; and green, of red.

A color wheel is an invaluable aid in designing, for it shows the relationships of the various hues. The colors next to each other on the wheel are *analogous.* For example, yellow, yellow-orange, and orange are analogous, since they all contain yellow. When analogous colors are used, a dash of complementary color will give a sense of balance.

Since neither pigments nor materials for coloring lights are likely to have pure color, endless experiments are required to get a desired effect. You can experiment with the effect of light on pigment on actual sets as they are built. Run through the color cycle of night to day — black, pale gray, light yellow, light red, deep red, orange, and full daylight. Then reverse this cycle and run from daylight to darkness through the sunset hues, ending with the green-blue conventionally used to simulate moonlight on the stage. A point to remember: Green-blue and blue-green are not the same color. The second named color is the dominant hue. Therefore, green-blue is blue with a tinge of green in it, and blue-green is green with a tinge of blue in it.

Colors are referred to as *warm* or *cool.* Red, orange, and yellow are warm colors. You see them in sunlight and fire. Blue, green, and violet are cool colors. You see them in deep pools and in shadows under leafy trees. Warm hues seem to advance, or move forward in space, because they attract attention quickly. Cool colors appear to recede, or move back in space, because they are less noticeable. However, a stage background or set piece painted in warm colors looks smaller because it seems nearer, while one painted in cool colors looks larger. A warm-colored costume or object generally catches the eye at once and looks important. Objects or persons dressed in cool colors are generally less noticeable to the audience. The warm colors are stimulating and exciting, appropriate for highly emotional scenes and for comedies. Cool colors give a sense of tranquility and are usually the predominant colors in serious comedies and in tragedies. One should bear in mind that too much stress on warm colors can be very irritating and too many cool colors are depressing.

Most people now accept that different hues of various intensity produce emotional responses. Certain stage traditions are based on known reactions to color. Following these traditions is an important means of getting satisfactory empathetic responses from the audience.

The following emotional values have been given to colors. These color meanings are useful in stage design.

blue — calm, cold, formal, spiritual, pure, truthful, depressing

orange — exhilarating, cheerful, lively

red — aggressive, passionate, bloody, angry, strong

yellow — cheerful, happy, youthful, cowardly

pink — fanciful, romantic

green — youthful, eternal, reborn, jealous

soft green — restful, soothing, tranquil

purple — mournful, mystic, regal

gray — neutral, depressing, negative, somber

brown — earthy, common, poverty-stricken

black — melancholic, tragic, gloomy, deathlike

white — truthful, pure, chaste, innocent, peaceful

In any stage set, there should be a controlling color scheme that carries out the predominant mood and atmosphere of the production. The most effective color schemes are those that give a single impression.

Other Aspects of Design

If a design is to be interesting, it must have variety coming from contrast and subordination. Too often high school stage settings give every scenic element equal strength and dominance. This is not to say that a single motif carried through an entire scene of a production will not effectively underscore the unity and harmony of design. The key word in good design is simplicity. Cluttered sets, "busy" walls, or too many colors are not found in artistic stage sets.

Constructing the Set

The most common sets involve draperies, flats, or drops. The flat is the basic unit of construction for box sets, screens, prisms, and cut-down scenery. Since the majority of plays require an interior set, you should learn the procedures in flat building, assembling, and painting.

These Wheaton College students are working on set pieces—in this instance, birch trees. The scene shop is conveniently located adjacent to the stage and includes a paint area.

The most satisfactory height for flats to be used on the high school stage is 12 feet, although 10-, 14-, and 16-foot flats are not uncommon. Large university and professional stages with high prosceniums may accommodate flats up to 24 feet high. There are two different approaches, each having definite advantages and disadvantages, in determining the width of flats. One system includes the following as a basic number of flats:

PLAIN FLATS		SPECIAL FLATS	
Width	*Number Needed*	*Type*	*Number Needed*
1 ft	2–4	Door flats, 5–6 ft	2–3
1½ ft	2	Window-bookcase flats, 5–6 ft	2
2 ft	2–4	Fireplace flat (optional), 5–6 ft	1
3 ft	6–8	Arch flat (booked), 8 ft	1
4 ft	6–8	French door-sliding door	1
5 or 6 ft	6–8	(booked), 8 ft	
	24–34		7–8

This system requires a total of thirty to forty flats, depending upon the size of the stage. One of the advantages of this system is that you would have matching flats for alcoves, bay windows, periaktoi, and columns. Another advantage is that it is easier to plan wall dimensions and designate flats accordingly. However, care must be taken that the set does not turn out nearly symmetrical.

The second system consists of twenty plain flats starting with a 12-inch flat. Each successive flat increases the width by 3 inches: 12, 15, 18, and so on, up to 72 inches. Since there are no two flats exactly the same width, variety in the shape of the set is reasonably assured. Proponents of this system claim that the audience will not notice a 3-inch difference when flats are used for an alcove or a bay window. There are many times, however, when flats are to be matched. Therefore, if this system is followed, it is wise to pair some flats. The special flats for this system are the same as those in the first system described.

Construction of a Flat

The materials needed to build a flat consist of lumber, fabric, hardware, rope, and glue. The best kind of wood for stiles (the frame of the flat) is 1″ × 3″ white pine because of its workability and light weight. Ideally, the grade of the lumber should be screen stock, clear, or #1. Although the cost of this grade of lumber may seem high, a properly built flat will last for many years. However, the high cost of lumber has made it necessary for most high schools to use lower grades of lumber, wider dimensions, and other types of wood. For example, today many flats are built of #2 grade, 1″ × 4″ yellow pine. The boards used for stiles and rails should be absolutely straight and free of any but tight knots. The corner braces are made from 1″ × 2″ stock or may be ripped from any piece of 1″ × 4″ lumber. The corner blocks, keystones, and mending plates are cut from ¼″ plywood. Refer to page 416 for a detailed illustration of a flat.

The best fabric is canvas, but its cost makes it prohibitive to most groups. The next best choice is unbleached muslin. The special stage hardware needed for a well-made flat includes three lash-line cleats, two tie-off cleats, and a stage-brace cleat. Corrugated fasteners are used at every joint. Clout nails (1¼″ soft nails that clinch themselves when a piece of heavy metal is placed under the stile or rail before hammering), three-penny box nails, or screws are used to attach the plywood to the frame. Staples or tacks and glue are used to fasten the cloth to the finished frame. Use diluted white glue to hold the cloth to the frame.

The first step in the construction of a flat is framing. The most common joint used is the butt joint. However, mitre joints are better, since they are stronger and do not chip or split as easily. When using butt joints, cut the top and bottom rails the exact width the finished flat is to be. This allows the flat to slide without splitting the stiles. This also means that the boards used for the stiles must be cut the desired height of the flat less the width of two rails. Bear in mind that common names for lumber sizes do not reflect actual width and thickness. For example, 1″ × 3″ lumber is always less than 1 inch by 3 inches. It is ¾ inch by 2⅝ inches or less. Check exact lumber sizes with the lumber yard. Always measure carefully. Then check your measurements again before and after cutting. An old rule of thumb is "measure twice; cut once." A board sawed too short can never be used.

After cutting the top and bottom rails and two stiles, assemble the frame. The most important tool for scenery building is the framing square. Unless you have a template, an adjustable framework serving as a mold, or can nail two boards at a 90° angle to serve as a square, framing is easier when one person can hold the square while another does the nailing. Then, keeping the square in place, a corner block is nailed on with eleven nails in the pattern shown on page 417. If you use a butt joint, the grain of the corner block must run across the joint.

Remember: Whenever you attach anything to the back of a flat, it must be set back ¾ inch from the edge. A scrap piece of 1″ × 3″ wood on edge will serve as a guide. This setting-back allows two flats to be joined at a right angle without a crack appearing between the flats. Place a corner block at each corner in the same manner.

Next, put in one or two toggle rails (bars). Toggle rails should be set at the same height so that keeper hooks may hold a stiffener board when the set is erected. Usually one toggle is sufficient for 8 to 10 foot flats, but for flats 12 feet and taller, use two toggles. The toggles should be cut the width of the flat less the width of the two stiles. Do not measure the toggle by the space between the stiles. If you have to, force the stiles in or out as necessary so that the total width is exactly the same as the top and bottom rails. Nail in the corrugators, and cover the joint with the keystones.

You can now install the corner braces. Notice that both are on the left side of the flat. If they were on opposite corners, the flat would torque (twist) diagonally. Corner braces need not be exact but are approximately the length of a rail and should extend from slightly past the midpoint of the rail to a point on the stile. A 40–60° angle is created if the corner braces are placed properly. Use corrugators and mending plates to secure the joint, and your flat is fully framed. Mending plates are 1½ × 5 inch pieces of ¼″ plywood cut lengthwise with the grain. Screw on the hardware as indicated in the drawing on page 417. You can approximate all measurements for the hardware except for the tie-off cleats, which must be exactly 2 feet from the floor to facilitate lashing.

Make the frame flameproof by washing it in a solution of 2 pounds of borax, 2 pounds of sal ammoniac, and 2 gallons of water. Then you may turn the flat face side up and cover it with muslin. The muslin should overlap all sides unless there is a finished edge, which you may place ¼ inch from the outer

THE FLAT

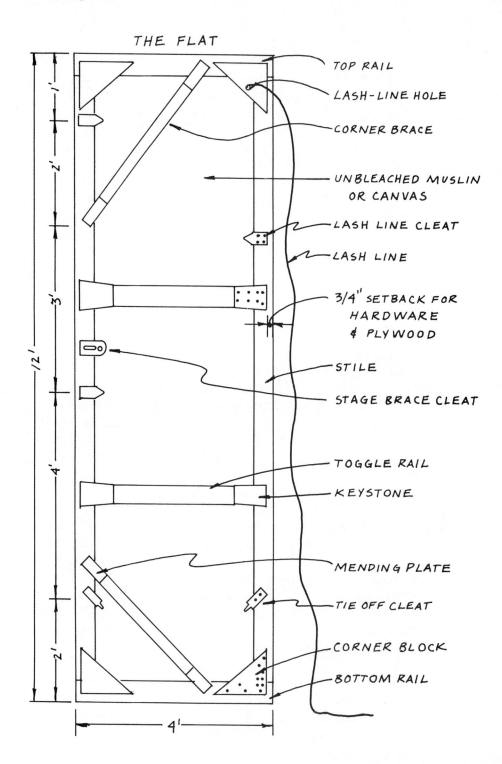

TOP RAIL

LASH-LINE HOLE

CORNER BRACE

UNBLEACHED MUSLIN
OR CANVAS

LASH LINE CLEAT

LASH LINE

3/4" SETBACK FOR
HARDWARE
& PLYWOOD

STILE

STAGE BRACE CLEAT

TOGGLE RAIL

KEYSTONE

MENDING PLATE

TIE OFF CLEAT

CORNER BLOCK

BOTTOM RAIL

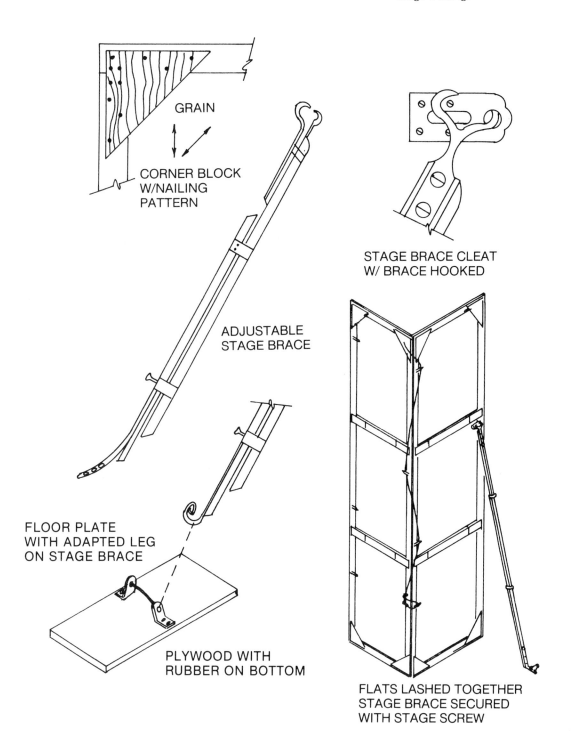

GRAIN

CORNER BLOCK
W/NAILING
PATTERN

STAGE BRACE CLEAT
W/ BRACE HOOKED

ADJUSTABLE
STAGE BRACE

FLOOR PLATE
WITH ADAPTED LEG
ON STAGE BRACE

PLYWOOD WITH
RUBBER ON BOTTOM

FLATS LASHED TOGETHER
STAGE BRACE SECURED
WITH STAGE SCREW

edge of one stile. Place staples or tacks every 4 inches, ¼ inch from the inner edge of the stile. Many set builders prefer to drive the staples or tacks only part way and remove them after the glue dries. Others drive staples all the way and leave them. Fold the muslin back over the staples, and spread glue on the stiles. As soon as you have applied the glue, fold the cloth back down on the glue and smooth the cloth down with a wood block. Carefully stretch the muslin across the frame, allowing it to "belly" to the floor in the center. Be especially careful at the corners. There will be extra material because of the bellying of the cloth. Be sure the fabric does not pull or wrinkle. Repeat the stapling-gluing process until both stiles and the top and bottom rails are glued. Do not place any glue on the toggles or corner braces. Now staple ½ inch in from the outer edge of the frame around all four sides. The cloth can be flameproofed with the same formula that was used on the frame. Do not wrap the cloth around the frame and staple it to the backside because the flat might bow.

You are now ready to **size** — to paint on a glue-water mixture that seals the pores, provides a good painting surface, and stretches the muslin like an artist's canvas. The easiest sizing to use is made from a commercial cold-water size to which a little whiting has been added. Some brands of sizing need a little more water than the directions on the box call for. Your fingers should just tend to stick together when the sizing is properly thinned. After the sized muslin dries, use a razor knife to trim the selvage (waste) off ¼ inch from the outer edge of the stiles and rails. Do not trim the cloth flush with the outside edge of the flat or the cloth will be pulled loose by the handling of the flat.

All that remains to be done is to put a length of ¼-inch rope through the hole drilled in the upper right corner block, knot the end, and pull back tightly. Cut the rope 6 inches longer than the flat.

You can build rigid flats from plywood instead of cloth. Such flats are strong, require little frame bracing, and last longer than those made of cloth. However, plywood flats are much heavier than cloth flats.

Erecting the Set

Flats may either be lashed or hinged together. If you plan to hinge all future scenery, every hinge should be matched, using loose pin (backflap) hinges. Tight pin hinges are good only if the hinges are to be removed after the production. If only one set is required for the play and if it is permissible to nail into the stage floor, it is usually advisable to **floor block** — tack a small block of wood to the floor on both sides or each union where two flats meet. This keeps the walls straight and strengthens them. Stop cleats or stop blocks may be placed on the back of flats to prevent one flat from being pushed back of the other at sharp angle junctions. Walls that shake and rattle when a door is slammed have been identified with amateur theater far too often. Proper bracing will eliminate nearly all such distractions.

Adjustable stage braces provide support for the individual flat. One brace is used for each flat except door flats and occasionally window flats, which need two braces. The hook of the brace is inserted upside down and turned over firmly against the stile as shown on page 417. It is very important that the brace be correctly installed. If it is not, a hole in the muslin and a wobbly flat will be the price paid by a careless grip. The brace may be anchored to the floor by stage screws or a floor plate. If stage screws can be used, drill a hole before inserting the screw. If the wood is reasonably close-grained, the same hole may be used over and over again for many years. (The dust from the stage will "fill" the hole sufficiently to secure the brace time after time.) If holes cannot be drilled in the floor, a wood block may be lightly tacked to the floor and the stage screw anchored into the block. Never nail stage braces directly to the floor.

When there are restrictions against the use of any nails or screws in the floor or when the wood is too soft to hold a stage screw, there is an easy solution, which may be the best answer in almost all situations — the floor plate as shown on page 417. A floor plate is simply a piece of plywood having a nonslip rubber pad on its under side and a special hardware adapter, which any school shop can make, bolted to the brace. Stage weights or concrete blocks are placed on top of the floor plate to hold it in place. However, a piece of 2" lumber will work satisfactorily if there is not enough time to make floor plates.

Another type of bracing is the jack such as the one shown on page 388. A jack is a triangular wooden brace hinged to fold out of the way or even placed on wheels to allow large units to be moved more easily. Jacks are often used with set pieces and ground rows. Similar in function to the jack is the foot iron. The foot iron is an L-shaped piece of strap iron attached to the back of the flat and anchored to the floor with a stage screw. Foot irons are used mostly when there is insufficient space for jacks or braces.

Another means of strengthening walls is to use keeper hooks. Wherever there are two or more flats in a straight line, these handy pieces of hardware can be hooked over the top and toggle rails of each flat and a stiffener board dropped into the notch, making that entire wall section one "solid" unit. Some technicians prefer hinged stiffeners, but keeper hooks are convenient, quick, and effective.

Once the set is assembled, apply the dutchman. A dutchman is a 4 to 5 inch strip of muslin used to cover the cracks between flats. A dutchman is never used on a set that is to be shifted except on booked flats or screens. Depending on whether the flats were painted before setup or are to be painted

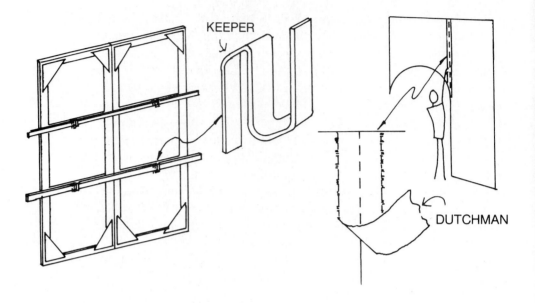

after being erected, the dutchman may be dipped in either scenic paint or sizing, placed over the crack, and brushed down smoothly. If flats are perfectly matched, a strip of masking tape can sometimes be substituted for the dutchman.

Handling Flats

Novice grips can have a difficult time trying to move flats. There are some simple techniques that make the task far less awkward. One person can lift a flat from the floor to a position for moving by *edging* — getting the flat up on one side. The grip puts one foot against the bottom rail, grasps the stile, and pulls the flat up. *Walking* a flat requires two or three grips. One grip puts a foot against the bottom rail and one or two others lift the top rail and gradually raise the flat by moving hand-over-hand toward the first grip. The best and safest way to lower a flat is *by floating*. To float a flat, simply place a foot against the back of the bottom rail and allow the flat to fall. It will gently "float" to the floor face down. Because dust will rise — even from a "clean" floor — it is wise to wear goggles during floating. Moving a flat is called *running* it. The grip takes an upright flat with both hands grasping the stile on the side that the flat is to go, lifts that edge slightly, and slides the flat along, not actually lifting or carrying it. A grip should not try to grasp both stiles and move the flat — the flat will act like a sail.

Painting Scenery

Painting the set is certainly one of the important steps in the completion of a set, but it should not be the chore it often seems to be. One of the problems faced by amateur theater is the handling of scenic paints and glue. It takes only one sour batch of scenery paint to strain the relationships between the drama department and the rest of the school.

There are four approaches that may be taken. The first is to use some of the new scenic paints that are available. Colors are pure, and costs are fairly reasonable.

A second method mixes dry scenic pigment with one of the polyvinyl glues now on the market. There are polyvinyl liquid glues that require no cooking, and there are polyvinyl alcohol resins that must be cooked, but once prepared, can be stored indefinitely without decomposing. Check with paint manufacturers for new developments in this area.

A third choice is the use of casein or acrylic paints. These paints are made ready to use simply by adding water, but their cost is several times that of dry color and fewer colors are available. Casein is more water-repellent than dry color and can be used for scenery placed out-of-doors or in damp locations.

The fourth choice is latex paint. Its advantages and disadvantages are nearly equal. Latex paint is most convenient when shop space is limited or only a small amount of scenery is to be painted. By shopping around, you can find fairly inexpensive latex paint, which can be diluted considerably for stage use.

The advantages of latex make it practical for many schools: it is readily available; it covers well and will not bleed through; it comes in basic tints, and with universal tinting colors, the spectral range is possible; any good paint or hardware store can mix latex paints to order. On the other hand, it is fairly expensive to paint with latex unless you can find some on sale. If you apply the paint too heavily, the muslin eventually absorbs so much that the life of the fabric is shortened. Universal tinting colors are very expensive in the deep tones. Finally, when tinting colors are used at nearly full strength for special touches and accents, the color may rub off unless you use a dryer.

Apply paint in random strokes or in figure eights. An uneven base coat is better than a smooth finish, which is "flat" and emphasizes all the flaws in the set. Some scenic painters **scumble** the base coat. Scumbling requires two or more brushes and two or more tones of the base color. Paint each tone on a small area and blend the tones together. You must work quickly or the paints will set.

After applying the base coat, highlight and shadow the set and then texture it. The texturing process is the most important for a good paint job. The texture coat covers flaws, dutchmen, patches, so that the audience does not even see them.

Texturing

The most common method of texturing is **spattering,** shown below. Use at least two colors, one a shade darker and the other a tint lighter than the base color. You may also use the complementary color to blend and harmonize the colors in the set. Dip a 4-inch brush into paint that has been diluted from ⅓ to ½, wipe it "dry" on the side of the pail, and shake the brush once on an old flat or dropcloth. Then stand a short distance from the set and strike the handle of the brush against the palm of the other hand, causing drops of paint to spatter the flats. This is a difficult technique to master, so

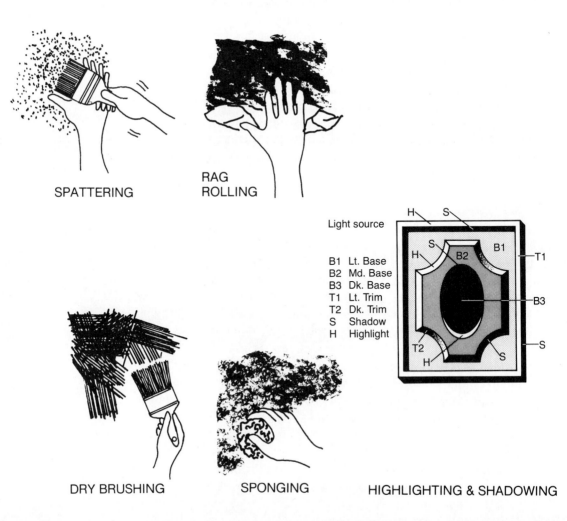

SPATTERING

RAG ROLLING

DRY BRUSHING

SPONGING

Light source

B1 Lt. Base
B2 Md. Base
B3 Dk. Base
T1 Lt. Trim
T2 Dk. Trim
S Shadow
H Highlight

HIGHLIGHTING & SHADOWING

practice on an old flat first. The dark spattering coat should normally be heavier at the top of the walls to make them appear shadowed.

Rag rolling, shown on page 422, is a second method of texturing. Dip a rag or rolled-up piece of frayed burlap in paint, then roll it over the walls to make them look like rough plaster.

Stippling is a texturing method in which the painter gently touches the flat with a sponge, a crumpled rag, or the tips of a dry brush, leaving clusters of paint drops. The painter turns whatever tool he or she is using to avoid creating a set pattern.

Featherdusting is another popular and quick texturing technique. Dip a featherduster into the paint, shake it off, and gently press it against the flat. By turning the handle slightly, you will get a different pattern each time the duster is applied. Featherdusting is especially good for foliage effects.

Dry brushing, as shown on page 422, may be used for wall texturing or for simulating wood grain. For walls, use a dry brush, stroke in one direction with a light color, and repeat with a dark color. For a woodgrain effect, use long, straight strokes with a dark color and then repeat the process with a lighter color.

Highlights and shadows are essential if the scenery is to be convincing and alive. Before painting these realistic dimensional touches, the painter must consider the primary light source, that is, the direction and cause of the predominant light. Moldings, paneling, wainscoting, shingles, siding, bricks, and rocks must be carefully painted, even when they are built in three dimensions. You can create realistic bricks by applying a base coat of mortar color and using a rubber sponge block cut to brick size. Press the bricks, dipped in paint, onto the scenery. Use from 2 to 4 colors such as red, gray, dark yellow, and green. You may cut three-dimensional bricks and rocks from Styrofoam and glue them to plywood. Cardboard makes good shingles.

Profile scenery and drops, shown on pages 400 and 407, are real challenges to stage painters because such scenery almost always represents some three-dimensional object or a perspective scene. **Gridding** is the process used to make the enlarging from a sketch to a drop. Mark the drop off into 1- or 2-foot squares and scale the sketch proportionally as shown. You may also transfer a drawing by using an overhead or opaque projector. A special copy machine can put the drawing on a piece of clear plastic. This copy may then be projected onto the drop and outlined. It is important, for any of these methods, that the drawing be a simple outline with clean lines.

One of the most challenging painting tasks for the amateur is the painting of rock walls. They often end up looking like strange "masses" randomly placed in an equal amount of gray mortar. On a real wall the rocks are laid in mortar, light causes highlights and shadows, and the texture and color of the rocks give the viewer the feeling of bulk and weight. Such scenery should be

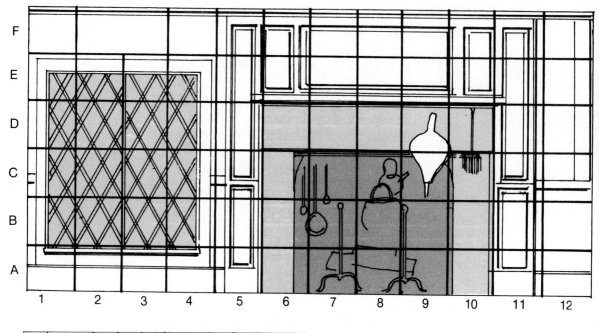

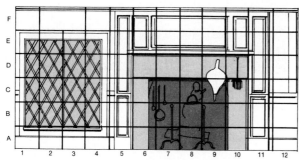

TRANSFERRING A BACKDROP
DESIGN FROM THE SKETCH TO THE DROP
THROUGH THE USE OF A SCALED GRID

Grid Transfer Technique

painted with a wet-brush technique using at least four colors and blending while the paint is wet.

Painted wallpaper patterns can be applied using stencils, carved sponge rubber blocks, carpet padding, pattern rollers, and old paint rollers. Stencils may be cut out of plywood or out of stencil paper which is strengthened by a coat of acrylic and placed in a wooden frame and supported by wires.

Scenery painting is an art that develops with time, experience, and experimentation. Watch what happens to color and textures under various lighting effects and consider how you would represent them scenically.

Shifting the Setting

The most important requirement for shifting scenery is a well-trained crew who know what their job is and how to get it done efficiently. The stage manager "runs the show" backstage. Backstage workers include grips, who move flats, prisms, and set pieces; the flycrew, who raise the lower flown scenery and draperies; the prop crew, who check properties in and out as they are set or struck; and the set dressers, who are responsible for setting and striking the finishing touches on a set, such as pictures, scarves, flowers, and so on.

Changing Scenery

There are many ways to change scenery, including those discussed earlier: unit, permanent, prism, and screen sets. A "booked" set may be dropped inside an existing set. Screens can also be used for a set within a set. Drops are the most frequently used type of flown scenery. Ground rows are usually brought in to mask the junction where drop meets floor, and wings or false prosceniums are used to mask the sides of the stage. Since most designers use wings sparingly, the masking of the wing areas is a real problem to the designer — the solution to which is often an even greater challenge to the crew. Masking the wings is a special problem associated with all exterior sets and now quite regularly with the musical play. Once again, a black cyclorama can help simplify the problems. Even a full sky cyc will close off the audience's view of the backstage areas. But a sky cyc may, in turn, make entrances and exits difficult.

Wagon sets are another means of executing scene changes. A set is placed on a wheeled platform, which can be rolled out on the stage. A type of wagon arrangement that often works quite well is the jackknife. The jackknife wagon, shown on page 426, is stored perpendicular to the curtain line on the side of the stage, usually behind the tormentor or false proscenium, and is pivoted out when needed. A second wall may be attached back-to-back to the wagon, making two sets possible for each wagon. Wagons require storage space in the wings, which may be lacking, but they are often the best solution when fly space is not available.

Some directors have complained that the elevation of the wagon destroys the illusion they desire and eliminates the use of the apron unless the actor steps down from the wagon. This problem may be corrected in one of two ways. First, you may treat the wagon as a natural elevation, like a hallway above a sunken living room, or as a porch, with the apron as the lawn. The second method takes more work, but the results are worth it. The apron floor is built up with platforms that are flush with the front edge of the wagon. The

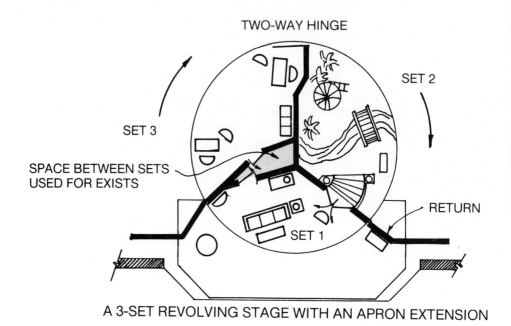

A 3-SET REVOLVING STAGE WITH AN APRON EXTENSION

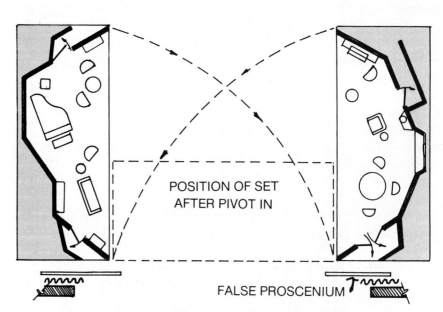

JACKKNIFE STAGING USING FALSE PROSCENIUM

TWO WAYS OF CHANGING COMPLETE SETS

apron is treated as an extension of the wagon set. Hinged returns may be added to the side walls of the set to frame the apron acting area.

A revolving stage may be used if you have the budget, equipment, time, and skill. As many as three sets may be placed on a revolving platform. However, revolving stages are expensive to build and take special mechanical equipment to rotate smoothly. It is possible to build stages that can be moved manually. If this is to be done, however, it would probably be simpler and certainly more economical to bolt wagons together to make a "revolving square." Such an arrangement allows four scenes to be placed on the platform. Of course, once a set is out of view of the audience, it can be redressed for a new setting.

On many stages, the counterweight systems have been replaced by electric winches. This has often caused more problems than it has solved. The winches are slow, and the number that can be operated at one time is often limited.

Special Set Pieces

Set pieces are scenery that may be carried or rolled on the stage, such as benches, lamp posts, rocks, and trees. Before designing and building set pieces, the scenic designer must decide how the unit will be used. Is it only for show or must it support weight or operate in some manner? Those pieces that operate, such as windows that will open, lamps that will light, or a tree that will support an actor sitting on a branch, are called practical or practical-usable. Because theater is illusion and time and expense are always to be considered, few set pieces are built to be practical unless the script requires it. Columns (shown below), rocks, and trees may be plastic, that is, three-dimensional, or simply two-dimensional cut-outs. Three-dimensional pieces allow for more light and shadow effects, but cut-outs may better convey a stylization and the feeling of illusion.

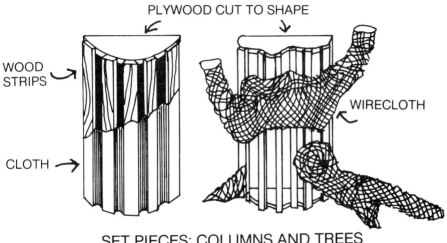

PLYWOOD CUT TO SHAPE

WOOD STRIPS

WIRECLOTH

CLOTH

SET PIECES: COLUMNS AND TREES

Styrofoam expands the repertory of materials that can be used to create three-dimensional props and scenery. It can be cut, carved, glued together, and painted to replicate many different textures.

• • • • • • • • • • • •

Special Materials

Plastics have many uses on the stage. Styrofoam can be cut or shaped and pressed. It can be made into fine bricks, molding, statues and ornate-appearing trim. Expandable plastics can be formed into rocks, or most anything for which a mold can be formed. Be sure you know the safety rules for handling plastics, that there is adequate ventilation, and that protective clothing and masks are worn.

Papier-mâché has long been a special effects material for the stage. Wheat paste or stage sizing and strips of newspaper or paper towels are all you need. For large projects, the papier-mâché is usually applied over formed chicken wire. Chicken wire and wire cloth are hard to shape and easily cut the hands. An easier material for many shapes such as rocks for a wall or fireplace is cardboard. A pattern can be drawn out on plywood. Next, the cardboard can be cut roughly to the shapes on the plywood. Slash the cardboard in a random zigzag fashion and nail one edge of the cardboard to the plywood using roofing nails. Then push the cardboard toward the nailed portion causing it to bulge. Tack down some depressions in the surface if you wish and then nail around the unnailed edges. When this process is completed, you may apply the papier-mâché. You will find that this procedure requires a thinner layer of papier-mâché and will dry faster than the chicken wire method.

Common Scenery Problems

One of the problems encountered on most stages is that of insufficient space, particularly if the stage is shallow or lacks wing space. Many plays and most musical plays call for several sets and many changes. Sometimes the stage may be extended out into the pit area or built out over the front center seats. A runway may be built out from the center or may enclose the pit and, at the same time, the orchestra. Acting areas can often be added to the sides of the apron with platforms. Inadequate fly space may force the use of *trip* drops — doubled up for storage — or the use of short drops that can be raised as high as possible and concealed with low-hung borders. It may even be necessary, as in arena staging, to make changes in full view of the audience. In some instances, the "invisible" stage hand may be your only recourse.

Your stage opening may be too large to make a standard set look its best. Many auditoriums have prosceniums as wide as 40 feet or more, yet most sets average 28 to 32 feet in width. You can sometimes lower the grand drape to change the height of the opening. You can add a false beam or ceiling to replace the first border. A false proscenium can decrease height and width, as can the teaser and tormentors.

Masking the side areas can be a serious problem in musical plays and exterior sets. Portals or drops with tabs similar to a false proscenium work reasonably well. Screens, wings, hanging banners, and backs of double-walled wagons may also work. Of course, a sky cyc can mask the wings quite well.

The acting surface in high school auditoriums often present difficulties, for stage and platform floors may be rough, slick, or noisy. A canvas floor cloth,

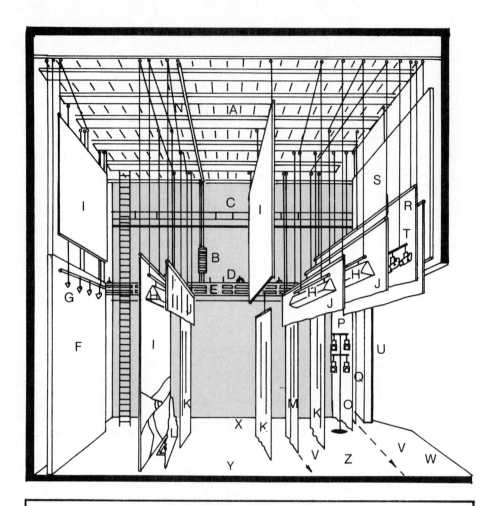

CUTAWAY OF A STAGE

A	Gridiron	N	Spare batten
B	Counterweight system	O	Tormentor
C	Weight floor	P	Tormentor "tree" or bommerang
D	Pin rail	Q	Act curtain
E	Fly deck (gallery)	R	Grand drape (valance)
F	Sky drop or cyc	S	Asbestos fire curtain
G	Cyclorama floods	T	Spotlight batten (bridge)
H	Border lights	U	Proscenium arch
I	Drop	V	Curtain line
J	Teaser (border curtain)	W	Apron
K	Leg	X	Wings
L	Ground row	Y	Acting Area
M	Traveler	Z	"In one"

especially one that is reversible — brown on one side and green on the other — covers the stage floor and replaces carpeting or "grass." Carpets are fine if they lie flat or can be tacked down. Carpets deaden sound and provide a realistic appearance to a room that otherwise may seem unnatural to the audience, who can see the stage floor. Even stairs, wagons, and parallels should be padded to lessen noise.

Stage Safety

The safety of actors, crew members, and the audience is always of great concern. Power equipment, stage weights, electric winch systems, paints, plastics, and protruding nails are but a few of the materials that may lead to physical injury.

Even safety devices themselves can be hazardous. The fire curtain should be checked on a regular basis to see that it is operating properly in conjunction with the fire doors. The deluge systems that are replacing the asbestos curtain have many problems in design and operation that often make them more of a threat than a safety feature. The emergency controls should not be situated so that they can be activated by accident. The shut-off crank must be accessible and never chained off. The water should not drain into the orchestra pit, but if it does, there should be several drains to carry off the water. The electric outlets in the pit should be at least a foot from the floor. Despite these

Appropriate scenery and set dressings should support the play, not overwhelm it. This Nickerson Theatre production of Hedda Gabler *is framed by correct period furnishings which add a rich element to the production.*

precautions, a pit-draining deluge system poses a real threat to musicians in the pit — with their electric cords that are attached to music-stand lights and musical instruments.

General Stage Safety Rules

1. Know the location and operation of all fire extinguishers and fire alarms.

2. Know what to do if sprinklers, the fire curtain, or deluge system were to set off.

3. When you hear "heads" move quickly out of the way.

4. When using a tool such as a wrench to adjust lights or tighten bolts, always tie the tool to a line attached to your belt so that it will not fall.

5. Be certain that weights are removed from the system as you remove weight from a batten.

6. If an imbalanced counterweighted line takes off, do not try to stop it by hand.

7. Always wear goggles when operating power equipment and floating flats.

8. Do not wear loose-fitting or fringed clothing or dangling jewelry when operating power equipment or when around gears or winches.

9. Always wear shoes, preferably safety shoes.

10. Remove all protruding nails in boards and keep nails swept up off the floor.

11. Be sure there is adequate ventilation when using materials that emit toxic fumes.

12. Know the number and wattage of instruments plugged into a circuit before turning it on.

13. Do not smoke backstage nor allow anyone else to.

14. Be alert and concerned about your safety and the safety of others.

Things to Remember

There are certain bits of information that come in handy to stage designers and crews. Among these are the common lumber measurements and nail sizes. These should be posted in the shop. Since muslin draws up when sized, the ends of drops should be tapered by cutting the fabric on a 1-foot diagonal from top to bottom on each end. Another method requires using *stretchers.* These are boards bolted to the top and bottom battens at the outer edge of the drop before sizing. The ends of the drops are stapled to the stretchers until all painting is completed. This will keep the drops from pulling and wrinkling. The stretches may be removed after the painting is finished.

It is not necessary to accept a set that shakes every time a door closes. Determine what bracing is needed and use it. Remember that standard dimensions apply to most common scenic props: chair seats are 16 inches from the floor; table and desk tops are 30 inches from the floor; chests are usually about 16 inches deep; stair treads are 10 or 12 inches deep with corresponding risers that are 6 to 7 inches high; finished door openings are 6 feet 8 inches high. Plywood comes in sheets 4' × 8' and may be $\frac{3}{16}$, $\frac{1}{4}$, $\frac{3}{8}$, $\frac{1}{4}$, $\frac{5}{8}$, or $\frac{3}{4}$ inch thick. Doorknobs and light switches also have standardized heights.

Use different levels, ramps, and stairs as much as possible for interest and variety. Stage doors normally open offstage-upstage except in mysteries when it is important that a character be concealed. Fireplaces are more usable on side walls than rear walls. Watch the location of mirrors so that they do not reflect lights or backstage areas into the audience's eyes.

Although most playbooks have a floor plan illustrated in the back, it is often foolish for schools to try to copy such a set. Most high schools do not have the time, budget, equipment, or space to build a Broadway set. The essential entrances, furniture, and props must be provided, but the creation of a scenic design should not be stifled by another designer's concept. If the audience spends much time looking at the set and not at the actors, it is a poor design no matter how elaborate or attractive it may seem. Researching for a play is part of the fun and part of the learning; the library is usually the designer's best friend.

A Summary Statement

The student of drama should recognize that scenery is an integral part of modern play production. However, scenic design has developed as a complement to the play itself and may lose its impact if looked upon as an end in itself. If scenery swallows up the performer, the costume, the makeup, or the acting; if the scenery is in poor taste or not aesthetically satisfying; if inappropriate sets cause the mood of the play to be lost; or if the set is a showpiece for a talented designer or exuberant art students — but does not serve the play — then the purposes and intent of the playwright and director become distorted and meaningless.

Good scenery should add to and never detract from the overall merit of a production. Much of the scenery found in high school productions is inex-

cusably poor and ineffective. A little imagination, some inexpensive materials and equipment, and the enthusiasm and talents of high school students can easily bring to the audience a setting that enhances the total production by making it an "everything-seemed-to-go-together" performance.

In order to accomplish this goal, high school directors, designers, and production committees should work together to carefully select scenic elements, emphasizing those they wish to convey to the audience and minimizing or eliminating those that would not make a positive contribution to the play. It is often the frequently overlooked little things that may make a realistic set look complete — the right number and kind of pictures on the wall; the knick-knacks on the shelf; the flowers in the vases about the room; the choice of carpets, drapes, lamps, and furnishings; a flickering fire in the hearth; the shadow lines and texturing on the walls.

Conversely, it is usually the smallest number of elements with the greatest impact of identification and meaning that make a nonrealistic set the most satisfying — a lonely, twisted cedar makes one think of barren wastes; three lofty, graceful poplars may suggest an Italian formal garden; six towering pines may take the audience into the heart of the Black Forest; the knothole eyes and mouths of frightening Tree-Monsters may make us want to run from the magical forest of Oz.

Selectivity, simplicity, and consistency are the guide words of the stage designer. In addition, sets should be planned so that they may be set up and struck rapidly, carried easily, and packed away efficiently. Naturally they should be built firmly enough to stand steadily. They also should allow the actors to move easily and safely and to be seen effectively.

Recalling Ideas

1. Why should students of drama study stagecraft?

2. What is the purpose of scenery? In what four areas does the scenic designer work?

3. Describe the stage of Renaissance Italy. When and why did the box set develop? For what kind of sets is David Belasco known?

4. Describe each of the following: box set, unit set, prism set, drapery set.

5. Tell five things the designer must know before designing a set.

6. What are four artistic considerations in building a set?

7. Describe two major differences between warm and cool colors.

8. What is the best fabric for flats? What is the next best choice?

9. Name three methods of texturing a flat.

10. What are three common scenery problems?

11. List six rules for backstage safety.

Discussing Ideas

1. How does the saying "use the least to say the most" apply to stagecraft?

2. How can a set design hamper or even ruin a play?

3. After watching a play, analyze the work of the set designer. How many sets were there? What type were they? What colors dominated? Were there any set pieces? Did the actors seem at home on the set? What did the set contribute or take away from the play?

4. Describe a realistic set for the balcony scene of *Romeo and Juliet*. Describe a symbolic set for the same scene.

5. Visit the stage area of your school. Discuss the problems a set designer would have in mounting a 3-act musical with 4 set changes and a cast of over 25.

Careers

Scenic designers, also known as **set designers,** design and may supervise the construction of movie, television, and theater sets. They study scripts, confer with the **director** and **technical director,** and conduct research to determine the proper architectural styles. For musicals, they also work closely with the **choreographer** and **musical director** in the planning stage. They make preliminary sketches of sets, draw them in perspective and color, and get the director's approval. They make floor plans and sometimes 3-D scale models of the sets, as well working drawings that show how each set will be built.

Scenic directors oversee the construction, painting, and installation of sets. They may hire a **construction head** to supervise the **painters, carpenters,** and other members of the **construction crew.** When selecting paint colors, they work closely with the **lighting director** to create proper moods.

During construction, scenic designers set up work schedules for construction crews. They have to coordinate that schedule with rehearsals that take place on the stage and be sure the sets are ready by the first technical rehearsal. They order all supplies, keep records of expenditures, check all tools, and supervise the clean-up after each work session. Most set designers have a 2- or 4-year education from a college whose drama department offers courses in theater production, or a professional school.

Property Masters and their teams collect, repair, and store for future productions hand props such as guns, flags, and swords, and set props such as couches, chairs, and tables. They may also design and build props. Many property masters have degrees or specialized training in theater production. Most have had previous experience working behind-the-scenes as a stagehand or crew member.

Chapter 13

Lighting

You Will Learn

About the special effects lighting can produce.

About basic lighting equipment.

How to prepare a lighting plan.

How to prepare a lighting cue sheet.

How to draw a light plot.

Vocabulary

light panel   dimming up   dimming down

*S*tage lighting is the most rapidly expanding phase of scenic art. It is taking the place of paint in many productions because white backgrounds can be instantly transformed by lighting in response to changes in mood, action, and location. In musical plays especially, dream sequences, dances, and tableaux are set apart by imaginatively designed lighting.

There is no more intriguing phase of play production than working out truly effective lighting for different scenes, whether you have the simplest or the most sophisticated equipment.

The area of action on this multi-level set for Death of a Salesman *is highlighted by controlled area lighting.*

Stage Lighting Effects

Suppose, as the curtain opens, we look in on an antiquated English manor house. The room is dark except for a flickering glow from the fireplace. A dim figure appears in the archway, silhouetted against the diffused light of the entrance hall. The room instantly comes to life as the young woman presses the wall switch and the chandelier and the two sconces over the fireplace illuminate the right half of the stage. She presses another switch, and the lamp by the chair at stage left brightens the rest of the room. The actress swiftly crosses upstage to the high window and pulls the drapery cord. Immediately, the stage is flooded by bright sunlight reflected off the snow-covered terrain outside. She crosses down right to the fireplace and places two more logs on the dying fire. As she stirs up the coals, a reddish glow warms her young face. She turns, takes two steps toward the table, center, looks at her watch, and utters the first line of the play: "I *do* wish Martin would hurry. It's been nearly three hours since he called."

The audience probably did not notice that, after the initial flash broke the darkness, the room continued to brighten. It is unlikely, too, that they noticed that the "sunlight" dimmed slightly after the first rays struck the heroine's face. Nor would we expect the viewers to question whether the fire glowed as brightly after she turned toward the middle of the room to deliver her first line. And, most assuredly, the audience never asked: "I wonder what lighting equipment was used for that effect?" The audience accepts the illusion created by modern stage lighting.

In the days of tribal ritual and primitive dance, the only lighting available was the natural light of the sun or moon and the artificial light provided by the campfire and torch. For hundreds of years, plays were performed almost exclusively in the daytime out-of-doors or in buildings open to the sky. The use of many candles and torches eventually made it possible to present plays in a completely enclosed structure. But it was not until gaslight replaced candles in 1803 that artificial light aroused much interest. By the 1820s, Thomas Drummond, an Englishman, had developed one of the earliest spotlights, an oxyhydrogen flame directed against a piece of lime. Actors soon learned how to play in the "limelight."

However, with the greater use of artificial lighting came the increased danger of fire. The history of theater has been blackened by the ashen shells of once active playhouses. By the end of the nineteenth century, electricity had revolutionized the lighting of the home and the stage. Today we present well-lighted plays that may, with proper equipment, be preset and computerized.

All students of drama — actors, directors, and crew — should understand the basic principles of light, its peculiarities, qualities, and effects on actor, audience, costumes, makeup, and pigments.

Lighting Terminology

amperage: The strength of an electric current flowing through a wire.

arc or *carbon arc spotlight*: A very powerful spotlight with carbon rods as electrical conductors, used primarily as a long-distance follow spot.

backlighting: The use of light and instruments above and behind performers to accent them and set them apart from the background.

barn doors: A metal frame with 2 or 4 flaps for shaping the light pattern that fits into a gel holder.

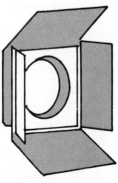

BARN DOORS

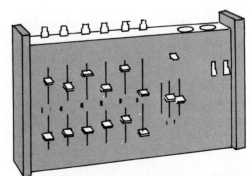

2 SCENE PRESET DIMMER CONTROLLER

boomerang (tree, boom): A polelike stand having horizontal arms (pipes) for hanging lighting instruments. A boomerang is usually located just upstage of the proscenium or tormentor.

border light or *borders*: A type of striplight hung from pipe battens above the stage.

breaker: An electrical device that cuts off the electric current when a circuit is overloaded. It may be reset once the problem is corrected.

bridge (x-ray): The first electrical pipe just upstage of the proscenium from which spotlights may be hung.

bump up: A quick increase in light intensity.

cable: Heavily insulated wire for joining instruments to electrical outlets or to a switchboard.

circuit: The complete path of an electrical current.

color frames: Metal holders that fit into a lighting instrument to keep a color filter in place.

connectors: Devices for joining cables to each other or for joining cables to instruments.

crossfade: The dimming of one set of instruments as another set comes up.

dimmer: An electrical device that controls the amount of current flowing into a lighting instrument, thus increasing or decreasing the intensity of the light.

ellipsoidal reflector spotlight: A highly efficient lighting instrument with a reflector shaped like an ellipsoid.

fill: The light that fills shadows aimed opposite a key light.

floodlight or *flood*: A high wattage (500 to 1,500 watts) lighting instrument with a metal shell open at one end, the inner surface of which is painted white, is polished metal, or has a mirror to reflect the nonfocused light.

floor pocket: A receptacle for stage plugs mounted in the floor.

follow spot: A long-range high-wattage (1,000 to 2,600 watts) lighting instrument capable of picking up or following a person moving on the stage, with a beam strong enough to stand out against normal stage lighting. These instruments may be either the zenon, carbon arc, quartz, or incandescent types.

footlights or *foots*: Striplights along the front of the apron that throw light up and back toward the acting area.

fresnel spot: A spotlight featuring a fresnel or stepped lens, which projects a clear, strong light with a soft edge.

funnel (top hat, high hat, snoot): A metal cylinder that can be placed in a gel holder to control the spread of light.

fuse: A protective device set in an electric current and destroyed by the passage of excessive current.

gelatin and *glass roundels*: Transparent color media placed on lighting instruments to produce different colors.

gobo: A cut-out placed in the gel holder of a spotlight to project a pattern.

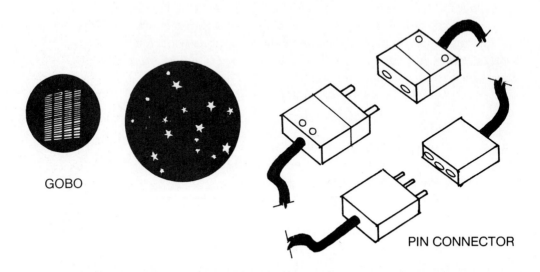

GOBO

PIN CONNECTOR

intensity: The brightness of light.

iris: A shutter device used to change the diameter of a beam of light.

key light: The strong source of light aimed at an acting area.

kill: Command to turn a light off.

light cue sheet: The lighting technician's guide for all dimmer readings and settings at act or scene openings and all lighting changes.

light plot: Diagram showing the placing of the instruments and plugging system and where the beams from all the instruments fall. See page 455.

linnebach projector: A lantern for projecting images from a slide onto a backdrop from the rear of the backdrop.

load: The wattage of lights and electrical pieces of equipment supplied by one circuit; an overload will burn out a fuse or trip a breaker.

pin connector or *slip pin connector*: A special stage connector used for joining cables or instruments.

preset dimmer: A type of dimmer board that allows two or more lighting patterns to be set in advance.

proportional dimming: A feature of many lightboards that allows several instruments to dim simultaneously at different intensities.

sidelighting: The placing of instruments behind the tormentor position for facial modeling and costume accent.

silicon-controlled rectifier (SCR): An electrical device that controls power flow; used in most modern dimmers.

splash (spill): Light that strikes outside the intended area — as on the grand drape, proscenium, or upper walls.

spotlight or *spot*: A metal-encased lighting instrument that can be focused, having a lens and a mirror that gives out a concentrated light and can be directed specifically. It is used to light acting areas. In wattage, it varies from 250 to 1,500.

stage plug: A special male connector consisting of a wood or fiber body and broad copper contact. Its use is declining.

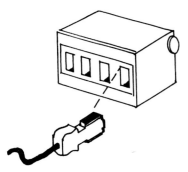

STAGE PLUG   TWIST LOCK CONNECTORS

striplights or *strips*: Lamps arranged in metal troughs, usually with three or four circuits.

switchboard: The panel that holds the dimmers, switches, and fuses. Ideally, all stage circuits are united in this one board so that they may be controlled at one location. A board may have any number of circuits and/or dimmers. A portable switchboard is often the most satisfactory type for a school theater.

throw: The distance from a lighting instrument to the area to be lit.

tower: A platform on which lights may be hung.

tungsten-halogen (T-H): A type of lamp now used in spotlights, floodlights, and follow spots.

twist lock connector: A type of stage connector that will not pull apart when inserted and twisted.

wash: A low-level fill light usually aimed from the balcony rails.

wash out: The drain (absorption) of color by light, leaving the actor, costume, or scenery lifeless.

wattage: The measurement of electric power. All lighting instruments, lamps, dimmers, and fuses are given wattage ratings to denote their electrical capacities.

Necessary Equipment

The ideal lighting equipment for the school stage is flexible, efficient, and economical. Of these, flexibility is the most important consideration. Flexibility is determined by (1) mobility: how easily you may move the instrument about the auditorium according to the needs of various productions; (2) control — how easily you may control the amount of light, usually by a dimmer panel; and (3) multiple service — how many different areas the instrument can light. The versatile spotlight meets these three needs most effectively and provides the best control of light distribution.

When determining the lighting equipment needed, you must consider the availability and number of dimmers, the size of the stage (especially the depth of the acting area as well as of the apron), the height of the theater ceiling or the distance to the balcony rail, the availability of mounting locations, and, of course, the budget. However, every high school should try to have the following minimum equipment.

The **light panel** is the first equipment of importance. Its dimmer board allows the operator to choose which dimmer will control the brightness of the light of any given instrument. One of the common types suitable for the high school stage has plugs, connected to each outlet or instrument in the auditorium, that may be inserted into a "patchboard," much like a telephone switchboard.

Despite all the technical advances, the stage cable and connectors are most important to the safe conduction of electricity. The danger of overloads, shorts, and fires is very great on the stage, and proper means of completing an electrical circuit are often overlooked.

Common lighting instruments are as follows:

1. Ellipsoidal reflector spotlight of 500 to 1,000 watts, which provides the most important lighting. (These spotlights are mounted in the ceiling or on balcony rails, behind the tormentor and on the first and second electric battens.) For front lighting, these instruments normally operate in pairs, each pair lighting an area approximately 8 to 10 feet in diameter, six are needed for the normal set opening of 28 to 32 feet. But stages having 40-foot prosceniums should have eight ellipsoidals if the entire width is to be illuminated. For washes, sidelighting, and backlighting, at least ten–twelve more are needed.

2. Fresnels — On a pipe just behind the grand drape a minimum of fourteen 500-watt fresnels should be located.

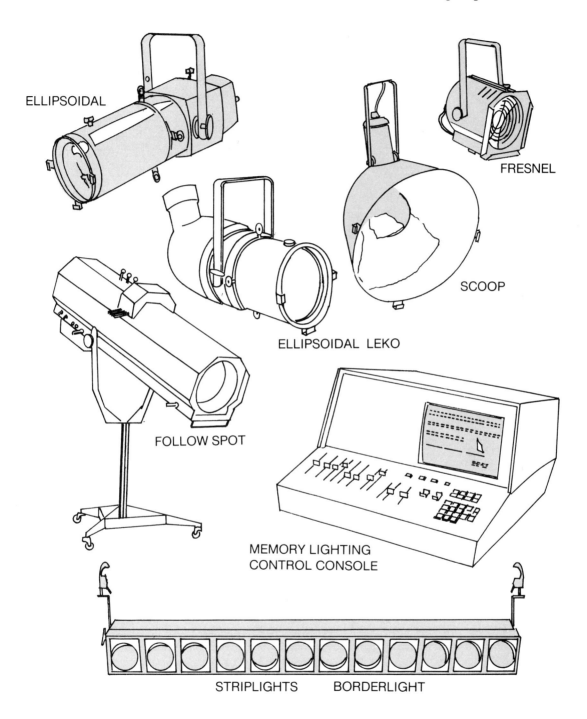

ELLIPSOIDAL

FRESNEL

SCOOP

ELLIPSOIDAL LEKO

FOLLOW SPOT

MEMORY LIGHTING
CONTROL CONSOLE

STRIPLIGHTS   BORDERLIGHT

3. Floodlights — Every stage needs at least four floodlights for special effects, such as sunlight and moonlight. If a cyclorama is to be lighted, more floods may be necessary. Some stage aprons are efficiently lighted by a special flood called a beam projector. Four beam lights are normally sufficient to cover the apron.

4. Border lights — Three to four 3-circuit border lights are necessary for general stage use and for scenic color blending.

5. Follow spot — At least one follow spot is essential for every stage, although its use is rather limited in play production.

6. Portable striplights — These are preferable to permanently mounted footlights. These may be used as footlights, backing or entrance lighting, or cyclorama lighting. Again, three circuits are necessary.

Other desirable equipment includes additional ellipsoidal reflectors for mounting on the side walls of the auditorium; additional fresnels for the first batten, including two 3-inch fresnels; the previously mentioned beam lights; a second follow spot; possibly black light units and special effects projectors. (These special effects instruments create the illusions of clouds, rain, flames, buildings, and scenic backgrounds but are quite expensive.)

Also needed are pipe clamps for hanging the instruments, color frames for each spotlight and flood, and color media (roundels for striplights; gelatin for the spots and floods). The best colors for the roundels in the borders and footlights are red, blue, and green because a combination of these three colors will make all the colors in the spectrum. Amber is sometimes substituted for the green, and this choice is wise if the light panel is one of toggle switches rather than dimmers or if a stronger overhead light is desired. However, the only way to produce green light is by using green color media. The delicate colors are the most preferred gelatins in use today. No-color pink, flesh pink, straws, ambers — especially bastard amber, a light scarlet — are some of the warm colors used. And special lavender, surprise pink, no-color blue, medium and daylight blue are some of the best cool color gelatins. Sometimes designers use frost and chocolate for special effects. Green-blue makes a better night scene than blues or violets. Many lighting designers prefer white light from an ungelled instrument as a cool light source.

You will find that new types of lighting equipment constantly appear. One of the most revolutionary is the tungsten-halogen equipment, which is expensive to purchase but more than pays for itself by providing a more efficient light at far less cost than incandescent bulbs. A 500-watt tungsten-halogen lamp will give 10 to 20 percent more light output than an incandescent lamp, and the T-H bulb will last four times as long as the conventional bulb. The T-H bulbs run very hot and require new types of gels that will not fade or warp.

The T-H lamp will crack or bulge if exposed to perspiration from fingers. Therefore, the lamps must be carefully installed with the protective covers in place. If the lamp is later removed, it should be cleaned with alcohol.

Basic Lighting Principles

Without a doubt, lighting is the most important element in scenic design, for it affects the creation of mood and atmosphere. The exuberant nature of a musical is enhanced by the gaiety of a brightly illuminated stage. A mystery takes on a spine-tingling quality when the high walls and deep recesses of a deserted mansion are lost in the depths of shadows. An eerie fog, an iridescent liquid in a witch's cauldron, the ghostly whiteness of full moon, the aura of intrigue and death in the shadowy alleys of counterespionage — you can create each of these on stage by the right distribution and brightness of light from carefully selected instruments. This is effective stage lighting.

Stage lighting is based on three qualities of light: intensity, or brightness; distribution, or area covered; and color. The most effective lighting considers the natural light sources on the set — the sun or moon, a streetlight, lamps, fireplaces, televisions, candles, lanterns. To avoid a pasteboard-figure effect, designers usually pair spotlights. One uses warm colors, and comes from the same side of the stage as the sources of natural light. The other comes from the opposite direction, the direction of diffused or reflected light and uses cool colors. Each spotlight is aimed in and down at a 45° angle toward the area to be lighted (see drawing on page 446). This results in the most dramatic effect of highlight and shadow. Designers usually avoid straight-on lighting from centrally located instruments because it serves as a general wash. A *wash* eliminates shadows and brings a strength of light to the central acting area. Spotlights used for the wash are best located on the balcony or on the sides of the auditorium aimed diagonally across the stage.

The most important acting areas need the most light. Bringing a greater quantity of light into a given acting area makes the actor playing in that area stand out. In any lighting plan, there is always *key light*, the strongest light aimed at each acting area, and *fill light*, light that fills in the shadows. *Side-lighting* from upstage of the tormentor, using different color than the front lighting can help model the actor's features and accent costumes. It also adds a touch of "life" to musicals. *Backlighting* comes from above and behind the actor and sets the performer off from the background. The technical director and the stage electricians may help shift the focus of attention back and forth by the smooth flow of light from one actor or area to another throughout the play.

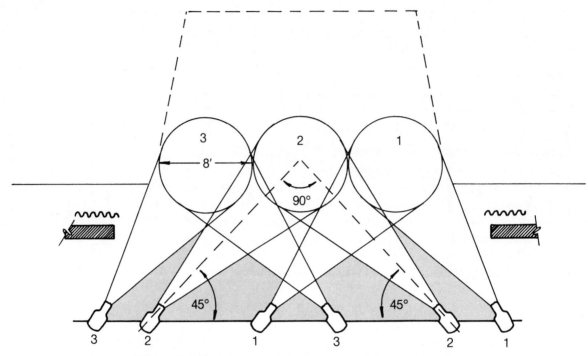

DIAGRAM OF A GENERAL LIGHTING PLAN FOR DOWNSTAGE AREAS

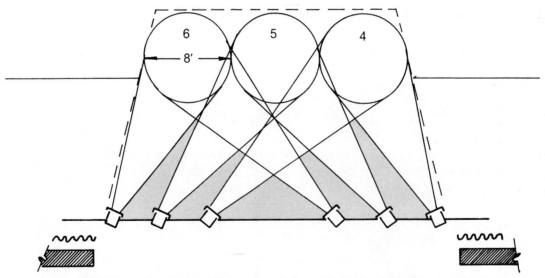

DIAGRAM OF A GENERAL LIGHTING PLAN FOR UPSTAGE AREAS

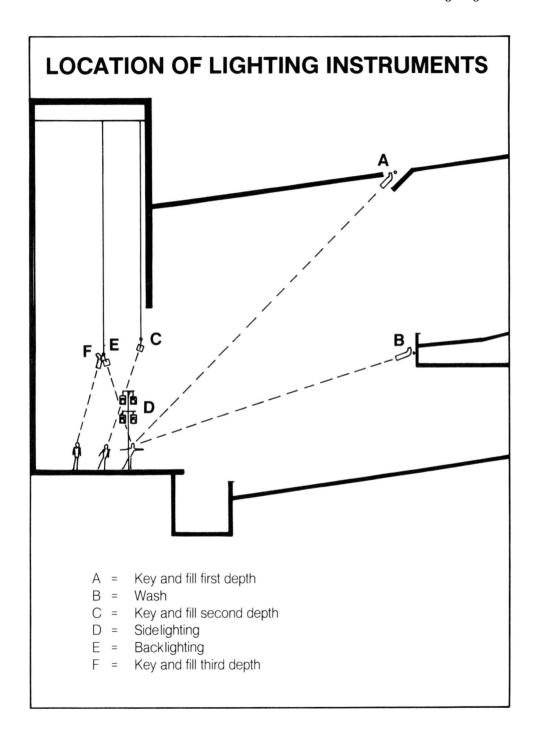

LOCATION OF LIGHTING INSTRUMENTS

A = Key and fill first depth
B = Wash
C = Key and fill second depth
D = Sidelighting
E = Backlighting
F = Key and fill third depth

As a general rule, tragedies and serious dramas emphasize cool colors, and comedies stress warm colors. However, the lighting designer should never allow actors to be lost in unintentional pockets of dark shadows. Nor should the lighting designer try to eliminate all shadows by generalized bright light. This results in one huge flat glow of light, which is the most common lighting error of the high school stage. This problem stems from the incorrect notion that lighting a set means turning all border and footlights on full. This garish amber-white light makes actors "dead" on the stage or makes them "disappear" into the set. Many of the most successful designers today use only spotlights and floods. Others add borders and foots for blending only. In any case, strong lights should be kept off the walls of a set. Most designers suggest keeping the upper walls in shadow.

Most lighting changes should happen gradually by **dimming up** or **dimming down.** Lights rarely pop on or off except when a light switch is flipped onstage. Even then, not all instruments come on at once. With a scene, lights normally change with a crossfade — some lights coming up at the same time others are dimming down. The audience should not consciously notice that a change is taking place. This means that the technicians must begin light changes far in advance in order to accomplish them smoothly.

A dramatic use of backlighting helps create a mysterious atmosphere in the Agatha Christie melodrama The Unexpected Guest, *presented by the Hartman Theater Company of Stamford, Connecticut.*

There are some general considerations to remember when working with stage lights. Brightly lighted scenes, especially of the type frequently found in musical plays, can cause changes in makeup and costumes. Strong amber can turn colorful fabrics into a drab brown; a strong red may wash the rouge out of the faces.

Night scenes are always difficult to light without having costumes and makeup turn black under a bluish light. When lighting scenes are to be played in the "dark," it is always best to have some light even if no attempt is made to represent natural light sources. An unlighted stage is dead. Figures outlined against a moonlit window, a shaft of light through a window or skylight, a crack of light from under a door, or the glow of an old-fashioned streetlight may provide a realistic source for the stage light. However, if no other choice is left, a beam or two of colored light that is there solely for the reason that the actors must be seen may meet the requirements for light. The audience should never be left completely in the dark for more than a few seconds.

The effect of light on color is difficult to predict accurately because of the relationship between light and pigments and dyes, but there are some generalizations that may be made:

red light on red	=	red
red light on blue	=	violet
red light on green	=	gray
red light on yellow	=	orange
red light on purple	=	red
blue light on red	=	violet-black

In the Yale Repertory production of August Strindberg's The Ghost Sonata, *the combined use of scrims and lighting create a ghostly, dreamlike scene.*
· · · · · · · · · · · ·

blue light on blue	=	blue
blue light on green	=	green
blue light on yellow	=	green
blue light on orange	=	brown
amber light on red	=	brown
amber light on blue	=	greenish-orange
amber light on green	=	greenish-orange
amber light on violet	=	red
green light on red	=	black
green light on green	=	green
yellow light on blue	=	blue-green
yellow light on green	=	green
yellow light on violet	=	brown

Curtains, costumes, and furnishings are affected by light. Smooth, shiny fabrics reveal light and shadows. Heavy, coarse materials, no matter how inexpensive, absorb much light and often appear quite expensive to the audience; outing flannel may look like expensive velour. The important consideration is the brilliance of the color of the material and the color of the stage lighting for the scene in which the material is to be used. Patterns and prints cause many problems, as do several colors in the same costume. Lighting of period plays is always difficult, for the mixture of lace, silk, velvet, wigs, and makeup is a technician's nightmare.

Special Lighting Effects

Lighting is probably the designer's most versatile source of special effects, accomplishing such feats as pinpointing a face in a crowd, changing the stage into a blazing inferno, "suspending animation" (as in the Soho Square scene of *My Fair Lady*), or creating the illusion of a silent movie by the use of a flicker wheel or strobe.

One of the most striking scenic-lighting combinations is that of using a scrim, or gauze drop. Lighting a scrim from the front makes it nearly opaque, and lighting it from behind makes it semitransparent. Scrims, properly lighted,

Lighting affects the creation of mood and atmosphere. The exuberant nature of a bouncy musical, such as the Broadway production 42nd Street, *is emphasized by a brightly illuminated stage.*
● ● ● ● ● ● ● ● ● ● ● ●

may help create fog, mist, and dream scenes. Actors and cut-out scenery may be silhouetted against the scrim by backlighting. In the Broadway presentation of *The Sound of Music,* the designer elected to represent the Austrian Alps by an outline silhouette of mountains and trees. Maria was nearly imperceptible as she reclined on a cut-out limb. Then both she and the lighting came to life with the song "The Sound of Music."

Painting or dyeing a scrim makes an impressive traverse curtain, which provides a fine background for short scenes, especially in musical plays. Such a painted scrim can also create the illusion of "passing through." In *The Music Man,* for example, a scrim might be painted to represent the outside of the Madison Public Library. With front lighting, the scrim looks like any ordinary drop, but when the lights come up in the library (behind the scrim), the watchers feel as if they have passed directly through the library's walls.

One of the more unusual effects possible with light uses what is normally considered a negative effect of light. A standard makeup is applied, over which makeup using colors washed out under the normal stage light is placed. Makeup the same color as the lights has a tendency to disappear. By changing the dominant lighting colors or by having the character move into the beam of a special spot, the actor may suddenly assume the mask of Death, the features of Satan, or the ugliness of a Mr. Hyde as the "invisible" makeup is seen.

When considering unique special effects, few techniques match the possibilities for the unusual that can be attained by the use of black light. Many new colors of luminous paint, paper, and fabrics have been developed, which have increased the flexibility and variety of black light (invisible ultraviolet or infrared lighting) uses.

Planning the Lighting

Just as soon as the director and crew have worked out the needs for costumes, makeup, scenery, and furnishings, it is time to begin work on the lighting. Using the information provided by the director and the scenic designer, the lighting technician works out the light plot and the lighting cue sheet (see pages 455 and 456). The light plot shows the location of each lighting instrument and the area or object each illuminates. Almost all important acting areas need paired spotlights. However, some locations, such as doorways and windows, may be adequately lighted by one spot.

Once the light plot is prepared, the lighting technician can work out the cue sheet. The light plot indicates how the light board is to be set up for each scene. The cue sheet shows what changes are to take place; which controls,

(ABOVE) *The* Talley's Folly *set—early evening. The dominant blue and soft greens convey a calm and spiritual atmosphere, while the browns project an earthy quality. At the start of the play, Matt is trying to woo Sally Talley, who remains aloof to him.* (BELOW) *As Matt begins to win Sally over, the atmosphere of the play changes to romantic fancy, and the lighting changes from cool blue to warm pink.*

The formal staging of this grouping is emphasized by the stark lighting.

The most appropriate lighting is often the most subtle. The audience needs to see the actors in a non-tiring light—not too dim to be frustrating nor too bright to be glaring. The lighting in Beckett's End Game *molds the acting area and complements the set.*

Lighting design should take into account not only the season and weather but, just as important, the time of day. In Mamet's The Woods, *the action takes place on an outdoor porch. Thus the impressionistic design implies natural light as the prime light source.*

The Crucifer of Blood *(a Sherlock Holmes mystery) by Paul Giovanni used striking special lighting effects to pull the audience into the supernatural atmosphere of the play.* UPPER LEFT: *The scene is Pondicherry Lodge late at night. Light streaming through the latticed window creates an eerie mood.* UPPER RIGHT: *The scene is the River Thames. A smoke machine and overhead lighting create the dense fog expected on the Thames late at night.* BOTTOM: *Light radiating upward casts a golden glow, making the actors stand out in the darkness.*

Beverly Emmons's lighting plays a dramatic role in the production of Amadeus.

LIGHTING PLAN FOR: "ONCE IN A LIFETIME"

FUNCTION	INSTRUMENT NUMBER	INSTRUMENT TYPE	LOCATION	LOAD WATTS	COLOR	DIMMER WATTS	NOTES
AREA 1 KEY	1	8" ELLIPSOIDAL	BEAM-L	750	34		FRAME OFF RETURN
AREA 2 KEY	2	"	BEAM-L	750	34		
AREA 3 KEY	3	"	BEAM-L	750	34		
AREA 1 FILL	4	"	BEAM-R	750	54		
AREA 2 FILL	5	"	BEAM-R	750	54		
AREA 3 FILL	6	"	BEAM-R	750	54		FRAME OFF RETURN
L. CENTER WASH	7	"	BALCONY R	1000	33		
R. CENTER WASH	8	"	BALCONY R	1000	33		
L. CENTER WASH	9	"	BALCONY L	1000	60		
R. CENTER WASH	10	"	BALCONY L	1000	60		
AREA 4 KEY	11	6" FRESNEL	1ST ELEC L	500	33		
AREA 5 KEY	12	"	1ST ELEC L	500	33		
AREA 6 KEY	13	"	1ST ELEC LC	500	33		
AREA 4 FILL	14	"	1ST ELEC RC	500	54		FRAME TO ENTRANCE
AREA 5 FILL	15	"	1ST ELEC R	500	54		
AREA 6 FILL	16	"	1ST ELEC R	500	54		
LEFT BACKLIGHT	17	6" ELLIPSOIDAL	2ND ELEC LC	500	33		
RIGHT BACKLIGHT	18	"	2ND ELEC RC	500	33		
STAIRCASE SPECIAL	19	"	BOOM VL	500	08		AT TOP OF BOOM
FOYER SPECIAL	20	"	BOOM UR	500	08		AT TOP OF BOOM
FIREPLACE SPECIAL	21	ROLL LOG	FIREPLACE	200	14		
SL. EXIT SPECIAL	22	6" ELLIPSOIDAL	1ST ELEC L	500	12		
SR. EXIT SPECIAL	23	"	1ST ELEC R	500	06		

Lighting Plan

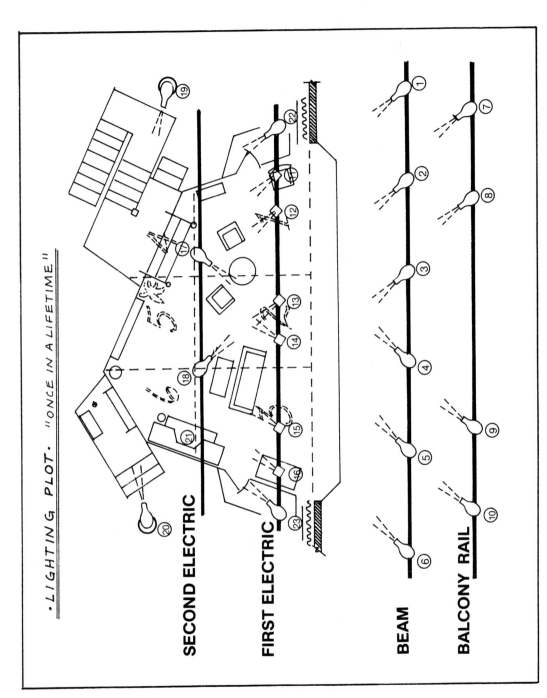

Lighting Plot

which instruments, what setting to use; and the length of time each change is to take. These are listed chronologically as they appear in the play, including warning cues, execution cues, and timing cues, that is, how to count the time during a change. The matter of timing is of great importance. One of the disadvantages of some electronic systems is that they are on timed settings, and if the production gets off schedule, the lighting cues do not synchronize and the lighting technician must override the system.

Lighting may be preplanned, but since the effects of light on any particular surface or color are unpredictable, the only way to properly light a production is to try out things under the lights.

LIGHTING CUE SHEET FOR:

CUE NO.	PAGE	CONTROL NO.	AREA	START CUE	RDG.	COMPLETE CUE	RDG.
1	3	$M_1 M_2 M_3$	1,2,3	FOGHORN	0	BOATSWAIN'S WHISTLE	8
2	3	12,14	6,8	FRANK: "DO YOU THINK..."	0	PHIL: "I DON'T BELIEVE IT"	10
3	5	$M_1 M_2 M_3$ 12,14	1,2,3 6,8,	SCREAM (KILL)	8 10	(IMMEDIATE BLACKOUT)	0
4	8	$M_1 M_2 M_3$ $M_4 M_5$	1,2,3 4,5	CAR COMING UP DRIVE	0	CAR STOP	10

All lighting cues need to be worked out in rehearsals, although it saves the time and the patience of the director and cast if most preliminary run-throughs and experimentations can be done in technical rehearsals held apart from the cast rehearsals.

The lighting technicians need to see that all equipment is in working order, that cables are not laid where they may be tripped over, and that exposed cables are taped down. Square knots or twist lock connectors should secure each connection, faded gels must be replaced, and any instruments that might have been accidentally moved by actors or crew during scene shifts have to be realigned. The lighting crew needs to be alert to the dangers of reflective surfaces — mirrors, highly polished furniture, glass-fronted cabinets, sequins, jewels, or anything else that might throw a blinding light into the eyes of the audience or reveal backstage areas.

There are three problems common to schools and little theater groups that should be discussed. The first concerns the matter of cues. The ideal location for the light panel is in a booth at the rear of the auditorium where the technician may watch the action on the stage and see the lighting effects as the audience sees them. However, most stages have the light panel at floor level or on an elevated platform stage right. Frequently the technician cannot see the actors and must depend on verbal cues, signals from other crew members in the wings or booth, or count cues.

There are two ways to avoid the embarrassment of an actor standing with a hand on a light switch for five seconds waiting for the lights to change. One solution, of course, is to wire the onstage lights directly to the power source so that they really work, as in a home. A second solution is to wire an onstage switch to a pilot or cue light located on the wall directly behind the switch or, better still, by the light panel itself. When a switch is thrown, the pilot operates just as the onstage lights do. The fraction of a second delay for the crew's reaction is imperceptible to the audience.

The second problem is more difficult to solve — that of the school having no dimmers or having the available dimmer linked directly to border or footlights only. An imaginative designer can devise various tricks to get the necessary lights on by flipping toggle switches, but, after a short time, the uniqueness of these tricks will wear off, and the designer must return to "lights on, lights off." Homemade dimmers can be used, but a couple of small auto transformers would probably be the best low-cost investment. Several lights can be wired in a bypass system that uses the same dimmer. Unfortunately, good lighting effects demand a flexible dimmer panel, and makeshift substitutes are only substitutes.

The third common problem faced by many schools and community theater groups is the limitations of a low budget. However, small spotlights and floods are not too expensive, even for small schools, and their purchase makes fine money-raising projects for drama clubs, parents' groups, or class gifts. Still, some fine effects can be achieved by imaginative use of 150-watt PARs or reflector floods, which call for a very nominal cash outlay. It has been so widely acknowledged that good lighting is essential to modern theater that a series of good productions may soon pay for a large portion of the cost of new equipment merely from increased ticket sales.

Recalling Ideas

1. What is the most versatile and easily controlled lighting instrument?

2. Describe the following lighting instruments: fresnels, floodlights, border lights.

3. What are the differences among key light, fill light, sidelight, and backlight?

4. What is the most common error in the lighting of high school plays?

5. Describe three lighting problems common to school and little theater groups.

Discussing Ideas

1. If you were given a single figure in a simple white costume standing against a white background on a fairly small stage, discuss how you could use lighting to create the following atmospheres: (a) supernatural — the figure is an angel or a benign alien; (b) eerie — the figure is evil, a murderer, perhaps; (c) circus — the figure is a happy clown; (d) serene beauty — the figure is of great and delicate beauty.

2. Why do people working on costumes, makeup, set painting, and other aspects of a production need to communicate with the lighting crew? What problems can last minute changes in set or costumes cause for the lighting?

3. Arrange a demonstration of the effect of different-colored lights on fabrics of different colors and textures.

4. Design the light plot for a play having an interior set, keeping in mind natural light sources (sunlight, lamps, fireplaces, etc.).

5. Use lighting as the basis for a set design to suggest depth, time changes, or acting planes.

6. Request catalogs from lighting companies. Discuss the advantages and disadvantages of three new lighting instruments.

Careers

Lighting designers analyze a play to determine its lighting needs. Lighting can be (1) specific illumination, (2) general illumination, or (3) special effects.

Specific illumination uses spotlights to light limited areas of the stage. General illumination uses striplights, footlights, and borderlights to light whole sets and backgrounds. It also blends light from brightly lighted acting areas to less brightly lighted backgrounds. Special effects use colored lights to create moonlight, sunlight, and firelight. They are also used for lightning. With the use of rotating disks or projectors, **lighting technicians** give the impression of movement, such as clouds blowing across a sky.

Lighting designers can create different light intensities in various parts of the same set. They can change the overall intensity of light to create sunrises and sunsets. They can give the impression of light coming from a single source, such as a lamp or moonlight coming through a window.

Because light helps establish mood, lighting designers work closely with the **scenic designer** and **technical director.** They make lighting plots on a floor plan to show how the stage and sets will look when lighted. They make a separate plot for each set and one plot for all the sets at the same time. They make out an instrument schedule that gives complete technical information about lighting needs. Lighting plans must be approved by the **director** of the play.

Lighting designers, who need a background in theater arts and electronics, can attend a 2- or 4-year college or professional school. Experience in or out of the theater as an **electrician** or **lighting technician** is helpful.

Chapter 14

Costuming

You Will Learn

Why costuming is so important to a good production.

What color coding is.

Why costume authenticity is good but not the most important consideration in a period costume.

Why costumes — or costume substitutes — need to be worn in rehearsals.

Why a complete costume, including accessories, is essential.

Why costumes need to be checked under stage lighting.

That silhouette is the key to a believable period costume.

How to determine whether to rent, borrow, or make costumes.

How to take measurements for costumes.

How to follow a costume pattern.

Vocabulary

color coding	building	Velcro
costume silhouette		

*C*ostuming is one of the integral parts of play production that suffers most on the high school stage. An actor must realize that the costume is not merely a means of characterizing a role as attractively as possible. In its color and silhouette, it is a vital part of the total stage design. If the color of a costume is not in harmony with other colors on the stage or if it is not appropriate to the historical period of the play, it can destroy the atmosphere of the production, no matter how beautiful it may be in itself or how flattering it is to the actor. The wise director will therefore work very early in the planning stages of the production with the designer and the person in charge of costumes to be sure that all costumes are appropriate in all respects. Because proper costuming is difficult and expensive, it is usually the first aspect of production to suffer because of budgetary limitations.

Effective Costuming

A costume should express the personality of the character. It should reveal social status, tastes, and idiosyncrasies. It should aid the audience's understanding of the actor's relationship to the other characters and to the play itself. The costume may be in harmony with others on the stage or in strong contrast to them. **Color coding** — matching characters by color or pattern — can provide a subtle means of identifying members of the same family or group, a pair of lovers, or masters and servants.

Since costuming is a part of the total design of a production, you will probably have little to do with the design of your costume. Too often, however, in high schools, costumes are designed or rented only for period or stylized plays. When it comes to contemporary plays, the actors are frequently asked what they have in their own wardrobes. This is acceptable only if the student is portraying someone of the same age, personality type, social position, and so on, and this is rarely the case. For most plays, the actor's personal wardrobe will never provide a suitable costume without some modifications. Therefore, costumes should be designed for all actors in all plays. In any production, the effect of a costume on both the actor and audience is what counts on the stage. The taste of the director and designer, not the actor, must govern the choice of material and color, and the meaning of the play must control all decisions. Valuable heirlooms, lavish designs, and expensive fabrics are of no value unless they are appropriate in color, period, and design.

Amateurs are usually reluctant to appear as anything but attractive on the stage, forgetting that the audience should react to the play, not to the individuals. No director will ever deliberately insist upon unbecoming or ludicrous lines or colors unless they are necessary to the correct interpretation of the play. However, the psychological reaction of being comfortably, becomingly, and suitably clothed greatly assists an actor's work. It is for this reason that you should understand the theories of costuming in order to cooperate intelligently in wearing whatever is designed for you in your role.

PEPLOS

CHITON

CHLAMYS

Ancient Greek dress

JERKIN

HOSE

Medieval dress
(fifteenth century, Burgundy)

RUFFS

FARTHINGALE

DOUBLET

PUMPKIN HOSE

CANIONS

Renaissance dress (1500)

Costume Design

The first step in costume design, as in all phases of theater production, is to study the play carefully. The costume designer should then meet with the director and technical director to discuss costumes in relation to the theme, style, period, colors, scenery, lighting, and budget. Together they can decide on types of materials for costumes that will suit the play in question in texture, finish, weight, fullness, and stiffness. Then measurements of the cast are taken and preliminary sketches are made.

Fabric samples should be tried under the lighting planned for the show. But remember that the lighting may be changed, and it is almost always the costumer who must make adjustments, seldom the painters or electricians. Once the fabrics are selected, the costumes may be sewn and fitted. It is wise to place the costumes on actors under the lights again before making the final fitting and adding the trim. This is called a *costume parade* and is part of the

SLASHED SLEEVE

PERIWIG

BODICE WITH PEPLUM

BREECHES

ROSETTE

Restoration dress (1660)

production schedule. Once each costume is completed, it should be checked one last time under the lights before the dress rehearsal.

Actors have a bad habit of not reporting lost buttons, tears, and other accidents to costumes. They should be reminded that such problems should be reported at once so that the necessary repairs may be made before the performance.

An important point to bear in mind is that a historically accurate costume is not always essential and might even have a negative effect on the production. Authentic costumes, especially those that expose parts of the body, such as Egyptian, Greek, or Roman costumes, may not look right on a particular actor. It is better to adapt the costume to the size, bone structure, and shape of the actor than to insist on historical correctness. Every historical or national costume has two or three identifying characteristics that are enough to give the impression of the era or geographical region. A collar, cape, belt, or hat may be all the audience needs to accept the costume as being of a given time

POWDERED WIG

TRICORN

JABOT

STOMACHER

FAN

PANIERS

CLOCKING

Eighteenth-century dress (1775)

and place. The addition of a few little touches, such as jewelry, handkerchiefs, or gloves, will make the costume seem complete.

A complete costume is essential. All accessories should be part of a properly designed costume and should be obtained early enough for use in some rehearsals. Neglect of such details as shoes, hats, purses, fans, and parasols can ruin the harmony of the design and mood. Masks, wigs, and hairpieces are part of both costume and makeup, creating the complete costume.

It is equally important for the actor to have some substitutes to rehearse with if the real accessories are not available for use. An actor needs to get the "feel" of a costume. For a hoopskirt, a hoop alone may be used for rehearsing and will remind the actress that she will not be able to see her feet, that she may have difficulty maneuvering a 110-inch hoop skirt through narrow passages, and that she may have trouble getting close to a person or an object without the back of the hoop tipping up embarrassingly. When accessories are added at the last minute, many beginning actors find they must change some of their stage business and even modify some of their blocking. It is a

CHEMISE

Empire dress (1815)

mistake to think that the addition of essential accessories on the day of dress rehearsal is good because it may give the performers a lift. Several weeks of rehearsal are necessary to develop the ease and naturalness essential to the use of a lorgnette, monocle, long cigarette holder, sword, or swagger stick.

The costume designer recognizes that clothing styles progress in definite patterns. This fact may be applied to the characters in a play. In any era, someone sets the fashion — perhaps a clothing designer, perhaps a person of renown, perhaps the star of a movie. This fashionable apparel is often first worn by professional models, then by the socially elite. Once a style is accepted in elite circles, fashionable people everywhere follow the new style, until finally the general population follows the trend. Then there are the people who are always outdated. They discard the previous style too late and consequently pick up the new style as it is waning. There are those who wear styles of a time ten to fifty years prior to the play; these are usually old-fashioned, eccentric, and economically or socially deprived people. Finally,

STOVEPIPE

FROCK COAT

CRINOLINE

Mid nineteenth-century dress (1850)

there are those people who wear offbeat, unusual, or bizarre clothing. These are the people who may be classified as eccentrics and nonconformists. Remember also that styles are often revived and that conservative and flamboyant styles occur in cycles according to the tone of the times.

It is usually safer to costume plays of the last two or three decades in present-day attire unless some aspect of the play hinges on authentic costuming. For example, the middies of the girls in *Cheaper by the Dozen* add to the humor of the play, but a long, straight-line dress of the twenties for Mrs. Gilbreth might seem ridiculously out of place.

Always consider the kind of action that will take place in the scene in which the costume will be used. A costume must be comfortable, easy to put on and take off, and strong enough to stand heavy strain. A skintight uniform may

CRAVAT

CORSET

BUSTLE

Late nineteenth-century dress (1890)

appear dashing, but may handcuff the actor completely in a fight scene. Costumes for dance sequences must be designed with the choreography in mind. If more than one costume is to be worn, each costume must be designed in such a way that the actor can change costumes in the time allowed. It must be admitted that playwrights do not always consider carefully the time needed for costume changes.

The total design of the play determines whether the costumes may be stylized. Some period plays adapt well to modern dress, the wearing of contemporary clothing instead of authentic period costumes. Formal attire (tuxedos and evening gowns) can be worn for many plays, particularly classical tragedies. Flowing robes, mosaic patterns, and variations in black and white fabrics may be used for certain stylized plays.

LEG O'MUTTON
SLEEVES

SACK SUIT

PARASOL

Dress 1905

Appropriateness

Each historic period has its own distinctive line and form in dress. This is the **costume silhouette.** Look carefully at the silhouettes in this chapter, and notice how each period has its own characteristics. If a costume does not recreate the basic silhouette of the period, it is not effective, no matter how beautiful or elaborate it may be. This is a very important principle.

In style, material, and cut, a costume must be appropriate to the social background and period of the play. On the stage, certain problems of dress are intensified. Actors and actresses should study their full-length reflections at a distance to get the proper perspective of themselves in costume. The director should observe every costume from various parts of the auditorium.

Small details become important onstage. For example, long skirts are more graceful than short ones, especially when the actress is seated. Draped

LOW CROWN DERBY

Dress 1910

HOBBLE SKIRT

DEEP CUFFS

SACK DRESS

Dress in the 1920s

DOUBLE BREASTED
JACKET

CUFFED TROUSERS

Dress in the 1930s

scarves and stoles are very effective if they are skillfully handled. Trimming, to be noticed, must be somewhat conspicuous. Lapels and pockets may be outlined with trim so that they may be distinguished from each other. However, if the trim is too gaudy, it should be discarded.

Most people want to look their best when appearing in public, so costumes should fit well and bring out the best physical characteristics of the actor — unless a particular role dictates otherwise. It takes time in rehearsal to make a different style of clothing feel natural. The actor must lose self-consciousness in the costume if it is to look right. Sometimes a high school performer "pulls back" in the role because the costume feels uncomfortable — a girl may be embarrassed by a gown that is too "revealing"; a boy may feel ill at ease in a Roman tunic. Often the student actors do not complain because they believe such a costume is what the director expects them to wear. But if the feelings of discomfort cannot be overcome by a better understanding of the role and the relationship of the costume to it, the director

Dress in the 1940s

should consider modifying the costume slightly rather than send a tense, ill-at-ease actor onto the stage. In real life, clothes may not make the person, but on the stage they do.

Color, Line, and Material

Costumes for comedies, farces, children's plays, and fantasies are normally made of light material, are bright or pastel in color, and are frothy in design. Restoration comedy calls for satins, laces, and brocades, which are usually as overconscious of style as the characters themselves. High comedy deals with persons of taste and social grace; costumes for fashionable characters require careful selection of color and material and also special attention to line. In realistic plays, almost any material that will create garments suitable for the character and for the stage picture can be used. Symbolic and allegorical plays require even more thought concerning fabric, texture, and pattern, because the audiences will assume that the costumes used in such plays will help them interpret the inner meanings. Tragedies use grayed colors or dark tones in heavily weighted materials. The color of the costume has much to do with the audience's response. A pale yellow will make a person appear younger and light in spirit. Maroon will suggest martyrdom. Refer to the list on page 412 for additional psychological values of colors.

The personality of the character and the style of the play will determine whether a tailored cut or a touch of lace is needed. Even in plays in which we think the styles of costumes are much alike, there must be variety in color, cut, line, material, and trim. The characters in every play must be treated as individuals to be identified in their stations of life, idiosyncracies, or philosophies by some aspect in their costume design. At the same time, all costumes for the same play must go with each other in basic design.

Garment lines should harmonize with those of the human body without constriction or exaggeration. A heavy-set person will seem more slender in costumes, hair styles, and hats accenting long, vertical lines. Tall, thin people will appear more "filled-out" in costumes, hair styles, and hats accenting horizontal lines, especially at the shoulder, and they should avoid long, clinging skirts, high hats, and V-necks. Black and dark colors are slenderizing, while white and light colors are broadening. Glaring colors, striking patterns, and lustrous materials attract attention and should be avoided by large persons unless they are especially appropriate to the characterization. Satin is a glossy material that in light colors makes a person appear larger, whereas velvet absorbs light, and dark velvet takes off pounds.

Prints must be carefully tested, for the stage lights turn small or light patterns into an undefined mass of color, which may create a grotesque effect. In general, blondes should wear cool colors, with touches of warm color contrast, and delicate designs and materials. Brunettes should wear warm colors, and they can risk brilliant fabrics and stronger color contrasts. Ordinarily red-heads should emphasize their coloring by wearing yellow, orange, green, and golden brown.

Texture not only determines the outline of the costume but also has much to do with the effects of a material under the lights. Heavy or soft materials, such as velvet, burlap, cheesecloth, and flannel, react well under stage lighting, and the more inexpensive materials often appear richer than many costly fabrics. Drapery material and even carpeting have been used for costumes for this very reason. Knitted materials drape beautifully and cling to the figure, emphasizing lines.

Oilcloth, cardboard, plastics, rubber sheeting, felt, and other similar materials, including the special plastic molding materials now available, can be used for trim, accent features, and appliqués. All sorts of familiar materials can be utilized in creating bizarre or unusual outfits.

Obtaining the Costumes

Work sheets and costume charts should be made for every costume in the production. The work sheets should describe the colors, fabrics, and accessories for each design. Ruled columns placed next to the items in the costume description are of great value. As each listed task is completed, the item can be checked off. Such charts can facilitate matters so that the costumes are ready before dress rehearsals.

One of the first problems to be settled is whether the costumes are to be rented, borrowed, adapted from thrift store clothing, or made. This decision must be made in time for the costumes to be collected with a minimum of effort and expense.

COSTUME PLOT FOR:							OUT	IN
CHARACTER	SCENE	COSTUME DESCRIPTION	MEAS. CARD	1ST FITTING	COMPLETE			
JULIE (CINDY PHELPS)	I, i	BLUE CHECKED GINGHAM PINAFORE w/WHITE BLOUSE AND WHITE APRON. WIDE BRIMMED STRAW HAT. PARASOL	✓	✓	✓	✓		
"	I, ii	LT. GREEN BLOUSE WITH PUFFED SLEEVES. PINK SKIRT w/BUSTLE. PURSE		✓	✓	✓		

Renting Costumes

If you decide to rent costumes, be careful. Rented costumes are very expensive. Many costume companies will not have what you want or all that you need when you need it. Be particularly cautious when costumers say that they do not have quite what you request but will fix you up with something else.

If you send out of town for costumes, they may not fit properly. This is usually due to inaccurate measurements. The costume supervisor needs to know what measurements to take and how to take them. Refer to page 475 for instructions on how to measure for proper costume fit. Some costume houses will send costumes that are in poor condition. Substitutions are common, accessories may not be what you expect, and the use of interchangeables — such as using the same hat for several purposes simply by changing the identifying trim — can result in a sameness you did not anticipate. Many costume houses send boot covers to be worn over regular shoes. Boot covers make poor substitutions for boots because they do not look natural when an actor walks. Also, boot covers are impossible to dance in. Wigs are usually considered part of a rented period costume. "Perforated" wigs made of human or animal hair are much preferred to cloth-based synthetic wigs. Only when you deal with very large firms can you hope to get the footwear, the wigs, the colors, or the patterns that you need. Otherwise, you take what they have.

One of the chief drawbacks of rented costumes is that they may be available for only one dress rehearsal or at most for only forty-eight hours prior to the first performance without additional charge. Most costume houses charge an additional fee for each performance day after the opening night. Some, however, will quote a flat rate per week including dress rehearsals and performances. Rental costumes are never available for publicity photos unless you rent them for that purpose. This can be done only if you are dealing with a local concern. In general, all costume orders should be placed well in advance of dress rehearsal and performance dates. This means that measurements must be taken shortly after casting. Before committing yourself to a costume house, check to find out how far in advance orders must be placed. Your schedule may not allow for ordering from costumers too far away.

With so many reasons against renting why consider renting? It is because fine costumes enhance the overall quality of a production. Formal evening dress, especially in period styles; uniforms and unusual national costumes; armor; and certain special properties are often unobtainable from any other source. If the budget is adequate, some of the leading costume houses can provide you with the costumes actually used in the Broadway or other well-costumed productions; such productions may have had a high enough budget to order the kind of costumes that no high school could afford to make. The trim for such elaborate costumes is quite expensive, and only large costumers can afford to trim the costumes properly.

When schools do not rent, there is always the temptation to take the easiest, cheapest route, which means you may make even more substitutions than the costumer or use some kind of apparel completely unsuitable for the play. Musical plays have sometimes lacked the sparkle and color so essential to their success simply because the costumes were arbitrary substitutions. If you

Taking Measurements

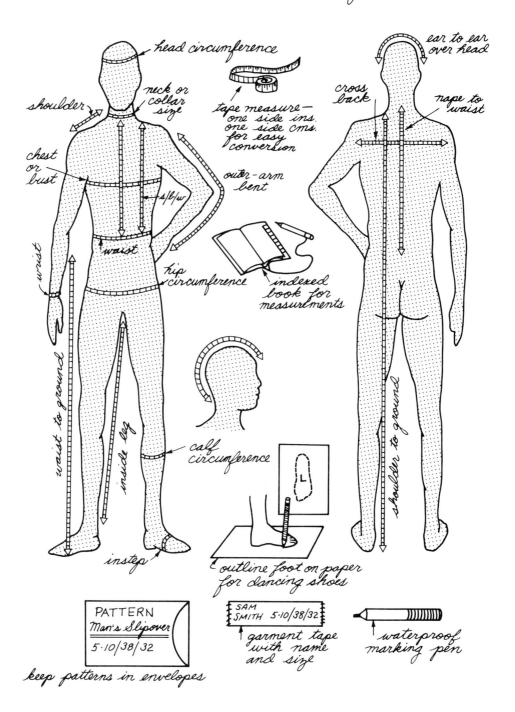

head circumference

neck or collar size

shoulder

tape measure— one side ins. one side cms. for easy conversion

chest or bust

s/b/w

outer-arm bent

wrist

waist

hip circumference

indexed book for measurements

waist to ground

inside leg

calf circumference

instep

ear to ear over head

cross back

nape to waist

shoulder to ground

outline foot on paper for dancing shoes

L

PATTERN
Man's Slipover
5·10/38/32

keep patterns in envelopes

SAM SMITH 5·10/38/32

garment tape with name and size

waterproof marking pen

do rent, often it is best to deal with a large firm or, better still, two reliable companies. The choice of costumes of each company for certain historical periods is usually limited, and you do not want your audiences to tire of seeing the same costume over and over again. If at all possible, the director, designer, and costume manager should go to the costume company personally to select the costumes to be used.

Borrowing Costumes

Having the members of the cast and committee buy or borrow their own costumes may seem to be the simplest method of costuming a production, but it seldom is. It is very difficult to obtain garments that will achieve the planned and desired effect, even those that at first seem easy to get. In period plays, suitable costumes lent by generous friends are apt to be valuable and fragile, and no assurance can be offered that they will not be soiled or torn. Makeup stains that will not come out, delicate lace that is snagged, and materials that disintegrate under the strain of a performance are hard to explain to the owner of such treasured heirlooms. If you borrow costumes, treat them carefully.

Of course, when students borrow or buy their own costumes, it is obvious there is little or no budgeting cost other than the cleaning of the borrowed costumes. As previously mentioned, it is not easy for students to look older in their own clothes, and seldom would the wardrobes of character and actor match. Also, the actor may be more careful with a purchased costume or one that belongs to a friend or relative. Since cost is always a major factor, most modern costumes are borrowed.

Making Your Own Costumes

Building is the term that costumers use for the making of costumes. It almost always outweighs renting and borrowing if you insist on good design, materials, workmanship, and a definite time schedule. The cost of making costumes may be about the same as, and sometimes a little more than, the rental fee, but the major difference is seen in the end result — welcome additions to the costume wardrobe, compared to a high bill with little to show for it.

Making the costumes serves several purposes. Those students who design and make them gain valuable experience and have the pride and satisfaction of seeing the part a good costume plays in creating an effective stage picture. A more uniform pattern for the play in both color and line is possible, and the costume is made to fit the individual actor. Both the costumer and the actor take a personal interest in this facet of production, bringing about a mutual respect for each other's contribution to the play. It is exciting for the designer, as well as a relief to the publicity director, to have the actual costumes avail-

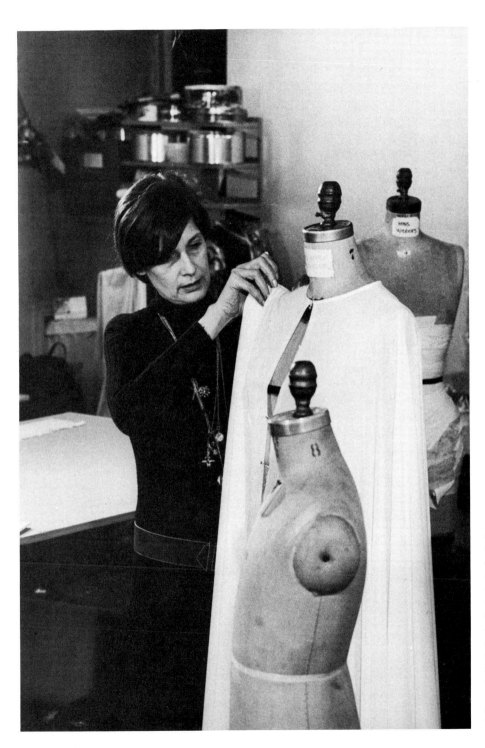

Professional designer Theoni Aldridge drapes material on a dress form as part of the initial design process. She has picked a model to work on that is close to the actual size of the actor who will wear the finished garment.

able for publicity photos. This is especially true if the publicity director plans to set up a poster featuring "real" scenes from the play.

If the costumes are to be made, a well-stocked wardrobe room is essential. If your school does not already have a costume room where costumes, accessories, materials, and supplies can be stored and cared for, you and your classmates should set up one. You will find your supply will grow quickly when the need for costumes becomes known in the community.

When you are ready to make costumes, individual sketches and costume charts and sheets should include notes on the kind, amount, and cost of materials. Dyeing makes possible a more satisfactory and unified costume scheme. However, it requires skill in a complex activity, a place for the dyeing, and people willing to work until the job is completed. Before the dyeing is done, patterns should be cut to the exact measurements of the actors and be approved by the director, scenic designer, and actors. When all material has been dyed and checked under the lights, it may be cut from the patterns and sewed together.

The completed garments must be strong enough to stand the strain of rehearsals and performances, but they do not need to have elaborate, ornamental sewing. Pinking edges and basting rather than stitching are quite acceptable for much of costume making. Details, such as a row of buttons, are usually nonfunctional or "dummied" in order to save sewing time and facilitate quick changes. **Velcro,** strips of material that adhere to each other instantly when pressure is applied, can replace unreliable zippers and allows for the fast removal of costumes. Costumes for dancers need extra material or stretch material under the arms for greater freedom of movement. For that matter, all costumes should be built with extra material in seams, darts, and hems so that the costume can be altered for another actor in the future. Do not build a costume that will only fit one person if you plan to use it again.

The main emphasis in costume planning should be on the total effect as seen from the auditorium. The perfection of a costume cannot be judged by the design alone. The costume must be observed in action on stage with the correct scenery and lighting. Costume design and construction are complex processes, but the effort is rewarded by the achievement of an original and artistic production.

Time is always the enemy in the production of a play, and this includes costuming. A schedule for measurement, fittings, and completion should be established and adhered to. Sufficient time must be allowed for checking material under lights, for alterations and corrections, and for the costume parade. One of the great advantages of making your own costumes is that if they are completed on schedule — at least a week before dress rehearsal — you can test them under the lights, make final adjustments, and add a touch of trim, accent, or jewelry as needed several days before rental costumes would be available.

In the long run, a combination of renting, borrowing, buying, and making your own costumes is probably the only satisfactory way to meet all your costume requirements, particularly if you present musical plays.

Never overlook the possibilities of making over old clothes or revamping old costumes. It is a good practice to save fabric remnants for trim or accessories or perhaps to add to a costume of the same material at a later date. Men's old suits can be cut and remade into cutaways without a great amount of work. Even beautiful hats — always a costume problem — can be made from a few materials, a little imagination, ten minutes in the library, and considerable patience. Thrift stores are often gold mines for old clothes that can be altered into costumes.

Following Costume Patterns

The sample patterns on pages 480 to 483 have been drawn to a scale of ¼ inch to 2 inches; each square represents 2 inches. To reproduce these patterns, or create ones of your own, start with plain brown paper. Mark off the paper in 2-inch squares by measuring outward from the center front and the center back of the pattern, adjusting the pattern according to the size of the actor. Pin the pattern to your fabric, which has been placed on a large table. Cut around the pattern allowing extra fabric for ⅝-inch seams.

The most important measurements for women are the following: height, bust, waist, hips (approximately 7 inches below natural waistline), back of neck to waist, waist to shoe tops, across back from shoulder to shoulder, and arm length from top of shoulder to wrist. The most important measurements for men are the following: height, chest, waist, inseam, back of neck to waist, across back from shoulder to shoulder, collar size, and arm length from top of shoulder to wrist.

The pattern on page 480 for a woman's Greek robe or a man's Greek tunic can be altered for different effects. Increasing the width of the fabric will increase the sleeve length. By changing the length of the fabric, you can make the garment reach the knee, calf, or ankle. Sew this garment at the side seams, and gather it at the shoulders with clasps or fancy buttons to fashion the armholes.

The pattern on page 481 is a medieval robe with Magyar sleeves. This garment, with adjustments in overall length, sleeve design, and decorations, is suitable for both men and women. Pieces X and Y add length and fullness to the sleeves for either a woman's or a man's garment. The use of dagged edges, mock buttons, and a belt dress the garment for a man.

The pattern on page 482 shows a nineteenth-century man's full-length coat

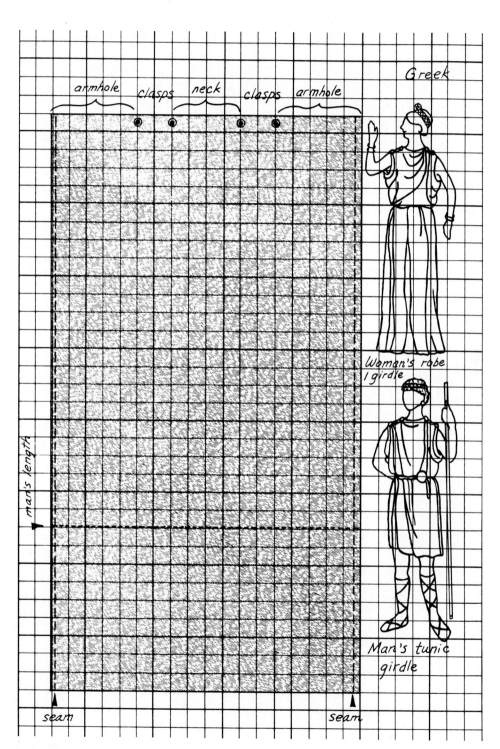

armhole | clasps | neck | clasps | armhole

Greek

man's length

seam | seam

Woman's robe
/ girdle

Man's tunic
girdle

Greek Pattern

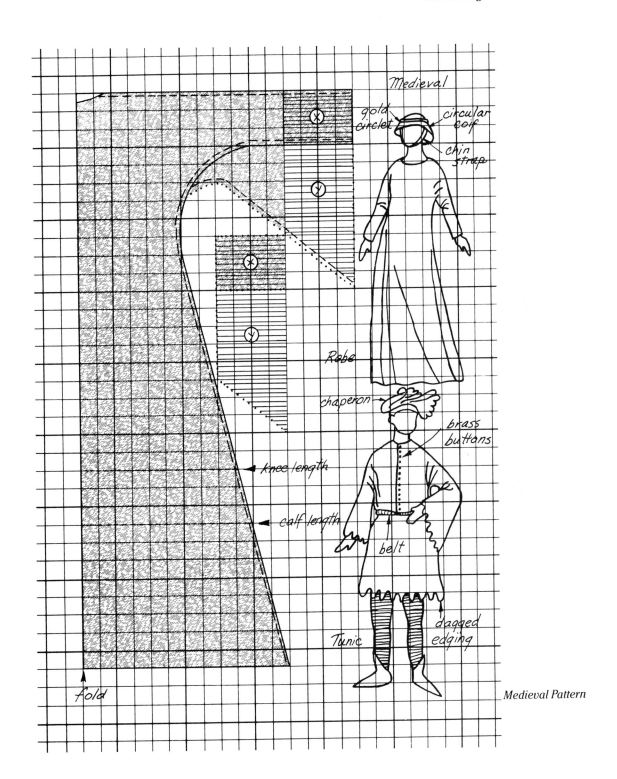

Medieval

gold circlet

circular coif

chin strap

Robe

chaperon

brass buttons

knee length

calf length

belt

Tunic

dagged edging

Fold

Medieval Pattern

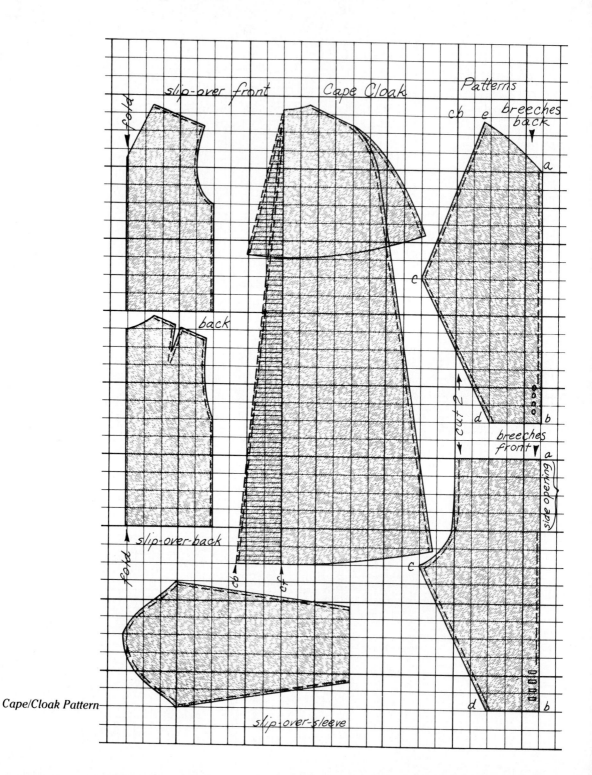

slip-over front   Cape Cloak   Patterns

fold

cb   e   breeches back

a

back

e

Cut 2

d   b

breeches front

a

side opening

slip-over-back

fold

cb   cf

c

Cape/Cloak Pattern

slip-over-sleeve

d   b

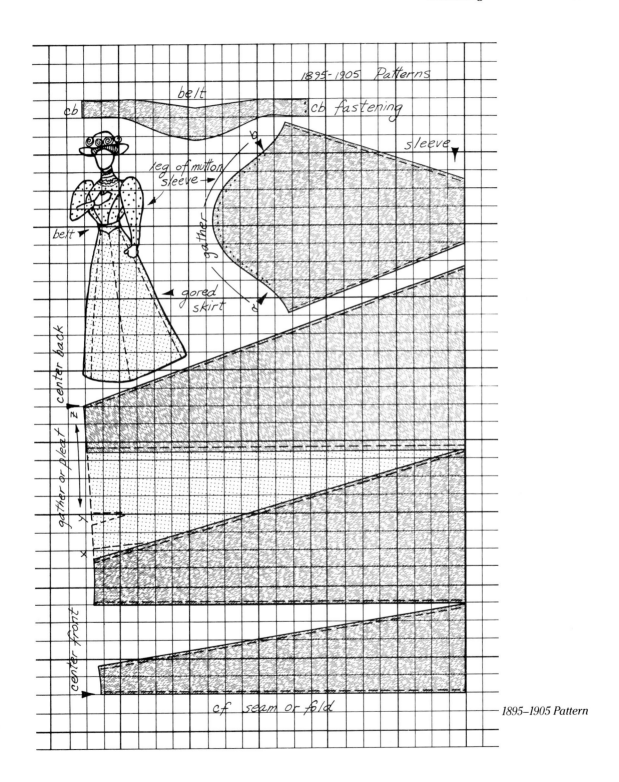

1895–1905 Pattern

(with or without cape), a jacket, and a pair of breeches. For the jacket, make a simple slipover garment. By using braiding along the collar, front, bottom, and sleeve edges, you will get the visual effect of a jacket without the tailoring problems of making a real jacket. Mock buttons down the front will complete the jacket look.

To make Victorian breeches, sew the center back (e–c on the pattern) and center front seams (f–c on the pattern) first. Then sew the inside leg seams (c–d on the pattern). Finally, sew the leg side seams (a–b on the pattern), leaving open the button fastenings at the knee and the placket at one side. Use braiding to make a mock drop flap in the front.

The cloak can be made full length, knee length, or any other length desired. The horizontal markings on the pattern show an allowance for extra fullness recommended for an overcoat. The cloak section can be eliminated for a straight-line coat. For this garment, you will have to sew a back seam (cb, center back, on the pattern). The center front of the coat is identified as cf on the pattern.

The pattern on page 483 is a gored skirt. You can fashion two types of skirts from this pattern: a six-gore skirt or a skirt with two darts at the hips. The darts are shown as X and Y on the pattern. The darted skirt requires gathering or pleating at the back, shown as Y–Z on the pattern. Also included are patterns for a belt or waistband and a leg-of-mutton sleeve.

For additional patterns and more detailed explanations, refer to Sheila Jackson's book *Costumes for the Stage*.

Care of Costumes

After the costumes have been obtained, they must be cared for during rehearsals and performances. A competent wardrobe manager should be chosen. The wardrobe manager will keep a costume plot as shown on page 473 and will choose responsible assistants in all the dressing rooms. The assistants help the actors with their changes, hang up clothes, keep all accessories close at hand, and see that everything is returned in good condition after the performance. The wardrobe manager sees that every costume is complete, in good repair, and identified by character and actor. Actors should have a designated place for their costumes, such as costume racks marked by tags or dividers. The wardrobe manager checks with the cast for problems that might have developed with zippers, tears, and the like, keeping needle and thread and a few handy supplies like hooks and eyes, buttons, Velcro, and elastic on hand during all performances. An ironing board, steam iron, spray starch, and a glue gun should also be readily available. All borrowed clothing should be

The costumes that transform the performers into roller skating trains in Starlight Express *are a compromise of form and function. Part armor, part athletic padding, the effect is sculptural.*

The cast of Godspell *traditionally wears colorful and imaginative combinations of street clothes that recall the free-spirit style of the late 1960s. In coordinating costumes that make use of the actors' personal clothing, every detail should be checked by the costume designer before the dress parade. Actors should be made aware that there should be no unapproved substitutions made during the run of the show.*

Disegno di Zama. Moglie del Gran Mogol Pr.a Donna non eseguito N. 59.

(ABOVE) *Costume for Zama, wife of the Grand Mogul, for* Tamas-Kouli-Kan, *1772, at the Royal Theater, Turin, Italy. (*AT RIGHT*) Costume for Prince of Turin for* Theodolinda, *1789, at the Royal Theater, Turin, Italy. The dominant colors in both costumes are red, orange, and yellow. Such warm colors usually arouse cheerful, passionate, and lively feelings in audiences.*

These are three different stages of a costume designer's creative process. (TOP LEFT) A rough sketch showing important details of the costume. (TOP RIGHT) A finished sketch that also shows important costume features—the bodice and hem design. (RIGHT) A finished watercolor showing the complete costume as well as the type of character intended to wear the costume.

The costuming of the quintet of vocalists that forms the chorus in A Little Night Music *must be approached as one would approach the dressing of a larger chorus. The ensemble must be unified yet retain, for the sake of interest, individuality. The proper effect is achieved in this design by the use of a formal design and a soft array of colors.*

dry-cleaned or washed before being returned to the owner. The wardrobe manager also sees that all school costumes are cleaned, repaired, and returned promptly.

Dressing room floors should be covered with paper if long trains or fine materials are worn. The stage floor should also be kept clean. It should be mopped or vacuumed before dress rehearsals and performances. Protruding nails, unexpected steps, low ceilings, and other backstage hazards should be eliminated.

The detailed design of these elaborate costumes from Follies necessitated additional dressing room care. Racks had to be constructed for the off-stage storage of the costumes.
. . . .

After almost every production, some costumes will need to be replaced or repaired. Decisions about how the costs of repair and replacement will be covered should be made when preparing the budget.

The Actor and the Costume

The actor must learn to wear a costume properly, bearing in mind the angle at which the audience will view the stage and performers as the actor turns, bends over, or crosses the legs. The actor should also consider the maximum stretch or reach taken in the costume, considering the extra stretch placed on the costume and the parts of the body that will be exposed. The actor must think of the other performers — that they are not jabbed unintentionally with a sword; that buttons, medals, or jewelry do not snag or catch on another's costume; or that another performer's cape or train is not stepped on. The actor must seem natural and at ease in a costume, learning how to make a turn in a flowing costume. Girls must learn how to sit gracefully while wearing a hoop or several petticoats, and boys must learn how a "man of quality" sits without pinning the tails of his full evening dress under him. Snapping fans, removing scarves and gloves, handling capes and finger rings must be second nature to the actor if that actor is to appear convincing in a role.

In addition, the actor should feel responsible for personal costumes and properties, remembering that some makeup, powder, spirit gum, and nail polish are almost impossible to remove and that torn fabrics can seldom be mended satisfactorily. Actors must personally see that every costume, accessory, and property is returned to the school, costumer, or friend exactly as it was received. But, above all, the actor should remember that the "total" actor is made up of a well-coordinated combination of voice, physique, makeup, and costume.

Recalling Ideas

1. Define *color coding*. Explain how it can be used for character identification.

2. What is a *costume parade?* When should it take place in the production schedule?

3. Explain how historically accurate costumes might have a negative effect on a production.

4. What does a *complete costume* include? Why is a complete costume essential?

5. What is a *costume silhouette?* Why must it be accurate for costumes to be effective?

6. What are *garment lines?* Tell why they are important.

7. Explain why costume rental must be carefully approached.

8. Identify some of the major benefits in making your own costumes.

Discussing Ideas

1. Costume designers realize that clothing styles progress in definite patterns. Discuss styles that have been popular during the last five years. What is the current most popular style?

2. Discuss the problems you would encounter in your own school if you chose to rent costumes for a production. Would renting be an intelligent thing for your school to do?

3. Discuss the feasibility of making your own costumes for a production. How would you go about getting it done? Whose help could you seek?

Careers

Costumes help identify the country, the period, and the location of a story. They help the audience understand the ages, occupations, personalities, and social and economic status of the characters.

Costume designers study the script to determine costume needs, taking into consideration special needs such as quick changes. They check their ideas with the **director, technical director, scenic designer, lighting designer,** and main **performers.** They make color sketches of the costumes and give them, with material samples, to the director for approval. Then they make a costume plot that shows what each character will wear in each scene.

Costumes may be made, rented, or assembled from existing wardrobe. They may be made at the theater or by a professional costume house. Most theater and motion picture studios maintain a wardrobe of costumes from previous performances.

During the dress parade, the performers, singularly and in groups, display their costumes under the lights. The director and all designers attend and suggest changes if necessary. A **wardrobe attendant** works backstage during performances to supervise costume changes and make adjustments and repairs.

Costume designers, who must be good researchers, study old paintings to see how people dressed. They must know how to draw and make the clothes they design. They and their crews are responsible for all fitting, cleaning, and storage of costumes.

Most costume designers attend a 2- or 3-year school of fashion design or get a bachelor's degree in fashion design from a 4-year college or university.

Chapter 15

. . . .

Makeup

You Will Learn

Why we use stage makeup.

The contents of a makeup kit.

The principles of highlight and shadow.

About special makeup problems.

About wigs and beards.

About makeup and the dark-skinned actor.

About the effects of stage lighting on makeup.

Vocabulary

chiaroscuro	highlighting	blender
foundation	shadowing	prosthetics
matte	facial mask	

*M*akeup should be one of the most rewarding phases of your dramatic experience, because it opens up a field of study that conveys the excitement, fun, and challenge of theater illusion and communication. Unfor-

Makeup plays an integral part in the development of the character Ariel in Shakespeare's The Tempest. *The impact of appearing from a trap in the stage is enhanced by makeup and costume design.*

● *489*

tunately, many students of drama do not fully realize that most stage actors must design and apply their own makeup. Makeup techniques cannot be mastered merely by watching a demonstration or reading about them. To help yourself acquire this skill essential to every performer, you should study faces to see how they show the effects of age and emotion. Observe portraits, cartoons, magazines, and photographs. Collect pictures of interesting faces that you might want to use as models.

Better still, observe real people. Take special note of differences in skin color and texture; where wrinkles occur, bones are prominent, and flesh hangs in folds; and the direction and patterns of hair growth. You will find that the changes that take place in facial expression are closely related to the changes in personality, stature, and voice that occur when an actor develops an effective characterization.

Bone structure is the key to facial makeup. Every student needs to know the bone-muscle relationship and how it alters with age and differs with nationality. It is essential that you study your own bone structure carefully before designing makeup for a role.

General Considerations

On the school stage, makeup must be handled with special care. Youthful faces do not always adapt themselves readily to older roles, and heavy makeup inexpertly applied looks "tacked on." Only a slight amount of foundation should be used. It is much better to use too little than to use too much. For classwork, a little makeup and an appropriate hairstyle can suggest age and nationality effectively. However, every student of the drama should study and practice elaborate as well as simple makeup.

When you are to design makeup for a large production, your makeup requirements change considerably. The larger the auditorium or the more lights to be used, the more makeup is needed. Stage lights can wash the color from an actor's face until the face has a pasteboard effect. Too much light from above results in deep shadows under all the bony prominences. Bright footlights make the face appear flat and lifeless. Most stages today do not have footlights. Without them, there must be proper lighting from the sides. Otherwise serious shadows distort the actor's face, the eyes can appear lost in deep sockets, and the nose may take on strange shapes.

The techniques of makeup application are closely related to the portrait artist's approach: the face is made a blank mask and then the principles of **chiaroscuro** — the use of highlight and shadow — are applied to model the features into the desired effect. Makeup should be designed on a makeup work sheet similar to the one on page 491. You may want to create your own

MAKEUP WORKSHEET

PLAY: _____

CHARACTER _____

ACTOR _____

Foundation: _____
Eye shadow: _____
Eye liner: _____
Moist Rouge: _____
Dry Rouge: _____
Shadow: _____
Highlight: _____
Powder: _____

Hair: _____
    Style: _____
    Color: _____
Beard/mustache: _____
Forehead: _____
Eyes: _____
Cheeks: _____
Nose: _____
Mouth: _____
Prosthetics: _____
Special treatment: _____

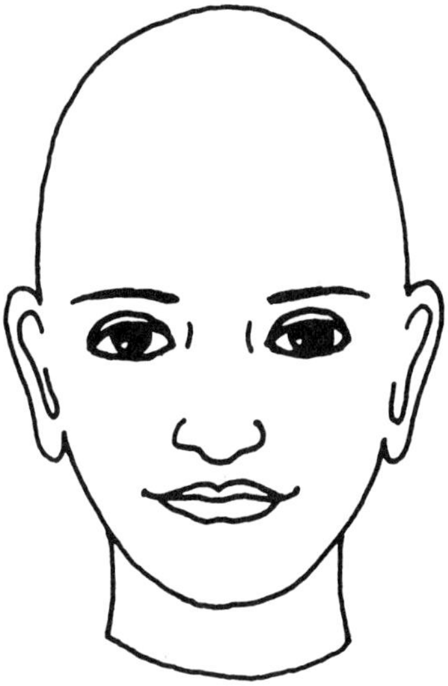

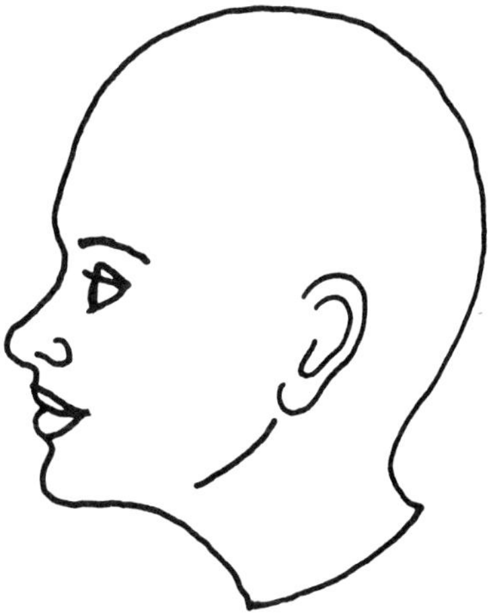

Makeup Worksheet

George Grizzard prepares for his role as Henry V in front of a dressing room mirror. Makeup should be a rehearsed and calm procedure before the performance.
. . . .

work sheet using a sketch of your own face as the model. Remember: Makeup does not make a character, but it does help present the external appearance of the internally created role.

The Makeup Kit

Since most high schools use makeup crews to apply makeup for an entire cast, a well-stocked makeup kit is essential to every drama department. However, makeup is a very personal thing, and many amateurs and all stage professionals have their own personal kits.

Makeup is very expensive and can be very messy. Proper care of the makeup supplies, the kit, and the makeup room is most essential. Materials should be carefully laid out, all containers and tables should be cleaned up after use, lids and caps must be replaced on the right containers, and all supplies should be put back in the kit or storage cupboards.

Before a rehearsal or performance, the makeup crew should place the supplies neatly on a covered table. When makeup is being applied by a crew, materials must never be taken by individuals. An ample supply of makeup remover and cleansing tissue is always important. Though not on the table, the complete makeup supply must be readily available for emergencies. Only one or two experiences will teach the person in charge of makeup that if all the supplies are in sight, every one of them will be used, even if only slightly.

Makeup essentials are usually handled by a special committee, whose members are headed by someone experienced in makeup techniques who can design the makeup for the production. This committee should see that the makeup kit contains the following essentials:

foundation: Foundation, or base, makeup comes in creme, stick, cake, or soft greasepaint. Shades ranging from light pink to dark sunburn to very dark brown are necessary for straight parts. For character parts, such as old age, there are various mixed tones. There are proper shades for different nationalities.

clown white: This is a special foundation color used for stylized makeup and highlighting. It comes in greasepaint or pancake form.

face powders: They come in translucent or in shades to harmonize with the foundation.

moist rouge: Light, medium, and dark.

liners: These are greasepaints in such colors as blue, brown, green, violet, maroon, yellow, and white.

lipsticks: Women use moist rouge or stage lipstick; men use brownish rouge.

makeup pencils: Brown, maroon, red, and black eyebrow pencils are needed.

dry rouge: Light, medium, and dark.

mascara: Black, brown, and white.

cold cream, Albolene, mineral oil, baby oil, or *makeup remover*: Used for dissolving and removing makeup.

powder puffs: Large and small.

roll of absorbent cotton

powder brush: Used for removing excess powder.

hair whitener: White mascara; liquid white shoepolish, clown white, or washout hair colorants.

hair colorants: Temporary hair color.

liquid body makeup: To match foundation.

eyeliner brushes or *round toothpicks, paper liners (stumps),* and *sable* or *camel's hair brushes*: For making wrinkles, painting lips, lining eyes, and filling in eyebrows.

crepe hair: Gray, gray blends, light brown, medium brown, dark brown, and black.

spirit gum and *alcohol* or *spirit gum remover*

liquid latex: For attaching beards and building up features.

nose putty or *derma wax, black tooth enamel, white tooth enamel,* and *artificial blood*: For building up features and making scars and wounds.

collodian: Flexible and nonflexible.

large mirrors

paper toweling: To protect the dressing tables.

cleansing tissues

hand mirror, comb, brush, scissors, needles, black and white thread, straight pins, hairpins, bobby pins, safety pins, and *soap*

Straight Makeup: Principles and Procedures

Before beginning to make up, put on a smock, an apron, or a makeup cape. Carefully bind back the hair or cover it with a cloth. Allow ample time for making up — at least half an hour for a straight role and an hour for a character part. Men should be clean-shaven but should never shave less than a half hour before applying makeup. Men should never get a full haircut less than three days before the production because the back of the head and the temples may appear "skinned" under the lights. Also, to protect the collars of white shirts and blouses, a piece of adhesive tape may be placed over the fold of the collar.

Preparation for Makeup

Before applying makeup, cleanse the face thoroughly, removing all cosmetics. Then moisten the fingertips with cold water and cool the surface of the face. Persons with oily skins may need to use an astringent to assure a dry surface before applying makeup.

Step One: The Foundation

The first step in the makeup process is the application of the correct **foundation** (base) color. The foundation turns the face into a blank mask upon which facial features are drawn with makeup. The foundation also provides pigment to replace that which is washed out by stage lights and gives a "character color" to help create a visual impression of a role.

There are three types of foundation in stage use today: creme makeup, soft greasepaint, and cake (pancake) makeup. *Creme* is the most preferred because of its ease of blending and use with soft liners. Creme comes in a plastic tube or jar and combines the advantages of soft greasepaint and cake. It is not overly greasy, but it does require powdering because it reacts to body heat and has a tendency to shine when moist. Consequently, some actors like to powder a creme foundation with translucent powder, pat the surface with a moist sponge, and then apply more makeup.

Creme base is usually applied directly with the fingers after a few spots have been dabbed on the face and neck. However, it may also be applied with a rubber or synthetic sponge. A thin coat should be spread over the face and all exposed parts of the head and neck areas, including the ears. The foundation should be worked gently into the hairline to avoid a halo effect around the face. Creme base should also be spread into the collar line, the back of the neck, and as far down the chest as is exposed or where body makeup will be applied. If the upper torso will be seen, stretch, gesture, or reach as you would in performance. This will help you determine how much of the chest and shoulders needs to be made up.

Stage makeup should be applied to a clean face. Use of a non-greasy moisturizer under a clown white or other full foundation will create a uniform facial texture and aid later removal.

The foundation (base) color used should be selected according to the age, nationality, health, occupation, and experiences of the character. Generally speaking, men use darker foundations than women. Pinks are used for blondes and for children's roles. Sallows (yellowish tones) are used for characters who are ill, anemic, or shut in. Tans are used by those who are healthy, active, and outdoorsy. Ruddy (reddish) foundations are used for individuals who are blustery, alcoholic, robust, or weather-beaten.

Soft *greasepaint* is preferable for its economy as well as its ease in blending. Do not use any cold cream before applying soft greasepaint. Dab or streak small amounts on the forehead, cheeks, chin, and neck. Use greasepaint sparingly. A thin, even coat is desirable; a heavy mask is not. Heavy greasepaint causes perspiration and running makeup. Also, lines will be difficult to draw, and the makeup will require constant retouching. Remove the makeup from your hands, moisten the fingertips with water, and begin spreading the greasepaint smoothly.

Cake (pancake) foundation was originally designed for motion picture makeup but has become quite popular with many actors, particularly school groups. Cake makeup goes on easily with a damp sponge or brush. A natural silk sponge works best for application. If cake highlights, shadows, and rouge are used, there is no need to powder. In fact, a light final coat of cake foundation sets and softens the total makeup effect. Since it is water-soluble, pancake makeup washes off without difficulty after the performance. However, in spite of ease of application and cleanup, the disadvantages of pancake makeup outweigh the advantages. Pancake melts under heat and runs under perspiration. In addition, pancake is very difficult to mix and does not blend well with soft liners. Since most high school makeup kits have only grease liners, the **matte** (flat) finish of cake foundation makes an incompatible combination. Therefore, most makeup experts do not recommend pancake for young, inexperienced actors.

Step Two: Shadows and Highlights

The application of shadow and highlight is really the most important aspect of modeling the face. **Highlighting** and **shadowing** are used for three purposes: (1) to bring out the features in order that they may be seen; (2) to correct the features; and (3) to change the features to indicate age, character, or physical impairments. For shadowing, use a greasepaint at least three shades darker than the foundation color, or use brown, reddish-brown, or maroon lining color. Never use gray except for extreme makeup, for it makes the face look skull-like or dirty.

Every shadow has its highlight. For highlighting, you may use a greasepaint at least three shades lighter than the foundation, or yellow or white liner.

White is usually the easiest to use because it will pick up enough of the foundation color to blend effectively without appearing garish. If your chin, nose, or brows are too prominent, blend a shadow over that part of the face. If, on the other hand, some part of your face is not dominant enough, apply a highlight to that area. It is almost always necessary to shadow the sides of the nose in order for it to be seen under bright stage lights.

A sable or camel's hair brush is the most satisfactory tool for lining, but a round toothpick may work quite well if you are careful to make the lines thin and sharp before blending them out. Also, a makeup pencil may be used if the point is kept wedge-shaped and sharp.

Step Three: Rouge

Now apply moist rouge to cheeks and lips. For a feminine straight part, select a color that blends with the foundation color and costume. You should place the moist rouge where it will help shape your face to that of your character. If you have an oval face, apply the rouge in a crescent shape to the cheekbones and blend up and out. For a round face, blend the rouge along the cheekbone and then downward closer to the nose. For a long face, place the rouge high on the cheekbones and blend out toward the temples.

Blending is always important in makeup, but it is especially so in the application of moist rouge. You should never see where the rouge ends unless your character is a person obviously over-made up. Men and boys should use moist rouge sparingly — just enough for a healthy glow. Although rouge may be washed out under strong light, it often gives the same effect as shadowing. Use very little, if any, rouge for night scenes, since both blue and green lights will turn the red into a dark brown or black.

Step Four: Eyes and Eyebrows

The eyes and brows are made up next. Remember that the eyes and the mouth are the most expressive feature of the face. Remember also that it is the brows that give the greatest character to the eyes. The purpose of the eye shadow is to beautify the eyes, to make them seem larger, and to indicate character. Eye shadow is applied to the upper lids only, beginning with a heavy application next to the eye and fading out, blending the color over the eyelid. The choice of color is determined by the color of hair and costume, the personality of the character, and whether the eyes are supposed to look "made up." Blue, blue-green, blue-gray, violet, or brown may be used. Brown is the safest and most flattering color and should always be used for corrective male eye shadowing. Violet is used only when a weepy appearance is sought or the character is a fragile old lady whose foundation color is a delicate pink.

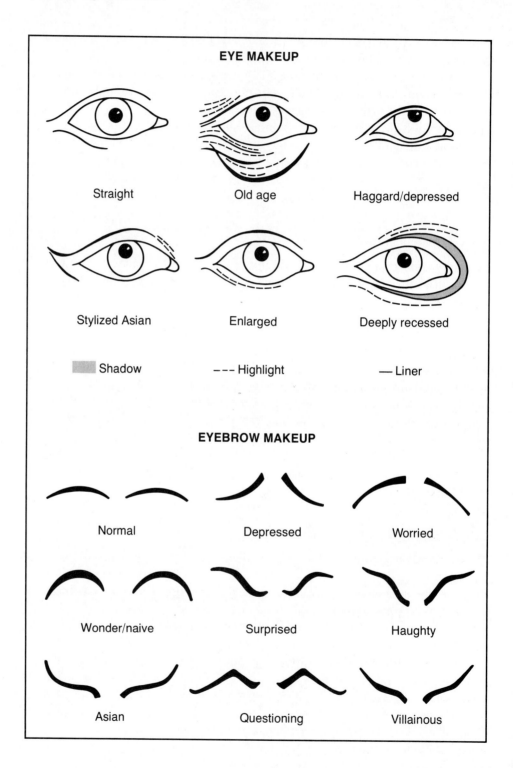

Be certain that the eye shadow does not kill any highlight below the eyebrow. The placement of the shadow can alter the appearance of the eyes to make them appear closer together or farther apart, or happy, sad, weary, suspicious, or squinty. In all cases, the shadow should be blended so no definite line is seen.

The eyes are enlarged and accented by lining. Makeup experts disagree sharply regarding both the technique and placement of eye lining. Brown or black lining color may be used, but black is acceptable only for dark-complexioned actors, characters who would use heavy eye makeup, or for oriental eyes. If false lashes or heavy mascara will be applied later, the upper line is omitted by many actresses. Otherwise, you should use a sable brush or round toothpick to draw a line close to the lashes starting about two thirds of the way in towards the nose and extending beyond the outer corner of the eye about ¼ inch and curving slightly upward. The lower line is drawn about one third from the outer corner out to the upper line, fading out before it reaches the top line. Both lines should be softened by running the finger gently over them. If an eyebrow pencil is used, it must be sharp, or the lines will be too heavy.

To add sparkle to the eye, some makeup experts suggest a small red dot in the inner corner of the eye; others recommend a touch of rouge just below the outer corner or below the outer edge of the brow. The red dot, or *life spot* as it has been called, may help to serve another purpose: it can aid in determining how close or far apart the eyes seem to be. For Asian makeup, when latex lids or adhesive tape is not to be used, a dot placed below the inner corner may contribute to the illusion of a slanted eye.

In straight parts, the eyebrows should frame the eyes rather than attract attention to themselves. Again, brown or black may be used in hairlike strokes following the shape of the eye. Most natural eyebrows do not have identical arches; therefore, by matching them, makeup can greatly improve their appearance. In character makeup, many different effects can be achieved by changing the eyebrows. Close, heavily drawn brows appear villainous. Lifting the brows into a round, thin arch gives an amazed or stupid expression. Twisted brows or brows dropped at contrasting angles make a face seem plaintive, menacing, or leering.

Step Five: Powdering

The most important step in the application of creme makeup or soft greasepaint is that of putting on the powder. Use translucent powder or a shade one tone lighter than the foundation. The powder, when properly applied, sets the makeup, softens the lines and colors, and gives a matte finish, which removes the shine of the makeup under the lights. Powder must be squeezed into the puff and the excess shaken off. Then the powder should be pressed or rolled into the makeup thoroughly but gently. Be very careful not to rub or smear the makeup.

The pressing in of the powder holds the makeup in place and prevents its running under the lights. Some makeup authorities suggest patting the powder on, but beginners often find that they can get spots of heavy powder that are difficult to remove, or they pick up globs of lining color on the puffs and transfer that color to the other parts of the face. Be certain that you have powdered all of the exposed skin areas that you have made up, including the eyelids, ears, neck, and lips. Brush off the extra powder very lightly with the powder brush, but do not disturb the lines or leave streaks and powder spots.

Step Six: Lipstick and Finishing Touches

After the powder, you may apply the finishing touches. If the powder dulled the cheeks, dry rouge may be used to restore the color, but be sure no lines or spots of rouge are visible.

Girls should now apply mascara or false eyelashes. Use brown mascara instead of black unless you are a real brunette. False eyelashes, put on with liquid adhesive and carefully trimmed to suit the character and lighting, are often very effective and in many ways preferred over mascara.

Girls should use moist rouge or stage lipstick for the lips, for with the many pigments found in commercial lipsticks today, it is impossible to predict how they will react under modern lighting effects. Therefore, it is dangerous to use your "street" lipstick unless you have tested it under the stage lights and the director has approved the color. Boys, if they use lip makeup, should use brown or reddish-brown lining color.

For sanitary reasons, it is best for the actor to apply lipstick with the little finger or a lipstick brush. Lipstick brushes may be used for group makeup provided they are wiped clean and sterilized after each use. Girls should remember that the shape of the lips is determined by the role and not by their ordinary street makeup. The lipstick should be blended on the inside so that a definite line is not visible when the mouth is open. It is also important that the corners of the mouth receive just enough rouge to define the mouth against the foundation. The lower lip should be lighter in color than the upper lip. If the lips are too full, the foundation may be extended over them and "new" lips created. If the lips are thin, the rouge may be extended beyond the natural lip line to any shape desired, but not widened beyond the natural corners of the mouth. For character emphasis, the lips can be outlined with dark red or brown. Sometimes the lips are more readily distinguished by applying a darker shade of red or brown to the lower edge of the upper lip where the natural shadow appears.

Makeup design considerations must balance the character traits of a role, the features of the actor, the style of the production, and the size of the theater. In this case, the actors, cast as King Lear and The Fool, makeup with enough definition to be seen by the middle of the house without being at odds with the tragic nature of the play.

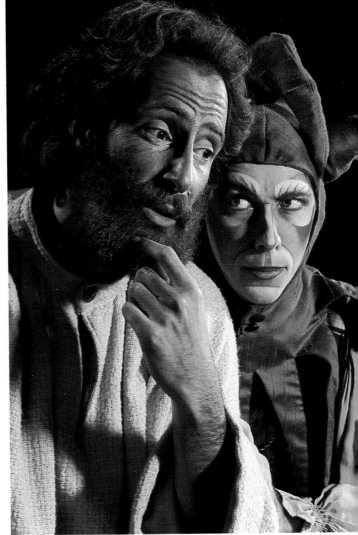

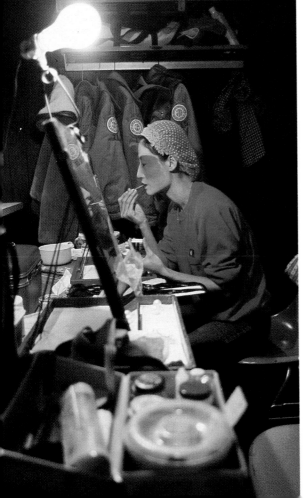

The makeup applied by this member of a Chinese troupe involves symbolism not readily understood by American audiences. Our perception of the universality of color and beauty must include an appreciation for diversity.

Realistic and nonrealistic makeup. (UPPER LEFT) *Medieval lady. Inspired by a fifteenth-century painting. Eyebrows and front hair soaped out. Makeup by student Dianne Hillstrom.* (UPPER CENTER) *Leopard makeup for children's play. Entire makeup applied with cake makeup, using sponge and brushes. Makeup by student Diane Harris.* (UPPER RIGHT) *Woman of Samoa. Shape of the face changed by highlighting cheekbones and shadowing jawbone and chin. Makeup by student Diane Harris.* (LOWER LEFT) *Portrait of a sixteenth-century lady. Inspired by a painting by Leonardo da Vinci. Creme makeup used for foundation, highlights, shadows, and rouge. Makeup by student Gaye Bowan.* (LOWER CENTER) *Stylized makeup based on an Asian mask. Makeup by student Lee Austin.* (LOWER RIGHT) *Portrait of a lady. Inspired by a painting by Chardin. Creme makeup used for foundation, highlights, shadows, and rouge. Makeup by student Ruth Salisbury.*

The Kabuki drama of Japan came into being in the sixteenth century and remains popular in Japan today. Traditionally, only men perform in Kabuki drama. The actors begin acting in Kabuki drama as children and continue to act in historical and domestic plays and dances until they are in their seventies. The makeup for each role is traditional and passed on to each new generation. The Kabuki performance of today gives us a glimpse of a past time.

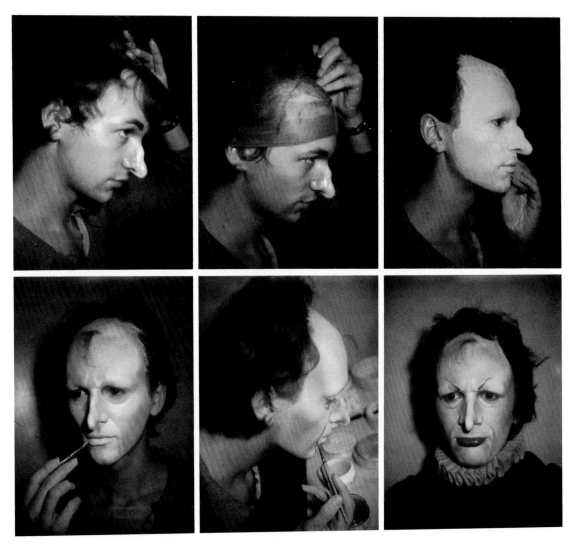

Nonrealistic makeup. An example of theatricalism. (UPPER LEFT) *Soaping out the front hair. Nose built up with nose putty.* (UPPER CENTER) *Making outline of bald area on nylon stocking, which will cover soaped-out hair.* (UPPER RIGHT) *Applying the foundation with a sponge. Eyebrows have been blocked out.* (LOWER LEFT) *Modeling the face with highlights.* (LOWER CENTER) *Applying shadows.* (LOWER RIGHT) *Completed makeup, with painted eyebrows, rouge, and full lower lip. Makeup by student Lee Austin.*

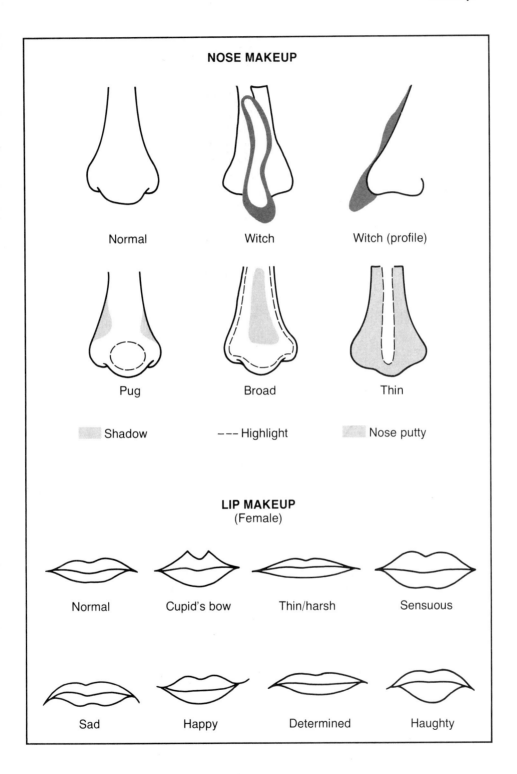

NOSE MAKEUP

Normal

Witch

Witch (profile)

Pug

Broad

Thin

Shadow

--- Highlight

Nose putty

LIP MAKEUP
(Female)

Normal

Cupid's bow

Thin/harsh

Sensuous

Sad

Happy

Determined

Haughty

Reshaping the mouth can do much to suggest character. For example, a full, sensuous mouth can be made puritanical by blocking out the curves and using light, straight lines in their place. By turning the corners of the mouth up slightly, an actor may be made to seem happy or pleasant even when not smiling. By turning the corners down, the actor may be made to seem always bitter or depressed. Avoid making your mouth the center of interest in your face, however, unless the part you are playing demands it.

Removing Makeup

After the performance is over, remove the makeup completely. Wearing makeup outside the theater marks you as an amateur and an exhibitionist. Use cold cream, Albolene, or makeup remover to soften the makeup and cleanse the skin. Use only the amount of makeup remover necessary to soften makeup. Too much makeup remover will dissolve the makeup so much that it will run and create a great smeared mess. Wipe off the liquified makeup with cleansing tissue or towels. Long strokes and a circular motion will prevent rubbing the makeup into the skin. Wash the face with soap and warm water and then rinse with cool water to close the pores.

Special Makeup Problems

Aging

Of all the makeup problems commonly encountered by the high school actor, the most difficult to handle effectively is the aging process. Young faces do not lend themselves well to the illusion of age. The methods suggested by some makeup authorities work well with older actors but do not result in a convincing appearance of middle or old age with most high school students.

The key to all makeup is bone structure. The actor needs to know her or his own bone structure before designing makeup for a role. Most serious acting students have facial masks made of their faces. A **facial mask** is a plaster casting taken of the face. The basic bone structure that the mask preserves does not alter much with time although the face may change considerably in appearance as years go by. These changes are due primarily to a pulling away of the muscles of the face, resulting in the sagging effect seen in old age.

Aging with makeup begins with the choice of foundation color. With age, the skin color tends to pale and deaden. Therefore, use light foundation colors, such as yellow, tan, or pale pink. However, it is through the modeling

Hal Holbrook prepares for his one-man show, Mark Twain Tonight. *Makeup transforms Holbrook into a seventy-year-old Mark Twain.*

of the face that the real effects of aging are portrayed. This modeling involves the following three basic principles: lines, highlights, and shadows. *Lines* create wrinkles; *highlights* and *shadows* create folds of the skin, which deepen the wrinkles.

There are two basic methods for applying wrinkles. The first assumes you have already applied the highlights and shadows. If you have natural wrinkles, you can usually "mark" them in the foundation by raising the brows, squinting the eyes, smiling, and pulling the chin in. Then, while the lines are still visible in the greasepaint, draw the wrinkles on with brown or reddish-brown liner. If you do not have natural wrinkles yet, you will have to follow the same procedure, but draw the lines while the muscles are still contracted.

The second method requires you to draw the wrinkles before applying the foundation. To use this method, spread brown liner over the areas where you plan to draw wrinkles. Form the wrinkles carefully, and wipe off the visible liner before relaxing the face. When you relax the muscles, the natural wrinkles should be clearly marked by the remaining liner. Form the wrinkles again, and apply the foundation greasepaint. After this step, highlight the folds of skin, relax, and blend the wrinkles into shadows.

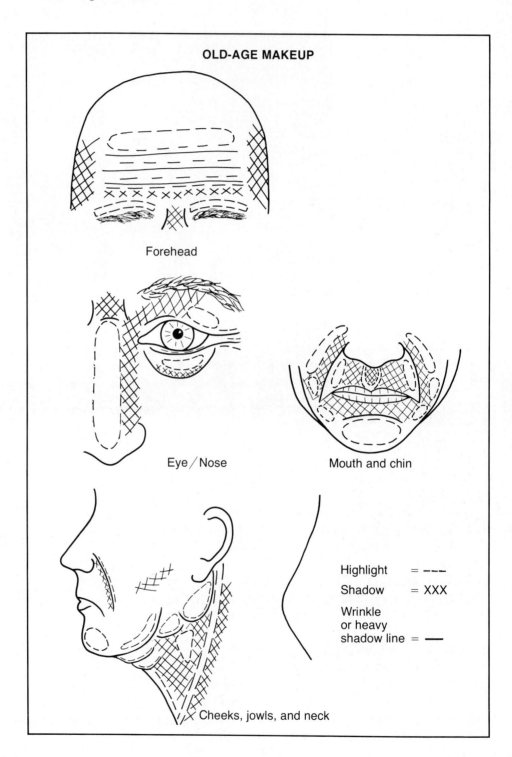

OLD-AGE MAKEUP

Forehead

Eye / Nose

Mouth and chin

Cheeks, jowls, and neck

Highlight   = ---
Shadow   = XXX
Wrinkle
or heavy
shadow line = ——

The most common locations for aging wrinkles are the forehead, between the brows, beneath the eyes (bags), the nasolabial folds (the smile wrinkle — from the nostrils extending to the outside corner of the mouth), vertically on the upper and lower lips, at the corners of the mouth, beneath the lower lip, under the jaw (the jowls), and horizontally on the neck.

Never draw too many lines on the forehead. Follow the natural wrinkle lines. You should also be especially careful when drawing age lines at the outer corner of the eye and below the eye, for if they are too heavy, they will appear as smudges rather than wrinkles. To emphasize sagging jowls, cotton, sponges, or tissues may be placed in the cheeks in addition to the use of highlights and shadows. If you elect this option, take extra care with your articulation since your mouth will be partially filled with cotton, sponges, or tissue.

It is the contrast in highlights and shadows that creates the illusion of old age. The older the character, the greater is this contrast. The bony prominences of the face receive the highlights, while the facial depressions receive the shadows.

The television production of Laurence Hausman's play Victoria Regina *won Julie Harris an Emmy Award. Here she is as the young queen and as the aging widow sixty years later. Helen Hayes played Victoria on Broadway.*

The areas of the face to highlight are the frontal crest (the area above and below the eyebrows), the outer half of the eyelid, the outer curve of the eye pouches (bags), the bridge of the nose, the cheekbones, the nasolabial folds, the chin, the jowls, the Adam's apple (men only), the wrinkles of the forehead and the eyes, and the tendon which runs from behind the ear to the breastbone. When highlighting a wrinkle to make the wrinkle deep and sharply defined, a thin line of highlighter is drawn above the wrinkle line and blended outward until the highlight gradually fades into the foundation color.

The areas of the face to shadow are the depression in the forehead, the temples, the inner half of the eyelid next to the nose, the pouch (the soft area) beneath the eyes, the sides of the nose, the inside edge of the nasolabial folds, the depression between the ridges above the upper lip, the depression beneath the lower lip, the hollows of the cheeks, the lower edges of the jowls, and the depressions of the neck.

There are additional factors to consider when creating an old-age makeup. As people age, their lips tend to become paler and thinner. To produce this effect with makeup, spread the foundation color to block out the edges of the mouth. Draw new lip contours by using a lighter foundation color, a reddish brown liner, or a light covering of white liner. Use darker rouge in old-age makeups. Apply the rouge lightly for a natural effect or more heavily if a "made-up" look is desirable. Hair changes with age. Gray, silver, or white the hair at the temples, in streaks, or overall. Brows may also be grayed or whitened and brushed gently inward toward the nose to give that shaggy appearance common in some older people.

Skin tone changes with age. Stippling with a plastic sponge helps age the skin and is particularly effective for aging the smooth skin of youth. To stipple the skin, use two or three colors. Place a dab of each color in the palm of the hand. Take the sponge and dip it into each color. Then lightly touch the sponge to the face so that the little holes in the sponge leave tiny dots on the face.

A technique that is popular in the theater today is using liquid latex to roughen skin texture. Liquid latex comes in tan, flesh, and white. Stipple the latex over a stretched section of skin and allow it to dry. When the skin relaxes, a wrinkled-textured face is the result, ready to be covered with greasepaint. However, this rough surface is more difficult to cover smoothly. A word of warning in using liquid latex. It must not get into the hair, even the "down" of a young face, because when the latex is removed the hair will be pulled.

Still another way to roughen the skin to show old age is to press cornmeal into a liquid latex base before it dries. For extreme old age, toilet tissue or cleansing tissue can be wrinkled and pressed into the latex. The cornmeal or tissue, whichever is used, is then covered with another coat of latex before applying the foundation color.

An often forgotten clue to age is the hands. They clearly reveal age and should always be made up for the portrayal of an older person. The tendons, knuckles, and other bones need to be highlighted. The sides, depressions, and wrinkles of the fingers need to be shadowed. To portray extreme old age, strongly pronounced blood vessels should appear on the backs of the hands.

One last word about old-age makeup. Like the hands, the legs are dead give-aways of age. A 16-year-old girl playing a 70-year-old woman must remember to change the appearance of her legs. One simple way is to wear cotton hose. A more dramatic solution may be required if the character will appear wearing sheer hose. In this situation, the legs must be aged by stippling and creating varicose veins.

Wigs and Beards

Hair is an integral part of both makeup and costume. Well-planned and carefully dressed coiffures can help transform high school girls into sophisticated middle-aged women, prim matrons, or exotic adventuresses. The use of easily removed hair tints can change a girl's stage personality. Hair whitener, white mascara, liquid white shoe polish, clown white, or wash-out colorants are used to gray or whiten the hair. The use of ordinary cornstarch or white powder is not wise. Cornstarch has a tendency to deaden the highlights of the hair, and a cloud of white powder arises if anyone touches it. Costume changes over whitened hair are not difficult, particularly if the hair is covered with a protective scarf.

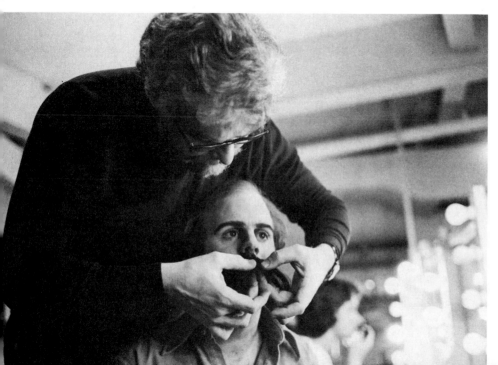

False beards made of crepe hair can be glued into place with spirit gum and then trimmed accordingly to the style appropriate to the character. Pre-trimmed mustaches, beards, eyebrows, etc. that are built on mesh or latex bases may be obtained and used repeatedly.

Wigs, hairpieces, and falls are quite helpful in changing hairstyles to fit character types and historical periods. However, only expensive wigs appear natural and effective. They should be individually fitted, if the budget permits, and they should be adjusted and handled with great care. Wigs are put on from the front and fitted back over the head. The real hair, if it shows, must be tinted to match the wig. A bald wig must fit perfectly, and the places where it meets the forehead and neck must be cleverly concealed by makeup. One way to do this is to place adhesive tape over the edge of the **blender** and work the foundation greasepaint up over the tape onto the cloth. If inexpensive cloth wigs are to be used, the forehead edge of the blender can be cut unevenly and then glued down with spirit gum.

For men, eccentric haircuts and hairdos are often more realistic than wigs. Boys' hair problems are important, for a perfect makeup and an impeccable adult costume can be ruined by a boyish contemporary hairstyle. A good barber may cut the hair to suit the characterization. Boys can easily change the color of their hair with mascara or wash-out colorants. The hair should be freshly washed so that there is no natural oil on it. The mascara may then be applied with a wet toothbrush, brushing it back from the forehead.

Beards, mustaches, and sideburns require time and practice to apply realistically. Too many beards seem tacked to the point of the chin — probably because they were. Although professionally prepared beards and hairpieces are available, most are too expensive for school use. Wool crepe hair is used to create beards for the stage. Crepe hair comes in many colors, including grays, salt-and-pepper blends, blondes, light and dark browns, and black.

Crepe hair comes braided and is sold by the yard. It is curly when unbraided and must be straightened for most use. Either dampen the crepe hair and tie it across the arms or back of a chair to dry overnight, or iron the damp hair dry. Then the hair may be cut into lengths somewhat longer than the trimmed beard or mustache is to be. Colors may be blended together for a more realistic appearance. Fan the hair between the fingers and thumb, and apply to the adhesive-coated area.

Spirit gum is still a popular adhesive, although liquid latex is being used by many actors. One disadvantage of latex is that it must never get into the actor's natural hair or brows. But it does have a strong advantage for those who must wear beards and sideburns for several performances. A piece of nylon stocking cut approximately the shape of the beard can be glued to the face with latex; the hair is then applied to the nylon. The beard and nylon are trimmed to shape, but instead of discarding the beard at the end of the performance, the nylon-backed hairpiece may be carefully peeled off to be used for the succeeding performances.

When making a beard, always consider the patterns and directions of natural hair growth. Before applying the hair, be certain that the face is clean-

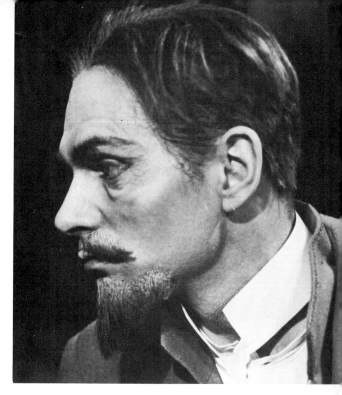

Laurence Olivier's performance is supported by makeup that transforms him into various characters. (Starting in the lower left and moving counterclockwise are: Sophocles's Oedipus, Sheridan's The Critic, Justice Shallow in Henry IV, Part II, and Chekov's Uncle Vanya.

shaven and that all skin areas to which hair is to be attached are free from makeup if spirit gum is to be used. Apply only a small amount of hair at a time, starting at the point of the chin and shingling upwards. In a similar fashion, apply the hair beneath the chin. However, the shingling is from the point of the chin downwards. When all the hair is in place, press it to the face with a towel. It can then be combed and trimmed to shape.

An unshaven effect can be created by stippling gray-blue or brown lining color on the foundation with a rubber sponge just before powdering. An even more realistic effect can be achieved by cutting crepe hair into tiny bits, spreading the shredded hair over the surface of a smooth towel, and transferring the hair to the face, which has been sparingly coated with spirit gum or latex. For a heavy stubble, use pulverized tobacco.

Facial Features

Liquid latex can be used for molding eyelids, cheeks, noses, and other built-up features attached to the skin with additional latex. These molded pieces are called **prosthetics.**

Prosthetics are best made on a facial mask by taking a plaster casting of the entire face, including the closed eyes. After the plaster has set you have an exact replica of the face. Shape the desired prosthetic piece in clay on the facial mask. Make a plaster casting of this clay model to provide a mold for the liquid latex. Pour the latex into the mold and allow it to set. When the hardened latex is removed, you have a prosthetic piece ready to be attached to the face.

When you use *nose putty* to change facial features, bear in mind that the putty must be kneaded into a pliable mass in the hands before it is placed on the face. Adding a little greasepaint or cold cream will make it more workable, and a little spirit gum will add to its adhesiveness. Nose putty may be used for building up noses, chins, cheekbones, and ears; for creating warts, scars, and other blemishes. Use alcohol or acetone to dissolve the spirit gum used to attach nose putty.

There are two types of collodion that are useful to the makeup artist — flexible and nonflexible. *Flexible collodion* is used for building up the flesh or texturing the skin. For example, a double chin may be built up with layers of cotton that have been coated with spirit gum. When the "chin" is as large as desired, the cotton is coated with diluted collodion (thinned with an equal amount of acetone), brushing outwards and extending the collodion about ½ inch beyond the cotton. *Nonflexibile collodion* is used for making indentations and scars and for drawing up the flesh. To form a skin depression, apply the nonflexible collodion with a brush and allow each layer to dry until the indentation is deep enough. To draw up the flesh, stretch the skin in the area to be painted and allow the collodion to dry. Then relax the skin. Collodion may be peeled off or removed with acetone.

Adhesive tape can be a very effective aid to character makeup. Asian eyelids can be created by placing tape over the lids; the lift of Asian eyebrows may be achieved by a piece of tape that pulls the outer brow toward the temple. Tape may also "pull" parts of the face to suggest the effects of scars or paralysis.

Tooth enamel comes in black, white, ivory, or cream. The black enamel is used to block out teeth, to make teeth appear pointed or chipped, and to make large teeth seem smaller. The "white" enamels are used to cover discolored, filled, or capped teeth and braces. The teeth must be dry before the enamel is applied.

Some other techniques, which take time and practice to master, can be used. It is sometimes necessary to block out part or all of the eyebrows. Foundation greasepaint is satisfactory if the brows are not too dark or heavy; otherwise nose putty or derma wax may be required. Then draw new brows with an eyebrow pencil.

Bizarre Makeup

Bizarre makeup may be tried if it is in keeping with the type of play and style of production. Stylized makeup, including "white masks," clownlike faces, and mosaics, can be quite effective on the stage. Special makeup has been developed for use with ultraviolet light. Changeable makeup really involves two makeup designs, one visible under ordinary light and the other visible under special lighting. For example, place a character wearing a special red greasepaint under red light, and that character will appear to be white or in straight makeup. Change to blue or green light and the red will appear to be black. Ultraviolet makeup can also be used for changeable illusions.

Animal makeup is fun and challenging. Most *animal makeup* can be suggestive rather than realistic. This allows the makeup designer to be creative in selecting makeup materials. For example, the designer can work with crepe hair, feathers, construction paper, foam rubber, Styrofoam, pipe cleaners, drinking straws, patches of cloth, and so on. Plastic bottles can be shaped into teeth. Liquid latex, nose putty, and derma wax can build up facial features or be molded into beaks, snouts, and horns.

Nonhuman illusions can be created with hoods and half masks. Upper head pieces constructed of foam rubber, Styrofoam, or paper can be worn like a hat or can be attached to a cap that will fit snugly on the actor's head.

The first step in creating an animal makeup is to develop a workable design that considers the identifying features of the animal and the actor. The

Precise makeup delineates specific characters and characterizations in the fantasy Cats.
• • • • • • • • • • • •

makeup designer should begin with a photograph or sketch of the actor. Then a makeup work sheet similar to that shown on page 491 should be made. Next the designer should make a drawing of the animal's face that is the same size as the drawing of the actor's face. The prominent features of the animal should be outlined.

The Dark-Skinned Actor

The same basic makeup principles apply to dark-skinned actors as to the Caucasian actor. However, light-skinned actors almost always need a base, while the dark-skinned actor's own skin color may sometimes serve as the makeup foundation. However, if a tone close to the natural color of the performer is desired, a darker foundation is required because every performer's pigments wash out under stage lights. Dark skin tones are not simply brown or black. There is as much variation in dark skin as there is in light, and the underlying red, yellow, and "copper" pigments are important to proper makeup. Very dark skin has a tendency to "bleed" through a lighter foundation. Consequently, it may be necessary to apply a makeup sealer before applying the base. White, "flesh," yellow, rose, or a lighter foundation color may be used for highlighting. Maroon or maroon mixed with brown or black works well as a shadow color. Dark brown, maroon, or violet are good eye shadows. Black or dark brown should be used for eyeliner. At proscenium distance, the facial features of a dark-skinned actor can be lost to the audience. Therefore, a highlighting of the nostrils and the jawline may be required. The rouge should match the foundation color, but dark-skinned actors can also use rouges with orange as well as red pigment. Since some dark-skinned people often have oily skins, careful drying or use of an astringent is recommended.

Makeup and Lighting

One must always be aware of the effects of light on makeup. Amber light, which is frequently used on the stage, causes the complexion to yellow, the rouge to fade, and blue eye shadow to gray. Green-blue, the gel most frequently used, will turn rouge purplish-black. Be certain that you know the lighting that will be used while you are on stage so that pigments can be selected or mixed in order that the light will reflect the proper colors. Finally, it is usually wise to plan a costume-makeup rehearsal to check the effects of light and costume on makeup.

Remember that in both class and school plays it is the actor, not the makeup and costume, who creates the real illusion. However, the care spent on a first-class ensemble of correct costume, makeup, hairdress, and accessories will give you an assurance that will help you create a convincing characterization. Makeup is an integral part of the actor's whole appearance. It is to be used and enjoyed as another tool in the actor's craft.

Makeup Projects
● ● ● ● ● ● ● ● ● ● ● ● ●

1. Draw a facial "mask" of your own face, carefully indicating bone structure and features.

2. On the facial mask indicate the types and colors of makeup you would use if you were to make yourself up for a specific part in a play. Carefully show where it should be applied.

3. Design the makeup for a young woman in a night scene.

4. Design the makeup for all the characters in a stylized production.

5. Present a demonstration of some unusual makeup technique, such as the use of latex, nose putty, or collodion.

6. Prepare a full beard and mustache on a nylon backing for yourself or a classmate.

Recalling Ideas

1. Define *chiaroscuro*.

2. What are the most expressive features of the face?

3. What is the key to facial makeup?

4. What is the first thing that must be done before any makeup can be applied?

5. Identify the six steps in applying makeup.

6. What are the purposes of highlighting and shadowing?

7. What is the most difficult makeup problem for the high school stage?

Discussing Ideas

1. Discuss the effect that lighting has upon stage makeup. What characteristics of lighting must you take into consideration in planning effective makeup?

2. Consider the problem of making a teenage actor into a seventy year-old man or woman. Discuss the kinds of things you could do with makeup so that the young actor would appear convincing.

Careers

Makeup is used to reflect the mood of the play and to be sure that facial expressions are visible to the audience. **Makeup designers** work closely with the **director** and **technical director** to plan the makeup of all the characters. They draw up a makeup plot for each character, order and inventory supplies, and oversee the clean-up after each makeup session.

Traditionally, makeup has been the responsibility of the actor or the **costumer.** In the professional theater, performers often apply their own makeup but often consult **hairstylists** and other specialists for advice and assistance.

Makeup is classified as (1) straight and (2) character. Straight makeup accentuates but does not change the appearance of the performers; character makeup alters the appearance of facial characteristics.

Makeup effects are created by painting. They are also achieved with plastic pieces such as beards, wigs, false noses, eyebrows, and "blemishes" such as warts and scars.

Members of the **makeup crew** are assigned certain characters to work with for the first makeup rehearsal. During that rehearsal, adjustments may be made to makeup that does not work well with the lights and costumes.

In the theater, in television, and especially in motion pictures, **cosmetologists** may work on the makeup crew. Cosmetologists care for the skin and nails of the performers and style and arrange their hair.

While a background in art or theater arts is helpful for makeup designers and crew members, training in a school of cosmetology is needed. Applicants need manual dexterity, stamina, and skill in dealing with people. Graduates receive a certificate and must pass a state examination for a license.

Glossary

A

action   that which happens on stage to hold the audience's attention

allegory   a form of storytelling that teaches moral concepts

ambiguity   double meaning

antagonist   the person or force working against the protagonist in a play

anticipation   looking forward to something

aside   a line spoken directly to the audience

assistant director   the person who acts as the liaison between the director, cast, and crew and takes charge of the rehearsal when the director is absent

atmosphere   the environment of the play created by staging and lighting

audition   a tryout for a position in a play

avant-garde   a group of people who are ahead of all others in using or creating new ideas

B

backlighting   light thrown on the performers from above and slightly upstage

balance   keeping sets symmetrical

blender   the edge of area where a bald wig meets the person's skin

blocking rehearsal   a rehearsal at which the movement and groupings on the stage are planned

body language   communication without the use of words

box set   a two-wall or three wall set composed of flats representing an interior room, often covered by a ceiling

building   the term used by costumers for making a costume

Bunraku   Japanese drama that features marionettes about four feet tall; also called the Doll Theater

burlesque   common form of low comedy, seen in television skits and in performances by stand-up comedians; exaggerated acting often referred to as "ham"

business manager   the person responsible for handling the financial part of a production — printing and selling tickets; paying bills; keeping financial records

C

callbacks   the cast selection process by which actors return for a second or third tryout

cast by type   actors cast in straight parts who really play themselves

catastrophe   an unlucky event in a play that may strike the leading character or one of the major characters

catharsis   a purging or cleansing that comes as a result of emotional release

central axis   the deepest point on stage that is just off-center

character-centered action   an approach to telling a story which places a character or group of characters in different situations

characterization   putting together all facets of a character to make that character a living, convincing human being

character parts   roles in which actors deal with traits that differ from their own to produce a desired character

cheat out   a stage technique where an actor pivots the torso and turns the face toward the audience

chiaroscuro   the use of makeup to highlight and shadow the face

circumflex inflection   using the voice to blend two or three sounds for a vowel that normally has a single sound, allowing the actor to stress a particular meaning or to change a word's meaning

climax   the turning point in a play

closed audition   a tryout open only to union members

closet dramas plays meant to be read rather than acted

cold reading a tryout when the actor uses material never seen before

color coding matching characters by color or pattern

comedy a play that deals with treating characters and situations in a humorous way

comedy of manners a play that laughs at a particular segment of society, usually the upper class

comic opera humorous or satirical operettas

commedia dell'arte professional improvised comedy that developed in Italy during the Renaissance

concentration the ability to direct all thoughts, energies, and skills toward a given goal

concept musicals a series of independent scenes loosely tied together

conflict a struggle between two opposing forces

constructivism an abstract style of stage setting that employs skeletal structures instead of realistic props

conventions special or traditional ways of doing things

coordinates costumes that are separates or interchangeable, sometimes reversible, such as ties, vests, etc.

costume silhouette each historic period's own distinctive line and form in dress

crisis a moment of decision for the leading character; the highest point of conflict

critic a specialist in judging plays

critique a positive or negative evaluation

cross to move from one position to another on stage

crossovers when characters walk across the stage together or enter from opposite sides and meet on the stage

curtain calls the appearance of a play's cast in response to an audience's applause

curtain sets the use of curtains as a backdrop for a play

cut-off lines lines interrupted by another speaker and indicated in the script by dashes (---)

cycle the entire sequence of plays performed from pageant wagons or stages on wheels by guilds in the twelfth century

D

dance pre-done ritualistic drama, such as traditional tribal dances

denouement an element of the plot that is the solution of a mystery and/or an explanation of the outcome

dialogue the lines of a play spoken by characters

diction the selection and pronunciation of words and their combination in speech

dimming down gradually reducing light

dimming up gradually increasing light

director the person in charge of molding all aspects of production — the acting, scenery, costumes, makeup, lighting, etc. — into a unified whole

drama a literary composition performed on stage

E

emotional or **subjective** the playing of roles in such a way that actors weep, suffer, or struggle emotionally

emotional memory recalling specific emotions, such as fear, joy, or anger

empathy the emotional identification with someone or something outside oneself. Ideally, the audience develops empathy with the characters in a play.

emphasis the focus of the audience's attention on some part of the stage

energy the fuel that drives acting, enlivens performances, creates empathy, and makes forceful characters

epic theater a learning theater that developed in Germany between the two World Wars that causes the audience to think deeply about important social problems in order to correct them

etiquette proper behavior

exaggeration an overstatement; an enlargement of the truth

existential theater theater that supports the philosophy that human beings do not really begin to live until they define their existence

exposition the information put before an audience that gives the *where, when, why,* and *who* facts of a play

expressionism a highly symbolic and poetic type of playwrighting, usually in revolt against realistic forms of drama

externalization when an actor shows the audience a character's true personality through interpretation, nonverbal expression, voice quality, pitch, rate, and physical action

F

facial mask a plaster casting taken of the face

fade-off lines lines that actors trail off because they do not finish them

falling action the series of events following the climax

falling inflection using the voice to signal the end of a statement or to express depression, finality, or firmness

fantasy a play that deals with unrealistic and fantastic characters

farce a kind of comedy when everything is done strictly for laughs

featherdusting a texturing method used by a painter using a featherduster dipped in paint to create a different pattern each time, such as foliage

floor block a small block of wood tacked to the floor on both sides of a flat or at each union where two flats meet

focus the direction of an actor's attention, action, emotion, or line delivery to a definite target

foundation a base color in makeup

G

gesture a movement of any part of the body to help express an idea

giving the scene shifting audience attention from one actor to another

gridding the process used to enlarge a sketch to a drop

grips stagehands who move scenery

grotesqueness an unusual or distorted feature

ground row a low profile of scenery that can stand by itself and is used to mask the bottom of the backdrop or background curtain

H

hanging plot a listing of all the flying scenery and what is on each piece, prepared by the technical director or the stage manager

high comedy a play that includes comedy of manners and satire and uses clever lines, word play, and allusions

highlighting the term used when applying makeup to bring out facial features

house manager the person responsible for distribution of programs, seating of the audience, and training the ushers

hue the purity of color

hues various colors seen in the spectrum of a beam of light that passes through a prism

humanities branches of learning having primarily a cultural character, such as drama, music, literature, and art

humor an appeal to the heart, where the audience feels tenderness, compassion, love, or pity

I

"illusion of the first time" making the audience believe that each performance is the first

impressionism a type of play which seeks to make the audience react and see as a character does when stirred by intense emotion

improvisation the impromptu portrayal of a character or scene without any rehearsal or preparation

improvisational audition a tryout at which the actor is assigned a character and given a brief description of a situation to perform with no preparation

improvising performing without preparation

inclination moving each body part one at a time

incongruity that which seems out of place, out of time, or out of character

inconsistent consistency that trait of a character

that an actor chooses to emphasize such as a dialect

inflection   modulation, variety in pitch

ingenue   a young romantic female lead between the ages of 16 and 30

initial incident   the first most important event in a play from which the rest of the plot develops

intensity   the brightness or dullness of a color

intent   inner force driving the character's behavior

internalizing   getting within a character to learn what the character is like

irrelevant   unimportant

isolations   separating parts of the body for individual development and expression

J

juvenile   a young romantic male lead between the ages of 16 and 30

K

Kabuki   Japanese drama from the sixteenth century, originally an imitation of both the Nō and Bunraku forms of drama

knap   the second sound after landing a blow — a sliding, slapping sound or clap

L

laugh curve   the audience's reaction that actors listen for in order to anticipate the length of time the audience will laugh

leading center   a slight or exaggerated movement of a part of the body that shows a character's personality, such as brave characters leading with their chests

leading roles   the main characters in a play

legitimate theater   originally, professional stage plays; now the term that is applied to regional and community theater, as well

light panel   a console from which the brightness of light is controlled

line   an artistic value in staging that alters proportion and affects the observer psychologically, such as the use of vertical lines in drapes to suggest dignity

low comedy   a play that is quite physical, sometimes vulgar, and highly exaggerated in style and performance

M

mansions   a series of acting situations placed in a line (the Miracle and Mystery plays of medieval drama were performed with mansions)

mass   an artistic value in staging that takes into consideration bulk and weight

master leading gesture   a distinctive action that is repeated and serves as a clue to a character's personality, such as a peculiar laugh or walk

matte   the flat or dull makeup that is achieved by powdering

melodrama   a serious play that arouses intense emotion and usually has a happy ending

memorizing   committing the lines of a script to memory

middle comedy   a kind of comedy that includes humor, such as romantic comedy, sentimental comedy, melodrama, and social drama

mime   an offspring of pantomime that gives the allusion to real-life action

Miracle and Mystery plays   plays based on the lives of the saints or on Bible stories

monotone   monotony in pitch; speaking continuously on one level; giving each sentence exactly the same inflection

mood   the emotional feeling of the play

Morality play   a play dealing with right and wrong, usually in the form of an allegory

motivated sequence   the natural way in which a person responds to an external stimulus — the brain registers, the body responds, and then reacts — as mirrored by an actor in an improvisation

motivation   the reason behind a character's behavior

musical comedy   a form of musical theater, a combination of operetta and musical revue — loosely connected production numbers

musical play   a form of musical theater where the emphasis is on real people in real situations

N

nasality the sound produced when nasal passages are blocked, leaving the voice flat

naturalism a style that grew out of realism that is often sordid and shocking

Nō (Noh) a six-hundred-year-old Japanese form of drama, the oldest form to be preserved in its exact form

nonverbal communication communicating without words, using facial expressions, gestures, and body language

O

observation the noting carefully of people's emotions, physical characteristics, and voice and diction patterns from which characters are modeled

open audition tryout open to nonunion actors

opera a form of musical theater, where all conversations are sung

operetta a form of musical theater in which the music is lighter than opera and conversation is spoken

optimum pitch the ideal highness or lowness of the voice

originality freshness of acting style

P

pantomime the art of acting without words

paraphrasing restating lines in your own words

part-whole memorization studying cues or lines of script line-by-line until committed to memory

pathos the power to arouse feelings of pity and compassion in an audience

pause a lull, or stop, in dialogue or action in order to sustain emotion

permanent set a set that never changes during a play, except when a set piece, such as a stairway, is brought in

picking up of cues speaking immediately on the last word of the previous speaker for rapid speech, or attaching your line to the former speech, with no space between

pitch the relative highness or lowness of the voice

playing the conditions the elements of time, place, weather, objects, and the state of the individual that help actors to interpret their characters

playing the moment responding to each line, action, and character in the permanent present, such as an actor not opening a door before the knock

playing the objectives methods used by characters to reach goals

playing the obstacles the ways a character faces each crisis or obstacle

plot the series of related events that take place in a play

polishing rehearsals the final rehearsals at which all parts of the play are brought together so that flaws can be discovered before the opening

preliminary situation a clearly defined explanation of the events in the lives of the leading characters before the start of a play's action

prepared audition a tryout when the actor uses material that has been memorized and thoroughly worked out

presentational a play in which the audience is recognized as an audience and the play as a play; consequently, the actors may speak directly to the audience

primary source observing a person's posture, movements, habits, voice inflections, and mannerisms in order to build a character

prisms or *periaktoi* sets made up of three 6-foot flats or of two 4-foot flats and one 6-foot flat, shaped as equilateral or isosceles triangles mounted to a wheeled carriage that can be pivoted

producer the person who finds the financial investors, hires the director and production staff, sets the budget, and pays the bills

profile sets two-dimensional pieces of scenery, such as hedges or bushes

projection controlling the voice's volume and quality so that it can be heard clearly

promptbook a script marked with directions and cues for use of the prompter

prompter the person who keeps the director's promptbook and makes penciled notes on cues, signals, etc.

pronunciation using the correct sounds in words and placing the accent on the stressed syllables

property chief the person who is in charge of getting the furniture and props, storing them, arranging them on the set, preparing the prop table, and giving the actors the props they need

proportion taking the human being as the unit measurement with regard to stage setting

prosthetics latex molded pieces of eyelids, cheeks, noses, and other features which are attached to the skin with additional latex

protagonist the main character in a play

protection factor when the audience is protected by knowing things are not really happening, such as when a character in a cartoon falls off a cliff and reappears in the next frame without a scratch

publicity manager the person who handles the advertising and promotion of the play in the press, radio, and other media

Q

quality the sound of a particular voice

R

rag rolling a method of texturing by using a rag or rolled-up piece of burlap that is dipped in paint and rolled on flats to give the painted flat the appearance of rough plaster

rate the speed at which words are spoken

reading rehearsal a rehearsal at which the play is read by the director or by members of the cast

realism a style that presents life as it actually is

recognition in tragedy, a scene in which the protagonist either achieves an inner awareness as a result of great personal suffering or identifies a lost loved one or friend

regional theaters theaters that present any type of play for as long as they wish, repeating plays when and if it is wise to do so

relief an easing of pressure

rendering a pencil sketch or watercolor that expresses the meaning of the play

repertory theaters theaters that present plays at regular intervals that are familiar to the actors

representational a play performed as if the audience is watching the action through an imaginary fourth wall

resonance the vibrant tone produced when sound waves strike the chambers of the throat, head, nose, and mouth

resumé a short account of a person's career and qualifications prepared by the applicant for a position; in the theater, an 8″ × 10″ headshot photograph is part of the resume

reversal a kind of incongruity that enables the audience to enjoy seeing the tables turned

reversible a costume that is double-faced so that by reversing, the illusion of a different costume is created

rhythm the overall blending of tempo, action, and dialogue

rising action the series of events following the initial incident

rising inflection using the voice to indicate questioning, surprise, or shock

romantic comedy a play that presents life as we would like it to be

romanticism the style of romantic comedies, showing life as we would like it to be

rotations moving each body part in smooth circles

S

satire a humorous attack on accepted conventions of society, holding up human vices and follies to ridicule

satires literary works that ridicule or scorn human vices and follies

saturation the brightness or dullness of a color

scene-stealing calling attention to your presence

on stage and diverting attention away from the main actors

scenic artist or **designer**   the person who designs the settings, and sometimes designs the costumes, makeup, and lighting

schwa   pronunciation symbol with the sound of "uh"; every vowel has a schwa sound

screens   two-fold and three-fold flats used either as walls against a drapery background or to cover openings or furnishings when changing scenes

script   the written text of a play

scumble   to use two or more brushes and two or more tones of the base color to make an uneven base coat of paint on a flat

secondary sources   books that help in characterization building

sentimental comedy   a play in which the need of people to have faith in others and to lose themselves in the lives of others like themselves is met

shades   dark or deep colors

shadowing   term used in applying makeup to bring out facial features

shape   an artistic value that influences both mass and the psychological reaction to objects on the stage, by using geometric or free-forms, such as a circle symbolizing the infinite

share a scene   two actors standing or sitting parallel to each other

situation   a problem or challenge the character or characters must face

situation-centered action   an approach to telling a story which takes a single situation or series of situations and places characters into them

situations   circumstances that are presented in dialogue and action, such as moments of danger or emotional upheaval

size   a glue-water mixture that seals the pores in the muslin covering a flat

social drama   a problem play which seeks to right the wrongs of society

soliloquies   speeches delivered by actors alone

on a stage which reveal the character's innermost thoughts aloud

spattering   a method of texturing in which paint is spattered onto the flat

spontaneity   naturalness

spoofs   literary works that poke fun at certain subjects or time periods

stage fright   the nervous anticipation of going on stage to perform

stage manager   the person who is in complete charge backstage during the rehearsals and performances

stippling   a texturing method used by a painter using a sponge, crumpled rag, or the tips of a dry brush, leaving clusters of paint drops

straight parts   roles in which the actor and the character are similar

stretching a character   making a role unique, individual, and interesting

style   the way in which a play is written, acted, and produced

stylization   a blending of script and production

substitution   the use by an actor of a personal experience to relate the experience of a character within a play

subtext   character interpretations which are not in a script but are supplied by an actor

supporting roles   those characters who act as contrasts to others — characters with whom other characters, usually the protagonist, are compared

sustained inflection   using the voice to suggest calmness, decisiveness, or steadiness of purpose by staying on the same note

symbolic   the use of characters, props, and sets to exemplify ideas, such as a blue bird symbolizing happiness

T

taking yourself out of a scene   the actor's turning away from the audience into a three-quarter back or full back position

technical director   the person who executes the

designs of the scenic artist with the help of a crew

technical or **objective acting** use of learned skills of acting, movement, speech, and interpretation to create roles; no emotional response is allowed

technical rehearsals rehearsals at which lighting, scenery, and props are used so that changes go smoothly

textual tryouts tryouts when actors use monologues or scenes

theater of the absurd a form of theater in which language becomes the unconventional, and in which political and social problems are examined and presented to the audience in unconventional ways

theater of involvement theater in which the members of the audience participate in the action of the play

theaters buildings where plays are performed

theatricalism the style that says "This is the theater. Accept it for what it is, as it is."

theme the basic idea of a play

tints light or pastel colors

total theater theater in which all the performing arts are fused into one presentation

tragedy a play in which the protagonist fails to achieve desired goals or is overcome by opposing forces

turning the scene in focusing audience attention on the actor who is the real center of dramatic action

twist the unexpected

typecasting identifying and casting an actor in the same kind of role over and over

U

uniqueness the actor's ability to shape a charac-

ter's personality into itself and not make it a copy of someone else's portrayal

unit set a basic stage setting from which several settings can be created

unity when all elements of the set form a perfect whole, centering on the main idea of the play

unnatural machinelike or puppetlike

unnatural sounds those sounds such as an undulating pitch that soars up and down like a slide trombone, that draws laughter from an audience

V

value a color's lightness or darkness

Velcro strips of material that adhere to each other when pressure is applied

versatility the ability to change style or character with ease

voiced those consonants, such as *b, d,* and *v,* that cause vibration of the vocal folds when sounded

voiceless those consonants, such as *p, t,* and *f,* that do not cause vibration of the vocal folds when sounded

volume the strength, force, or intensity with which sound is made

W

whole-part memorization committing to memory individual lines of a script after whole units of the play have been read several times

working backwards a technique in which an actor prepares the audience for what a character will do later

working rehearsal the rehearsal at which interpretation of the play is developed and words and actions are put together

INDEX

Page numbers in **boldface** indicate illustrations

Photo Credits

Part One Opener   Pp. xii–1   ©1987 Martha Swope

3: Boston Athenaeum;   **5:** Lauren Kurki;   **7:** Richard Wood/The Picture Cube;   **8–9:** Nancy McFarland;   **14:** New York Public Library/Picture Collection;   **15:** Henry E. Lowenstein/Bonfils Theater;   **16:** Martha Swope;   **20:** Ken Firestone/Peter Arnold, Inc.;   **27:** Bert Andrews;   **30:** Liamute E. Druskis;   **31:** NBC Photo;   **34:** Hartke Theater;   **37:** Martha Swope;   **38:** Martha Swope;   **40:** Culver Pictures;   **43:** Courtesy of Caedmon Records;   **49:** Martha Swope;   **54:** James Karales/Peter Arnold, Inc.;   **60:** ©Frank Siteman MCMLXXX/The Picture Cube;   **61:** Jane Caminos;   **63:** New York Public Library/Picture Collection;   **65:** The Picture Cube;   **69:** Martha Swope;   **72:** Martha Swope;   **77:** Martha Swope;   **80:** Martha Swope;   **84:** Martha Swope;   **87:** Carl Davis/Alley Theater;   **94:** Martha Swope;   **97:** Bettmann Archive;   **98:** Tass/Sovfoto;   **98r:** Don McKague;   **100:** Roger Greenwalt/Hunt, Pucci Associates;   **101:** Martha Swope;   **103:** Zodiac Photographers;   **104:** Jane Caminos;   **106:** Carl Davis/Alley Theater;   **108:** Jane Caminos;   **110:** Bert Andrews;   **111:** Robert Houser/Photo Researchers, Inc.;   **113:** Jane Caminos;   **115:** Henry E. Lowenstein/Bonfils Theater;   **116:** Jane Caminos;   **117:** The Picture Cube;   **119:** Bert Andrews;   **120:** Martha Swope;   **122:** Nancy Hereford/Mark Taper Forum;   **123:** Jane Caminos;   **124:** Jerry Goldstein;   **125:** Martha Swope;   **127:** ©James Foote 1973/Photo Researchers, Inc.;   **129:** Martha Swope;   **130:** Bert Andrews;   **131:** Henry E. Lowenstein/Bonfils Theater;   **133:** Martha Swope;   **135:** William Nelson/Carnegie Mellon University;   **137:** Jane Caminos;   **138:** Lauren Kurki/Boston University;   **141:** Martha Swope;   **143:** Richard Feldman/American Repertory Theater;   **147:** Richard Feldman/American Repertory Theater;   **149:** Jeff Albertson/Stock, Boston;   **150:** ©1985 Maureen Fennelli/Photo Researchers, Inc.;   **156:** ©Kathrina Thomas 1973/Photo Researchers, Inc.

Part Two Opener   Pp. 158–159   The Bettmann Archive, Inc.

231: The Bettmann Archive, Inc.

Part Three Opener   Pp. 232–233   American Repertory Theater

236: Don McKague;   **238:** The Bettmann Archive, Inc.;   **240t:** DonMcKague;   **240b:** The Bettmann Archive, Inc.;   **241:** Jane Caminos;   **242:** Don McKague;   **243:** Don McKague;   **245:** The Bettmann Archive, Inc.;   **246:** Don McKague;   **251:** The Bettmann Archive, Inc.;   **256:** The Bettmann Archive, Inc.;   **258:** Richard Feldman/American Repertory Theater;   **259:** Joseph P. Schuyler/Stock, Boston;   **263:** Henry E. Lowenstein/Bonfils Theater;   **264:** Richard Feldman/American Repertory Theater;   **265:** Zodiac Photographers;   **267:** Martha Swope;   **268:** Joseph Schuyler;   **270:** The Bettmann Archive, Inc.;   **271:** : The Bettmann Archive, Inc.;   **272:** Cary Wolinsky/Stock, Boston;   **274:** Martha Swope;   **276:** Photo Researchers, Inc.;   **277:** Arvine Garg/Photo Researchers, Inc.;   **282:** The Bettmann Archive, Inc.;   **284:** Mark Taper Forum;   **285:** Martha Swope;   **287:** Ray Munro, Lauren Kurki/Clark University;   **288:** Richard Feldman/American Repertory Theater;   **294:** The Bettmann Archive, Inc.;   **295:** D. A. Harissiadis, Athens;   **298:** The Bettmann Archive, Inc.;   **299:** The Bettmann Archive, Inc.;   **300:** German Information Center;   **302:** Richard Feldman/American Repertory Theater;   **304:** The Bettmann Archive, Inc.;   **306:** The Bettmann Archive, Inc.;   **308:** New York Public Library/Picture Collection;   **309:** New York Public Library/Picture Collection;   **310:** The Bettmann Archive, Inc.;   **312:** New York Public Library/Picture Collection;   **313:** New York Public Library/Picture Collection;   **315:** The Bettmann Archive, Inc.;   **316:** Richard Feldman/American Repertory Theater;   **318:** Michael Romanos/Ideas Associates;   **319:** Ideas Associates/Nickerson Theater.

Part Four Opener   Pp. 322–323   Denver Center Theater Company

326: Richard Feldman/American Repertory Company;   **328:** Lauren Kurki;   **329:** Lauren Kurki;   **332:** Jane Caminos;   **335:** The Wang Center;   **343:** Martha Swope;   **345:** Mark Taper Forum;   **351:** Liamute E. Druskis;   **353:** Lauren Kurki/Clark University;   **355:** Richard Feldman/American Repertory Theater; **357:** Joseph Schuyler; **358:** Martha Swope; **360:** Hartke Theater; **364:** Plymouth Theater; **367:** Martha Swope; **368:** Martha Swope; **370:** William Nelson/ Carnegie-Mellon University; **371:** Martha Swope; **373:** Martha Swope; **375:** Zodiac Photographers; **380:** Martha Swope; **382:** Ideas Associates; **386:** Lauren Kurki; **387:** Lauren Kurki; **388:** Lauren Kurki; **389:** Lauren Kurki; **390:** Lauren Kurki; **391:** Graphic House, Inc.; **393:** The Bettmann Archive, Inc.; **395:** The Bettmann Archive, Inc.; **396:** Stock, Boston/The Williamstown Theater; **402:** Lauren Kurki; **406:** Lauren Kurki; **407:** The Bettmann Archive, Inc.; **413:** Lauren Kurki/Wheaton College; **416:** Lauren Kurki; **417:** Lauren Kurki; **420:** Lauren Kurki; **422:** Lauren Kurki; **424:** Lauren Kurki; **426:** Lauren Kurki; **427:** Lauren Kurki; **428:** Marvin Lazurus/Photo Researchers, Inc.; **430:** Lauren Kurki/Jane Caminos; **431:** Ideas Associates/Nickerson Theater/Michael Romanos; **434:** Richard Feldman/American Repertory Theater; **437:** Coleman Photography; **438:** Lauren Kurki; **440:** Lauren Kurki; **441:** Lauren Kurki; **443:** Lauren Kurki; **446:** Lauren Kurki; **447:** Lauren Kurki; **448:** Jerry Goldstein; **449:** Theater Collection/New York Public Library, Astor, Lenox & Tilden Foundations; **450:** Bruce Siddons/Yale Repertory Theater; **451:** Martha Swope; **453:** Martha Swope; **454:** Lauren Kurki; **455:** Lauren Kurki; **461:** Jane Caminos; **462:** Jane Caminos; **463:** Jane Caminos; **464:** Jane Caminos; **465:** Jane Caminos; **466:** Jane Caminos; **467:** Jane Caminos; **468:** Jane Caminos; **469:** Jane Caminos; **470:** Jane Caminos; **471:** Jane Caminos; **474:** Jane Caminos; **477:** Margot Granitsas/Photo Researchers, Inc.; **480:** Jane Caminos; **481:** Jane Caminos; **482:** Jane Caminos; **483:** Jane Caminos; **485:** Martha Swope; **488:** Martha Swope/American Shakespeare Theater; **491:** Jane Caminos; **492:** John Engh/Photo Researchers, Inc.; **495:** Ken Firestone/Peter Arnold, Inc.; **503:** Courtesy of Harvey Sabinson; **504:** Lauren Kurki; **505:** NBC Photo; **507:** Frank Siteman/The Picture Cube; **509:** The Bettmann Archive, Inc.; **512:** Jeffrey Dunn Studios/The Picture Cube

Color Inserts

I-1 Martha Swope; **I-2** Lauren Kurki/Ann Mantel/Clark University; **I-3** Lauren Kurki/Ann Mantel/ Clark University; **I-4** Martha Swope.

II-1 Martha Swope; **II-2t** Lauren Kurki; **II-2b** Martha Swope; **II-3tl** Martha Swope; **II-3tr, bl, br** Lauren Kurki; **II-4** Martha Swope.

III-1t Robert Capece/McGraw-Hill; **III-1b** Martha Swope; **III-2t** Lauren Kurki/Boston Shakespeare Company; **III-2b** Lauren Kurki/Clark University; **III-3t** Lauren Kurki/Clark University; **III-3b** Lauren Kurki/Boston Shakespeare Company; **III-4t** Jeff Albertson/Stock, Boston; **III-4b** Martha Swope.

IV-1 Martha Swope; **IV-2** Lauren Kurki; **IV-3t** Lauren Kurki; **IV-3b** Martha Swope; **IV-4** Robert Capece/McGraw-Hill.

V-1t Martha Swope; **V-1b** Cary Wolinsky/Stock, Boston; **V-2** New York Public Library/Picture Collection; **V-3** New York Public Library/Picture Collection; **V-4t** Martha Swope; **V-4b** Steve Hanson/Stock, Boston.

VI-1t Ellis Herwig/The Picture Cube; **VI-1b** Dede Hatch/The Picture Cube; **VI-2** Richard Corson; **VI-3** Bruno Zehnder/Peter Arnold, Inc.; **VI-4** Richard Corson.

ican Repertory Theater; **357:** Joseph Schuyler; **358:** Martha Swope; **360:** Hartke Theater; **364:** Plymouth Theater; **367:** Martha Swope; **368:** Martha Swope; **370:** William Nelson/ Carnegie-Mellon University; **371:** Martha Swope; **373:** Martha Swope; **375:** Zodiac Photographers; **380:** Martha Swope; **382:** Ideas Associates/; **386:** Lauren Kurki; **387:** Lauren Kurki; **388:** Lauren Kurki; **389:** Lauren Kurki; **390:** Lauren Kurki; **391:** Graphic House, Inc.; **393:** The Bettmann Archive, Inc.; **395:** The Bettmann Archive, Inc.; **396:** Stock, Boston/The Williamstown Theater; **402:** Lauren Kurki; **406:** Lauren Kurki; **407:** The Bettmann Archive, Inc.; **413:** Lauren Kurki/Wheaton College; **416:** Lauren Kurki; **417:** Lauren Kurki; **420:** Lauren Kurki; **422:** Lauren Kurki; **424:** Lauren Kurki; **426:** Lauren Kurki; **427:** Lauren Kurki; **428:** Marvin Lazurus/Photo Researchers, Inc.; **430:** Lauren Kurki/Jane Caminos; **431:** Ideas Associates/Nickerson Theater/Michael Romanos; **434:** Richard Feldman/American Repertory Theater; **437:** Coleman Photography; **438:** Lauren Kurki; **440:** Lauren Kurki; **441:** Lauren Kurki; **443:** Lauren Kurki; **446:** Lauren Kurki; **447:** Lauren Kurki; **448:** Jerry Goldstein; **449:** Theater Collection/New York Public Library, Astor, Lenox & Tilden Foundations; **450:** Bruce Siddons/Yale Repertory Theater; **451:** Martha Swope; **453:** Martha Swope; **454:** Lauren Kurki; **455:** Lauren Kurki; **461:** Jane Caminos; **462:** Jane Caminos; **463:** Jane Caminos; **464:** Jane Caminos; **465:** Jane Caminos; **466:** Jane Caminos; **467:** Jane Caminos; **468:** Jane Caminos; **469:** Jane Caminos; **470:** Jane Caminos; **471:** Jane Caminos; **474:** Jane Caminos; **477:** Margot Granitsas/Photo Researchers, Inc.; **480:** Jane Caminos; **481:** Jane Caminos; **482:** Jane Caminos; **483:** Jane Caminos; **485:** Martha Swope; **488:** Martha Swope/American Shakespeare Theater; **491:** Jane Caminos; **492:** John Engh/Photo Researchers, Inc.; **495:** Ken Firestone/Peter Arnold, Inc.; **503:** Courtesy of Harvey Sabinson; **504:** Lauren Kurki; **505:** NBC Photo; **507:** Frank Siteman/The Picture Cube; **509:** The Bettmann Archive, Inc.; **512:** Jeffrey Dunn Studios/The Picture Cube

Color Inserts

I-1 Martha Swope; **I-2** Lauren Kurki/Ann Mantel/Clark University; **I-3** Lauren Kurki/Ann Mantel/ Clark University; **I-4** Martha Swope.

II-1 Martha Swope; **II-2t** Lauren Kurki; **II-2b** Martha Swope; **II-3tl** Martha Swope; **II-3tr, bl, br** Lauren Kurki; **II-4** Martha Swope.

III-1t Robert Capece/McGraw-Hill; **III-1b** Martha Swope; **III-2t** Lauren Kurki/Boston Shakespeare Company; **III-2b** Lauren Kurki/Clark University; **III-3t** Lauren Kurki/Clark University; **III-3b** Lauren Kurki/Boston Shakespeare Company; **III-4t** Jeff Albertson/Stock, Boston; **III-4b** Martha Swope.

IV-1 Martha Swope; **IV-2** Lauren Kurki; **IV-3t** Lauren Kurki; **IV-3b** Martha Swope; **IV-4** Robert Capece/McGraw-Hill.

V-1t Martha Swope; **V-1b** Cary Wolinsky/Stock, Boston; **V-2** New York Public Library/Picture Collection; **V-3** New York Public Library/Picture Collection; **V-4t** Martha Swope; **V-4b** Steve Hanson/Stock, Boston.

VI-1t Ellis Herwig/The Picture Cube; **VI-1b** Dede Hatch/The Picture Cube; **VI-2** Richard Corson; **VI-3** Bruno Zehnder/Peter Arnold, Inc.; **VI-4** Richard Corson.